South Sefton
6th Form College

south sefton
college

# International Relations
## 1879–2004

Collins

Published by Collins
An imprint of
HarperCollinsPublishers
77–85 Fulham Palace Road
Hammersmith
London
W6 8JB

Browse the complete Collins
catalogue at
www.collinseducation.com

10 9 8 7 6 5 4 3 2

ISBN-13 978 0 00 726871 9

British Library Cataloguing in
Publication Data
A Catalogue record for this
publication is available from the
British Library

Edited by Graham Bradbury
Commissioned by Michael
Upchurch
Design and typesetting by Derek Lee
Cover design by Joerg
Hartmannsgruber, White-card
Map Artwork by Tony Richardson
Picture research by Celia Dearing
and Michael Upchurch
Indexed by Christine Bernstein
Production by Simon Moore
Printed and bound in Hong Kong

ACKNOWLEDGEMENTS
Every effort had been made to
contact the holders of copyright
material, but if any have been
inadvertently overlooked the
publishers will be pleased to make
the necessary arrangements at the
first opportunity.

HarperCollins for the extract from
*Lyndon Johnson and the Exercise of
Power* by Rowland Evans and Robert
Novak (1966) and *A People's History
of the United States* by Howard Zinn
(1980). Heinemann for the extract
from *The Cold War* by Hugh Higgins
(1993). Henry Holt and Company
for the extract from *France 1940–55*
by AlexanderWerth (1957). Hodder
for the extracts from *The Cold War
1947 to 1991* by Simon Ball
(Headline 1998) and *The USA and
Vietnam, 1945–1975* by Vivienne
Sanders (Hodder and Stoughton,
Access to History series, 1999).
Houghton Mifflin for the extract
from *The Imperial Presidency* by
Arthur M. Schlesinger (1973). Keele
University Press for the extract from
*Vietnam: American Involvement at
Home and Abroad* (British
Association for American Studies
Pamphlets 1992). Little, Brown for
the extract from *Hitler's Willing
Executioners* by David Goldhagen
(1996). Longman for the extract
from *The Origins of the Second World
War* by R.J. Overy (1987).
Macmillan for the extract from *The
Economic Consequences of the Peace*
by J.M. Keynes (1920). Methuen for
the extracts from *Peacemaking, 1919*
by Harold Nicholson (1967). Oxford
Press for the extracts from *The
Unfinished Journey: America Since
World War II* by William H. Chafe
(1999). Pearson Education for the
extracts from *The Hitler State* by
Martin Broszat (Longman 1981),
*Kennedy* by Hugh Brogan (Longman
1996) and *Russia, America and the
Cold War 1949–1991* by Martin
McCauley (Longman Seminar
Studies series 1998). Penguin Books
Ltd for the extracts from *The Pity of
War* by Niall Fergusson (Allen Lane
1998), *Rise to Globalism* by Stephen

Ambrose and Douglas Brinkley
(1997), *Hitler: A Study in Tyranny* by
Alan Bullock (1962), *The Origins of
the Second World War* by A.J.P. Taylor
(1964), *The War against the Jews
1933–45* by Lucy Dawidowicz
(1975) and *The Making of the Second
World War* by Anthony Adamthwaite
(Allen and Unwin 1977). Routledge
for the extracts from *France and the
Coming of the Second World War* by
Anthony Adamthwaite (1977) and
*The Cold War 1945–1991* by John W.
Mason (Lancaster Pamphlets 1996).
Twayne Publishers Inc for the
extract from *Big Daddy from the
Pedernales* by Paul K. Conkin
(1986). The University of California
Press for the extract from *The
Nationalist Revival in France* by
Eugen Weber (1959). University
Press of Kansas for the extract from
*The Presidency of John F. Kennedy* by
James N. Giglio (1991), *The
Presidency of Lyndon B. Johnson* by
Vaughn Davis Bornet (1986) and
'The War in Vietnam' in *The Johnson
Years: Foreign Policy, the Great
Society and the White House v. 1* by
George C. Herring (1981).

The publishers would like to thank
the following for permission to
reproduce pictures on these pages.
T=Top, B=Bottom, L=Left, R=Right,
C=Centre

akg-images/ullstein bild 125R; ©
CORBIS 69, 166; © Baldwin H.
Ward & Kathryn C. Ward/CORBIS
140; © Bettmann/CORBIS 125L,
153, 154, 167, 177B; © Hulton-
Deutsch Collection/CORBIS 105;
Imperial War Museum, London 86;
DPA DEUTSCHE PRESS-
AGENTUR/DPA/PA Photos 193B;
EVAN VUCCI/AP/PA Photos 204;
SCOTT APPLEWHITE/AP/PA
Photos 206; © popperfoto.com 171;
HIP/ TopFoto.co.uk 26;
© ullsteinbild / TopFoto 56, 192,
202; © 2001 Topham / AP 169;
© 2004 TopFoto 185; © 1999
Topham Picturepoint 193, 194;
TopFoto.co.uk 198; © 2005
TopFoto/ImageWorks 205; unknown
65, 104, 172, 176, 177T.

# Contents

Study and examination skills                                          4

1 International Relations, 1879–2004: A synoptic overview             12

2 The causes of the First World War                                  20

3 International relations, 1919–1941                                  45

4 The Second World War                                               81

5 The Cold War in Europe, 1945–1991                                 110

6 The USA and the Cold War in Asia, 1945–1973                       136

7 Crisis in the Middle East, the state of Israel and Arab
  nationalism, 1945–2004                                            180

Index                                                               208

# Study and examination skills

This section of the book is designed to aid Sixth Form students in their preparation for public examinations in History.

- Differences between GCSE and Sixth Form History
- Extended writing: the structured question and the essay
- How to handle sources in Sixth Form History
- Historical interpretation
- Progression in Sixth Form History
- Examination technique

## Differences between GCSE and Sixth Form History

- The amount of factual knowledge required for answers to Sixth Form History questions is more detailed than at GCSE. Factual knowledge in the Sixth Form is used as supporting evidence to help answer historical questions. Knowing the facts is important, but not as important as knowing that factual knowledge supports historical analysis.

- Extended writing is more important in Sixth Form History. Students will be expected to answer either structured questions or essays.

Structured questions require students to answer more than one question on a given topic. For example:

(a) Why was the League of Nations created after the First World War?

(b) How successful was the League of Nations in maintaining international peace from 1920 to 1939?

Each part of the structured question demands a different approach.

Essay questions require students to produce one answer to a given question. For example:

To what extent was the outbreak of the First World War due to German foreign policy?

### Similarities with GCSE

- Source analysis and evaluation

The skills in handling historical sources, which were acquired at GCSE, are developed in Sixth Form History. In the Sixth Form, sources have to be analysed in their historical context, so a good factual knowledge of the subject is important.

- Historical interpretations

Skills in historical interpretation at GCSE are also developed in Sixth Form History. The ability to put forward different historical interpretations is important. Students will also be expected to explain why different historical interpretations have occurred.

# Extended writing: the structured question and the essay

When faced with extended writing in Sixth Form History students can improve their performance by following a simple routine that attempts to ensure they achieve their best performance.

## Answering the question

*What are the command instructions?*
Different questions require different types of response. For instance, 'In what ways' requires students to point out the various ways something took place in History; 'Why' questions expect students to deal with the causes or consequences of an historical event.

'How far' or 'To what extent' questions require students to produce a balanced, analytical answer. Usually, this will take the form of the case for and case against an historical question.

*Are there key words or phrases that require definition or explanation?*
It is important for students to show that they understand the meaning of the question. To do this, certain historical terms or words require explanation. For instance, if a question asked 'how far' a politician was an 'innovator', an explanation of the word 'innovator' would be required.

*Does the question have specific dates or issues that require coverage?*
If the question mentions specific dates, these must be adhered to. For instance, if you are asked to answer a question on Hitler and foreign policy it may state clear date limits, such as 1935 to 1939.

## Planning your answer

Once you have decided on what the question requires, write a brief plan. For structured questions this may be brief. This is a useful procedure to make sure that you have ordered the information you require for your answer in the most effective way. For instance, in a balanced, analytical answer this may take the form of jotting down the main points for and against an historical issue raised in the question.

## Writing the answer

*Communication skills*
The quality of written English is important in Sixth Form History. The way you present your ideas on paper can affect the quality of your answer. Therefore, punctuation, spelling and grammar, which were awarded marks at GCSE, require close attention. Use a dictionary if you are unsure of a word's meaning or spelling. Use the glossary of terms you will find in this book to help you.

*The introduction*
For structured questions you may wish to dispense with an introduction altogether and begin writing reasons to support an answer straight away. However, essay answers should begin with an introduction. These should be both concise and precise. Introductions help 'concentrate the mind' on the question you are about to answer. Remember, do not try to write a conclusion as your opening sentence. Instead, outline briefly the areas you intend to discuss in your answer.

*Balancing analysis with factual evidence*

It is important to remember that factual knowledge should be used to support analysis. Merely 'telling the story' of an historical event is not enough. A structured question or essay should contain separate paragraphs, each addressing an analytical point that helps to answer the question. If, for example, the question asks for reasons why the Cold War began in Europe, each paragraph should provide a reason. In order to support and sustain the analysis evidence is required. Therefore, your factual knowledge should be used to substantiate analysis. Good structured question and essay answers integrate analysis and factual knowledge.

*Seeing connections between reasons*

In dealing with 'why'-type questions it is important to remember that the reasons for an historical event might be interconnected. Therefore, it is important to mention the connections between reasons. Also, it might be important to identify a hierarchy of reasons – that is, are some reasons more important than others in explaining an historical event?

*Using quotations and statistical data*

One aspect of supporting evidence that sustains analysis is the use of quotations. These can be from either an historian or a contemporary. However, unless these quotations are linked with analysis and supporting evidence, they tend to be of little value.

It can also be useful to support analysis with statistical data. In questions that deal with social and economic change, precise statistics that support your argument can be very persuasive.

*The conclusion*

All structured questions and essays require conclusions. If, for example, a question requires a discussion of 'how far' you agree with a question, you should offer a judgement in your conclusion. Don't be afraid of this – say what you think. If you write an analytical answer, ably supported by factual evidence, you may under-perform because you have not provided a conclusion that deals directly with the question.

## Source analysis

Source analysis forms an integral part of the study of History.

In dealing with sources you should be aware that historical sources must be used 'in historical context' in Sixth Form History. This means you must understand the historical topic to which the source refers. Therefore, in this book sources are used with the factual information in each chapter. Also, specific source analysis questions are included at the end of most chapters.

# How to handle sources in Sixth Form History

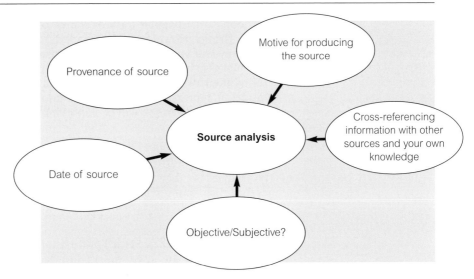

In dealing with sources, a number of basic hints will allow you to deal effectively with source-based questions and to build on your knowledge and skill in using sources at GCSE.

## Written sources

### Attribution or Provenance and date

It is important to identify who has written the source and when it was written. This information can be very important. If, for instance, a source was written by Kaiser William II, in 1914, this information will be of considerable importance if you are asked about the usefulness (utility) or reliability of the source as evidence of German policy in that year.

It is important to note that just because a source is a primary source does not mean it is more useful or less reliable than a secondary source. Both primary and secondary sources need to be analysed to decide how useful and reliable they are. This can be determined by studying other issues.

### Is the content factual or opinionated?

Once you have identified the author and date of the source, it is important to study its content. The content may be factual, stating what has happened or what may happen. On the other hand, it may contain opinions that should be handled with caution. These may contain bias. Even if a source is mainly factual, there might be important and deliberate gaps in factual evidence that can make a source biased and unreliable. Usually, written sources contain elements of both opinion and factual evidence. It is important to judge the balance between these two parts.

### Has the source been written for a particular audience?

To determine the reliability of a source it is important to know to whom it is directed. For instance, a public speech may be made to achieve a particular purpose and may not contain the author's true beliefs or feelings. In contrast, a private diary entry may be much more reliable in this respect.

### Corroborative evidence

To test whether or not a source is reliable, the use of other evidence to support or corroborate the information it contains is important. Cross-referencing with other sources is a way of achieving this; so is cross-referencing with historical information contained within a chapter.

### Visual sources

*Cartoons*

Cartoons are a popular form of source used at both GCSE and in Sixth Form History. However, analysing cartoons can be a demanding exercise. Not only will you be expected to understand the content of the cartoon, you may also have to explain a written caption – which appears usually at the bottom of the cartoon. In addition, cartoons will need placing in historical context. Therefore, a good knowledge of the subject matter of the topic of the cartoon will be important.

*Photographs*

'The camera never lies'! This phrase is not always true. When analysing photographs, study the attribution/provenance and date. Photographs can be changed so they are not always an accurate visual representation of events. Also, to test whether or not a photograph is a good representation of events you will need corroborative evidence.

*Maps*

Maps which appear in Sixth Form History are predominantly secondary sources. These are used to support factual coverage in the text by providing information in a different medium. Therefore, to assess whether or not information contained in maps is accurate or useful, reference should be made to other information. It is also important with written sources to check the attribution and date. These could be significant.

*Statistical data and graphs*

It is important when dealing with this type of source to check carefully the nature of the information contained in data or in a graph. It might state that the information is in tons (tonnes) or another measurement. Be careful to check if the information is in index numbers. These are a statistical device where a base year is chosen and given the figure 100. All other figures are based on a percentage difference from that base year. For instance, if 1900 is taken as a base year for arms production it is given the figure of 100. If the index number for arms production in 1905 is 117 it means that iron production has increased by 17% above the 1900 figure.

An important point to remember when dealing with data and graphs over a period of time is to identify trends and patterns in the information. Merely describing the information in written form is not enough.

# Historical interpretation

An important feature of both GCSE and Sixth Form History is the issue of historical interpretation. In Sixth Form History it is important for students to be able to explain why historians differ, or have differed, in their interpretation of the past.

### Availability of evidence

An important reason is the availability of evidence on which to base historical judgements. As new evidence comes to light, an historian today may have more information on which to base judgements than historians in the past.

### 'A philosophy of history?'

Many historians have a specific view of history that will affect the way they make their historical judgements. For instance, Marxist historians – who take the view from the writings of Karl Marx the founder of modern socialism – believe that society has been made up of competing economic and social classes. They also place considerable importance on economic reasons in human decision making. Therefore, a Marxist historian of fascism may take a completely different viewpoint to a non-Marxist historian.

### The role of the individual

Some historians have seen past history as being moulded by the acts of specific individuals who have changed history. Bismarck, William II and Hitler are seen as individuals whose personality and beliefs changed the course of German history. Other historians have tended to 'downplay' the role of individuals; instead, they highlight the importance of more general social, economic and political change.

### Placing different emphasis on the same historical evidence

Even if historians do not possess different philosophies of history or place different emphasis on the role of the individual, it is still possible for them to disagree because they place different emphases on aspects of the same factual evidence. As a result, Sixth Form History should be seen as a subject that encourages debate about the past based on historical evidence.

## Progression in Sixth Form History

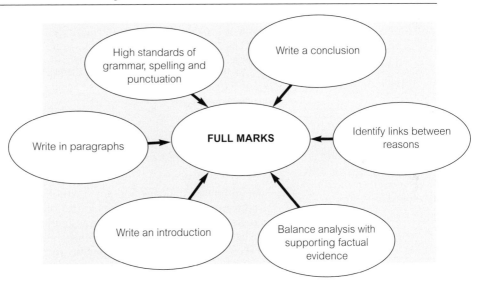

The ability to achieve high standards in Sixth Form History involves the acquisition of a number of skills:

● Good written communication skills

● Acquiring a sound factual knowledge

● Evaluating factual evidence and making historical conclusions based on that evidence

● Source analysis

● Understanding the nature of historical interpretation

● Understanding the causes and consequences of historical events

- Understanding themes in history which will involve a study of a specific topic over a long period of time

- Understanding the ideas of change and continuity associated with themes.

Students should be aware that the acquisition of these skills will take place gradually over the time spent in the Sixth Form. At the beginning of the course, the main emphasis may be on the acquisition of factual knowledge, particularly when the body of knowledge studied at GCSE was different.

When dealing with causation, students will have to build on their skills from GCSE. They will not only be expected to identify reasons for an historical event but also to provide a hierarchy of causes. They should identify the main causes and less important causes. They may also identify that causes may be interconnected and linked. Progression in Sixth Form History will come with answering the questions at the end of each sub-section in this book and practising the skills outlined through the use of the factual knowledge contained in the book.

## Examination technique

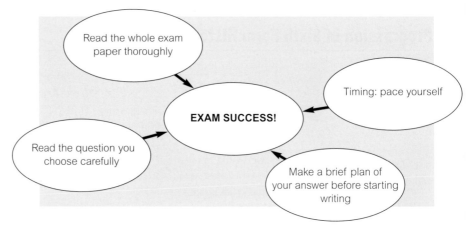

The ultimate challenge for any Sixth Form historian is the ability to produce quality work under examination conditions. Examinations will take the form of either modular examinations taken in January and June or an 'end of course' set of examinations.

Here is some advice on how to improve your performance in an examination.

- Read the whole examination paper thoroughly
  Make sure that the questions you choose are those for which you can produce a good answer. Don't rush – allow time to decide which questions to choose. It is probably too late to change your mind half way through answering a question.

- Read the question very carefully
  Once you have made the decision to answer a specific question, read it very carefully. Make sure you understand the precise demands of the question. Think about what is required in your answer. It is much better to think about this before you start writing, rather than trying to steer your essay in a different direction half way through.

**Revision tips**

Even before the examination begins make sure that you have revised thoroughly. Revision tips on the main topics in this book appear on the Collins website:

www.collinseducation.com

● Make a brief plan
Sketch out what you intend to include in your answer. Order the points you want to make. Examiners are not impressed with additional information included at the end of the essay, with indicators such as arrows or asterisks.

● Pace yourself as you write
Success in examinations has a lot to do with successful time management. If, for instance, you have to answer an essay question in approximately 45 minutes, then you should be one-third of the way through after 15 minutes. With 30 minutes gone, you should start writing the last third of your answer.

Where a question is divided into sub-questions, make sure you look at the mark tariff for each question. If in a 20-mark question a sub-question is worth a maximum of 5 marks, then you should spend approximately one-quarter of the time allocated for the whole question on this sub-question.

# 1 International relations: A synoptic overview

## Key Issues

- How did the political balance of power change in the world between 1879 and 2004?

- How successful were attempts to maintain international peace in the period from 1879 to 2004?

- What impact did the changing nature of warfare have on international relations?

**1.1** How far did Europe dominate international relations in the period from 1879 to 1945?

**1.2** Why and how were the two superpowers able to dominate international relations in the period from 1945 to 1991?

**1.3** How did regional disputes affect international relations in the period from 1879 to 2004?

**1.4** To what extent were international attempts to maintain peace a success in the period from 1879 to 2004?

**1.5** In what ways did the changing nature of warfare affect international relations?

## 1.1 How far did Europe dominate international relations in the period from 1879 to 1945?

**Autocratic monarch**: a monarch with complete political power.

In 1879 Europe was dominated by five Great Powers – Britain, Germany, France, Russia and Austria-Hungary.

In geographical size, Russia was the largest power. It comprised 20% of the world's land surface and was ruled by an **autocratic monarch**, the Tsar.

Britain, however, had the largest Empire. By 1914 the British Empire covered 25% of the world's land surface and contained one third of the world's population. It was the empire 'on which the sun would not set'. The jewel of the Empire was India. The British Indian Empire comprised the present-day countries of India, Pakistan, Bangladesh, Sri Lanka and Myanmar. However, Britain also had colonies on other continents. Some of these – Australia, New Zealand, Canada and South Africa – contained large numbers of European immigrants.

The dominant continental power from the mid-seventeenth century to 1870 was France but, following the Franco-Prussian War of 1870–71, the newly formed German Empire replaced France in that position. Finally, Austria–Hungary was the weakest of the Great Powers. It was a multi-racial empire of thirteen nationalities, dominated by Germans in Austria and Hungarians.

In the period from 1879 to 1918 Europe dominated international relations. The main international phenomenon in this period was the 'New Imperialism', with European states rapidly acquiring colonial possessions across the globe.

By 1914 most of the world was under the control of a European power. The main exceptions were China and the Americas, but even here European influence was considerable. In the Americas, the various states were created by the descendants of Europeans. The most striking examples were the United States and the Spanish- and Portuguese-speaking states of Latin America. However, even here the largest American state of all –

Canada –was part of the British Empire. In China, European powers acquired trading rights and coastal towns as trading bases.

The best example of the New Imperialism was the partition of Africa. Between 1880 and 1914 the vast majority of Africa was acquired by European states. Only Liberia (guaranteed independent by the USA) and Ethiopia (one of the world's oldest nations) remained outside direct European control. The acquisition of African territory involved a wide variety of European states. Great Powers such as Britain, France and Germany were joined by Spain, Portugal, Italy and Belgium in acquiring African colonies.

Why did European states acquire so much of Africa during this period? This is the centre of considerable historical controversy and debate. To some historians, European rivalry for colonies was merely an extension of rivalry between European states beyond Europe. France, for instance, having been defeated in the Franco-Prussian War, 1870–71, attempted to regain international prestige by gaining a large overseas empire. Others have seen the acquisition of colonies in economic terms. From 1873 to 1896 the European economy faced a major slowdown, known at the time as the 'Great Depression'. In a bid to acquire raw materials and potential markets for goods, European states acquired overseas colonies. Perhaps the most interesting explanation of the partition of Africa came from two British historians, Robinson and Gallagher. They contended that the British government had to protect and maintain the seaways to and from her Indian Empire – her main overseas interest. This meant acquiring control over the Cape of Good Hope, in southern Africa and the Suez Canal area (Egypt). Having acquired political control over these areas by the early 1880s Britain then began to move inland to ensure that these areas were secure. This sparked retaliation by other European states, most notably France and Germany. The speed of the process has led many historians to call the development the 'Scramble for Africa'.

Underlying European imperial growth was the economic power of Europe. From 1760 Britain became the world's first industrial state. In the nineteenth century Britain was joined by Belgium, Germany and France. By 1914, Britain was the world's greatest economic power, followed by Germany. The only non-European power to rival European dominance was the United States.

In addition to economic power, Europe contained states which were the world's dominant military powers. Britain was the world's greatest naval power. In 1889 Britain's government passed the Naval Defence Act, which declared that the Royal Navy should be at least as large as the world's next two largest navies combined. In 1889 this meant France and Russia. The German Empire had the world's greatest army. All Europe's major powers, except Britain, had compulsory military service (conscription) which meant that they could field armies of millions of men. The largest of all was the Russian army.

In 1914 Europe was dominant in military, economic and colonial power. However, the First World War of 1914–18 transformed this position. By 1918 four European empires had collapsed – the Russian Empire, the German Empire, the Ottoman (Turkish) Empire and Austria–Hungary.

The major European powers had lost millions of men dead and wounded. Even the victorious Allied powers of Britain and France owed millions in war loans to countries like the USA. By 1918 the USA was the world's dominant economic power. In the Far East, Japan was emerging as both a major regional military and economic power.

From 1919, European states still dominated international relations. They were able to do this for various reasons. After the First World War, apart from Germany, European states still possessed vast overseas colonies. Also, in the period 1919 to 1941 the United States adopted an isolationist approach to world affairs. The turning-point in international relations came following the onset of world economic depression from 1929. In 1931, Japan invaded and occupied the Chinese province of Manchuria. In 1933, Hitler came to power in Germany with the aim of destroying the First World War peace settlement and making Germany the dominant European power.

By 1939 Europe faced another world war. The Second World War caused widespread devastation, right across Europe – far greater than the war of 1914–18. In the USSR alone, 25 million died. Huge areas of Germany were destroyed by aerial bombardment by 1945. The greatest crime of the Second World War was the destruction of European Jewry. By 1945, 6 million Jews had been exterminated by Nazi Germany.

By 1945 all Europe had been occupied by two vast armies. In the East, the Soviet Red army occupied all eastern and central Europe. In the West, the armies of Britain, the USA and Canada had liberated all western Europe and Italy from Nazi rule.

**1. In what ways did European states dominate international relations in the period from 1879 to 1945?**

**2. What do you regard as the most convincing reason for the development of European colonial empires from 1879?**

**3. Why do you think European dominance came to an end by 1945?**

Although Britain was one of the victorious Allies, it was economically bankrupt by the end of the war. Germany and Austria were divided into four military zones (British, French, American and Russian). In the Far East, the Japanese Empire had been destroyed and was occupied by British, Commonwealth and American troops.

By 1945, European dominance of international relations was coming to an end. From 1945 to 1991 world affairs were dominated by two super-powers – the USA and the USSR. Also from 1945 European states such as Britain and France began a process of decolonisation, whereby their over-seas possessions were given independence. And by 1975 European overseas empires had all but disappeared.

## 1.2 Why and how were the two superpowers able to dominate international relations in the period from 1945 to 1991?

1945 was a major turning-point in international relations. European states ceased to dominate world affairs, and international relations was domi-nated by two world superpowers – the USA and the USSR.

These two states had dominated the defeat of Germany in the Second World War. (The USA had also been dominant in the defeat of Japan in the Far East and Pacific.) These two states were the world's greatest military powers. The Soviet Red Army numbered its troops in several millions. The USA had surpassed the Royal Navy as the world's greatest military force.

In addition, the USA, in 1945, possessed nuclear weapons. These had been used to end the war with Japan. Hiroshima and Nagasaki were the only cities on earth to be attacked using nuclear weapons. However, by 1949 the USSR had begun testing its own nuclear weapons, and from then on the world was subjected to an international arms race in nuclear weapons.

The domination of the superpowers was linked directly to the Cold War – a period of international tension which lasted from 1945 to 1991. In the Cold War both the USA and the USSR were in a constant state of war preparation. Both superpowers built up huge arsenals of weapons and both engaged in propaganda warfare. The USA represented the capitalist economic world, while the USSR represented the communist world. From 1945 to 1991 both superpowers attempted to spread their views and their particular political and economic structures. In 1945 the USSR and Mongolia were the only two communist states in the worlds. By the 1970s they had been joined by China, North Korea, Cuba, Vietnam, Laos,

Cambodia and all the states of eastern Europe that had been occupied by the Soviet army at the end of the Second World War. In addition, there were struggles across Africa between supporters of the USA and supporters of the USSR in the 1960s and 1970s.

The domination of the superpowers was aided by the decline of European states. Germany had been defeated and divided in 1945. Britain and France found it increasingly difficult to maintain their overseas empires after 1945. In 1947, Britain gave independence to India and Pakistan, beginning a process of decolonisation. By 2004 the once great British Empire had all but disappeared. France, after 1945, fought two major wars in order to preserve its empire. From 1946–54 it fought a war in **Indo-China**, losing to the communist Vietnamese, and in Algeria France faced another bitter colonial war, which led to French withdrawal in 1962.

In addition to the collapse of their overseas empires, Britain and France could not compete either militarily or economically with the two super-powers. Both feared the USSR and were willing to follow the USA's lead in opposing Soviet power.

After decades of tension, the Cold war came to an end in 1991. By the 1980s the USSR was no longer in a position to compete with the USA either militarily or economically. Under the leadership of Mikhail Gorbachev the USSR began the process of ending tension between the two superpowers. However, this process helped spark off open opposition to communist rule in the Soviet **satellite states** of central and eastern Europe. In 1989 communist rule collapsed in all the Soviet satellite states and, in 1991, communist rule collapsed within the USSR itself.

**Indo-China**: Modern-day Vietnam, Laos and Cambodia.

**Satellite state**: A state under the influence and control of another.

---

1. What do you regard as the most important reason why the two superpowers dominated international relations from 1945?

2. In what ways did the competition between the two superpowers affect international relations?

---

## 1.3 How did regional disputes affect international relations in the period from 1879 to 2004?

In the period from 1879 to 2004, international relations was dominated by the major powers. From 1879 to 1918, the major powers were the five Great Powers of Europe. Within this framework, regional disputes threat-ened to increase tension between the Great Powers. Between 1879 and 1914 the major regional dispute affecting European powers was in **the Balkans**. This peninsula in South East Europe was an area of interest for Britain, Austria–Hungary and Russia. For much of the nineteenth century the area had been controlled by the Ottoman Empire. However, with the rise of Balkan nationalism, the Ottomans found it increasingly difficult to maintain control of the region. In 1875–78 a major international crisis developed in the Balkans which almost brought war between Russia, on the one side, and Britain and Austria–Hungary on the other. From 1879 to 1914 the Balkans were a major cause of tension between Russia and Austria–Hungary. And in 1914 it was a crisis in the Balkans that was the immediate cause of the outbreak of the First World War.

In the inter-war period (1918–1939) regional disputes continued to have a major impact on international relations. In 1931 Japan occupied the northern Chinese province of Manchuria – an action which had a major impact on the international prestige of the League of Nations. Together with the Italian invasion of Abyssinia in 1935, these disputes revealed the inability of the League to prevent war and to punish aggressive powers.

The most significant regional disputes in the 1930s, however, involved Germany. Hitler's aim to destroy the Paris Peace Settlement of 1919–20 led directly to the Munich Crisis of 1938. This crisis brought Europe to the brink of war. However, the policy of **appeasement** adopted by Britain and France averted war in 1938. But it did not stop Hitler's aggressive foreign

**The Balkans**: Peninsula of South East Europe. Today it comprises Greece, Macedonia, Bulgaria, Romania, Albania, Montenegro, Serbia, Bosnia-Herzegovina ,Croatia and Turkey-in-Europe.

**Appeasement**: Policy of avoiding war by granting concessions.

**Bohemia and Moravia**: Part of the modern-day Czech Republic.

policy, and when he occupied **Bohemia and Moravia** in March 1939, Britain and France abandoned appeasement. In September 1939 both powers declared war on Germany, following Hitler's invasion of Poland.

After 1945 regional disputes were usually linked directly to the Cold War between the USA and the USSR. In June 1950, when North Korea invaded South Korea, the resulting war was a confrontation between the communist and non-communist worlds. This situation was repeated in Vietnam in the years 1964 to 1973. Although it began as a regional dispute, the Arab–Israeli conflict had become linked to the Cold War by the 1960s, with the USA supporting Israel and the USSR the Arab states.

Following the end of the Cold War in 1991 the Arab–Israeli conflict continued to be a major issue in international relations. Attempts by the UN and the USA to end the dispute ensured this regional dispute remained at the centre of the international stage. Conflict in the Middle East was widened in the 1980s with the outbreak of the Iran–Iraq War. In 1990 Iraq again became a centre of international concern when it invaded Kuwait. The 1991 Gulf War saw the intervention of UN forces – under US leadership – engaged in a major Middle Eastern war.

The 9/11 attack on the USA in 2001 transformed the international scene. From 2001 the USA led a 'war against terror' where Islamic extremists were targeted by the USA and its allies as enemies of international peace.

In 2001–02, US-led forces overthrew the Taliban regime in Afghanistan. In 2003, war again involved Iraq. This time a coalition of forces led by the US and UK toppled Saddam Hussein, only to become embroiled in a protracted guerrilla war against Iraqi and Islamic insurgents.

By 2004 the Middle East was the major area of international instability, with the capacity to involve the world's major powers and the UN.

---

**1. What do you regard as the most important regional dispute which affected international relations in the period 1879 to 2004? Give reasons for your answer.**

**2. What impact did the Cold War have on regional disputes?**

---

## 1.4 To what extent were international attempts to maintain peace a success in the period from 1879 to 2004?

In the period 1879 to 1918, European powers dominated international relations. In this period the main guarantor of peace was the European balance of power. Created after the Napoleonic Wars, in 1815, the balance of power was the idea that no one European power had the capacity to dominate the European continent. The mechanism used to ensure peace was the Concert of Europe. Whenever a regional dispute threatened European peace, the Great Powers were meant to act 'in concert' to solve it. This occurred in 1878 with the Treaty of Berlin – a five-Power agreement bringing peace to the Balkans. However, from 1879 Europe was divided by the development of the Alliance System. By 1894 Europe was faced with two rival military alliance systems – the Triple Alliance of Germany, Austria–Hungary and Italy, and the Franco-Russian Alliance. And in 1914, during the July Crisis, the balance of power failed to stop Europe descending into a major war.

Because of this catastrophic failure of the balance of power, moves were made after the First World War to create a completely new international organisation to preserve peace – the League of Nations, formed in 1920. Unfortunately, the League did not possess any military resources to enforce its decisions. Some major powers – such as the USA – refused to join. The USSR only joined in 1934, and Japan, Germany and Italy all left the League in the 1930s. By the late 1930s Britain and France abandoned the League, choosing instead to follow their own policy of appeasement to maintain European peace. When war broke out in September 1939 the League of

Nations lost any remaining credibility as a guarantor of international peace.

In 1945 a new international organisation to preserve peace was assembled – the United Nations (UN). This time the two superpowers were members and, unlike its predecessor, the UN had the ability to raise peace-keeping forces from amongst its members to preserve peace. In 1950, the Korean War proved that the UN could stand up to military aggression by defending South Korea against North Korean and Chinese attack. However, for most of the period 1945 to 2004 the UN proved unable to prevent wars, as was illustrated by the Vietnam War, the Arab–Israeli wars and the wars involving Iraq from 1980 to 2003.

A major reason preventing wars between the major powers was the existence of nuclear weapons. The existence of nuclear weapons led to the development of the concept of 'MAD' (mutually assured destruction). Both the USA and the USSR believed that if either side used nuclear weapons against the other, both superpowers would face complete annihilation.

1. What do you regard as the most effective method of maintaining international peace in the period from 1879 to 2004?

2. Which organisation was more successful – the League of Nations or the United Nations? Explain your answer.

## 1.5 In what ways did the changing nature of warfare affect international relations?

In the years from 1879 to 2004, warfare went through a revolution. In 1879 armies comprised infantry, cavalry and artillery. Infantry used rifles – machine guns were still in their infancy. However, all major European countries, except Britain, had compulsory military service. This meant that the Great Powers had the ability to field armies of hundreds of thousands of men. In addition, the speed at which armies could reach the battle front was greatly enhanced by the development of railways. In the mid-nineteenth century, wars in Europe were associated with the rapid movement of armies. Most wars were swift, lasting in some cases just weeks (seven weeks in the case of the 1866 war between Prussia and Austria) or sometimes months (eighteen months in the case of the Franco-Prussian War).

In 1914 all the Great Powers expected the First World War to be a rapid war of movement. The development of trench warfare and the war of attrition – which lasted four and half years – was unexpected. In the 1914–18 war defensive weapons – such as machine guns, artillery and trenches defended by barbed wire – were far more effective than the main offensive weapon, mass infantry assaults. As a result, the death rate in the First World War was tremendous and far greater than any previous war. The nature of warfare in the First World War put great strains on each of the combatants.

As a direct result of defeat in the war, political revolutions occurred. In February 1917 the Tsar was overthrown in Russia, and in the following October the Bolshevik Revolution created the world's first communist state. In October 1918 revolution spread across Austria–Hungary, and by 1919 the empire had fragmented into a number of smaller states. In November 1918 a political revolution in Germany overthrew the Kaiser and created a democratic republic.

In the inter-war period a new effective offensive weapon was developed – the tank. The tanks first used in 1916 had been slow and liable to mechanical failure, but by 1939 tanks had become more mobile and reliable. In addition, the Germans had developed a method of warfare which used mass formations of tanks to break through enemy lines. This *Blitzkrieg* (lightning war) was used to great effect in the German attacks on Poland in 1939 and on France in 1940. In their 1941 attack on the USSR *Blitzkrieg* almost brought the Germans victory.

However, German failure to defeat the USSR in 1941 was linked to another major development in warfare – 'total war'. In the twentieth century the entire economies of warring countries were geared towards the maximum production of war material. As a result, the USA and USSR, as the world's greatest economic powers were able to out-produce Germany and its allies, and this was a major factor behind the Allied victory.

The other major development in twentieth-century warfare was the use of aerial warfare. In 1914–18 the Germans had used airships (Zeppelins) to bomb civilian targets. In the Second World War the advance in plane technology meant that large formations of bombers could devastate whole cities. From 1942 to 1945 Britain and the USA destroyed most German cities by bombing. In Japan, one US air force raid in 1945 killed over 100,000 civilians in Tokyo.

The biggest change in the nature of warfare came in August 1945, when the US dropped atomic bombs on the Japanese cities of Hiroshima and Nagasaki. In 1949 the USSR tested its first atomic weapons, and from 1949 to the 1980s the USA and the USSR engaged in a nuclear arms race. By 1988 both superpowers had sufficient nuclear weapons to destroy the entire world several times over. By the 1980s the superpowers had been joined in the nuclear weapons 'club' by Britain, France, China, India and Israel. In an odd way, nuclear weapons made war less likely, because fear of massive retaliation prevented the major powers from going to war with each other.

In naval warfare, most navies in 1879 had ironclad or iron battleships which were steam powered. By 1900 developments in naval weaponry meant that warships could fire one-ton shells at each other from several miles apart. In 1904 Britain revolutionised battleship design with the launch of HMS *Dreadnought*, a heavily armoured steel ship with large-calibre guns.

By 1914 naval warfare between the Great Powers envisaged battles between large formation of *Dreadnought*-like battleships. However, the First World War saw the introduction of a completely new naval weapon which would revolutionise warfare – the submarine. German submarine warfare had a devastating effect on Allied merchant shipping, which almost forced Britain out of the war by the end of 1917.

In the Second World War more advanced submarines almost repeated the German attacks of the 1914–18 war. However, the most effective naval weapon of the Second World War was the aircraft carrier, which replaced battleships as the premier naval weapons. This change was most apparent in the Pacific war between the USA and Japan.

From 1945 both the submarine and aircraft carrier became the dominant naval weapons. By the 1960s many submarines were nuclear-powered and carried nuclear weapons. By 2004 the supreme naval weapon in terms of sheer military power was the submarine. However, like land-based nuclear weapons, it was difficult to envisage their use without involving global nuclear war. Therefore, the aircraft carrier remained the most effective naval weapon in terms of its impact on war. The aircraft carrier gave countries like the USA the means to use carrier-based aircraft to attack opponents across the globe. Aircraft carriers played a major role in the Korean War, the Vietnam War and the Gulf wars of 1991 and 2003.

**1. What do you regard as the most significant development in warfare in the period from 1879 to 2004?**

**2. To what extent has the development of nuclear weapons affected international relations?**

1. Re-arrange the points in the grid so that the left-hand column consists of what you regard as major factors affecting international relations, and the right-hand column shows examples of each one.

If you feel there are not enough specific examples of the major factors, pick other examples from this synoptic overview chapter. You may include more than one specific example for each major factor.

International relations
1879–2004

| | |
|---|---|
| New Imperialism | Maintaining international peace |
| Scramble for Africa | Balance of power |
| Alliance System | League of Nations |
| Regional disputes | United Nations |
| Korean War | Changes in the nature of warfare |
| Cold War | *Blitzkrieg* |

# 2 The causes of the First World War

## Key Issues

- How far did the alliance system increase tension in Europe between 1879 and 1914?

- How important were the Balkans to the outbreak of war in 1914?

- To what extent was Germany most responsible for the outbreak of war in 1914?

2.1 International relations in Europe in 1879

2.2 What was the impact of the alliance system on European international relations from 1879?

2.3 Why did Germany embark on *Weltpolitik* (world politics) after 1897?

2.4 What were the main causes of tensions between the European powers in the decade before 1914?

2.5 What impact did the Balkans have on international relations in the period 1912–1913?

2.6 Why did the July Crisis lead to the outbreak of European war?

2.7 Historical Interpretation: Was Germany completely to blame for the outbreak of war?

## Framework of Events

| | |
|---|---|
| 1879 | Dual Alliance between Germany and Austria–Hungary |
| 1881 | Renewal of the *Dreikaiserbund* (Three Emperors' League) |
| 1882 | Triple Alliance (*Triplice*) between Germany, Austria–Hungary and Italy |
| 1885–86 | Bulgarian Crisis |
| 1887 | Reinsurance Treaty between Germany and Russia |
| 1890 | Germany fails to renew Reinsurance Treaty |
| 1894 | Franco-Russian Alliance |
| 1902 | June: Renewal of Triple Alliance between Germany, Austria and Italy for six years |
| | November: Franco-Italian Entente |
| 1904 | February: Outbreak of Russo-Japanese War |
| | April: *Entente Cordiale*: Britain and France resolve colonial tensions |
| 1905 | Russian defeat in Russo-Japanese War |
| 1906 | First Moroccan crisis resolved in favour of France |
| | June: Third German naval bill |
| 1907 | July: Further renewal of Triple Alliance |
| 1908 | June: Fourth German naval bill |
| | October: Austria annexes Bosnia and Herzegovina |
| 1911 | July: Agadir Crisis |
| | August: Military conversations between France and Russia |
| | September: Outbreak of war between Italy and Turkey |
| 1912 | October: Outbreak of First Balkan War |
| 1912 | 8 December: German War Cabinet meeting |
| 1913 | June: Outbreak of Second Balkan War |
| | November: Zabern incident in Alsace-Lorraine heightens Franco-German tensions |
| 1914 | June: Assassination of Archduke Franz Ferdinand in Sarajevo |
| | July: Austro-Hungarian ultimatum to Serbia, followed by declaration of war. Russian mobilisation |
| | August: German declaration of war on Russia. French mobilisation. German ultimatum to France, followed by declaration of war. German invasion of Belgium, followed by British declaration of war on Germany. Russian defeats in East Prussia |

| 1914 | September: Germany's Schlieffen Plan thwarted by French victory in First Battle of the Marne and by British resistance in First Battle of Ypres |
|------|------|
| 1915 | February–December: Allied offensive against Turkey at Gallipoli |
| | April: Second Battle of Ypres |
| | May: Italian declaration of war on Austria–Hungary |
| | August: German forces capture Warsaw |
| 1916 | February–November: Battle of Verdun |
| | May: Battle of Jutland |
| | June–September: Brusilov Offensive on Eastern Front |
| | July: Major allied offensive on the Somme |
| 1917 | March: Revolution in Russia forces abdication of Nicholas II |
| | April: USA declares war on Germany |
| | July–November: Third Battle of Ypres |
| | November: Bolsheviks seize power in Russia |
| 1918 | January: Woodrow Wilson publishes '14 Points' |
| | March: Treaty of Brest-Litovsk. Beginning of German Spring Offensive |
| | July: Second Battle of the Marne |
| | September: German retreat to Siegfried (Hindenburg) Line |
| | 3 November: Austria–Hungary withdraws from the war |
| | 11 November: Germany signs armistice. |

**1 Which of the reasons in the mind map was the most important in explaining the outbreak of the First World War? Give reasons for your answer.**

**2. Can you link any of the reasons in the mind map? For instance, German *Weltpolitik* and the Agadir Crisis are linked. Can you identify any other links?**

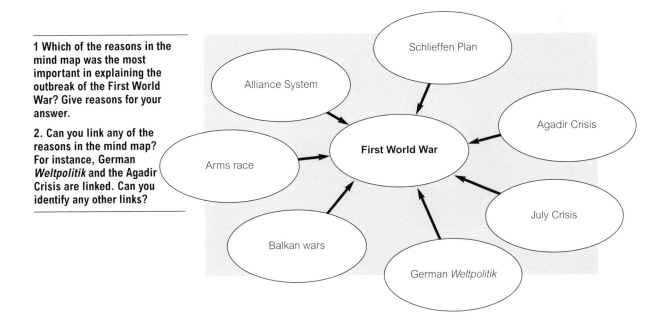

## Overview

THE First World War was one of the most important events in modern world history. As a result of the war, four empires collapsed – Germany, Austria–Hungary, Russia and the Ottoman Empire. A by-product of these changes was the replacement of monarchic governments by republican governments across Europe. The war also cost the lives of 9 million people. Before 1914 the biggest battle in the western world had been the Battle of Gettysburg in the American Civil War. It lasted three days, and involved 230,000 soldiers. In the First World War the Battle of Verdun lasted 11 months, involved over 1 million troops and cost the lives of hundreds of thousands. No wonder, after 1918, people referred to the conflict as 'the Great War'.

Between 1815 and 1914 very few wars took place between Europe's major powers, and these had been limited to the period 1854 to 1871. How did such a destructive war occur? Ever since the end of the First World War historians have been trying to answer this question.

**Treaty of Versailles**: Peace treaty between the Allies and Germany at the end of the First World War. Germany was forced to sign.

**Reparations**: Payments by the defeated power to the victorious powers.

In June 1919, the first official verdict was made on the causes of the First World War – in the **Treaty of Versailles**. Under Article 231 of the Treaty (the 'War Guilt' clause) it was claimed that Germany and its allies had caused the war. To confirm this view, Germany was forced to pay huge **reparations** to the Allied powers. It took until 1921 to come up with the final amount to be paid – £66 billion. Opinion in Germany was outraged. Ordinary Germans thought they had been fighting a defensive war against aggression from the Allied powers, most notably Russia. Following the Treaty of Versailles successive German governments attempted to show that they did not cause the war. Germany was the first country involved in the war to release thousands of official documents for the pre-1914 period in an attempt to 'clear their name'.

**Memoirs**: Someone's personal reminiscences, written down and published.

**Diplomatic system**: The conduct of foreign relations.

The German case was aided, in 1929, by former British war leader, David Lloyd George. In his **memoirs** he claimed that no one country was responsible for the outbreak of the war. Instead, the war occurred because the European **diplomatic system** had failed to prevent its outbreak. His views were supported by many historians during the 1930s. An American historian, Sidney Bradshaw Fay, claimed that a variety of factors all combined to cause the war. He cited the 'alliance system' before 1914 as a cause of increasing tension. He also mentioned the arms race between Germany and France, and Germany and Britain. Finally, he mentioned the chronic political instability in the Balkan area of Europe, in the decade before 1914. The Balkans became the setting for the crisis – the 'July Crisis' – which caused the outbreak of war. On 28 June 1914, the assassination of Franz Ferdinand, the heir apparent to the Austro-Hungarian throne, sparked off a series of events which led to war between the **Great Powers** by August.

**Great Powers**: The five major powers in Europe before 1914 – Britain, France, Germany, Russia and Austria–Hungary. Great Power status was based on military power.

Fay's views were supported by other historians. In 1951 an international meeting of historians held to discuss the causes of the First World War claimed that there were a wide variety of reasons and that all the Great Powers and Serbia were in some way involved in the outbreak of war.

**Mobilisation**: The process of calling up reserve soldiers to the army. By 1914 it took Germany and France approximately two weeks to mobilise; Austria–Hungary four weeks, and Russia six weeks. To many in 1914 mobilisation meant war. Once mobilisation was activated it was virtually impossible to stop.

An interesting addition to the debate was made by British historians A.J.P. Taylor. In *War by Timetable* he claimed that the **mobilisation** plans of the Great Powers limited greatly the ability of diplomats to provide a peaceful solution. Once one Great Power mobilised its armed forces it forced the other powers to do the same. In the critical period from 28 July to 4 August 1914, claimed Taylor, the diplomats lost control of events. Once Austria–Hungary had declared war on Serbia a series of mobilisation orders, by Russia, Germany and France transformed a local Balkan war into a major European war.

The debate on the causes of the First World War took a radical turn in 1961. In that year a German historian, Fritz Fischer, produced *Grasp for World Power: German War Aims 1914–1918*. The book, as its title suggests, was about the war itself. However, Fischer claimed that the main set of German war aims in 1914, the 'September Programme' was so detailed that it could not have been produced between the outbreak of war and September 1914. The implication – that Germany had drawn up its war aims before the war – caused outrage in Germany. It suggested that Germany had been more responsible than any other Great Power for the outbreak of war.

This had the added impact of placing Hitler's rule in Germany in a different perspective. Until 1961 many Germans had claimed that Hitler's rule was the exception to the development of German history. Hitler's decision to launch aggressive war was completely at odds with the rest of modern German history. Now Fischer was suggesting that Germany was willing to launch aggressive war in 1914 and 1939!

With such an intense debate about his book, Fischer was asked to justify his views. His reply came in 1967 with *War of Illusions*, a study of German Foreign Policy 1911–1914. With access to a wide variety of German documents Fischer claimed that Germany was willing to risk a major European war to solve its problems in foreign policy. These had begun with the launch of *Weltpolitik* (world politics) in 1897. From that year, Germany attempted to become a world power alongside other world powers, such as Britain and the USA. To achieve this end it attempted to acquire a large overseas empire. To assist in this quest it planned to build a world-class navy to rival the Royal Navy. From 1897 to 1912 Germany attempted, with very limited success, to acquire overseas colonies. Other Great Powers were so alarmed by Germany's actions that they sank old differences and began to ally with each other. In 1904 Britain signed the Entente Cordiale with France. In 1907 it signed the Anglo-Russian Entente. By 1912, Germany was feeling encircled by 'hostile' Great Powers. To the German government, other Great Powers were jealous of Germany's economic and military strength, and they were trying to prevent Germany taking its 'rightful' place as a world power. So in 1914 Germany went to war to achieve its aims.

In support of Fischer's view came another German historian, Immanuel Geiss. In 1978, in *German Foreign Policy 1871–1914*, he produced evidence of a War Cabinet Meeting of the German government held on 8 December 1912. Geiss claimed that this meeting discussed Germany's international position and came to the view that it should solve its problems through aggressive war. Evidence came from the diary of Admiral Muller, second in command of the German Navy, and from the diary of the Bavarian State representative, both at the meeting.

An important addition to the historical controversy was made by another historian, Volker Berghahn, in 1973. In *Germany and the Approach of War, 1914* he claimed that the decision to go to war was as much to do with Germany's domestic problems as with its international position. Berghahn noted that Germany was ruled by an elite of German aristocrats and landowners, mainly based in eastern Prussia. They dominated the government and the officer class of the army. Although Germany was ruled by the Kaiser it had a democratically elected national parliament, the Reichstag. By 1912 the largest party in the Reichstag was the Social Democratic Party (SDP). It was a left-wing party which wanted major social, economic and political change in Germany.

By 1912 the German government feared the growth of the SDP. They believed that a short, successful European war would unite the German people behind the

Kaiser. This would then allow the Kaiser and his government to ban the SDP. A similar problem had faced Bismarck and the Prussian king in the early 1860s. At that time the opponents were the Prussian liberals. In the successful wars of 1864, 1866 and 1870 Bismarck won over the majority of liberals in return for achieving German unity.

Even though many historians believe that Germany was more responsible than other countries for causing the war it does not mean other European countries were blameless. Serbia, supplied the assassins of Franz Ferdinand with arms and training. Austria–Hungary was determined to go to war with Serbia in order to prevent a unification of Austria–Hungary with Serbia. Russia's decision to call a general mobilisation of its army on 30 July forced Germany to retaliate. France was Russia's main supplier of arms. During the July Crisis, Britain's failure to make clear to Germany its plans to support France if attacked by Germany, helped force Germany to make the wrong assumption that Britain might stay neutral in a major war.

**1. Draw a timeline highlighting the main stages of the historical debate on the causes of the First World War.**

**2. Explain why Germany has been singled out as the Great Power most responsible for the outbreak of the war.**

## 2.1 International relations in Europe in 1879

### Who were the five Great Powers?

In 1879, Europe was dominated by five Great Powers – Britain, France, Germany, Russia and Austria–Hungary. These states held their position because of their military power, and since 1815 it had been their responsibility to ensure European peace. When political crises threatened to erupt into wider conflict, the Great Powers were expected to act, in concert, to prevent major war. This 'Concert of Europe' worked well in the period 1815 to 1854. Conflicts over Belgium (1830–39) and the Middle East (1839–41) were settled in this way. However, from 1854 to 1871 the Concert of Europe collapsed and a series of major European wars occurred. These included the Crimean War (Russia against Britain and France) the Franco-Austrian War of 1859, the Austro-Prussian War of 1866 and the Franco-Prussian War of 1870–71. The main result of this period of warfare was the unifications of Italy and Germany. By 1871 Prussia had united most of Germany into the German Empire, under its leadership.

*Britain*
Britain's claim to Great Power status was its navy. The Royal Navy's physical size dwarfed all other European navies, and it dominated the seas around Europe. Britain had naval bases in Heligoland, off North Germany, and in Gibraltar, Malta and Cyprus. In 1882 it added Alexandria, in Egypt. As a result, the Royal Navy controlled the North Sea, Atlantic Ocean and Mediterranean Sea.

Britain was also the world's most advanced economic power and the centre for world finance. Britain had a vast overseas empire which included India, Australia, Canada and large parts of Africa.

Unlike the other Great Powers, Britain had a parliamentary government. Although it was a monarchy, Queen Victoria (1837–1901) had little political power, and the government was decided through general elections for the House of Commons.

Also unlike the other Great Powers, Britain did not have compulsory military service (conscription). British armed forces were volunteers. Compared to the continental Great Powers the British army was extremely

## Otto Edouard Leopold von Bismarck (1815–1898)

Born in Brandenburg, Bismarck studied law and agriculture before becoming a member of the Prussian parliament in 1847. He was Prime Minister of Prussia (1862–90) and Chancellor of the German Empire (1871–90). He became Prince von Bismarck in 1871. After successfully waging wars with Denmark in 1863–64, he went to war with Austria and its allies (the Seven Weeks' War, 1866). His victory forced the unification of the north German states under his own chancellorship (1867). He was then victorious against France, under the leadership of Napoleon III, in the Franco–Prussian War (1870–71), proclaiming the German Empire and annexing Alsace-Lorraine. His priorities as Chancellor were to preserve Prussian leadership within Germany, and to guarantee German security through alliances with Russia and Austria. He was forced to resign by Wilhelm II on 18 March 1890.

**Serfs**: People who were the personal property of others, usually landowners. Similar to slavery.

small, its main task being to preserve law and order within the Empire – in India, in particular.

### Germany

The German Empire was proclaimed in January 1871 at the height of Prussia's victory over France. After Britain, Germany was Europe's major economic power, rivalling Britain by 1914. It was also Europe's greatest military power – the German army was the best in the world. In 1866 Prussia had defeated Austria in a mere seven weeks. In 1870 the Prussians destroyed the French armed forces. As a result, Prussia united most German states into an empire, which it dominated. The Prussian king was German emperor, and the government was dominated by Prussians. From 1871 to 1890 the German Chancellor was Otto von Bismarck, who had been the Prussian minister president (prime minister) since 1862.

Germany was a monarchy where the Emperor chose the government and was 'supreme warlord' in charge of the armed forces.

### France

Until 1870–71 France had been Europe's dominant military power, but its humiliating defeat by the Prussians had destroyed the French army. Also, in the 1871 Treaty of Frankfurt, which ended the Franco-Prussian War, France lost its eastern provinces of Alsace and Lorraine to Germany. Resentment at this territorial loss and the country's decline in international prestige following military defeat were dominant themes in French foreign policy after 1871.

Unlike the other four Great Powers, France was a democratic republic. The Third French Republic had been created in 1870 at the height of the Franco-Prussian War. From 1870 to 1914 France acquired a large overseas empire in Africa and east Asia.

### Russia

Russia was the largest Great Power in geographical area – it comprised 20% of the world's land surface – and it had the largest population. However, Russia was also the most economically backward of the Great Powers. Until 1861, 80% of the Russian population were **serfs** – predominantly landless agriculture workers. They were literally 'owned' by their aristocratic masters. In 1861 the Tsar (Emperor) of Russia freed the serfs, but up to 1914 most of the Russian population remained illiterate and poor.

Russia's great military asset was the size of its army, which numbered more than two and half million men by 1914.

Russia was the most conservative Great Power. The Tsar had absolute political power until 1906, when a national parliament with very limited powers was created.

### Austria–Hungary

Austria–Hungary was the weakest of the Great Powers. It was a multi-racial Empire comprising twelve major ethnic groups. Since 1867 the Empire had been divided into two administrative units, Austria and Hungary. The two dominant ethnic groups were the Germans in Austria and the Hungarians. However, the whole Empire was ruled by an Emperor – Franz Josef from 1848 to 1916 – and it had a combined central government and armed forces.

Also known as the 'Habsburg Monarchy' the Empire had once been dominant in Italy and Germany from 1815 to the 1860s. However, the unifications of Italy (1859–61) and Germany (1866–71) had greatly reduced Habsburg power. From the 1870s Austria–Hungary looked for political expansion into South East Europe, in the Balkan peninsula. This brought it into direct conflict with the Ottoman Empire, which controlled

**Balkan nationalism**: The idea that the various ethnic groups of the Balkan peninsula should form their own independent states, based on race. The groups included Serbs, Bulgarians, Greeks, Albanians.

most of the peninsula. It also brought Austria–Hungary into conflict with Russia which also wanted to expand at the Ottoman Empire's expense. Finally, this policy brought Austria–Hungary into conflict with **Balkan nationalism**.

### The impact of Bismarck on international relations

The German Chancellor, Otto von Bismarck, dominated European international relations from 1871 until his resignation in 1890. His reputation as an exceptional diplomat developed when he was minister president of Prussia from 1862 to 1871. During this period he united Germany under Prussian domination. In the process, Prussia defeated two Great Powers, Austria and France.

After 1871, Bismarck had one major aim – to maintain European peace. This would allow the newly created German Empire time to develop. To ensure European peace he adopted two policies – the diplomatic isolation of France, which he saw as Germany's main potential opponent, and his plan to ally Germany with Russia and Austria. Britain, meanwhile, was seen as more interested in Empire and world trade than European affairs.

In 1873 Bismarck helped create the *Dreikaiserbund* – the 'Three Emperors' Agreement'. This agreement was a general understanding of

Cartoon from *Punch*, 1887. Germany's Prince Bismarck sidles up to France and pays lavish compliments. The caption underneath says: 'Madam, you are great, powerful, warlike and it was by meanest accident that we happened to get the better of you!' France (aside) 'Methinks the gentleman doth protest too much!!'

**" VELVET AND IRON ! "**

Prince B-sm-rck (*with the utmost courtesy*). " MADAME, YOU ARE GREAT, POWERFUL, WARLIKE, AND IT WAS BY THE MEREST ACCIDENT THAT WE HAPPENED TO GET THE BETTER OF YOU ! "
France (*aside*). " METHINKS THE GENTLEMAN DOTH PROTEST TOO MUCH !! "

**How reliable is this cartoon as evidence of Bismarck's aims and plans in foreign policy in 1887? Explain your answer.**

---

### Bismarck's alliance system

**1879** Dual Alliance between Germany and Austria–Hungary. Secret military alliance renewed every three years until 1918.

**1881** *Dreikaiserbund* (Three Emperors' alliance) of Germany, Austria–Hungary and Russia. Alliance of friendship renewed in 1884 but collapsed as a result of the Bulgarian Crisis in 1887.

**1882** Triple Alliance of Germany, Austria–Hungary and Italy. Secret military alliance, renewed every three years until 1914.

**1883** Romania becomes an associate of the Triple Alliance.

**1887** Reinsurance Treaty. Secret military alliance between Germany and Russia. Lasted three years. Not renewed by Germany after Bismarck's fall.

Mediterranean agreements between Britain, Austria–Hungary and Italy, formed in response to potential Russian naval threat to eastern Mediterranean.

**1889** Britain offered associate status in Triple Alliance. Britain refused.

---

friendship between Germany, Austria–Hungary and Russia. However, this understanding collapsed with the outbreak of a major crisis over the Balkans, which began in 1875.

The ethnically diverse population of the Balkans revolted against Ottoman (Turkish) rule in 1875. The crisis escalated when Serbia and Montenegro sided with the rebels. The climax came in 1877 when Russia declared war against the Ottoman Empire in defence of the ethnic minorities of the Balkans. The Russo-Turkish war of 1877–78 ended in Russian victory and the subsequent Treaty of San Stefano gave Russia enormous influence in the Balkans. The treaty caused outrage in Britain and Austria–Hungary. War between Russia on one side and Austria–Hungary and Britain on the other seemed a possibility.

But in 1878 Bismarck organised the Congress of Berlin. It was a triumph of Bismarckian diplomacy. War was averted and a new treaty, the Treaty of Berlin, brought peace between the Great Powers. However, the peace came at a cost. Austria–Hungary and Russia refused to renew the *Dreikaiserbund* of 1873. This was a turning-point in Bismarck's foreign policy. It led directly to the creation of a military alliance system which was to have a profound impact on the causes of the First World War.

> 1. What do you regard as the main issue facing each Great Power in the 1870s?
>
> 2. Why do you think Germany was seen as the greatest Great Power after 1871?

## 2.2 What was the impact of the alliance system on European international relations from 1879?

### Why did Bismarck sign the Dual Alliance of 1879?

Bismarck was an exponent of *Realpolitik* (The politics of realism). To achieve his aims Bismarck would use a variety of policies. He usually chose the least risky policy first. If this did not work, he would try more risky options. Before 1871 Bismarck chose the most risky course of all when dealing with **Austria** in 1866 – he went to war.

**Austria**: name of Austria–Hungary before 1867

After 1871, Bismarck chose a general agreement between Germany, Austria–Hungary and Russia to achieve his aim of isolating France. Unfortunately this policy collapsed in the Balkan Crisis of 1875–78. So, in 1878 Bismarck adopted a different course, planning a formal, secret military alliance with Austria–Hungary – the 'Dual Alliance'.

There are several reasons why Bismarck chose Austria–Hungary rather than Russia. First, there were close historical links between Germany and Austria–Hungary. Following 1866 Bismarck feared Austria–Hungary might attempt to avenge its defeat. To prevent Austria–Hungary from following this course a close alliance was adopted.

Secondly, Bismarck was considering abandoning free trade and adopting protection for the German economy. Austria–Hungary was a much more important market for German goods than Russia, which had the highest protection in Europe. Also, East Prussian farmers (*junkers*) feared economic competition from cheap Russian wheat.

Thirdly, Bismarck regarded Russia as a potentially more difficult partner to work with. Russia was seen as an expansionist power. It had ambitions to expand in the Balkans and Central Asia. Bismarck felt Germany would be able to have greater influence over Austria–Hungary, which would be regarded as a junior partner.

### How did the Dual Alliance affect European international relations?

The Dual Alliance was a secret, military alliance, committing both parties to action in a future crisis. If Germany and France went to war, Austria–Hungary would remain neutral. If Russia attacked Austria–Hungary, Germany would aid Austria–Hungary.

Normally such detailed commitments were made either on the eve of war or just after war had been declared. An example was the Anglo-French alliance in 1854 in the Crimean War. The Dual Alliance was a completely new departure because it was signed in peacetime, and committed both parties to action in some future, unforeseen crisis. This would greatly limit the normal diplomatic processes designed to avoid war.

Finally, as a secret alliance it caused considerable unease in the international community. Other Great Powers were aware an alliance had been made but they were unaware of its contents. A clause in the alliance stated that if war seemed imminent the terms of the Dual Alliance would be disclosed to a potential foe. This occurred in the Bulgarian Crisis of 1885–87, when Russia was informed of its contents.

### In what ways was Bismarck able to keep France isolated after 1879?

Even though Germany had made a formal alliance with Austria–Hungary it still attempted to retain close relations with Russia. In 1881 Bismarck helped create a new version of the *Dreikaiserbund*. This was a much more detailed agreement than the original *Dreikaiserbund* of 1873. It aimed to prevent future conflict between Austria–Hungary and Russia in the Balkans. Russia was keen to keep close links with Germany and Austria–Hungary. The three states were empires where the ruler retained considerable political power. Russia, the most conservative and **autocratic** Great Power was unlikely to ally with France, which was a democratic republic.

**Autocratic**: Describes the form of government in which the ruler exercises absolute political power, unlimited by other factors such as a parliament or a constitution.

In 1882 Bismarck exploited Franco-Italian problems to extend the Dual Alliance into a 'Triple Alliance'. Italy had aimed to acquire colonial control over the Ottoman region of Tunis, but in 1881 France moved first and made Tunis part of its own Empire. Bismarck used this conflict to attach Italy to the Alliance in 1882. In the following year, Bismarck exploited Romanian fears of Russian expansion to make Romania an associate member of the Triple Alliance.

Finally, in 1887, Bismarck encouraged Britain, Austria–Hungary and Italy to sign a naval agreement against Russia. All three signatories feared Russia might persuade the Ottoman Empire to allow Russian warships to enter the Mediterranean Sea via the Straits. The Agreement was an attempt to force the Ottoman Empire to resist Russian pressure.

## A Bismarckian gamble – the Reinsurance Treaty of 1887

**Eastern Rumelia**: An area of the Ottoman Empire – inhabited by Bulgarians – which was given self-government in the Treaty of Berlin 1878.

The diplomatic system created by Bismarck between 1879 and 1887 to isolate France was on the verge of collapse because of the Bulgarian Crisis of 1886–87. The union of **Eastern Rumelia** and Bulgaria and the overthrow of a pro-Austrian Bulgarian king by a pro-Russian rival created a major crisis.

The conflict between Austria–Hungary and Russia prevented a renewal of the *Dreikaiserbund*, in 1887. As an attempt to keep Russia as an ally Germany signed the 'Reinsurance Treaty'. This treaty suggested that Germany would stay neutral in any future war between Austria–Hungary and Russia. But this contradicted the Dual Alliance.

To some historians the Reinsurance Treaty was the beginning of the end of Bismarck's plans to be allies with all of Europe's continental Great Powers, except France. However, in 1890 Russia wanted to renew the Reinsurance Treaty. It was Bismarck's successor, Caprivi, who refused to do so.

Yet by 1890 problems had already begun to arise. In 1887 the *Lombardverbot* meant that Germany would no longer offer loans to the Russian government. As a result, Russia turned to France. Also by 1890 Russia had begun to import arms from France, with the condition that they would never be used against the French.

## The end of Bismarck's alliance system: the Franco-Russian Alliance

Once Germany refused to renew the Reinsurance Treaty, Russia began to look for a potential ally. By 1893 the unthinkable had occurred – republican democratic France had made a military alliance with autocratic, monarchic Russia. In 1893 the Tsar, Alexander III, visited France and stood to attention when the French national anthem – *La Marseillaise* – was played. This anthem dated from the French Revolution.

On 27 December 1893 the two Great Powers signed a military agreement. It declared that France or Russia would only aid the other power if either were attacked by Germany or Austria–Hungary. It also declared that the agreement would last as long as the Triple Alliance. This agreement was followed by a formal treaty in 1894.

## How far was the alliance system a cause of the First World War?

In 1894 Europe was faced with two opposing military alliances, the Triple Alliance and the Franco-Russian Alliance. Germany now faced the prospect of a two-front war. From 1894 onwards German military thinking was linked directly to this prospect, and by 1906 the Germans had produced an appropriate war plan: the Schlieffen Plan. This plan was based on the supposed mobilisation timetables of France and Russia. It was believed that France would take two weeks to mobilise and Russia six weeks. This difference was due in part to Russia's immense size and its limited number of railway lines. Germany decided to attack and defeat France first, then turn their entire army eastward to confront the Russians.

To defeat France the Germans planned to outflank the French armies by attacking through Holland and Belgium. By 1914 the plan was amended to omit Holland. On 31 July 1914 the Schlieffen Plan was activated. The movement of the German army into Belgium led directly to the British decision to declare war on Germany by 4 August.

The alliance system meant that both alliances were placed on a war footing. Central to preparation for war was the mobilisation timetable. Once a political crisis occurred any move by one of the alliance partners towards mobilisation would spark off mobilisation across both alliances.

This occurred on 30 July 1914, when Russian general mobilisation led to German mobilisation against France and Russia.

The rival alliance system also sparked off an arms race. Both alliance systems expanded their armies. In 1912 Germany became aware that France wanted to extend its conscription period. This would expand the French Army by approximately 250,000. Also Russia embarked on the 'Great Programme', which would modernise and expand the Russian army by 1917. As a result, on 8 December 1912, a meeting of the German War Cabinet took place. Believing that war with France and Russia was inevitable, German military leaders calculated that it had to take place by 1914 to ensure a German victory.

The alliance system, therefore, was linked directly to the outbreak of war.

The alliance system also meant that all parties were committed to action in an unforeseen future crisis. On 28 June 1914, Archduke Franz Ferdinand was assassinated by a Bosnian Serb terrorist. It sparked off a Balkan Crisis.

It was the alliance system, however, that helped to turn this crisis into a major European war. Even though France was not directly involved in the 1914 Balkan Crisis, it was the first Great Power to be attacked by another, as a result of the Schlieffen Plan.

**Archduke Franz Ferdinand (1863–1914)**
Nephew of Franz Josef, and heir to the throne of Austria–Hungary from 1896. Inspector General of the army (1913). Assassinated at Sarajevo on 28 June 1914.

**1. Why did Bismarck form alliances with other European powers?**

**2. How far do you think Bismarck was responsible for the outbreak of war in 1914?**

## 2.3 Why did Germany embark on Weltpolitik (world policy) after 1897?

Following the resignation of Bismarck, in March 1890, German foreign policy went through a period of transition. It was not until 1896–97 that a new radical foreign policy was developed. *Weltpolitik* (world policy) was closely associated with Kaiser Wilhelm II. Its main architect was von Bulow, the Kaiser's foreign policy adviser.

The aim of *Weltpolitik* was ambitious. It planned to make Germany a world power. This was to be achieved through the acquisition of a large overseas empire. From 1880 to 1896 other European states had acquired overseas colonies, mainly in Africa. Even France, which Germany had defeated in 1870, had a large overseas empire.

To acquire and defend this large empire, Germany decided to greatly expand its navy. The aim was to produce a navy to rival the Royal Navy.

Why did Germany adopt such an ambitious policy?

i)   The expansion of Germany overseas was seen as a natural development in German history. Prussia united Germany. Now Germany would expand beyond Europe.

ii)  This idea was linked with the prevailing idea of social Darwinism. This idea suggested that the history of mankind was a constant struggle between different racial groups. In this conflict some racial groups had innately superior qualities which would make them dominant. In Germany it was believed that the German race was superior to other races. It was Germany's destiny to rule large parts of the world!

iii) An important influence on the Kaiser was a book published in 1890 by an American admiral, Alfred T Mahan. *The Influence of Sea Power upon History* suggested that empires rose and declined over time. An important element in developing an empire was a powerful navy. The Kaiser believed that Germany, through naval power, could rival other world powers such as Britain.

iv)  In the period before 1914 the German government was dominated

*Sammlungspolitik* (German – 'policy of gathering together'): Term used to describe the attempt by the German government in the 1890s and 1900s to pursue policies that would have an equal appeal to the many different political and economic interest groups that existed within the Reich.

by aristocratic landowners – who comprised only a small percentage of the population. The government wanted to win support from other sections of the German population. The building of a great navy would win support from industrialists who would win contracts to build the fleet. The navy would provide opportunities for middle-class men to become naval officers. The prestige that Germany would receive from its new large fleet and overseas empire would win support from most Germans. This policy was called *Sammlungspolitik* (the policy of bringing together).

v)     The Kaiser was the nephew of Queen Victoria. Throughout his life he had a love–hate relationship with Britain. He admired Britain's Empire and navy. (On several occasions he competed in the Cowes Yachting Regatta on the Isle of Wight.) However, he was also jealous of Britain's imperial and naval power. He wanted Germany to equal Britain.

### How successful was Weltpolitik ?

In 1898 the Reichstag passed the German Navy Law. This was the first in a series of laws which created a large ocean-going fleet. The Navy Law alarmed Britain. Since 1889 Britain had adopted the 'two-power standard' which aimed to make the Royal Navy as large as the next two largest navies combined. In 1889 this had meant France and Russia, but now Germany became a threat. During the first decade of the twentieth century Britain and Germany engaged in a naval arms race, concentrating in particular on building battleships. In 1904 Britain made a major advance in naval technology with the launch of HMS *Dreadnought*. This was a heavily armed and armoured battleship. The Germans then passed another Navy Law in 1906 to build German dreadnoughts. By 1912 Germany had the second largest navy in the world, but they failed to 'outbuild' the Royal Navy. By now Britain no longer regarded France and Russia as its main rivals – they had been replaced by Germany.

Germany's quest for colonies was a failure. By 1914 it had acquired the Marshall and Caroline Islands in the Pacific and a part of French Cameroon – hardly the 'world empire' envisaged by the Kaiser.

Also, as a result of Germany's attempts to acquire colonies, Britain, France and Russia buried their colonial differences and became allies. In 1904 Britain and France signed the Entente Cordiale. This was an agreement to end colonial differences. Britain withdrew objections to French influence in Morocco. France accepted the British occupation of Egypt. In 1907 British and Russia signed an entente about spheres of influence in Iran.

If Germany was to achieve *Weltpolitik* it would have to break these agreements, especially the Entente Cordiale. The opportunity to do this arose in 1904 to 1905 in the First Moroccan Crisis.

1. In what ways was *Weltpolitik* different from Bismarck's foreign policy?

2. '*Weltpolitik* was the main reason for the outbreak of war in 1914.'

How far do you agree with this view?

## 2.4  What were the main causes of tensions between the European powers in the decade before 1914?

### The origins of the first Moroccan crisis

Sultanate: A state or country subject to a sultan (king or chief ruler of Muslim country).

Between 1905 and 1914, tensions between the European powers centred upon two disputed areas: the North African **sultanate** of Morocco, and the Balkan states that had emerged from the wreckage of the Turkish Empire.

**Théophile Delcassé (1852–1923)**
French Radical deputy (1889). Colonial Minister (1894–95). Foreign Minister (1898–1905), during which time he played a major role in developing French understanding with Italy (1898) and Russia (1900) and in instigating the *Entente Cordiale* with Britain. He was forced to resign in 1905, largely to satisfy German opinion. Subsequently Naval Minister (1911–13), Ambassador to Russia (1913–14), and briefly Foreign Minister once again in 1914.

Attention was first focused on Morocco by a German initiative that typified the incoherence and illogicality of *Weltpolitik*. In the course of a Mediterranean cruise, the Kaiser was prevailed upon by his chief ministers to land at Tangier (31 March 1905). There, his public speeches and behaviour implied that he recognised the Sultan of Morocco as an independent monarch, and called into question the recent Anglo–French agreements over the colonial status of these territories.

The motives of the Kaiser and his ministers are not altogether clear. They were probably keen to demonstrate, as was now usual, that no international question could be resolved without reference to Germany. They possibly also entertained hopes, by forcing France to give ground, of weakening its credibility as an ally in the eyes of Great Britain and Russia. The Kaiser's coup was followed by the formal demand that the status of Morocco should be referred to an international conference of the major powers. As that status was formally governed by an international agreement of 1880, Germany looked to be in a strong position, and the prospects of a notable triumph seemed bright. Indeed, when Théophile

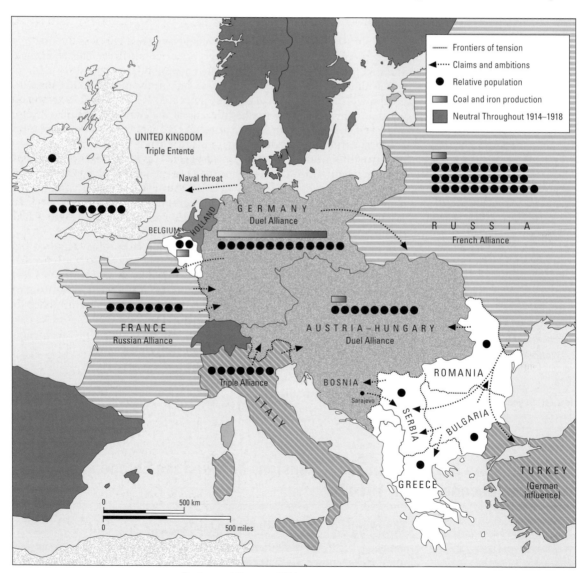

European Alliances, 1914

Delcassé, France's anti-German Foreign Minister and architect of the Anglo–French Entente counselled resistance to German projects, he failed to win general support and resigned his office.

The outcome of the conference convened at Algeçiras in Spain (January–March 1906) was, however, very different from that anticipated by Germany. Far more impressed by the bullying manner of the Germans than by the justice of their case, Spain, Italy, Russia, Great Britain, and even the USA, all supported French rights in Morocco. Isolated but for the faithful support of Austria–Hungary, Germany had to accept confirmation of French predominance in the sultanate, now strengthened by its control over the Moroccan police.

### How significant was the outcome of the Algeçiras Conference for the future growth of international tension?

The Algeçiras Conference played only a limited role in preparing the ground for international conflict. No military preparations were made by any power, British public opinion showed a marked lack of concern over Morocco, and subsequent Anglo–French military conversations come to nothing. Nevertheless, the impact of this diplomatic defeat upon Germany should not be underestimated. It ended Holstein's career and left Bülow in a state of physical collapse. More important, the rebuff did much to confirm German fears that the unreasonable jealousy of its neighbours was leading them to pursue a deliberate 'policy of encirclement' (*Einkreisungspolitik*), aimed at stifling Germany's natural growth and vitality. From this point, the historian Imanuel Geiss claims, in *German Foreign Policy, 1871–1914* (1976), Germany turned its back upon international conferences as a means of settling international disputes.

Lastly, it should be noted that diplomatic co-operation between the French, the British and the Russians at Algeçiras also had a number of side-effects. The discussions between the **General Staffs** of Britain and France were inconclusive. Colonial discussions between Britain and Russia ended, however, with an agreement (August 1907) that solved many of the outstanding disagreements over rival spheres of influence in Persia. British control over south-eastern Persia kept Russia at a safe distance from Afghanistan, and thus from India, and thus did much to remove the Asian tensions that had dogged Anglo–Russian relations at the time of the Russo–Japanese War.

### Why did a crisis arise over Bosnia in 1908–1909?

By 1908, the Balkans had been free of major political crises for a little more than a decade, despite the emergence of an ambitious and expansionist government in Serbia. In July of that year, however, revolution by the 'Young Turk' movement overthrew the corrupt rule of Sultan Abdul Hamid and offered the prospect to other powers of easy gains in the Balkans while Turkey was preoccupied with domestic upheavals.

The opportunity coincided broadly with the appointment to high office in Austria–Hungary of men eager to re-establish the prestige of the Dual Monarchy. Conrad von Hötzendorf had been Chief of Staff since late 1906, much more confident than his predecessor, General von Beck-Rzikowsky, of the Empire's military capacity. At the same time, Aloys von Aehrenthal had succeeded Count Goluchowski as Foreign Minister. Aehrenthal came to office envisaging an energetic foreign policy as a useful means of submerging the nationalist tensions within the Dual Monarchy. The joint project of these two men for the re-establishment of Habsburg prestige involved the formal **annexation** of the Turkish provinces of Bosnia and Herzegovina that had been under Austrian administration since 1878. Certainly this was seen as a

**General Staffs**: The groups of senior officers responsible for the planning, organisation and overall command of their national armies.

**Conrad von Hötzendorf (1852–1925)**
Chief of Staff of the Austro-Hungarian army (1906). Highly suspicious of Serbia and of Italy, he devised plans for war in the Balkans, catering for Russian involvement. His wartime campaigns in the Balkans failed, although he enjoyed some success against Russia and against Italy. Dismissed from overall command upon the accession of the Emperor Charles (1916).

**Aloys von Aehrenthal (1854–1912)**
Austrian diplomat. Ambassador to Romania (1895) and to Russia (1899). Foreign Minister (1906), responsible for expansionist policies, including the annexation of Bosnia-Herzegovina (1908).

**Annexation**: Taking possession of territory, and adding it to another, existing state. The annexed areas are then integrated into the state, and ruled as part of the state.

counter to growing Serbian influence over the Empire's Slav population, and it may even have been envisaged as the first move in a programme leading ultimately to the eventual partition of Serbia itself.

## The annexation of Bosnia-Herzegovina

In September 1908, Aehrenthal sought the compliance of Russia. Meeting its Foreign Minister, Alexander Izvolski, at Buchlau, he concluded an agreement. By this agreement Russia would accept the new status of Bosnia and Herzegovina in return for Austro-Hungarian support for Russian designs on the **Dardanelles** (see map on page 36).

**Dardanelles**: The straits linking the Black Sea and the Mediterranean.

By accepting this agreement, Izvolski committed a diplomatic blunder of the first order. Evidently, he had expected the matter to be referred first to an international conference on the lines of 1878. On 5 October, however, Aehrenthal proclaimed the annexation of Bosnia and Herzegovina, leaving Izvolski to seek his part of the bargain single-handed. In this, he not only encountered hostile reactions in London and Paris, but had his policy disowned by his own prime minister as outdated and irrelevant to current Russian priorities. Izvolski's attempts to soften his defeat, by demanding that a conference be convened to discuss the annexation, only increased and broadened the international tension. In response, Austria–Hungary sought clarification of the position of its German ally, and received assurances of support. 'I shall regard whatever decision you come to as the appropriate one,' wrote Bülow to Aehrenthal at the end of October, while Hötzendorff received assurances from his German opposite number that Germany was prepared to mobilise in support of the Dual Monarchy.

These assurances represented a significant deterioration in the international situation. Motivated primarily by the hope of humiliating Russia, and perhaps of weakening its links with France, Germany was sacrificing another essential Bismarckian principle. It was involving itself in the Eastern Question where no fundamental German interest was involved, and where Austria–Hungary had acted without any consultation with its ally whatsoever.

**Alexander Izvolski (1856–1919)**
Russian statesman and diplomat. Foreign Minister (1905). Sought improved relations with Britain and Japan, but was outmanoeuvred by Austria over the Balkan crisis in 1908–09. As ambassador to Paris (1910–16) he was a key figure in the construction of the wartime alliance between the two states.

## The humiliation of Serbia and Russia

Thus emboldened, Germany and Austria–Hungary felt strong enough to rub both Serbia's and Russia's noses in their defeat by demanding from them a formal acknowledgement of Habsburg authority over Bosnia and Herzegovina. In March 1909, both states gave such an acknowledgement, and the crisis was over. Its legacy, nevertheless, was substantial. Russia suffered a humiliation far greater than that suffered by Germany over the Moroccan question. It could ill afford a further reverse if it was to retain any influence in the politics of the Balkans. Aware of its weaknesses in 1908–09, Russia was to embark upon a programme of military reconstruction to ensure that a future confrontation would not find it wanting.

Austria's success and the unconditional nature of German support for its aims were to embolden it in future Balkan adventures. Serbia's reverse, meanwhile, was to stimulate the growth of nationalist terrorist organisations of the kind responsible for the assassination at Sarajevo in 1914. Although the crisis had given rise to little in the way of serious military preparations, we may accept the logic of Imanuel Geiss's judgement, in *German Foreign Policy, 1871–1914* (1976), that 'the Bosnian crisis in the East was a kind of dress rehearsal for the First World War'.

## The occupation of Fez and the Agadir crisis, 1911

In May 1911, the focus of European tension switched once more to Morocco. The cause was the French occupation of Fez, the major city of

**Protectorate**: A country that is controlled and protected by a more powerful country.

the territory – a move that was widely thought to indicate that France was preparing to establish an overall **protectorate**. Given that France was exceeding the limits of its agreed role in Morocco, and that relations between its international partners, Britain and Russia, were once again strained, the prospects for German compensation seemed good. It has been argued that Germany's Foreign Minister, Alfred von Kiderlen-Wächter, was interested in more than compensation. Historian Fritz Fischer stresses the enthusiasm of expansionist elements in Germany for the establishment of permanent influence in North Africa, and has attached sinister importance to Kiderlen's apparent willingness to use force to gain Germany's ends. Similarly, a great community of interest and aims existed between Kiderlen-Wächter and the Pan-German League. Whatever its motives, the German Foreign Ministry once again acted aggressively and clumsily. The dispatch of the gunboat 'Panther' to the Moroccan port of Agadir, seemingly to protect German interests there, immediately resurrected British fears of a hostile naval presence in the Mediterranean, and of a threat to Gibraltar.

Unambiguous statements of British support for France, such as that contained in Lloyd George's Mansion House speech (21 July 1911) weakened the resolve of the less chauvinistic elements in Germany, including that of the Kaiser himself. A compromise settlement in November did grant Germany compensation in the form of territory in the French Congo. However, the maintenance of French influence in Morocco, culminating in the establishment of a formal protectorate (March 1912), clearly demonstrated that German aims in the crisis had failed.

### What was the impact of Agadir upon the alliance system?

This second Moroccan crisis was unlikely to lead to a general war, mainly because of the lack of Russian interest in the affair. 'Russian public opinion,' Izvolski informed the French, 'could not see in a colonial dispute the cause for a general conflict.' Nevertheless, the crisis contributed to the likelihood of a future breakdown of international relations in several important ways. Firstly, it worsened relations between Britain and Germany for no good reason, and weakened the support in both countries for reductions in naval building programmes. Indeed, the next two years were to witness the height of the naval 'arms race'.

Secondly, French reaction to the compromise settlement destroyed the administration of Joseph Caillaux (January 1912), whose main aim had been to achieve some measure of reconciliation with Germany. 'The events of 1911', in the opinion of historian Eugen Weber, in *The Nationalist Revival in France* (1959), 'persuaded many of the pacific, the hesitant and the indifferent that the threat to France was real and that war was only a matter of time.' The succession of the more aggressively patriotic Raymond Poincaré can be seen as the beginning of the 'national awakening' that led France into war by 1914.

Thirdly, stimulated by the increased German naval estimates of 1912, the crisis led to a degree of formal military co-operation between Britain and France. This took the form primarily of the naval agreement of March 1912 whereby Britain confided its central Mediterranean interests to the protection of the French fleet, and concentrated its resources in home waters and at Gibraltar. Such an agreement still did not amount to a formal alliance, but indicated clearly Britain's awareness of the German threat to its interests.

Lastly, the Agadir crisis dealt a blow to the prestige of the German government similar to that suffered by the Russians in the Balkans. Germany, too, if faced with a similar crisis, might feel that the cost of further compromise might justify the risk of war.

1. What issues were at stake between the great European powers in the years 1900–14 (a) in North Africa and (b) in the Balkans?

2. Why did the confrontations between France and Germany over Morocco in 1905 and 1911 not lead to a European war?

3. Would you agree that the crisis in the Balkans in 1908–09 was more dangerous than the crisis over North Africa? Explain your answer.

## 2.5 What impact did the Balkans have on international relations in the period 1912–1913?

The Agadir crisis brought European politics to a pitch of tension from which it was not released before the outbreak of general war. Its implications spread eastwards down the Mediterranean. A direct result of the extension of French influence in Morocco was Italy's attempt in 1911 to improve its own standing in North Africa. To this end it launched an unprovoked attack upon the Turkish possession of Tripoli. This stretching of Turkish resources provided an irresistible temptation to the Balkan states to free themselves forever from the influence of Turkey. From this temptation there emerged, in the early months of 1912, the Balkan League of Serbia, Bulgaria, Greece and Montenegro.

### The First and Second Balkan Wars

The First Balkan War, between the Balkan League and Turkey, began in October 1912. By the end of that month the Turks had suffered a string of defeats and had been driven out of their European possessions, apart from

The Balkans, 1912–13

0 / 300 km
0 / 300 miles

AUSTRIA – HUNGARY

BOSNIA (ann. 1908)

Sarajevo

Belgrade

ROMANIA

Bucharest

Galatz

Constanza

SERBIA

MONTENEGRO

Cetinje

Navibazar

BULGARIA

Sofia

Burgas

Black Sea

Scutari

Dulcigno

ALBANIA

Tirana

(indep. 1913)

Janina

CORFU

ITALY

Adrianople

Lule Burgas    Constantinople

Kavalla

Salonika

Lemnos

Mytilene

TURKEY

Smyrna

Chios

GREECE

Athens

Samos

Mediterranean Sea

MOREA

Rhodes (Italian 1912)

cauton. 1898: to
CRETE    Greece 1908

National boundaries in 1914
National boundaries in 1911
Turkish in 1911

Constantinople, the peninsula of Gallipoli and the fortresses of Scutari, Adrianople and Janina. Renewed hostilities in early 1913, however, transferred those last two strongholds to the Bulgarians and the Greeks respectively. Now tension centred upon the division of the spoils. Already, in late 1912, Austria–Hungary had attempted to maintain its prestige and security by insisting upon the establishment of an independent Albanian state, and upon the exclusion of Serbia from the Adriatic coastline.

More immediate tensions arose, however, between the victors. Serbia, thwarted over designs on Albania, and acting in partnership with Greece, occupied territory in Macedonia originally earmarked for Bulgaria. Bulgaria's attempts to clear Macedonia of Serbian and Greek forces in June 1913 started the Second Balkan War. The move was disastrous for Bulgaria. By the Treaty of Bucharest (August 1913), it had to cede territory to Serbia, Greece and Romania, which had seized the opportunity to intervene. Even Adrianople, won earlier at great cost from the Turks, was now returned to its former masters.

## The status of Serbia and Austria–Hungary

The renewed Balkan crisis of 1912–13 contributed to the advent of general war in numerous important respects. Most obviously, Serbia emerged from these events with both its prestige and its power enormously increased. It had added some million and a half people to its population, and could now mobilise an army of some 400,000 men. Conversely, as A.J.P. Taylor put it, 'the victory for Balkan nationalism was a disaster beyond remedy for the Habsburg monarchy'. Even with Serbia preoccupied, its foreign policy had appeared frozen into inactivity. This was partly due to the indecision of the new Foreign Minister, Count Berchtold, partly to Magyar distrust of actions that might create more Slav subjects for the Dual Monarchy, and partly to uncertainty as to Germany's attitude. By mid-1913, it was clear that the government of Austria–Hungary could not afford further retreat. When Serbian troops entered Albanian territory in October to 'mop up' partisan resistance, the Dual Monarchy issued an ultimatum, which foreshadowed that of 1914. On this occasion, Serbia yielded and withdrew its troops.

## Political and popular attitudes among the leading powers

To what extent did this crisis make the leading European powers more willing to accept the prospect of war? There is certainly evidence of heightened tension at top political levels in Germany and France, and of increased military preparation. France, for instance, sought closer military ties with Russia, and showed less interest in restraining its major ally. When President Poincaré visited Russia in August 1912 he left his hosts in no doubt about France's attitude. Although their formal agreements only committed France to support Russia if it were attacked by Germany, Russia could expect French help in the event of a clash with Germany triggered by a confrontation with Austria–Hungary. In Germany the government remained reluctant initially to become involved in Balkan hostilities, but there were clear signs, nevertheless, of political unease and of military preparation to meet a future crisis. The government had already been attacked from all sides in the Reichstag (November 1911) when the compromise settlement over Morocco was debated. The next year and a half saw substantial increases in military estimates. In July 1913, the Reichstag sanctioned the addition of 130,000 men to the army in the biggest army estimate in German history. By October 1913, at the time of Vienna's ultimatum to Serbia over Albanian independence, the Kaiser was urging his ally to take a firm stance, and assuring it of unswerving German

**Leopold von Berchtold (1863–1942)**
Entered Austro-Hungarian diplomatic service in 1893. Ambassador to Russia (1906). Succeeded Aehrenthal as Foreign Minister (1912). Co-operated with Conrad von Hötzendorf in issuing ultimatum to Serbia, underestimating the danger of Russian mobilisation. Dismissed from office in 1915.

support. He informed Berchtold that month, in a fateful statement, that 'you can be certain that I stand behind you and am ready to draw the sword whenever your action makes it necessary. Whatever comes from Vienna is for me a command.'

Recent historians, however, have been at pains to point out that this does not necessarily mean that enthusiasm for war existed at more popular levels of society. In particular, Niall Ferguson provides a good deal of evidence (*The Pity of War*, 1998) to counteract the notion that popular support for militaristic policies was creating an irresistible impetus towards war. He emphasises, for example, that three consecutive general elections were won in Britain between 1906 and 1910 by a Liberal Party committed to expensive social reform. Similarly, the last pre-war elections in France and Germany brought considerable success for socialist parties officially committed to the cause of peace. In Germany, although much noise was made by such patriotic organisations as the Naval League, their combined membership amounted to little more than half a million Germans. In France, at the height of European tension, 236 deputies voted against a reform of the laws on military service, proposed by the government to increase the numbers recruited into the army. 'The evidence,' he concludes, 'is unequivocal: Europeans were not marching to war, but turning their backs on militarism.'

It is doubly tragic, therefore, that in diplomatic and military terms, by October 1913, many of the ingredients of the following year's catastrophe were present. Franco–Russian and Austro–German commitments were tighter than ever, the confidence and daring of Serbia were at a peak, and the prestige of Austria–Hungary and of Russia was at so low an ebb as to make them unable to tolerate any further blow. Only the attitudes of Great Britain and Italy remained uncertain.

> **1. Why was there a further political crisis in the Balkans in 1912–13?**
>
> **2. Explain the reactions of the major European powers to the Balkan crisis in 1912–13.**
>
> **3. In what respects was the second Balkan crisis in 1912–13 more dangerous for the general peace of Europe than the first Balkan crisis (1908–09) had been?**

## 2.6 Why did the July Crisis lead to the outbreak of European war?

### Sarajevo and the response of Austria–Hungary

'Fifty years,' wrote Basil Liddell Hart, in *History of the First World War* (1972), 'were spent in the process of making Europe explosive. Five days were enough to detonate it.' On 28 June 1914, the final crisis was triggered by the assassination in the Bosnian town of Sarajevo of the Archduke Franz Ferdinand, nephew of the Austrian Emperor. His murderer was Gavrilo Princip, a member of a Serbian terrorist organisation known as the 'Black Hand'. Although it has proved impossible to establish any clear responsibility on the part of the Serbian government, it is clear that its intelligence chief, Colonel Dimitrievich, played a leading role in the conspiracy, and that its Prime Minister had some foreknowledge of the attempt. Ironically, as historian Norman Stone points out, in *The Eastern Front, 1914–17* (1973), the death of the Archduke removed one of the strongest influences for peace at court.

The opinion was now widespread that Serbian pretensions had to be checked. In this resolution the Dual Monarchy received backing from Berlin. Historians Fritz Fischer, Imanuel Geiss and others have interpreted this as showing the willingness, even the eagerness, of the German government to accept the consequences of general war. On the other hand, Germany could hardly accept the further humiliation of its only firm ally. Other authorities have produced evidence to indicate that Germany still hoped that the coming conflict might be confined to the Balkans. Nevertheless, Austria–Hungary was sufficiently encouraged to deliver an ultimatum to Serbia (23 July) framed in such extreme terms that it was almost impossible for Serbia to accept. Serbia's government was required, for instance, to suppress all anti-Austrian organisations and propaganda, and to dismiss any officials to whom the Vienna government might object.

## The spread of the Balkan crisis

Within a week, Europe was at war. The first factor to determine this outcome was the reaction of Russia. Although Serbia's reaction to the ultimatum was conciliatory, it did not satisfy Austria–Hungary's demands, and it declared war on 28 July. For Russia to remain inactive would have stripped it of any influence in the Balkans and could have devalued it as an ally in the eyes of France. Thus Russia chose to mobilise its forces on its southern borders. Automatically, such action triggered the Austro–German alliance, and raised the question of German support for its ally.

The escalation of the crisis caused last-minute hesitations in Berlin, while the generals advised energetic action. Essentially, German military plans obliged it to act rapidly to deal with France before the Russian machine was fully operative. Germany thus took three fateful steps:

● On 31 July, it demanded the suspension of all Russian mobilisation.

● The following day, when mobilisation continued, Germany declared war.

● Lastly, it demanded from France a formal declaration of neutrality, and the surrender of the border fortresses of Toul and Verdun as guarantees.

Acceptance would have been incompatible with France's 'great power' status, and its inevitable refusal led to a further declaration of war by Germany (3 August).

Now German diplomacy centred upon attempts to keep Britain out of the war. Bethmann-Hollweg had already promised not to annex French territory and to restore the integrity of Belgium after the war. German military strategy, however, depended heavily upon the violation of Belgian neutrality for the purposes of the attack on France. When Germany invaded Belgium on 3 August, Britain's course was decided by its treaty obligations to Belgium, and the following day it, too, entered the war.

## Why did the powers go to war?

Although the victors in 1918 were quick to formulate questions of 'war guilt', the outbreak of the conflict makes more sense if it is seen as a monstrous combination of miscalculations. The government of Austria–Hungary erred in believing that a clash with Serbia could be settled without wider complications. Russia's partial mobilisation on 30 July was undertaken without sufficient awareness of its effect upon German policy. In Berlin there was a whole series of misjudgements:

● the hope that an Austro–Serbian clash could be localised;

● the failure to appreciate that the invasion of Belgium would bring Britain into the war;

● the long-term failure to anticipate foreign reaction to the bullying tone of *Weltpolitik*;

● The further naive supposition that a brief and successful war might ease domestic difficulties was an error shared with Vienna and St Petersburg.

1. Describe the steps by which the murder of the Archduke Franz Ferdinand in Sarajevo led to general war between the European powers.

2. Are there any grounds for claiming that any one of the major European powers acted less responsibly in the 1914 crisis than the others?

The historian A.J.P. Taylor made an extremely important contribution to the understanding of events in 1914 when he argued that the conflict arose from feelings of weakness rather than feelings of strength. Russia and Austria–Hungary felt that compromise would destroy their credibility as major powers. France and Germany felt that valuable allies had to be supported lest they themselves be left in isolation. In the German army, too, the feeling predominated that war in 1914 was preferable to war in two or three years' time, when the Entente powers would be much stronger. Lastly, all the participants misjudged the nature of the conflict to which they were committing themselves. They anticipated campaigns as sharp and decisive as those of the Balkan Wars, or of the wars of 1859, 1866 or 1870. They anticipated no great strain upon society, and would have been horrified to think that four years of trench warfare, technological revolution and economic attrition were about to tear apart the fabric of European society.

## 2.7 Was Germany completely to blame for the outbreak of war?
### A CASE STUDY IN HISTORICAL INTERPRETATION

### History and politics in the inter-war years

Although 1918 marked the end of the military contest, it marked the beginning of a fierce war of words concerning the causes of the conflict, and the dealing out of 'war guilt'. Clause 231 of the peace treaty forced the defeated Germans to admit that they bore the moral responsibility for the bloodshed by virtue of their aggressive policies before 1914. If the politicians of the Weimar Republic were forced publicly to accept that interpretation, German historians were not. The analysis of German diplomatic archives began immediately, undertaken to prove German claims of innocence, and culminated in a 40—volume work entitled *The Grand Policy of the European Cabinets 1871–1914* (1922–27). The inter-war years also saw many interpretative works by German historians, such as H. von Delbrück's *The Peace of Versailles* (1930) and H. Oncken's *The German Reich and the Prehistory of the First World War* (1932). These stressed the validity of Germany's fear of encirclement, and sought to lay greater emphasis on French desires to regain Alsace-Lorraine, and Russian designs upon Constantinople.

In the course of the 1930s it became politically acceptable, and even desirable, to share the responsibility for the outbreak of war. The American historian Sidney Fay, in *The Origins of the World War* (1930), caught the mood of the time by interpreting the disaster as an unfortunate succession of accidents. Austria–Hungary started a crisis in the Balkans without anticipating that it would escalate as it did; Germany was then trapped by its close links to Austria–Hungary, which operated in much the same way as the links between France and Russia, to drag the states into the conflict. Even contemporary French writers, originally the firmest advocates of German war guilt, were forced to admit that although 'the immediate origins suffice to tilt the balance [of guilt] to the side of the Central Empires, ... one does not discern in the other camp any miraculous will for peace' (J. Isaac, *A Historical Debate, 1914: The Problem of the Origins of the War*, published in 1933).

### The Fischer thesis and its critics

The compromise widely accepted as orthodox by western historians for 30 years was challenged dramatically in the 1960s by the work of the German historian Fritz Fischer. In *Germany's Aims in the First World War* (1961), he shifted a great deal of responsibility for the outbreak of war back on to German shoulders, claiming that its leaders had deliberately accepted the risk of war for the furtherance of their political ambitions during the course of the July Crisis of 1914. Fischer later claimed, in *The War of Illusions* (1969), that German actions since 1911 proved a desire, a preparation and a provocation of war. Naturally, such an interpretation provoked great opposition in Germany. Gerhard Ritter, then completing his masterpiece on German militarism – *The Sword and the Sceptre* (1954–68) – led the counter-attack. Ritter accepted that it was sadly true that the civil authorities had steadily abdicated their responsibilities in the face of military pressures during the reign of Wilhelm II, but argued that this did not amount to premeditated aggression. Another of Fischer's critics was Egmont Zechlin. In *The Outbreak of War in 1914* and the *Problem of War Aims in International Policy* (1972), Zechlin argues that although Bethmann-Hollweg took a calculated, and ultimately disastrous, risk in 1914, his objectives were essentially defensive, aiming to break the diplomatic encirclement which he believed to be stifling Germany.

More recently, the Fischer thesis has been modified by Hartmut Pogge von Strandmann, in *Germany and the Coming of War* (1988), and by H.W. Koch, in *The Origins of the First World War: Great Power Rivalry and German War Aims* (1984). Strandmann seeks to modify the nature of German war guilt by stressing that the error of its leaders was that they anticipated a short war with limited human costs. Koch's emphasis has been upon Germany's fear of isolation, and upon the concern of its leaders with the consequences of staying out of the conflict.

Yet Fischer has received much influential support among German historians. For instance, Imanuel Geiss, in *German Foreign Policy, 1871–1914* (1976), presents a modified version of Fischer's interpretation which still heartily condemns the conduct of Germany's leaders. Geiss concludes that Germany's unconditional support for Austria–Hungary was the decisive factor in the July Crisis, not only encouraging politicians in Vienna to take violent action, but also convincing Russian and French leaders that their countries were at risk, and that they needed to defend themselves. The German action in 1914 was compatible with its previous foreign policy, and thus implies a considerable degree of responsibility for the outcome.

Beyond Germany, the most frequent criticism of the Fischer thesis has been that it considers German actions and responsibilities too much in isolation from those of the other combatants. Some historians have been eager to stress the irresponsible actions of other states, and indeed of groups whose mentalities were not peculiar to individual states. Some have focused attention upon the intricate system of alliances that connected the interests of the major powers and on the considerable influence that military commanders exercised over many European governments. In *The Struggle for Mastery in Europe* (1954), A.J.P. Taylor played down the importance of the system of alliances that existed in 1914, stressing how loose and informal much of it was. Indeed, so loose was the system that one state, Italy, could actually change sides after the outbreak of the war. On the other hand, Taylor laid great stress upon the role of military commanders who advocated war in 1914, because they believed that the balance of military power was temporarily in their favour, and who argued against delay because their plans for mobilisation operated to a strict timetable.

Of the other European states, Austria–Hungary and Serbia have been criticised most for their irresponsible behaviour in the course of the Balkan crisis. Following the lead of Sidney Fay in the 1930s, Gordon Martel in *The Origins of the First World War* (1987), Fritz Fellner in *1914: Decisions for War* (1995) and others have blamed Serbian and Austro-Hungarian nationalists for plunging recklessly into a 'Third Balkan War', which spilled over to engulf the rest of the continent.

It is interesting to note that some recent work has revised views on the Balkan crisis in two important respects. It suggests that Serbia was too greatly drained by earlier Balkan wars to plan actively for a third. At the same time, there is some documentary evidence that Austria–Hungary's undoubted enthusiasm for a Balkan struggle was focused firmly upon Serbia until it was deflected and re-routed by German enthusiasm for a wider confrontation with Russia. While alternatives certainly exist to placing the blame on the shoulders of the German leaders, the role that they played continues to be regarded as central to the events that precipitated the war.

## Marxist historians and the guilt of capitalism

For Marxist historians, of course, the issue of German war guilt was largely irrelevant in explaining the outbreak of the First World War. The favoured Marxist interpretation was that put forward by Lenin himself in his essay, 'Imperialism, the Highest Form of Capitalism' (1916). Lenin's case was that the war was the inevitable result of the development of capitalism into the monopoly stage, wherein capitalists were bound to compete aggressively for limited resources and markets. European imperialism in the decades before 1914 was the result of the final stages of monopoly capitalism, because colonies represented new markets and new resources to these advanced capitalists. The First World War, in Lenin's view, had to be seen as a clash between states goaded into confrontation by the selfish interests of their capitalists.

Popular as such an interpretation remained for many years in left-wing circles, many objections have since been raised to it. Historian David Fieldhouse, in *The Colonial Empires* (1966), led the way in showing how small the extent of investment in the new colonies was and how Great Britain, for example, invested far more in the USA than in any new acquisition. Russia, too, remained far more popular with investors, especially French ones, than any African or Asian territory. Further objections were based upon emerging evidence that the major European powers were by no means locked into cut-throat competition with each other, as Lenin imagined. In particular, the French economic historian Raymond Poidevin showed, in *Economic and Financial Relations Between France and Germany from 1898 to 1914* (1969), strong links and substantial community of interest between the business communities of the rival belligerent states. Between 1893 and 1913, French exports to Germany doubled, while trade in the opposite direction trebled. More recently, the work of the American, Carl Stirkwerda, has indicated that such economic links occur between all of the European states that clashed in 1914–18. Raymond Poidevin's picture is one of politicians leading reluctant capitalists into confrontation, rather than the other way around. His categorical conclusion is that 'economic and financial questions are not at the root of Germany's declaration of war on France [in 1914].'

1. What different attitudes have historians taken over the issue of German 'war guilt'?

2. What are the main arguments against the proposition that Germany was responsible for the outbreak of war in 1914?

3. Why has the issue of responsibility for the First World War caused so much controversy among German historians?

## Source-based questions: The Sarajevo crisis, 1914

### SOURCE A

The annexation of Bosnia and Herzegovina was only one of the blows which Austria as the enemy of Serbia has aimed at this land. Many blows preceded it, and many will follow it. Work and preparation are necessary so that a new attack may not find Serbia equally unprepared. A new attack must be met by a new Serbia, in which every Serbian, from child to old man, is a rifleman.

The Austrians want to take our freedom and our language from us and to crush us. The Serbian people are faced by the question 'to be or not to be?'

The Narodna Odbrana proclaims to the people that Austria is our first and greatest enemy. If the Narodna Odbrana preaches the necessity of fighting Austria, she preaches a sacred truth of our national position. For the sake of bread and room, for the sake of the fundamental essentials of culture and trade, the freeing of the conquered Serbian territories and their union with Serbia is necessary to gentlemen, tradesmen, and peasants alike.

A publication of the Narodna Odbrana (Defence of the People), a secret Serbian patriotic society, 1911. Gavrilo Princip, the assassin of the Archduke Franz Ferdinand, was a probably a member.

### SOURCE B

The history of recent years, and especially the painful event of the murder of the Archduke Franz Ferdinand, has demonstrated the existence of a terrorist movement in Serbia whose aim is to separate certain territories from the Austro-Hungarian Empire. This murder, which has developed under the eyes of the Serbian government, has found expression beyond the territory of the kingdom in acts of terrorism, a series of assassinations and murders.

The Serbian government has done nothing to suppress this terrorist movement. She tolerated the criminal doings of the various societies and associations directed against the Habsburg Monarchy, the extreme language of the press, the glorification of the assassins and the participation of army officers and state officials in plots. The guilt of the Serbian government lasted up to the moment of the murder of the Archduke Franz Ferdinand.

It becomes plain from the evidence and confessions of the criminal authors of the outrage that the murder at Sarajevo was planned in Serbia, that the murderers received the arms and bombs with which they were equipped from Serbian officers and officials and that the transportation of the criminals and their arms to Bosnia was arranged and carried out by leading Serbian officials.

Letter from the Austo-Hungarian government to Serbia, 23 July 1914.

### SOURCE C

The Serbian Government has been painfully surprised at the allegations that citizens of Serbia have participated in the crime committed at Sarajevo. The Serbian Government will co-operate in an investigation of all that concerns this crime and it stands ready, in order to prove the entire correctness of its attitude, to take measures against any persons who are alleged to have been involved.

It is prepared to commit for trial any Serbian subject, regardless of his rank, whose involvement in the crime of Sarajevo shall be claimed.

If the Habsburg Government is not satisfied with this reply, the Serbian Government is ready to accept a peaceful understanding by referring this question to the decision of the International Tribunal at the Hague, or to the Great Powers.

Serbian response in reply to the letter from Austria–Hungary, 25 July 1914.

### SOURCE D

We did not hate Austria, but the Austrians had done nothing to solve the problems that faced Bosnia and Herzegovina. Nine-tenths of our people are farmers who suffer, who live in misery, who have no schools, who are deprived of any culture. We sympathised with them in their distress.

We heard it said that the Archduke Franz Ferdinand was an enemy of the Slavs. Nobody directly told us to kill him; but we arrived at the idea ourselves.

I would like to add something else. Although Princip is playing the hero, and although we all wanted to appear as heroes, we still have profound regrets.

We are anything you want, except criminals. I ask the children of the late successor to the throne to forgive us. As for you, punish us according to your understanding. We are not criminals. We are honest people, motivated by noble sentiments; we are idealists; we wanted to do good; we have loved our people; and we shall die for our ideals.

The statement in court of Nedjelko Cabrinovic, accused of the murder of the Archduke Franz Ferdinand, 23 October 1914.

---

**Source-based questions: The Sarajevo crisis, 1914**

### SOURCE E

Although the horrible murder was the work of a Serbian secret society with branches all over the country, many details prove that the Serbian government had neither instigated nor desired it. The Serbs were exhausted by two wars. The most hot-headed among them might have paused at the thought of war with Austria–Hungary, so overwhelmingly superior.

From the memoirs of the German Field Marshal Karl von Bulow, written after the end of the First World War.

'Serbia was responsible for the Sarajevo crisis of 1914.' Use Sources A–E to show how far the evidence confirms this statement.

---

## Further Reading

*Texts designed for AS and A2 Level students*

*The Origins of the First World War* by Gordon Martel (Longman, Seminar Studies series, 1987)

*Rivalry and Accord: International Relations 1870–1914* by John Lowe (Hodder & Stoughton, Access to History series, 1996)

*Origins of the First World War* by Ruth Henig (Routledge, Lancaster Pamphlets, 1984)

*More advanced reading*

The historical literature on the First World War is enormous and is fed by a constant flow of new works. What follows is only a small sample of the works available:

*Origins of the First World War* edited by H.W. Koch (Macmillan, 1972) deals in depth with the controversy launched by Fritz Fischer.

*The Origins of the First and Second World Wars* by Frank McDonough (Cambridge University Press, Perspectives in History series, 1997) provides a concise guide to the historiographical arguments surrounding the causes of the war.

*The Pity of War* by Niall Ferguson (Allen Lane, 1998) takes a broader view, addressing a series of questions concerning the mentalities that surrounded the declaration, the fighting and the organisation of the war.

*Sites of Memory, Sites of Mourning: The Great War in European Cultural History* by Jay Winter (Cambridge University Press, 1995) explores the emotional and cultural impact of the war.

# 3 International relations, 1919–1941

## Key Issues

- What were the strengths and weaknesses of the peace settlement of 1919–20?

- How successful was the League of Nations?

- Why did the Second World War take place?

**3.1** What forces shaped the terms of the Treaty of Versailles?

**3.2** Why was the Versailles settlement unsatisfactory?

**3.3** How effective was the League of Nations?

**3.4** To what extent had international relations been stabilised by 1929?

**3.5** What was the impact of the Wall Street Crash upon international relations?

**3.6** Why was it not possible to form a European alliance against Hitler between 1933 and 1935?

**3.7** In what respects had Hitler changed the Versailles settlement by 1938?

**3.8** Why did war break out in 1939?

**3.9** Historical interpretation: Did Hitler plan the outbreak of war in 1939?

**3.10** Why did the USSR and USA become involved in the Second World War?

## Framework of Events

| | |
|---|---|
| 1919 | June: Signature of Treaty of Versailles |
| | September: Signature of Treaty of St Germain |
| 1920 | Establishment of League of Nations |
| 1922 | Treaty of Rapallo between Germany and USSR |
| 1923 | French occupation of the Ruhr |
| 1924 | Introduction of Dawes Plan |
| 1925 | Locarno treaties |
| 1926 | Germany admitted to League of Nations |
| 1928 | Signature of Kellogg–Briand Pact |
| 1929 | Introduction of Young Plan |
| | October: Collapse of US stock market, the 'Wall Street Crash' |
| 1931 | Hoover moratorium on German reparation payments. Japanese invasion of Manchuria |
| 1932 | Lausanne conference on reparation payments |
| 1933 | January: Adolf Hitler appointed Chancellor of Germany |
| | July: Four Power Pact between Britain, France, Italy and Germany |
| 1934 | German–Polish non-aggression pact |
| 1935 | Saar returned to Germany. Germany introduces military conscription. Stresa agreement |
| | October: Italian invasion of Abyssinia |
| 1936 | March: German remilitarisation of the Rhineland |
| | July: Outbreak of civil war in Spain |
| | November: Anti-Comintern pact between Germany and Japan |
| 1937 | Japan–China War begins with Japanese invasion of northern China. Italy joins Anti-Comintern pact and withdraws from League of Nations |
| 1938 | March: German occupation of Austria |
| | October: Munich Conference, followed by German occupation of Sudetenland |

| 1939 | March: German occupation of Bohemia and Moravia in Czechoslovakia |
| | May: 'Pact of Steel' between Germany and Italy |
| | August: 'Ribbentrop–Molotov' pact between Germany and USSR |
| | September: German invasion of Poland. Declaration of Second World War by Britain and France on Germany. |
| 1940 | April: Germany invades Denmark and Norway |
| | May: Germany invades Holland, Belgium and France |
| | June: Italy enters war against Britain and France |
| | Fall of France |
| | September: Battle of Britain |
| 1941 | Lend-lease agreement between USA and Britain |
| | Atlantic Charter between Britain and USA |
| | Germany invades Yugoslavia and Greece |
| | June: Germany and its allies invade the USSR |
| | December: Japan attacks Pearl Harbor |
| | Germany declares war on the USA. |

**1. Which of the factors in the mind map was the most important in explaining the outbreak of war in 1939? Give reasons for your answer.**

**2. How far were Britain and France responsible for causing the Second World War?**

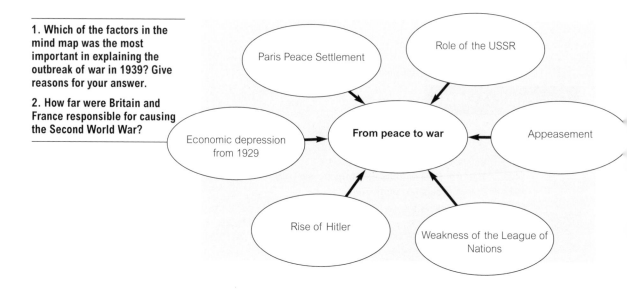

Paris Peace Settlement

Role of the USSR

Economic depression from 1929

**From peace to war**

Appeasement

Rise of Hitler

Weakness of the League of Nations

## Overview

Isolationism: A policy by which a state (e.g. the USA in the early 1930s) pursues its own domestic interests in isolation from the wider considerations of international politics.

I N November 1918, the powers that had fought the First World War emerged into a world quite unlike that which they had fought to protect. The degree of potential instability that existed in the aftermath of the First World War was without precedent in recent European history. The Austro-Hungarian Empire had collapsed, to be replaced by a collection of smaller states, more viable in terms of national identity than in terms of military strength or of defensible borders. The Russian Empire had not only given way to a collection of new states, but also to a new political, social and economic system that declared itself hostile to all others in Europe. The United States of America, whose intervention in the war had been decisive, withdrew immediately into **isolationism**. Britain and France, who had lacked the means and the desire to direct European affairs in 1914, were certainly in no position to do so five years later. Between 1919 and the mid-1930s Europe was essentially a power vacuum.

The 1920s can be seen, in retrospect, as a 'false start' to attempts to solve the terrible problems created, or left unsolved, by the First World War. The victorious allies approached the problem of political reconstruction in Europe with two assumptions that proved to be false:

1. that they had won a clear-cut victory;

2. that the ground was now clear for a just and enlightened re-ordering of European politics.

The perception that Germany had been defeated may have been partly true in the military sense (although Germany had clearly defeated Russia on the Eastern Front), but it was distinctly false in terms of its economic potential, and in terms of the political ideas that had driven its recent expansion. Even in the 1920s the assumptions of the allies were undermined by the bitter resentment felt by Germany at the terms of the peace treaty, and at the presumption of German 'war guilt' upon which the treaty rested. This contributed directly to the second problem, that of how the hated peace treaty could be enforced. Neither of the alternative strategies employed by the allies – to force the terms upon Germany, or to persuade the Germans into grudging acceptance – proved altogether successful. A third strategy – of employing the resources of American capitalism to fund German, and thereby European stability – seemed to show distinct promise in the years 1924–29. When that option was wrecked by the collapse of the American stock market, the major powers of Europe found themselves plunged back into a political world dominated by national self-interest and the rule of military force.

In the aftermath of the Second World War it was broadly acceptable to attribute all the tragedies and failures of the past decades to the evil expansionism of the Nazi regime. More recently, however, some historians have placed greater emphasis upon the context in which that regime operated, and upon the opportunities that it was able to exploit. They have become increasingly aware of the complexity of the problems posed for the western European powers by the economic collapse of 1929. Their understandable preoccupation with their domestic economies made them sympathetic to programmes of **disarmament**. In the cases of several powers, notably Britain and France, independence movements within their Asian colonies, and the willingness of Japan to exploit these movements, seemed to pose a threat to their interests as serious as that posed by the resurgence of Germany. At the same time, the destabilisation of western capitalism renewed fears about the intentions of Soviet Russia. It is of the greatest importance that, with the establishment and consolidation of the Soviet Union, Europe had to take into account a force that threatened not only the existing balance of power, but all existing social and economic structures. It is only with hindsight that we can identify Nazism as the major challenge that those powers faced in the 1930s.

It is no wonder that the states of Europe employed a number of strategies to deflect the German threat, as alternatives to confrontation. The most familiar and traditional of these was the formation of alliances that might deter Germany from aggressive action. By 1937, however, it appeared that none of the western European powers really had the stomach for the task. Besides, some states seemed

**Disarmament**: The act of reducing the number of weapons that a country has.

**Unilateral**: Countries make decisions without waiting for agreement from other countries.

**Maginot Line**: A line of military fortifications along the eastern and north-eastern borders of France, to defend against invasion. It was named after André Maginot, French politician (1877–1932).

**Vichy government**: The term used to describe the regime that governed the 'free' zone of France during the early part of the Nazi occupation. It took its name from the spa town of Vichy, in which it established its headquarters. It was largely dependent upon German goodwill, and was overthrown when German forces occupied the 'free' zone in 1943.

to pursue this strategy at the same time as they made **unilateral** arrangements for their own security. It was hard to believe in France, for instance, as an international peacekeeper, as it retreated behind the barrier of the **Maginot Line** (see map on page 94). The second strategy was to appease Germany, to offer concessions in the hope that this would satisfy its revisionist demands and encourage it to act once again as a responsible member of the international community. In many respects it was an honourable and justifiable policy, but its effect was largely to convince Hitler that he had a free hand in Europe. A third strategy was to recognise Nazi Germany as the dominant European power of the future, and to align one's state with Hitler. Italy had taken this course voluntarily by 1938. France followed a similar course in 1940, under the **Vichy government**, forced into it by the discovery to its cost that the other methods did not work.

The declaration of war by Britain and France against Germany's invasion of Poland did not lead to all-out European War. From September 1939 to May 1940 a period of 'phoney war' ensued. The 'real' land war occurred in May/June 1940, with Germany's attack on the West. France fell within six weeks, leaving Britain to fight on alone. From 1940 to June 1941, under the leadership of Winston Churchill, Britain survived – but only with US support.

However, what greatly increased the size and scale of the war was the German invasion of the USSR in June 1941, the greatest land invasion in world history. By December 1941 the German army had reached the outskirts of Moscow.

In the Far East the Japanese occupation of French Indo-China in 1940 provoked US sanctions against Japan. In order to break US opposition to Japanese policy in the Far East the Japanese attempted to destroy the US Pacific Fleet at Pearl Harbor in Hawaii on 7 December 1941.

By 8 December 1941 the world was faced with two major wars: one in Europe and one in the Far East. What united the two wars was the USA's commitment to Britain's defence and Hitler's decision to declare war on the USA on 8 December.

## 3.1  What forces shaped the terms of the Treaty of Versailles?

November 1918 brought an armistice rather than a definitive peace. Some of its terms – such as the withdrawal of German forces beyond the Rhine, and the internment of its fleet – made it a foregone conclusion that Germany would be unable to restart hostilities. In effect, the leaders of the four main allied powers – France, Britain, the USA and Italy – were concerned during their six months of deliberation (13 January – 28 June 1919) with the preparation of the terms for peace that would be dictated to the representatives of Germany when at last they were allowed to appear in France. Rarely has the preparation of peace been attended by such high hopes and rarely has the feeling been so quickly apparent that the outcome of negotiations had fallen far short of initial expectations. 'We arrived,' wrote the British historian and diplomat Harold Nicolson, in *Peacemaking, 1919* (1967), 'determined that a peace of justice and wisdom should be negotiated: we left it conscious that the treaties imposed upon our enemies were neither wise nor just.' Others saw the price that Europe would pay for the shortcomings of the peace. 'This is not peace,' Ferdinand Foch is reported to have exclaimed when he heard the terms, 'it is a truce for 20 years.'

## The political pressures

**Scuttling**: The act whereby naval commanders order the sinking of their own ships. This is usually done to prevent them from falling into enemy hands.

The first problem that handicapped the leaders of the allied powers in their search for a lasting peace was that they were not always free agents. The British Prime Minister, David Lloyd George, was in the process of fighting a general election in which popular anger produced such emotive slogans as 'Hang the Kaiser' and 'Squeeze the German lemon until the pips squeak'. In France, President Georges Clemenceau had to contend with anger and anxiety that the losses of the war should never be repeated. The priorities of the delegates also differed. French policy was dominated by an overwhelming desire for future security, for the achievement of which almost no imposition upon the German aggressor would be too great. Britain's view was moderated by a number of considerations. The **scuttling** of the German fleet at Scapa Flow (31 June 1919) guaranteed its own national security. At the same time, its traditional concern with the balance of power on the continent made Britain wary of weakening Germany excessively, especially as it became ever clearer that the Soviet regime in Russia was there to stay.

It was always likely that both sets of vested interests would be overridden by the concerns of the American President, Woodrow Wilson. He hoped to replace the outdated and corrupt criteria of European diplomacy with a lasting and just peace, based upon the satisfaction of justifiable national claims. He hoped for 'a peace without victory', a settlement that would not be dominated by selfish demands by the victors. Wilson was the central figure of the peace conference, partly because the USA alone had the manpower and financial resources to continue the struggle if necessary, and partly because of the enormous popularity that he enjoyed as 'the prophet of peace'. He could not, however, expect to impose his views upon the hard-bitten statesmen of Europe.

## The desire to punish Germany

The 440 clauses that constituted the peace treaty with Germany were concerned with four major issues.

- At the heart of the treaty lay the contention that Germany bore the main burden of guilt for the outbreak of the 'Great War'. Clause 231 was a key element in the treaty, forcing Germany to acknowledge this guilt and responsibility. Without this 'war guilt clause' there would have been little moral justification for the other impositions upon Germany, and it is little surprise that this was a prime focus for German resentment in the inter-war years.

- Secondly, although the Treaty of Versailles made allowance for eventual general disarmament, Germany was to be disarmed immediately. As its armed forces were in future to cater only for the defence of its own territory, they were restricted to an army of 96,000 men and 4,000 officers, all serving for a period of 12 years. This was to prevent the build-up of experienced reserves. These armed forces were forbidden the use of any purely offensive weapons – tanks, heavy artillery, powered aircraft, submarines and capital warships.

- The boundaries of the German state were also adjusted to satisfy the demands of neighbouring nationalities. In the west, Alsace-Lorraine returned to France and the small regions of Eupen and Malmedy became Belgian territory. Ideally, France would have wished to make greater inroads for its future security, either to advance its own border to the Rhine, or to create an independent and neutral state in the Rhineland. Both plans were opposed by Britain and America on

Territorial changes, 1919–24

ideological and rational grounds, and France had to be satisfied with a three-point settlement. The Rhineland was temporarily occupied by allied forces, all German forces were permanently banned from the Rhineland, and Britain and America promised their future aid in maintaining this settlement. To the north and east, Germany suffered further losses. North Schleswig once more became Danish territory, and territory in Posen and West Prussia was transferred to Poland, notably the infamous 'Polish corridor' giving the new state access to the sea. At the end of the 'corridor', the distinctly German city of Danzig became a 'free city' with Poland granted the use of its port facilities, its only access to the sea.

● Germany's 'war guilt' also provided justification for the allied demand for reparations. This was not the first time that victors in European wars had claimed material compensation from the conquered, but the scale of the demands, like the scale of the war, was unprecedented. The allies proposed to charge Germany for the material damage done to them during the hostilities, a very considerable figure in the case of France. They also proposed to charge future expenses on such items as

**Tomas Masaryk (1850–1937)**
Advocate of Czech independence during the First World War. Elected President of Czechoslovakia in 1920, 1927 and 1934, before retiring through ill health in 1935.

**Edvard Beneš (1884–1948)**
After working with Masaryk in the cause of Czech independence, Beneš served as Foreign Minister of Czechoslovakia (1918–35). President of the Republic (1935–39). Leader of the Czech government in exile (1941–45). Briefly president of liberated Czechoslovakia until ousted by communists in 1948.

1. What steps did the victorious allies take in the Treaty of Versailles to limit the future power of Germany?

2. How effectively did the terms of the Treaty of Versailles serve the interests of Britain and France?

pensions for their widows and war wounded. This last item alone constituted nearly half the total bill of £6,600 million which was handed to the Germans by the Inter-Allied Reparations Commission when the task of estimation was eventually completed (May 1921).

### Dismantling the Austro–Hungarian Empire

Although the peace settlement with Germany naturally dominated the attention of European statesmen, it was accompanied by a collection of other treaties made with Germany's former allies:

● with Austria at St Germain en Laye

● with Hungary at Trianon

● with Turkey at Sevres

● with Bulgaria at Neuilly.

The disappearance of the Habsburg Empire, that dominant feature of central Europe for five centuries, was central to these treaties. In its place stood the German state of Austria, specially forbidden by the treaties to unite with its fellow Germans to the north, and a number of new states. Yugoslavia, Czechoslovakia and Poland represented the fulfilment of national aspirations that had rumbled on throughout the 19th century. In the cases of Yugoslavia and Czechoslovakia the delegates around Paris had been able to do little but accept the actions of such national leaders as Tomas Masaryk and Edvard Beneš, who had seized their opportunities with the collapse of the Austro–Hungarian war effort. Hungary, after a century of increasing national fulfilment, now found itself stripped of Croatia, Slovenia, Slovakia and Ruthenia by these new states. Its resentment of these losses was to be a significant factor in the politics of central and eastern Europe over the next two decades.

## 3.2  Why was the Versailles settlement unsatisfactory?

The peace settlement of 1919 was unsuccessful. The historian A.J.P. Taylor's blunt judgement, in *The Origins of the Second World War* (1961), that 'the Second World War was, in large part, a repeat performance of the first' conveys clearly the extent to which the problems of 1919 were left unresolved. In part, its failure may be attributed to the enormous complexity of the problems facing the delegates. In 1815, at Vienna, European statesmen needed to regulate the territories of one state, Napoleonic France. In 1919, at Versailles, it was the empires of Germany, Turkey, Austria-Hungary and Russia – a large proportion of the European landmass – that lay in ruins. Several other distinct weaknesses in the final drafts of the treaties can also be identified.

### German resentment

The main problem that was to haunt Europe for the next two and a half decades was German resentment of the terms imposed upon them. Although on the verge of military defeat in November 1918, German troops were still on foreign soil, and their representatives had approached the allies confident that a settlement would be offered based upon Wilson's '**Fourteen Points**'.

Instead Germans found themselves presented with a dictated peace which stripped the Reich of 25,000 square miles (64,750 square kilometres) of territory and 7,000,000 inhabitants, about 13% and 10% of its

**Fourteen Points:** The 'Fourteen Points' were listed in a speech by President Woodrow Wilson in January 1918, intended to set out a blueprint for lasting peace in Europe after the First World War.

respective totals. They found that, in many cases, Germany was treated according to principles quite different from those that governed the settlements with other states. Nationality was the proclaimed principle behind most territorial settlements, yet union between Germany and the German-speakers of Austria was specifically forbidden. Germany was disarmed and stripped of its colonies, while the victors retained their weapons and in some cases actually added to their colonial empires. Yet, although Germany was treated as a defeated power, it retained the means to become a great force in the world once more. It was not partitioned, as it was eventually to be in 1945, and it retained nearly 90% of its economic resources. Germany was deprived of its weapons, but retained the potential to produce modern replacements at a later date. As early as 1925, Germany's production of steel, for instance, was twice that of Great Britain. Its relative position in the European balance of power had hardly suffered from the collapse of the Russian and Austrian empires, that left a collection of relatively weak 'successor states' on its eastern borders.

'**Successor states**': Those states that filled the vacuum left by the collapse of the Habsburg Empire in the aftermath of the First World War.

## The disintegration of the wartime allied alliance

In 1918 the allied alliance that had fought the war was already in the process of disintegration. By 1920 it was in ruins. Firstly, the great power of Russia, a key factor in the considerations of 1914, was completely excluded from the deliberations of 1919. The 1917 Bolshevik revolution removed Russia temporarily from the diplomatic scene, but its eventual success, and its brief imitations in Hungary (March 1919) and Bavaria (April 1919), profoundly shocked the governing classes of Europe. As a result of the revolution, the attitudes of these classes towards Germany often became ambiguous. With Germany defeated, might not Communist Russia now be seen as the major threat to Europe's stability and security? If a relatively strong, conservative Germany were not preserved as a bulwark in central Europe, what would prevent the westward flow of the Communist tide? By mid-1919 it was clear that the USA would not fulfil this role, for it had turned its back on Europe as abruptly as it had intervened in the first place. The considerable prestige of President Wilson at Versailles had hidden the true weakness of its domestic position. Involvement in Europe had never been universally popular in the USA, and the prospect of a permanent peacekeeping role there was quite unacceptable to many American politicians. Accordingly, the Senate refused to ratify the treaties that Wilson had negotiated (November 1919). A year later, Wilson's party was out of power, and America was once again on the path of isolationism. In short, the implementation of the peace treaty had to be undertaken from 1919 without the participation of either of the powers that were to decide Europe's fate in 1939–45.

| John Maynard Keynes (1883–1946) |
| --- |
| British economist; a fierce opponent of the allies' reparations policy at Versailles. Keynes proposed (1936) new theories on economic thinking and employment policy. He was an important figure in the organisation of international monetary arrangements in 1945. |

## Keynes and the controversy over reparations

There has been little historical dispute about the importance of German resentment or the problems of enforcement in the failure of the Versailles settlement. The same cannot be said for the third area of objection that was raised to the peace terms. In an influential work, *The Economic Consequences of the Peace* (1920), the English economist J.M. Keynes denounced what he saw as the folly of the treaty's reparation clauses. By putting such intolerable pressure on the German economy, he concluded, the allies threatened the stability of the whole European economy of which it was part. 'This treaty,' he argued, 'ignores the economic solidarity of Europe, and by aiming at the economic life of Germany, it threatens the health and prosperity of the allies themselves.' Although influential in Britain and in the USA, Keynes' arguments aroused great opposition in

France, the country most in need of reparations. There, they were most effectively answered by E. Mantoux, in *The Economic Consequences of Mr Keynes* (1944). The central part of Mantoux's argument was that the productivity of German industry during the 1930s, especially armaments manufacture, showed that the levels of reparations set in 1921 were, after all, within Germany's capacity.

### Was the Versailles settlement doomed from the outset?

Mantoux's work is part of a substantial literature, written largely since the end of the Second World War, that has modified the earlier condemnation of the Versailles treaty. Where Winston Churchill saw 'a turbulent collision of embarrassed **demagogues**', where Keynes saw profound economic ignorance, and where Harold Nicolson saw a sad failure to stick to original high ideals, more recent writers have often cited extenuating circumstances. The French historian, Maurice Baumont, in *The Origins of the Second World War* (1978), has stressed that the shortcomings that survived the peace conference should not blind us to the fact that 'as a whole the treaties righted age-old wrongs', especially with regard to the subject nationalities of central Europe. The English historian Anthony Adamthwaite, in *The Making of the Second World War* (1977), has claimed that the main fault in 1919 lay, not with the terms of the treaties, but with the hopes that preceded them, so high that they were bound to be disappointed. 'No peace settlement could have fulfilled the millennial hopes of a new heaven and a new earth. It was the destruction of these Utopian hopes that provoked the denunciations of the settlement.' In addition to these criticisms, it is also possible to argue that the main problem with the treaty lay not in its terms but in the subsequent failure to enforce it effectively.

**Demagogues**: Political leaders who try to win support by appealing to people's emotions rather than using rational arguments.

1. What features of the Versailles Treaty were most resented by Germany? Give reasons for your answer.

2. Why did the peace settlement with Germany prove so difficult to enforce in the years after 1918?

## 3.3 How effective was the League of Nations?

### What was the purpose of the League?

The League of Nations was a central element in Woodrow Wilson's ideas on the establishment and maintenance of European and world peace. He believed in the concept of an international organisation able to rise above the selfish motives and the misunderstandings that, in his view, were the root causes of international conflict. In general, the idea was greeted with enthusiasm by the nations represented at the Versailles peace conference. Two distinct schools of thought developed as to the form it should take. France took the realistic view that such a body could only be influential if equipped with sufficient armed force to enforce its decisions. This was opposed by Great Britain, uneasy at the idea of an international armed force possibly under French command, and by other states who baulked at the idea of portions of their own forces coming under international control. Above all, President Wilson refused to allow his 'brain child' to become simply another weapon of traditional power politics, or one with which the victors could torment the defeated. Thus, the body whose Covenant, or constitution, was written specifically into each of the peace treaties, and which met for the first time in Geneva in December 1920, was primarily a forum to which nations in dispute could bring their problems for advice and settlement.

### How was the League intended to work?

The Covenant of the League of Nations defined four main aims for the organisation:

- to prevent future wars by the peaceful settlement of international disputes;

- to promote disarmament;

**Mandated territories**: Areas placed under the supervision of the League of Nations at the end of the First World War.

- to supervise the **mandated territories** referred to it by the peace treaties, such as the former German colonies and the Saarland;

- to promote general international co-operation by its various organisations for social and economic work.

Its powers and the obligations of its members in these tasks were also clearly defined. Members in dispute with one another were obliged to refer their differences to one of three processes provided by the League:

- to the Permanent Court of International Justice;

**Arbitration**: The judging of a dispute between nations or states by someone not involved, whose decision both sides agree to accept.

- to **arbitration**;

- to enquiry by the Council of the League, its executive committee.

**Sanctions**: Measures taken by countries to restrict or prohibit trade and official contact with a country that has broken international law.

**Embargoes**: A non-violent form of political action in which pressure is placed upon a state by banning trade with that state.

Failure to do so, or failure to take reasonable account of the resulting decisions, rendered offending members liable to **sanctions**. The allies had been so impressed by the effect of economic **embargoes** employed against Germany in the war that economic sanctions were chosen as the League's main weapon. The possibility of military sanctions was admitted, but their extent was left undefined, and they could only ever be applied if a member state agreed to put its own forces at the disposal of the League. In its 20—year life, the League never once sought to apply military sanctions.

Forty-two states originally subscribed to these terms, but there were some notable absentees. The USA, because of the Senate's refusal to ratify the peace terms, never became a member of the organisation inspired by their President. Soviet Russia did not become a member until 1934, the year after Japan left the League. Germany was a member only between 1926–33, its initial absence confirming the impression that the League

The major institutions of the League of Nations

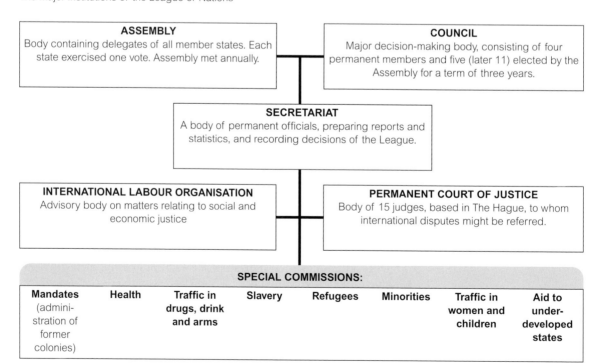

stood in essence for the preservation of the 'status quo' established in 1919. None of the powers dissatisfied with either the terms or the principles of the peace settlement could happily accept or further the aims of the League of Nations.

### What did the League achieve and what did it fail to achieve?

**1. By what means did the League of Nations hope to preserve peace in the post-war world?**

**2. How much justification is there for the statement that 'the League of Nations failed because its aims were neither popular nor achievable'?**

The League was not a total failure. When states accepted its mediatory functions it could and did reach notable settlements, as over the Åland Islands claimed by Sweden and Finland (1921), and in border disputes between Greece and Bulgaria (1924) and between Hungary and Yugoslavia (1934). When European statesmen such as Ramsay MacDonald, Gustav Stresemann and Aristide Briand worked with it in the late 1920s, it seemed to stand at the centre of European diplomacy. Its international bodies, such as the Health Organisation and the Advisory Committee on Traffic in Women and Children, still function today (as the World Health Organisation and UNICEF). It failed in its primary task, to prevent further war, due to the fact that the League represented a new concept of international relations in a world where most major powers were content to stick to the old selfish methods of force and *Realpolitik*.

In the major confrontations of the inter-war period the League failed, not because it could not find common ground between disputing parties, but because it was totally ignored by one or more of those parties. The League was bypassed in the case of Polish seizure of the town of Vilna (1920), Japanese aggression in Manchuria (1931), Italian attacks on Abyssinia (1935) and all of Hitler's expansionist moves. It had no means in its Covenant to prevent that. Two contemporary verdicts illustrate the League's weakness in the face of selfish acts of aggression. In all the cases just mentioned the judgement of Lord David Cecil held good, that 'the League of Nations has not been tried and found wanting; it has been found inconvenient and not tried'. Prominent among those who found the 'peace-mongering' of the League inconvenient was Benito Mussolini. He fully appreciated that, especially in the 1930s, the machinery of the League appealed only to those nations too weak to look after their own interests. 'The League is all right,' he declared, 'when sparrows quarrel. It fails when eagles fall out.'

## 3.4  To what extent had international relations been stabilised by 1929?

### Continuing confrontation: why did France invade the Ruhr in 1923?

In the years immediately after the conclusion of peace, it was France that faced the biggest problems over the enforcement of the treaty. For France, the questions of reparation payments, of post-war reconstruction and of German economic potential were not questions of morality or of theory, but of national survival. By 1920, however, the bases of French security proposed at Versailles lay in ruins. America had withdrawn from European involvement, Britain showed little interest in continuing the co-operation of wartime, and domestic developments in Germany offered little prospect of its willing acceptance of the settlement. Most serious for France's recovery and prosperity, Germany showed increasing reluctance to maintain its reparation payments. By the Wiesbaden Accords (October 1921), France agreed to help German payments by accepting a proportion in raw materials and industrial produce, rather than in cash, but in the next year, these payments in kind had also slipped steadily into arrears.

Faced with the choice of using conciliation or confrontation to exact its

**Raymond Poincaré (1856–1934)**
A hard-headed politician, a native of Lorraine who remembered Germany's past offences towards his home region, and was determined that Germany should not escape its due punishment. Member of the French Assembly from 1887. Finance Minister (1894–95). Prime Minister (1912–13). President of the Republic (1913–20), Prime Minister (1922–24).

**Passive resistance**: A form of political resistance based upon peaceful actions (e.g. strike action), as opposed to acts of violence.

How successful was German resistance to French and Belgium occupation of the Ruhr in 1923–4?

due from Germany, public and political opinion in France inclined more and more toward the latter solution. This tendency was strengthened by the appointment of Raymond Poincaré as Prime Minister (January 1922).

The crisis in French–German relations erupted in November 1922 when Germany requested a suspension of its payments for up to four years in the face of domestic economic difficulties. It was Germany's third such request in three years and strongly suggested that the whole question of enforcing the Versailles settlement was at stake. It was this vital issue, rather than the trivial pretext of non-delivery of a batch of telegraph poles, that prompted France, with support from Italy and Belgium, to send troops across the Rhine into the industrial heartland of the Ruhr (January 1923). Protesting, with justification, that the invasion of its sovereign territory was against the terms of the peace treaty, the German government of Chancellor Cuno appealed with great success for a policy of **passive resistance** in the Ruhr. In February 1923, coal production there fell to 2.5 million tons, where 90 million had been mined in 1922. Three iron-smelting furnaces operated in March, where 70 had worked the previous year. Occasional terrorist attacks on troops and military action against German demonstrators raised the overall tension.

Protest poster from 1923 against the French politics of occupation in the Rhine and Ruhr area with the inscription 'The Rhine will remain German!'

To overcome the effects of strikes and passive resistance, Poincaré appealed, with equal success, for unemployed Frenchmen and Belgians to operate mines, furnaces and railways in the Ruhr. Faced with the success of this ploy, with the total collapse of the German currency, and with the ominous spread of separatist movements in Germany, the government conceded defeat. Although it never became official French governmental policy, commanders in the Ruhr certainly showed some sympathy to political movements that proposed the establishment of an independent Rhineland state. With a united Germany at risk, Gustav Stresemann replaced Cuno as Chancellor in August 1923 and decreed the end of passive resistance within a month.

### Was French intervention in the Ruhr successful?

What had Poincaré achieved in the Ruhr? Economically, he seemed to have triumphed, with France guaranteed 21% of the region's production up to December 1923 and 27% thereafter. Against this, Poincaré had reinforced the mistrust and apprehension among his former allies at the French threat to the balance of power, and had made difficult, if not impossible, any future co-operation between France and Germany. 'France,' wrote the Italian minister Count Sforza, 'has committed the supreme error of polarising against her the hostility of all the patriotic elements in the Reich.' The economic gains, important as they were, were largely invalidated by France's subsequent political isolation. In his own country, Poincaré came under attack, from the left wing for high-handed action in the interests of French capitalists, and from the right for withdrawing when the chance existed finally to break the unity and economic backbone of Germany. In terms of its political consequences it must be considered highly doubtful whether the Ruhr gamble was worth the cost.

### Economic stabilisation: the Dawes Plan

At least France learned its lesson from the Ruhr adventure. The hostility of the British and American reaction, the dramatic decline in the franc (from 70 to the pound in 1922 to 240 to the pound in 1926), and the defeat of the National Bloc in the 1924 elections, all brought home the point that France could not safely rely upon unilateral action. The agreement between France, Britain and the USA (November 1923) to replace the reparations question upon an international footing, represented not only French misgivings, but British and American fears as to where unilateral action might lead in the future.

The result of this decision was the formation of the commission, chaired by the American economist Charles Dawes, which produced in April 1924 the so-called 'Dawes Plan' for the future regulation of redemption payments. By the Dawes Plan, which was to operate for five years, reparation payments would be guaranteed by two mortgages, one on Germany's railways, and the other on certain German industries, supplemented by deductions from certain German taxes. An American 'General Reparations Agent', Parker Gilbert, was to be installed in Germany to supervise payments. The amounts to be paid by Germany were substantially reduced, but this was outweighed in the French view by the facts that much of its post-war reconstruction was nearing completion, and that the plan once more involved its wartime allies in the collection of reparations. Thus, France accepted the Dawes Plan.

The five years of the Plan's operation have been described as the 'Golden Age' of reparations, with the allies receiving payments, in cash and in kind, with greater regularity than before. It was, however, a temporary measure, and was still accompanied by German complaints both at the level of payments and because no definite date had been fixed for their end. From the allied point of view, the plan also failed to provide any link between German payments and their own repayment of war debts to the USA.

### The Young Plan (1929)

The Young Plan (June 1929), which was proposed to succeed the Dawes Plan, set out to tackle these questions. Although it further reduced the total to be paid by Germany, it linked French and British debts to the level of German payments, and set 1988 as the final year of reparation payments. It also continued American commitment and involvement in this vital area of European politics.

In both the Dawes Plan and the Young Plan the fatal weakness was that they were largely dependent upon the huge sums of foreign capital, two-thirds of it American, that were being invested in Germany in the late 1920s to stimulate and sustain its industries. J.M. Keynes had already written in 1926 that the duration of these arrangements was 'in the hands of the American capitalist'. Within three years, the great crisis of American capitalism was finally to wreck these hopeful prospects of economic reconciliation.

### Diplomatic stabilisation: the Locarno Pact (1925)

For the German government, the primary objective of their agreement to the reparations plans was to clear their territory of foreign troops and to guard against their return. The first aim was only partially achieved. Although French and Belgian troops had withdrawn from the Ruhr by August 1925, allied troops remained in other Rhineland cities, such as Cologne, under the direct terms of the peace treaty. To complete the process, and to guard against the dangers of separatism in the Rhineland, Stresemann approached the allies with the boldest proposal of his political career and one that was by no means universally popular in Germany. At a meeting in Locarno, in Switzerland (February 1925), he proposed a voluntary German guarantee of its western borders. For France and Belgium, this meant that Germany freely gave up its claims to Alsace and Lorraine and to Eupen and Malmedy. For Germany, it meant that France would no longer be able to use the weapon of invasion, or harbour hopes of an independent Rhineland state – factors that also made the proposals highly acceptable to Britain.

There were, however, shortcomings in the 'package' from the French viewpoint. Would Germany similarly acknowledge its eastern frontiers? Would it acknowledge the peace treaties as a whole? Italy, also party to the proposals, was equally keen that Stresemann should acknowledge Germany's southern border with Austria. The German government would not go so far, and the Locarno Pact agreed by Germany, France, Britain, Italy and Belgium (October 1925), apart from guaranteeing the current western borders of Germany, merely recognised France's treaty commitments to Poland and Czechoslovakia. These were commitments, however, that France would now find very hard to carry out without violating Germany's western frontiers.

### The 'Briand–Kellogg' Pact (1928)

It must be understood that the French government accepted the Locarno terms, not because it misunderstood their implications, but because it had undertaken a significant change in its foreign policy. France had now deliberately abandoned attempts to control Germany in favour of attempts to draw Germany into international undertakings guaranteed by other powers. Locarno has to be seen as part of that programme. Germany's entry into the League of Nations (September 1926) was another essential element in the same programme. So, too was the 'Briand–Kellogg' Pact (August 1928) whereby the French Foreign Minister (Aristide Briand) and the American Secretary of State (William Kellogg) agreed to 'the renunciation of war as an instrument of national policy'. Of the 64 states invited to subscribe to this agreement, 62 did so. Brazil and Argentina were the exceptions. Although it has been widely attacked for its apparent naïvety, the pact was interpreted at the time as an important commitment to peace by the world's leading powers.

### Conclusion

1. Explain the means by which France sought to deflect the threat of German recovery in the 1920s.

2. In what respects, and for what reasons, were international relations in Europe more stable in 1929 than they had been in 1923?

3. Why did the crisis in the American economy in 1929 make it so much more difficult to maintain the peace settlement in Europe?

By the summer of 1929, when a conference at The Hague reached agreement on the evacuation of the Rhineland, five years earlier than envisaged at Versailles, the policy of reconciliation seemed largely vindicated and its future prospects inspired confidence. Locarno and German membership of the League of Nations seemed to create political stability in Europe; the Dawes Plan and its successor seemed to prove that reparations could be paid on a regular basis; the consultative spirit of the League of Nations seemed to be accepted by all major powers. The disintegration of this reassuring 'scenario' was abrupt. In July, the retirement of Poincaré removed the major source of stability in French politics. On 3 October, Stresemann died of a heart attack, aged 51, and exactly three weeks later, on 'Black Thursday', share values on the Wall Street Stock Market went into a disastrous decline. The 'Great Depression' had begun.

## 3.5 What was the impact of the Wall Street Crash upon international relations?

### The political impact of economic depression

The large-scale withdrawal of American capital from European investment, and the general fall in prices of industrial and agricultural goods, had serious implications for international relations. Any spirit of international co-operation that may have been emerging gave way to a desperate sense of 'every man for himself'. Nation after nation, for example, abandoned the **Gold Standard**, and most states hurriedly enclosed themselves behind tariff barriers in an attempt to minimise the domestic effects of the crisis.

**Gold Standard**: The convention whereby the value of a state's national currency is based upon the amount of gold held by that state. Abandoning the Gold Standard means that the state may issue a larger quantity of paper money than it would otherwise do.

By 1931, only France, Italy and Poland of the major European states continued to base their currencies upon gold. The economic crisis played a direct role in the rise of the Nazi Party to power in Germany between 1930 and 1933. Quite apart from aiding the spread of Fascism and self-interested nationalism, the Depression also prepared the ground for international appeasement of those forces. As Britain, America and other states slowly recovered, they sought safety in economic retrenchment and carefully balanced budgets. There seemed no room, at a time of careful housekeeping, for heavy arms expenditure, and the expense of another war was unthinkable. Besides, as the domestic affairs of France and Spain showed, the apparent failure of existing regimes to cope with the ills of capitalism caused many people to think of Bolshevism or of Fascism as an alternative. France, Spain, Belgium and even Britain were not immune from the forces that had engendered Nazism in Germany.

### The Hoover Moratorium and the end of reparations

A direct casualty of the economic catastrophe was the Young Plan for reparation payments. In October 1930, German representatives had approached the US President Herbert Hoover, as the peace treaty entitled them to do, to request a suspension (or 'moratorium') of reparation payments in the light of increasing economic difficulties. The resultant Hoover Moratorium covered all inter-state debts from mid-1931 to mid-1932. By December 1931, however, it was clear that Europe was not experiencing the 'relatively short depression' for which a moratorium was designed. In that month the powers involved with the Young Plan met in Basle (Switzerland) to consider the reparations question. They concluded that 'an adjustment of all inter-governmental debts is the only lasting measure which is capable of restoring economic stability and true peace'. The Lausanne Conference (June 1932) agreed that reparations should be ended by a lump-sum payment of 3,000 million marks, relieving Germany of 90% of its outstanding debt. To the anger of the USA, its European debtors insisted that their war-debt repayments should also end. That anger was heightened when the French Assembly vetoed the government's proposal to make one final debt repayment to America. Thus, the financial clauses of the Treaty of Versailles ceased to exist. If France had gained on an economic level, its diplomatic account was left badly in debt by renewed isolation from the USA. The final lump-sum payment by Germany, incidentally, was never made.

### The failure of disarmament

The principle of international disarmament was the second major casualty of the early 1930s. By the terms of the Versailles Treaty, in theory, the disarmament of Germany was merely a preliminary to a general disarmament. Not until 1926, however, did a 'Preparatory Commission' meet in Geneva, and not until February 1932 did the conference finally gather there to begin deliberation. On the surface, the prospects seemed bright, for the renunciation of expensive armaments made good sense at a time of economic recession. France, consistently one of the most positive members of the conference, explored three different routes to the goal.

1. The original plan was that each nation should submit its major offensive weapons, planes, capital ships and heavy artillery to the control of the League of Nations, in order to provide a force to oppose aggression. It was, in short, a revival of the 1919 idea of a 'League with Teeth', and fell foul of the same objections about the infringement of national sovereignty. In the face of division among the wartime allies, Germany played its 'trump' card, demanded equal treatment with the allies on the question of armaments, and withdrew from the conference.

2. An agreement without Germany was so pointless that France effectively conceded the radical idea of German equality in its new 'Constructive Plan' (November 1932). This combined the idea of a League of Nations force with the maintenance of national defensive militias, and Germany's would be as large as that of any other state. The principle of German equality was also acknowledged within 'a system which would comprise security for all nations'. Germany returned to the conference but, with Italy, showed little interest in the 'Constructive Plan'.

3. After the failure of a British plan to establish a common limit of 200,000 men on the forces of France, Germany, Italy and Poland, the third

1. In what ways did the Wall Street Crash cause European states to change their political and economic policies?

2. Why was it so difficult after 1930 for states to agree (a) on the regulation of reparations and war debts and (b) on disarmament?

French plan came close to success (June 1933). It proposed an eight-year period, during the latter half of which the continental armies would conform to the figures suggested by the British. With Britain, France, Italy and the USA in agreement, and Germany in danger of becoming trapped, Adolf Hitler withdrew finally from the conference (October 1933). Within five days he turned his back on international co-operation completely by quitting the League of Nations.

## 3.6 Why was it not possible to form a European alliance against Hitler between 1933 and 1935?

### The role of Mussolini

Collective security: A form of international security based upon the collective undertakings and co-operation of a large number of states, rather than reliance upon one's own military and economic resources, or upon those of the world's greatest powers.

The collapse of two essential parts of the **collective security** envisaged at Versailles caused the major powers of Western Europe to turn to the alternative form of security already explored with some success at Locarno. This form of security was provided by traditional pacts and alliances. The initiative this time came primarily from Mussolini who, in separate conversations with British and French ministers (March 1933), proposed the idea of a joint undertaking by Italy, France, Germany and Britain to take no unilateral action that might disturb the peace of Europe.

The motives of the four powers in following up the suggestion were various. Britain, in the words of the then Foreign Secretary, Sir John Simon, saw Italy as 'the key to European peace', and was willing to work with it to maintain a traditional balance of power. France shared these motives to an extent, although opinion there was by no means united as to the value of such a pact. Hitler, so soon after coming to power, was happy to take any step that reassured European opinion while he tackled domestic problems. Only in the case of Italy has there been real disagreement among historians. Those who have regarded Mussolini as cynical have seen his proposals as a means of separating France from its allies in eastern Europe, where Italy of course had ambitions, and perhaps from Britain. Others have regarded Mussolini as genuinely perturbed by the resurgence of Germany. They saw his proposals in 1933 as a genuine attempt to appease Hitler, by recognising Germany's great power status, while restricting its freedom of action by international guarantees.

### The Four Power Pact between Britain, France, Italy and Germany

This pact, concluded in July 1933, committed the contracting states to co-operation for a period of ten years to preserve the peace of Europe. On the other hand, as a further step away from the Versailles settlement, it acknowledged the principle of 'reasonable revision' of the peace treaties. In fact, the pact was a 'dead letter' almost as soon as it was agreed. In October Hitler felt confident enough to leave the Disarmament Conference and the League of Nations. Within 18 months (March 1935) he had reintroduced conscription in Germany, which said little for his desire to co-operate with his neighbours. In the light of these events, the Four Power Pact was never ratified by the other powers. Its effects were wholly negative, providing a nasty shock for the eastern European states, who now found themselves excluded from the 'great power club'. The Soviet Union's reaction was to enter negotiations with France for a mutual assistance pact, possibly with a view to splitting this new capitalist bloc. Poland, apparently let down by

France, reacted differently and concluded a non-aggression pact with Germany in January 1934.

## The Stresa Front, 1935

Italy, France and Britain did not yet despair of combined action to preserve their security. Contacts between Mussolini and France's pro-Italian Foreign Minister, Pierre Laval, were fuelled by an attempted Nazi 'coup' in Austria (July 1934). This resulted in a set of Rome Agreements (January 1935) in which the parties seemed to have reached an understanding on European security and Italian colonial ambitions. With Britain drawn in once more, the Stresa Conference (April 1935) produced a three-sided agreement to oppose 'by all practical means, any unilateral repudiation of treaties, which may endanger the peace of Europe'. In theory, this 'Stresa Front', formed by the leaders of the three powers, was an imposing structure. In reality, it had a number of weaknesses. Far from preparing to fight Hitler, all the members hoped that the very existence of the 'Stresa Front' might discourage the German dictator from risking dangerous adventures. Mussolini, although his concern at Germany's rise was genuine, specifically desired this agreement to gain such European security as would enable him to pursue Italy's 'imperial destiny'. The reaction of his Stresa partners to his colonial policy was shortly to put this final attempt at great power equilibrium to the test.

## Italy's invasion and conquest of Abyssinia

In October 1935 Italian forces began the pursuit of Mussolini's colonial plans by an open assault upon the East African state of Abyssinia (modern-day Ethiopia). The long-term motives for this attack reached back to the 19th century when Italy had marked out this region as its sphere of influence in the general 'scramble for Africa', and had suffered the humiliation of defeat at the hands of Abyssinian tribesmen at Adowa (1896). Not only did national pride demand some compensation for Adowa, but the aggressive nature of Italian Fascism demanded, in Mussolini's words, 'war for war's sake, since Fascism needs the glory of victory'. Besides, since Britain and France showed no signs of reducing their empires, was not Italy entitled to equal colonial status? Evidence suggests that Mussolini had determined his course by 1932. The precise timing of his attack, however, was dictated by various factors: by the rate of military preparation, and especially by Mussolini's conviction that his agreement with France and Britain at Stresa had ensured that Hitler would take no revisionist initiatives while his back was turned.

> **Haile Selassie (1892–1975)**
> Designated heir to the Empress of Abyssinia (1917). Abolished slavery in Abyssinia (1924). Emperor of Abyssinia (1930). Deposed by an army coup in 1974.

The new phase of Italian policy opened with a border incident at Wal-Wal (November 1934) and proceeded with a steady and obvious build-up of arms in Italian Somalia and Eritrea. On 2 October 1935, Italian troops invaded Abyssinia on the pretext that they were 'restoring order in a vast country left in the most atrocious slavery and the most primitive conditions of existence'. When local geography and the courage of the local tribesmen caused temporary embarrassment, Mussolini poured in huge resources: 400,000 men and the full weight of modern weaponry, aerial bombardment and the use of poison gas. The flight of the Abyssinian Emperor, Haile Selassie, and the capture of his capital, Addis Ababa, confirmed Italy's victory in May 1936.

*What were the diplomatic implications of the Italian invasion?*
The implications of the conquest of Abyssinia were not confined to East Africa. Abyssinia, despite its vague boundaries and semi-feudal government, had been admitted to the League of Nations in 1923. It now

Italian invasion of Abyssinia, 1935–36

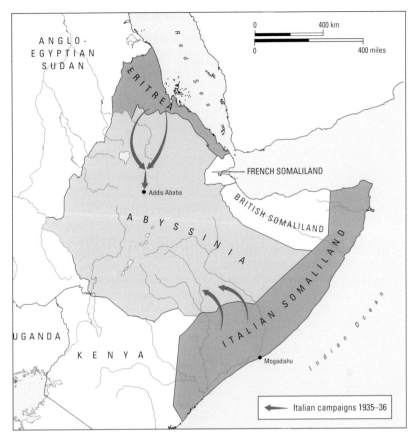

Italian campaigns 1935–36

demanded that the League apply the prescribed economic sanctions against the aggressor. Britain and France thus found themselves committed, with differing degrees of enthusiasm, to a boycott of all Italian goods and to a ban on exports of arms, rubber, and metal ore to Italy. The attempts of their foreign ministers, Samuel Hoare and Pierre Laval, to buy off either Mussolini or Haile Selassie ended in embarrassing failure. Worse still, their apparent 'double game' of applying sanctions and negotiating at the same time behind the back of the League of Nations effectively discredited both the League and the Stresa Front.

Furthermore, the sanctions were largely ineffective. The vital commodity of oil was not among the prohibited items and, in any case, non-members such as Germany, Japan and the USA were not committed to sanctions. Although Mussolini's whole policy over Stresa and Abyssinia was one of calculated deception, it seems likely that he was genuinely shocked by the imposition of economic sanctions. His assumption that Laval had granted him a 'free hand' by the Rome Agreements seemed confirmed by British and French silence at Stresa on the Abyssinian question, despite the contemporary build-up of Italian forces in Africa. Surely this had indicated their consent. To Mussolini, a League of Nations that allowed the Japanese to escape unpunished for their aggression in China, and then turned on Italy, was a 'front of conservation, of selfishness, and of hypocrisy'. Whatever their limitations, the 1935 agreements between France, Italy and Britain perished not necessarily because of Mussolini's deviousness, but because of the extraordinary confusion of British and French foreign policy.

## Mussolini and Italian isolation

The key feature of European diplomatic relationships, and a major factor in the collapse of the balance of power in Europe after 1935, was the movement of Italy out of the orbit of London and Paris and into that of Berlin. Superficially appealing as the attraction of one Fascist dictatorship for another may have been, the coming together of Italy and Germany had little to do with ideology. According to the French commentator Maurice Baumont, Mussolini 'wanted to be on the side of power, the only decisive attraction for him'. In this context of power politics, he had drawn four lessons from the events of 1935–37.

1.  It had become clear that the statesmen of Britain and France, and even less those of the League of Nations from which Italy withdrew in November 1937, had neither the will nor the means to check the resurgence of Germany.

2.  It was evident that Italy could not pursue its interests in Abyssinia and in Spain and, at the same time, guard its security in central Europe.

3.  Involvement in Spain had badly weakened Italy's international position. It had shown up weaknesses in its army, absorbed half of its foreign currency reserves, and established a gulf between Mussolini and the democracies without guaranteeing any gain or support from General Franco.

4.  Perhaps most important of all, just as he became disgusted at the weakness of the western powers, so Mussolini was at once seduced and horrified by the power of Germany. After a relatively unsuccessful visit to Rome in 1934, Hitler had spared no effort to demonstrate German military strength when Mussolini came to Berlin (September 1937).

### The Spanish Civil War

Civil War broke out in Spain in July 1936, when 'Nationalist' forces under General Franco attempted to launch a coup to overthrow the existing Republican government. This was the culmination of several years of tension, arising from the fall of the Spanish monarchy (1931) and the implementation of socialist and anti-Catholic reforms by the Republic that replaced it. Franco and the Nationalists enjoyed a distinct military superiority, but the conflict was complicated and prolonged by the fact that many foreign observers saw the war as part of a wider struggle between socialism and fascism. On the one hand, this led to the intervention of the 'international brigades', bodies of left-wing volunteers who travelled to Spain to fight for the Republic. On the other hand, both Hitler and Mussolini saw advantages in supporting Franco. Hitler limited himself to undercover intervention, sending 'volunteer' forces, such as the famous 'Condor Legion' to Spain to try out the new weapons with which German forces were being re-armed. Mussolini, however, committed substantial forces from the Italian regular army to the struggle, as part of his stance as the driving force behind right-wing politics in Europe. Britain and France remained strictly neutral in the conflict, while the Soviet Union only sent material aid to the Republicans under the strictest secrecy. This combination of factors confirmed the superiority of the Nationalists, and their victory was sealed by the fall of Madrid in March 1939.

### The development of the German–Italian alliance

This alliance had its origins in the 'October Protocols' signed by Count Ciano in Berlin in 1936. They contained little more than vague anti-Bolshevik phrases, but gave the relationship the name by which it is known to history, by declaring that the Berlin–Rome line was now 'an axis

A Soviet view of western politics in 1936. The infant Hitler is protected by France, Britain, 'Wall Street' and the 'Ruhr magnates'.

**How justified was this interpretation?**

**1. What were the main aims of Italian foreign policy between 1933 and 1936?**

**2. Why did Italy, France and Britain form pacts with each other in 1933–34 and why had these agreements fallen apart by 1936?**

**3. In what respects might the Italian invasion of Abyssinia be seen as a turning point in European international relations in the 1930s?**

around which can revolve all those European states with a will to collaboration and peace'. In November 1937, shortly after Mussolini's fateful visit to Germany, this 'Axis' took on wider implications when Italy subscribed to the Anti-Comintern Pact, originally concluded between Germany and Japan (November 1936) to present a united front against Bolshevism.

The *Anschluss* of March 1938, and Italy's meek acceptance of it, indicated the extent to which Italian policy was already subject to that of Germany. Within two months, Hitler began to pressurise the Italian government to accept a full military alliance. Mussolini's initial reluctance to commit himself was worn down by May 1939, when he allowed Ciano to conclude the alliance known as the 'Pact of Steel'. This committed both sides to help each other in the event of one of them becoming 'involved in warlike complications'. The terms made no pretence to be merely defensive. The Pact of Steel constituted a triumph for Hitler in his re-orientation of European diplomacy, and completed Mussolini's loss of control over his own policy. 'In point of fact,' as Elizabeth Wiskemann has written, by underwriting all future German schemes, 'Mussolini gave Hitler *carte blanche* [complete freedom of action] to attack Poland and to plunge into the Second World War.'

## 3.7  In what respects had Hitler changed the Versailles settlement by 1938?

### The remilitarisation of the Rhineland, 1936

The Abyssinian crisis preoccupied European statesmen for eight months (October 1935–May 1936), during which time Hitler struck his first blow at the territorial clauses of the Treaty of Versailles. On 7 March 1936, he ordered a force of 22,000 men into the Rhineland in direct defiance of those treaty terms that declared it a demilitarised zone. As pretext, he claimed that the French pact with the Soviet Union had breached the Locarno understanding. A more realistic explanation of his timing would, of course, take into account Italy's involvement in Abyssinia and the resultant weakening of the Stresa Front. Europe was taken by surprise, not by the fact of remilitarisation, but by the method. Diplomats had expected Hitler to negotiate; instead he took swift, decisive action, and offered negotiations afterwards – a method soon to become familiar. The operation succeeded through a combination of Hitler's boldness and French miscalculation. France's military leaders estimated that up to 295,000 German troops were available to Hitler and that their intervention would lead to a major conflict. Its political leaders thus concluded that they could intervene only with British aid, which was not forthcoming. It is now known that the German forces were under direct orders to withdraw if they met resistance. In Britain and France alike much public opinion felt that confrontation with Germany and Italy at the same time was folly, and that French friendship with the Soviet Union was unwise. In short, Hitler's move did not cause widespread popular outrage because, in the words of the French historian Maurice Baumont, 'a blow had been aimed, not at French territory, but only at the Treaty of Versailles, in which no one believed any longer'.

### The results of the remilitarisation

The implications of the remilitarisation were substantial and complex. In combination with the Abyssinian affair, it seemed to show that the western powers were as unwilling as the League of Nations was unable to act against unilateral revision of the treaties. The effect on France's strategic position was disastrous. Hitler's action provided further disillusionment for nations such as Poland and Czechoslovakia, and the rapid fortification of Germany's frontiers now made it extremely difficult for France to fulfil its eastern pacts by attacks against Germany in the west. French reluctance to act alone also provided proof that it had become the junior partner in its relationship with Britain. Lastly, Hitler's bold gamble, like that of Mussolini in Abyssinia, was invaluable in strengthening his prestige and authority at home, especially in military circles. If Abyssinia destroyed the League of Nations, the remilitarisation of the Rhineland destroyed Locarno, and the way was thus open to the disaster of 1939.

### Why did *Anschluss* not take place before 1938?

The question of union (*Anschluss*) between Austria and the German Reich was nearly a century old when Hitler came to power. It had its roots in the 19th-century contest for German leadership, seemingly settled by the triumph of Bismarck's Prussia and his careful exclusion of Austria from the German state. The loss of Austria's non-German territories in 1919, and the rise of Hitler, raised the question anew. At the beginning of the 1930s the long-established factors of language, and the memory of centuries during which Vienna had been the chief of the German cities, combined with the more modern consideration that many Austrians would undoubtedly be economically better off as part of a greater state. All were factors in favour of *Anschluss*.

The main factors against *Anschluss* were the desire of many Austrians to remain independent, still resenting the ascendancy of Berlin over Vienna, and the implacable hostility of the Versailles allies, especially of France and Italy. The project for a customs union between Germany and Austria (March 1931) had been undermined by French suspicion. 'They must take us for asses,' wrote the French politician, Édouard Herriot, 'if they think that we are able to forget that the political union of Germany was reached by way of a customs union.' The mismanaged coup by Austrian Nazis, with the knowledge of Hitler (July 1934), which ended in the murder of the Austrian Chancellor, Engelbert Dollfuss, foundered upon the prompt action of Mussolini who mobilised the Italian army on the Austrian frontier.

### Why was *Anschluss* possible in 1938?

By the end of 1937 the situation had changed. French inactivity over the advance of German troops to its frontiers did not suggest that it would act energetically over Austria. Indeed, British and French diplomats, beset with domestic problems, had even indicated to their German counterparts that they had 'no objection to a marked extension of German influence in Austria obtained through evolutionary means'. Most significant was the changed attitude of Italy. Deeply committed to intervention in the Spanish Civil War, Mussolini was impressed by the shows of military power staged for him in Germany and had already begun his drift into Hitler's wake. Count Ciano, his son-in-law and Foreign Minister, expressed the hopelessness of Italy's position over Austrian independence: 'What in fact could we do? Start a war with Germany? At the first shot we fired every Austrian, without exception, would fall in behind the Germans against us.'

These developments might suggest that Hitler deliberately set out to absorb Austria in 1938. Indeed, the very first page of *Mein Kampf* made clear his attachment to the principle of German–Austrian unity. In *The Origins of the Second World War* (1961), however, A.J.P. Taylor set out a convincing argument to suggest that this was not the case. Although Hitler had hoped to be able to deal first with the question of the **Sudetenland** (see below), the argument runs, his hand was forced by two factors. The first of these was the continuing agitation by Austrian Nazis led by Arthur Seyss-Inquart, and the second was the rash decision of the new Austrian Chancellor, Kurt von Schuschnigg, to confront Hitler and force him to disown the agitators.

If Schuschnigg and Seyss-Inquart caused the crisis, Hitler nevertheless acted to exploit it, partly in the interests of *Anschluss*, but partly to distract attention from contemporary domestic disagreements. In a violent interview at Berchtesgaden (12 February 1938), Hitler accused Schuschnigg of racial treason, and demanded that Seyss-Inquart be admitted to the Austrian government. Although Schuschnigg accepted this demand, he attempted to defend his position by holding a referendum on the question of union with Germany. Unable to risk an anti-German vote, Hitler's hand was now forced. Successively, the German government demanded the postponement of the referendum, the replacement of Schuschnigg by Seyss-Inquart, and finally threatened military intervention. On 11 March, the Austrian Nazi leader, having formed a 'provisional government' of doubtful legality, requested the dispatch of German troops 'to restore order and save Austria from chaos'. Even so, it is doubtful whether Hitler envisaged more than a 'puppet' government under Seyss-Inquart. On 13 March, encouraged by the enthusiastic reception from Austrian crowds at Linz, and by Mussolini's meek acceptance of the principle of *Anschluss*, Hitler proclaimed the formal union of his native Austria with the German Reich.

**Sudetenland**: An irregular ribbon of territory around the northern, western and southern periphery of Bohemia and Moravia.

**Arthur Seyss-Inquart (1892–1946)**
Leader of the Austrian Nazi Party. Served briefly as Austrian Minister of the Interior and Chancellor in March 1938. After *Anschluss*, he served as a senior Nazi official in the Ostmark (1938–39) and in the Netherlands (1940–45). Condemned and executed at Nuremberg.

## What was the impact of *Anschluss*?

The *Anschluss* marked a clear escalation in Nazi policy as it involved the actual obliteration of an independent state set up by the peace treaties. Still, Hitler's action did not excite united European condemnation. The approval registered in the referendums Hitler now held (99.08% in Germany and 99.75% in Austria) was obviously in part the result of pressure and fear, but it probably also had a sound basis in pan-German feeling. 'In Austria,' claimed Hermann Goering at Nuremberg in 1945, 'we were not met with rifle shots and bombs; only one thing was thrown at us, flowers.' The British government merely made a formal protest. There was no French government. Camille Chautemps had resigned four days earlier and Leon Blum had yet to take office. Once again, rapid and risky action had reaped a rich reward. Hitler's confidence in such action was now to put the peace of Europe in increasing danger.

## Czechoslovakia and the Sudetenland

If Hitler was serious in his desires either to unite all Germans in a single Reich, or to expand the territories of that Reich eastwards, the state of Czechoslovakia constituted a substantial obstacle in his path. It possessed a mountainous and easily defensible frontier with Germany, an army of 34 divisions well supplied by the Skoda arms factories at Pilsen, and enjoyed membership of a diplomatic system comprising France, Britain, Poland and the Soviet Union.

It also had its weaknesses. Czechoslovakia was, for instance, a state of minority groups. Apart from the uneasy union of Czechs and Slovaks at the heart of the state, Hungarians, Poles and Ukrainians had been placed under the authority of Prague to give the new creation territorial and economic viability. In fact, 35% of the population was neither Czech nor Slovak. The greatest of these minorities were the Germans of the Sudetenland. Spread through these regions were 3.25 million Germans, resentful that they no longer enjoyed the privileges that had been theirs under Habsburg rule. They were regarded with suspicion by the Czech government. Furthermore, the events of the mid-1930s isolated Czechoslovakia and increased its vulnerability. It had no border with friendly states such as France and the Soviet Union, could expect no help from Italy, as Austria had received none and, after the *Anschluss*, had a southern border with the enlarged Reich devoid of any natural defences.

As with Austria, Hitler did not so much cause a crisis over Czechoslovakia, as exploit one that was already developing. A key factor was the Sudeten Party, formed in 1935 by Konrad Henlein. Its political demands had grown by the time of Henlein's 'Karlsbad Programme' (April 1938) from a claim for equal treatment with the Czechs to a demand for full independence from Czechoslovakia. Still confident of French and British backing, the Czech President, Edvard Beneš, was happy to confront the Sudeten Germans. Hitler, more confident than ever after his Austrian successes, had no objection to confrontation. He was aided by a new turn in British and French policy.

> **Konrad Henlein (1898–1945)**
> Founder of the Sudeten German Party (1933). After the Nazi seizure of the Sudetenland, Henlein served as the senior Nazi official there until 1945.

> 1. By what stages did Hitler destroy the Versailles settlement between 1936 and 1938?
>
> 2. Why did Britain and France do so little between 1936 and 1938 to prevent Germany undermining the Versailles settlement?

# 3.8  Why did war break out in 1939?

### What was the significance of the Munich conference for the policy of appeasement?

For at least two years up to 1938, the governments of Britain and France had inclined increasingly towards a policy of appeasement. That is to say

**Neville Chamberlain
(1869–1940)**
British Conservative politician.
Chancellor of the Exchequer
(1923–24, 1931–37) and Prime
Minister (1937–40).
Chamberlain is particularly
associated with the re-
establishment of economic
stability after the 'Great
Depression' and with the policy
of appeasement.

**Edouard Daladier
(1884–1970)**
French radical politician. Prime
Minister of France (1933,
1934). Minister of Defence
(1936–38). Held the two offices
combined between 1938 and
1940.

that they were increasingly willing to make concessions to Germany, in the hope that Hitler's ambitions would be satisfied without the disaster of a military confrontation. It was in this spirit that they approached the question of the Sudetenland. Britain and France were committed by the second half of 1938 to a policy of persuading Beneš to grant Sudeten German demands. They were convinced by the events in Austria and by rumours of German troop movements (May 1938) that, if Hitler was determined to support Henlein, the choice lay between Czech concessions and a general war. Henlein's policy, however, and that of Hitler, was to 'demand so much that we never can be satisfied'. Thus, when the Czech President conceded the principal demands of the Sudeten Germans, their leaders started unsuccessful risings in Karlsbad, Eger and other centres (13 September) to sustain the tension. The danger that Hitler would intervene as he had in Austria broke the British and French nerve. Their respective premiers, Neville Chamberlain and Edouard Daladier, plunged into direct negotiations with Hitler, and Hitler correspondingly raised the stakes. At Berchtesgaden (15 September) and at Bad Godesberg (22 September), Chamberlain heard Hitler's demands escalate through direct German annexation of the Sudetenland, to immediate military occupation.

Six days later, Hitler agreed to a conference between himself, Chamberlain and Daladier, to be held in Munich with Mussolini as mediator. It has been suggested either that Hitler had become aware of the lack of enthusiasm in Germany for a military solution, or that he was disturbed by Mussolini's reluctance to give military support, or simply that he knew that his shaken opponents were willing now to allow him the bulk of his demands. Certainly the Munich Conference (29–30 September 1938) granted Hitler far more than he had been demanding a few weeks earlier. It was agreed between the powers that, although Germany would receive all Czech territory where Germans were in a majority, the transfer would be by stages, and under international supervision. In none of these negotiations was the Czech government consulted or allowed to participate. It was simply presented with the alternatives of acceptance or single combat with Germany.

Both morally and practically, the implications of the Munich agreement were enormous. The allies, especially the French with their direct treaty obligations, had betrayed Czechoslovakia. Although Britain, France, Italy

The meeting in Munich, September 1938. In the front, from the left, Neville Chamberlain, Edouard Daladier, Adolf Hitler and Benito Mussolini.

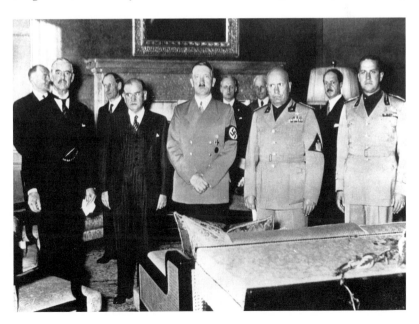

and Germany all formally guaranteed its remaining territory, the state was in fact doomed by its losses. It no longer had a defensible frontier, it had lost 70% of its iron and steel resources, and the Skoda works. In addition, the Sudeten success provided great encouragement to other separatists. Hungary and Poland both revived claims to Czech territory, and the cause of Slovak separatism took on a new lease of life. In March 1939, having failed to cause the collapse of Czechoslovakia by the Sudeten crisis, Hitler was to cause a new crisis over the Slovak demands, and to force the Czechs to accept a German 'protectorate' over Bohemia and Moravia, while Hungary, Poland and the Slovaks achieved their desires. Czechoslovakia, therefore, like Poland in the past, died of partition. The tremendous popular relief at the avoidance of war was short-lived, and certainly did not survive Hitler's seizure of Prague in March. Despite the weakness displayed at Munich, and the loss of Czechoslovakia's 34 divisions to their cause, the subsequent military co-ordination between Britain and France, and their renewal of guarantees to Poland, Greece and Romania (March–April 1939) strongly suggested that the next crisis would be confronted with greater resolution.

## The Soviet Union and the western allies

An undoubted casualty of the Munich surrender was the relationship between the western democracies and the Soviet Union. The relationship had suffered from mutual suspicion for a decade; suspicion on the Soviet side that the British and French secretly preferred German resurgence to the existence of a stable Soviet regime; suspicion in London and Paris either that Stalin still favoured the international spread of communism, or that his vicious domestic purges had destroyed the USSR's viability as an ally. The Munich agreement, made without any reference to the Soviet Union, showed at best that the diplomacy of the western powers was incapable of checking German ambitions, and at worst represented a tacit agreement to Germany's quest for 'living space' in eastern Europe. Either way, the Soviet Union could no longer trust its security to Paris and London.

## The German–Soviet pact (August 1939)

The first Soviet overtures for a more positive relationship with Nazi Germany came in May 1938, when the new ambassador to Berlin, A. Meretalov, received instructions to press for better commercial relations. At a time when he was increasingly preoccupied with the problem of Czechoslovakia, Hitler reacted favourably to anything that might separate the Soviet Union from his immediate enemies. In July, the governments reached an oral agreement on the ending of their hostile press campaigns. With the allied abandonment of Czechoslovakia, the Soviet government began to knock harder on Germany's door. The replacement of Maxim Litvinov as Commissar for Foreign Affairs by Vyacheslav Molotov (May 1939) was invested with great significance by foreign observers. Molotov, as a member of the Politburo, had the necessary power to engineer major policy changes, whereas Litvinov had been an advocate of collective security, and was furthermore a Jew. Nevertheless, it was widely agreed that Stalin at this stage was merely keeping open his option of choosing between Germany and the western democracies. In mid-August, when British–French–Soviet military negotiations in Moscow collapsed over the reluctance of Poland to allow Soviet troops to cross its territory in the event of an attack on Germany, Stalin and his advisors drew the conclusion that they had one remaining option for their national security.

Hitler responded far more rapidly and favourably than the allies had, for his short-term purposes were also served by a change of policy. With his sights now set on Poland, and with Britain and France renewing their pledges to the Poles, it was an urgent priority to ensure that his ambitions would not encounter Soviet opposition. This, and Stalin's desire for greater security for the Soviet frontiers, resulted in the startling agreement reached after only one day's negotiation in Moscow between Molotov and the German Foreign Minister, Joachim von Ribbentrop (23 August 1939).

## The terms of the German–Soviet pact

To the outside world, the Ribbentrop–Molotov Pact took the form of a non-aggression treaty lasting ten years. Secretly, however, it divided the territories between the German and Soviet borders into 'spheres of influence'. Germany's comprised Poland, west of the rivers Narew, Vistula and San, and part of Lithuania. The Soviet zone comprised the rest of Poland and Lithuania, and the states of Estonia, Latvia and Finland. Germany expressed its disinterest in the Balkans and recognised Russia's interest in the Romanian territory of Bessarabia. Hitler, in short, received tacit Soviet approval to fulfil his designs on Danzig and the Polish 'corridor'. In return, Stalin not only triumphantly reversed the losses suffered by Russia during the Revolution and Civil War 20 years earlier, but seemed to have won a breathing space in terms both of time and of territory. With the Soviet occupation of their sphere of influence between June and August 1940, the amount of territory between a future invader and the vital centres of Leningrad and Moscow was increased by 300 kilometres.

To western commentators, this was seen as one of the most cynical treaties in world history, a complete reversal of the ideologies of both states. As the historian A.J.P. Taylor commented, however, 'it is difficult to see what other course Soviet Russia could have followed' in the light of western indifference. It was difficult, too, to see why their part in the destruction of Poland was worse than that of the allies in the destruction of Czechoslovakia. Doubtless both Hitler and Stalin believed that the pact ensured that the Polish question could now be solved without general war. In the event, by giving Hitler the confidence to attack Poland, without diverting Britain and France from their renewed guarantees, Stalin's signature made war in Europe inevitable.

## The issue of Danzig

In the German view, the collapse of Czechoslovakia left one major element of the Versailles Treaty standing in eastern Europe. Hostility between Germans and Poles had a far longer history than the life of the post-war Polish state, but the treaty had created a new focus of hostility in the form of the 'free city' of Danzig. Even more resentment, perhaps, was caused by the 'corridor' of territory transferred in 1919 from Germany to Poland to connect Danzig with the Polish heartland. Although the treaty gave the Poles complete control of Danzig's docks, its customs duties, its railway system and foreign relations, Danzig was undeniably a German city. It was inhabited by 400,000 Germans and without a name in Polish until 'Gdansk' was invented in 1919. Similarly, the 'corridor' contained the homes of one million Germans. It was not a settlement that the majority of Germans were willing to tolerate freely.

## The dual threat to Poland

Despite gaining its independence in the aftermath of the Russian Revolution, Poland was trapped between an unforgiving Germany to the west and a resentful Russia to the east. Polish apprehension was heightened in the 1920s by the Russo–German agreement at Rapallo and by the failure of the Locarno Pact to guarantee Germany's eastern borders. Thus Poland sought security through its own armed forces and through treaties with France.

By the mid-1930s, however, Poland's international position had been greatly complicated by the rise of Hitler, the bankruptcy of French policy towards eastern Europe, and the entry of the Soviet Union into the diplomatic arena. In general, under the direction of General Beck between 1932 and 1939, the Polish foreign ministry proceeded upon the assumption that the Soviet Union posed the greater threat to Poland. 'With the Germans,' he reputedly declared, 'we risk losing our liberty. With the Russians we lose our souls.' From this line of thought sprang the Polish–German non-aggression pact of 1934 and the persistent refusal to allow passage to Soviet troops across Polish territory in the event of war. Furthermore, overestimation of his nation's strength led Beck into the cynical policy whereby Poland participated in the partition of Czechoslovakia, gaining the region of Teschen (March 1939) and staking an unsuccessful claim to Slovakia.

Throughout this period Danzig, its local government in the hands of the local Nazi party since May 1933, remained a thorn in Polish–German relations. After the completion of his destruction of Czechoslovakia, the signs accumulated that Hitler intended next to turn his attentions towards Poland. As with Austria and Czechoslovakia, his initial policy was that of a war of nerves. In April 1939, Hitler not only renounced Germany's non-aggression pact with Poland, but renewed German claims to Danzig. In May, the 'Pact of Steel' agreement committed Italy to follow Hitler's path, and by August he was assured that the Soviet Union would not stand in his way. Meanwhile, the German press conducted a campaign of accusations concerning alleged persecution of Poland's German minority. Surely, under these circumstances, Britain and France would not risk themselves on Poland's behalf?

## The crisis of August–September 1939

The last week of August 1939 was occupied by Anglo–French efforts to persuade Poland to sacrifice Danzig. This time, however, the situation differed in important respects from that at Munich the previous year. Poland, aware that surrender had not saved Czechoslovakia, refused now to compromise its national sovereignty. The two democratic governments, although eager to avoid war, refused to repeat their Munich performances. Perhaps they were encouraged by increasing evidence of Mussolini's reluctance to commit himself to war. Perhaps, as A.J.P. Taylor stressed, the political conservatives of Britain and France, rather than being terrified by the Russo–German agreement, became more hostile to Hitler now that he no longer posed as a defence against Communism. Maybe Chamberlain and Daladier recognised the futility of their Munich policy. General war, in the event, resulted from the conviction of both sides that the other was bluffing. 'The men I met at Munich,' Hitler declared to his generals, 'are not the kind to start another world war.'

So, on 1 September, German troops invaded Poland on the false pretext of Polish border violations. Only two days later did Britain and France issue separate ultimatums for German withdrawal, perhaps encouraging Hitler by their delay. Nevertheless, upon the expiry of the ultimatums, both powers declared war on Germany, ending the 'Twenty Years' Truce'.

1. What did Hitler wish to gain in 1938–39 (a) from Czechoslovakia and (b) from Poland?

2. Why did Britain and France abandon their policy of appeasement after the Munich Conference?

3. What grounds are there for claiming that 'the Nazi–Soviet Pact of 1939 made European war inevitable'?

## 3.9  Did Hitler plan the outbreak of war in 1939?
## A CASE STUDY IN HISTORICAL INTERPRETATION

For some years after the conclusion of the Second World War this would not have appeared to be a controversial issue. Although a great deal was written about the war's origins, there was little historical objectivity in these accounts. Such documents as those edited by E.L. Woodward and Rohan Butler (*Documents on British Foreign Policy*, 1946 onwards) tended to present a favourable view of allied policy, and to confirm the validity of the charges made against German leaders at the Nuremberg war crimes trials. E.M. Robertson, in *The Origins of the Second World War* (1971), characterised this lack of objectivity when he described such historians as 'intelligence NCOs [non-commissioned officers] in plain clothes'. The conclusions reached during these decades were consistent and predictable. While the majority of states worked for peace, war had been started by a German government dedicated to the principle of overturning the Versailles settlement and fulfilling the racial claims of its leader. The historian T.D. Williams, commenting in 1958 on the work of Sir Lewis Namier (*In the Nazi Era*, 1952) stated that 'he has proved that Hitler wanted war. Nobody would, on the whole, now contest this fact.'

In 1961, however, in *The Origins of the Second World War*, A.J.P. Taylor did contest the fact. Refusing to see in *Mein Kampf* anything more than the daydreaming of a frustrated revolutionary, Taylor stressed the continuity between Hitler's foreign policy aims and those of earlier German politicians. He also dismissed the notion of a German master plan for conquest and viewed Hitler's policy in 1938–39 primarily as a skilful exploitation of openings offered to him by the errors and hesitations of British, French and Italian leaders. Although Hitler undoubtedly wanted to change the map of Europe, Taylor concluded, he did not necessarily seek war. War in 1939 did not result from Hitler's long-term determination to begin one, but from his short-term miscalculation of allied reaction to the Polish crisis.

Many writers accepted that Taylor had shed important light on some of the individual crises that preceded the Second World War, but his overall thesis provoked widespread controversy. Many prominent historians refused to accept that major pieces of evidence, such as Hitler's statements in *Mein Kampf* and in the **Hossbach Memorandum**, could simply be set aside. Hugh Trevor-Roper argued strongly that Hitler considered himself not merely a practical politician, but 'a thinker, a practical philosopher, the *demiurge* of a new age of history'. Some leading German historians, such as Andreas Hillgruber and Klaus Hildebrand, in *The Foreign Policy of the Third Reich* (1973), put forward the view that Hitler's long-term plans stretched beyond domination of eastern Europe, and aimed ultimately at world domination. They envisage Hitler pursuing these massive goals by a series of distinct stages, the first of which certainly involved aggression in eastern Europe in the early 1940s at the latest. Other authorities, such as Alan Milward in *The German War Economy* (1965), stressed that Taylor's preoccupation with diplomacy blinded him to the steady economic and social progress towards a war footing made since 1933.

The most important outcome of the Taylor controversy was that historians were now forced to consider other factors that contributed to the outbreak of war in 1939. Above all, he had drawn attention to the encouragement that Hitler derived from the hesitant and timid policies of other European states, such as Britain and France. Is it possible to claim that the policy of appeasement made a serious contribution to the collapse of the peace? The policy has, indeed, been widely criticised

**Hossbach Memorandum**: A memo written by Colonel Hossbach in November 1937 to summarise the content of a meeting between Hitler and leading military commanders. Its content suggests that at this stage Hitler was making long-term preparations for war.

*Demiurge*: An independent creative force, or decisive power.

since the war, especially for such immoral aspects as the abandonment of Czechoslovakia in 1938.

Recent writers have argued, however, that it is unsatisfactory to view the policy of appeasement merely as a show of weakness and indecision, and that to see it in this way is to be wise after the event. In particular, Richard Overy in *The Origins of the Second World War* (1987) and *The Inter-War Crisis, 1919–1939* (1994) has insisted that the policy was formulated in just the same way as any other foreign policy, in order to defend the particular vested interests of the states concerned. 'British diplomacy', he wrote, 'was based on a global strategy of which the German question formed a part, and until 1935 a subordinate part.' With extensive imperial interests in Asia, which needed to be defended against the threat of Japanese expansion and aggression, it is unsurprising that the government showed reluctance to confront Hitler over his attitude to eastern Europe. While France was more directly threatened by German resurgence, it too had imperial interests to defend. It had also suffered so grievously in the First World War that its politicians could scarcely be blamed for wishing to avert a second conflict. Instead of dismissing appeasement as a bankrupt and cowardly policy, it might be more useful to conclude that it was part of an unfortunate but unavoidable conjunction of events. The 1930s found the leading powers of western Europe preoccupied with economic recovery and with the defence of imperial interests at the very moment when Hitler began to threaten the peace of Europe.

Important as the controversy over the Taylor thesis is in terms of detail, it is still possible to find agreement on the broad causes of the outbreak of war in 1939. The responsibility of expansionist elements in German policy has not seriously been questioned, and the less the outbreak is attributed directly to the 'evil genius' of Hitler himself, the more the historian is bound to concentrate on the continuous theme of expansion in recent German history and thought. This theme occupies the attention of the American journalist William Shirer in *Rise and Fall of the Third Reich* (1962). Returning to Hitler's aims and motives in the late 1930s, a sound compromise has been established by Alan Bullock (*Hitler: A Study in Tyranny*, 1962 and *Hitler and Stalin: Parallel Lives*, 1991) and by Donald Watt (*How War Came*, 1989). On the question of a Nazi master plan for aggression and aggrandisement, Alan Bullock concludes that 'Hitler's foreign policy combined consistency of aim with complete opportunism in methods and tactics'. The weakness of his opponents dictated the timing, but not the initial conception of Hitler's policy. On the specific problem of the outbreak of hostilities in 1939, Donald Watt resolves the question 'Did Hitler want war?' with the plausible conclusion that he did indeed desire an armed clash with Poland, and certainly envisaged a subsequent war of conquest against the USSR. Where the element of miscalculation and accident occurred was that he had not expected the violent destruction of Poland to involve him in a general European war with Britain and France, and did not foresee the eventual involvement of the USA in a global conflict.

**1. What different interpretations have historians made of Hitler's conduct of German foreign policy in the late 1930s?**

**2. In what different ways have historians viewed the policy of appeasement since the publication of A.J.P. Taylor's controversial work in 1961?**

## 3.10 Why did the USSR and USA become involved in the Second World War?

### The 'Phoney War', 1939–1940

Germany defeated Poland within three weeks, a major reason being the entry of the USSR into the war in mid-September. Under the Ribbentrop–Molotov Pact of August 1939, Germany and the USSR had agreed on the partition of eastern Europe, and by the end of September Poland was divided between them. Over the winter of 1939–1940 the USSR went to war with Finland to gain territory north of Leningrad. In June 1940 the USSR occupied the Baltic States of Estonia, Latvia and Lithuania and the province of Moldavia in Romania.

Although Britain and France had declared war on Germany, they did not intervene to defend Poland. From September 1939 to April 1940 German land forces did not fight British or French troops. However, from September 1939 onwards, the longest battle in the Second World War raged between Britain and Germany – the 'Battle of the Atlantic', with German U-boats and surface raiders attempting to prevent convoys reaching Britain.

In April 1940 Germany invaded Denmark and Norway. For the first time in the war, Britain and French troops fought the German forces in Norway. However, Germany's rapid movement of troops and their effective use of air power led to swift victory.

## Why did France fall in 1940?

The 'real' war began on 10 May 1940, when German forces attacked Belgium, Holland, Luxembourg and France. Within six weeks all four countries had been defeated. A British Expeditionary Force, sent to aid France, had to be evacuated from Dunkirk in May/June 1940. Why was this German victory so spectacular?

The main answer is the development of blitzkrieg (lightning war). Used with great effect against Poland, the Germans had developed a way of waging fast moving, aggressive attacks. The essence of blitzkrieg was the mass use of tanks and armoured vehicles – supported by air attack – to smash a hole in the defence lines of the enemy. Once a breach had been made in the enemy defences, massed infantry units would break through the gap. Germany adopted this style of warfare partly because of its limited ability to wage a long, protracted war.

The policy worked to great effect in May 1940. The German air force (*Luftwaffe*) destroyed the air forces of France, Holland and Belgium. German panzer (tank) units attacked through Belgium, outflanking the Maginot Line.

Under the leadership of General Heinz Guderian, German panzer forces rapidly moved across northern France and southern Belgium to split the Allied front in two. The Manstein Plan had effectively destroyed British, French and Belgian defences.

However, to see German victory solely in terms of blitzkrieg would be simplistic. The French armed forces were regarded as one of the best in Europe in 1940. Stalin, the Soviet leader, had hoped that Germany would be faced with a long, protracted war in the west, similar to the First World War. What shocked the world was the speed at which French forces collapsed. Part of the problem was the French emphasis on the Maginot Line as their main defence. Unfortunately, this defensive line did not extend to Luxembourg and Belgium. As a result, German forces outflanked the Maginot Line by attacking through Belgium. The French armed forces had better tanks than Germany, but were never used in mass formations like the German tanks.

A major problem faced by Britain and France was the capitulation of Belgium at the end of May 1940. This forced Britain to evacuate its army through Dunkirk. In June 1940 Germany launched its final offensive against France. By mid-June the French army had collapsed and Paris was occupied by German troops. France called for an armistice (ceasefire). The armistice was signed in the same railway carriage as the German request for an armistice in 1918. By the end of June, Britain was left to fight Germany alone.

## Why did Britain survive between June 1940 and June 1941?

For one year in the Second World War Britain stood alone against Germany. From June 1940 they were also at war with Fascist Italy. The relatively small British army had been evacuated from Dunkirk in May and June 1940, leaving behind all its heavy weapons and transportation.

The German army then began planning an invasion of Britain – Operation Sealion. But the invasion never came, and Britain survived. Why?

First, for a German invasion to succeed they needed to gain air supremacy over Britain. From July to September 1940 an air war developed – the Battle of Britain. By the end, the RAF had not been destroyed, and had caused heavy losses to the German *Luftwaffe*.

Also, Britain was able to keep open its supply lifeline – the sea lanes across the North Atlantic. Britain was aided in its attempt to survive by the USA, which from 1939 to early 1941 adopted a policy of 'Cash and Carry'. This enabled Britain and France to buy US military equipment, even though the USA itself was neutral. By early 1941 Britain could no longer pay for US supplies. As a result, US President F. D. Roosevelt persuaded the US Congress to agree to the policy of 'Lend-lease', which allowed US supplies to be given to Britain without payment until after the war. With Lend-lease Britain was able to rearm – and feed itself – through 1941.

However, from the late autumn 1940, Hitler's main attention had turned eastward. In his book **Mein Kampf**, Hitler had stated that Germany wanted living space (*Lebensraum*) in eastern Europe. He also hated communism.

From the end of the Battle of Britain to the summer of 1941, Germany planned to attack the USSR. This would be the greatest land attack in world history.

In the spring of 1941, the planned attack had to be delayed for two months because Germany became involved in two other problems – subduing an anti-German uprising in Yugoslavia and aiding Italy against Greece.

But by June Germany was ready to attack the USSR. It was joined by Finland, Hungary and Romania, and military units were also supplied by Italy, Spain and Slovakia. On 22 June 1941 'Operation Barbarossa' was launched – a surprise attack on the USSR.

Much debate surrounds the decision by the Soviet leader, Stalin, not to take more resolute action against possible German aggression. From August 1939 to June 1941 the USSR was in alliance with Germany (the Molotov–Ribbentrop Pact). Also Stalin feared provoking a German attack if he had prepared the USSR for a possible war. Stalin had remembered that in July 1914 the Tsar's decision to mobilise the Russian army forced Germany to declare war on Russia.

The Soviet–German War (known as the 'Great Patriotic War' in the USSR) was the greatest conflict in world history. In the war, from 1941–45, the USSR lost 25 million people (including 13 million in the Soviet Army). Germany and its allies lost 6 million. However, 1941 saw the Second World War spread across the globe to the Far East and Pacific Ocean.

## Why did Japan attack Pearl Harbor in December 1941?

War in the Far East pre-dated the outbreak of the Second World War in Europe. In 1931 Japan occupied the north Chinese province of Manchuria and in 1937 it began a major war of conquest against the rest of China. By 1940 Japan had occupied most of the Chinese coastline and had advanced

**Mein Kampf**: A book (My Struggle) written by Hitler in 1924–25 which sets out his ideas about German domination of Europe.

**French Indo-China**: The modern day countries of Vietnam, Laos and Cambodia.

**Embargo**: a restriction on trade by one country on another.

1. Why were the Germans so successful during the Second World War up to June 1940?

2. Explain why Hitler decided to invade the USSR in June 1941.

3. Why had the Second World War become a global war by December 1941?

inland up the Yangtze river valley. In 1940 Japan took advantage of the fall of France by occupying **French Indo-China**.

These Japanese advances alarmed the USA. In response to the Japanese move into French Indo-China the USA began an economic **embargo**, culminating in a ban on oil exports to Japan. By the autumn of 1941 Japan faced a major dilemma. It could either wind down its military operations because of a lack of oil and raw materials or it could force the USA to end its embargo.

By December 1941 the Japanese planned a lightning strike against the US Pacific Fleet which was based at Pearl Harbor, in the Hawaiian islands. At the same time, Japan planned to launch attacks against Malaya, the Philippine Islands and the Dutch East Indies. Conquest of these areas would give Japan access to the oil and raw materials it needed.

On 7 December 1941 Japanese carrier-borne aircraft attacked Pearl Harbor and sank several US naval vessels. Although Japan had disabled part of the fleet, the US aircraft carrier force had not been there, and six months later, in June 1942, this carrier force was able to destroy the Japanese carrier force at the Battle of Midway.

In South East Asia the Japanese attacks met with spectacular success. British Malaya and Singapore fell by February 1942, followed shortly afterwards by the US-controlled Philippines and the Dutch East Indies.

The impact of the Japanese attack on Pearl Harbor was to bring the USA into the war on the Allied side. Of equal significance was the decision by Hitler to declare war on the USA shortly afterwards.

By December 1941 Hitler's action had transformed the Second World War in Europe. Instead of fighting just Britain, Germany now faced the world's two greatest economic powers, the USSR and USA. And the Japanese attack on Pearl Harbor had turned the Second World War into a truly global war.

## Source-based questions: The policy of appeasement

**Study the following FOUR passages – A, B, C and D – and answer both of the sub-questions which follow.**

### SOURCE A

The German visit was from my point of view a great success, because it achieved its object, that of creating an atmosphere in which it is possible to discuss with Germany the practical questions involved in a European settlement. Both Hitler and Goering said separately, and emphatically, that they had no desire or intention of making war, and I think that we may take this as correct, at least for the present. Of course, they want to dominate eastern Europe; they want as close a union with Austria as they can get without incorporating her in the Reich, and they want much the same things for the Sudeten Germans as we did for the *Uitlanders* [the name given by the Boers to British settlers in South Africa] in the Transvaal.

*From a memorandum written by Neville Chamberlain in November 1937. Chamberlain accepts the need to make concessions to Germany in order to preserve the peace of Europe.*

### SOURCE B

The word that British statesmen chose to describe their response was 'appeasement'. It was an unfortunate choice, for it came to imply a weak and fearful policy of concession to potential aggressors. In fact appeasement was far more than that. It was more or less consistent with the main lines of British foreign policy going back into the 19th century. By appeasement was meant a policy of adjustment and accommodation of conflicting interests broadly to conform with Britain's unique position in world affairs. It involved no preconceived plan of action, but rested upon a number of political and moral assumptions about the virtue of compromise and peaceableness. It involved using the instruments of British power – trading and financial strength, and a wealth of diplomatic experience – to their fullest advantage. But it also implied that there were limits to British policy beyond which other powers should not be permitted to go.

*From R.J. Overy, The Origins of the Second World War, published in 1987. This historian argues that the policy of appeasement made good sense in the context of previous British foreign policy.*

### SOURCE C

It did not occur to Chamberlain that Great Britain and France were unable to oppose German demands; rather he assumed that Germany, and Hitler in particular, would be grateful for concessions willingly made – concessions which, if Hitler failed to respond with equal good will, could also be withdrawn. On 19 November 1937 Halifax [the British Foreign Secretary] met Hitler at Berchtesgaden. Halifax said all that Hitler expected to hear. He praised Nazi Germany 'as the bulwark of Europe against Bolshevism'; he sympathised with past German grievances. England would not seek to maintain the existing settlement in central Europe. There was a condition attached: the changes must come without a general war. This was exactly what Hitler wanted himself. Halifax's remarks were an invitation to Hitler to promote German nationalist agitation in Danzig, Czechoslovakia and Austria; an assurance too that this agitation would not be opposed from without. All these remarks strengthened Hitler's conviction that he would meet little opposition from Great Britain and France.

*From A.J.P. Taylor, The Origins of the Second World War, published in 1961. Taylor argues that the policy of appeasement served positively to encourage Hitler in his expansionist plans.*

### SOURCE D

Timidity was the dominant characteristic of [French] political leadership. At the critical moments – in March 1936 and September 1938 – ministers shrank from any suggestion of constraining Germany by force. This timidity had three main causes. Firstly, there was the caution of the military chiefs. Early in 1936 before the Rhineland coup, Marshal Gamelin considered that France could not fight Germany with any certainty of victory. Secondly, French public opinion was deeply divided on social and economic issues and the lack of national unity prevented a forceful reposte to German initiatives. Thirdly, from September 1935 onwards, military and political leaders were convinced that France could not contemplate war with Germany unless assured of active British help. British assistance was judged essential for the protection of French shipping and supplies in the Mediterranean.

*From Anthony Adamthwaite, France and the Coming of the Second World War, published in 1977. This historian argues that French foreign policy in the 1930s was based essentially upon feelings of weakness.*

**Source-based questions: The policy of appeasement**

(a) Compare Passages B and D on the motives that lay behind policies of appeasement in Britain and France.

(b) Using these four passages and your own knowledge, evaluate the claim that the policy of appeasement deserves a large proportion of the blame for the outbreak of the Second World War.

## Source-based questions: The end of the Twenty Years' Truce

Study the two sources and answer the questions which follow.

### SOURCE 1

Living space proportionate to the greatness of the state is fundamental to every power. One can do without it for a time, but sooner or later the problem will have to be solved by hook or by crook. The alternatives are rise or decline. It is not Danzig that is at stake. For us it is a matter of expanding our living space in the east and making food supplies secure and also solving the problem of the Baltic States. No other opening can be seen in Europe. There is therefore no question of sparing Poland and we are left with the decision to attack Poland at the first suitable opportunity.

Hitler in conference with his military commanders, 23 May 1939

### SOURCE 2

The following special reasons strengthen my resolve. There is no actual rearmament in England, just propaganda. The construction programme for the Navy for 1938 has not yet been fulfilled. Little has been done on land. England will only be able to send a maximum of three divisions to the continent. A little has been done for the Air Force, but it is only a beginning. France lacks men due to the decline in the birth rate. Little has been done for rearmament. The artillery is antiquated. France does not want to enter upon this adventure. The enemy had another hope, that Russia would become our enemy after the conquest of Poland. The enemy did not count upon my great power of resolution. Our enemies are little worms. I saw them at Munich.

Minutes of a speech by Hitler to his military commanders,
27 August 1939

(a) Study Sources 1 and 2.

What reasons does Hitler give for his decision to attack Poland?

(b) What steps had Hitler already taken before 1939 to revise the terms of the Versailles Treaty?

(c) Were diplomatic attempts to preserve European peace in the 1930s doomed to failure? Explain your answer.

# Further Reading

*Texts designed for AS and A2 Level students*

*The Inter-War Crisis 1919–1939* by R.J. Overy (Longman, Seminar Studies series, 1994)

*The Origins of the First and Second World Wars* by Frank McDonough (Cambridge University Press, Perspectives in History series, 1997)

*Versailles and After, 1919–1933* by Ruth Henig (Routledge, Lancaster Pamphlets, 1995)

*Origins of the Second World War 1933–1939* by Ruth Henig (Routledge, Lancaster Pamphlets, 1985)

*Hitler, Appeasement and the Road to War 1933–1941* by Graham Darby (Hodder & Stoughton, Access to History series, 1999)

*Hitler* (Book 2) by Mary Fulbrook (Collins Historymakers, 2004)

*Mussolini* by Derrick Murphy (Collins Historymakers, 2004)


*More advanced reading*

*The Making of the Second World War* by Anthony Adamthwaite (Allen & Unwin, 1977) includes a useful selection of documents.

*The Foreign Policy of the Third Reich* by Klaus Hildebrand (Batsford, 1973)

*The Nazi Dictatorship: Problems and Perspectives in Interpretation* by Ian Kershaw (Arnold, 1993)

*Germany and Europe 1919–1939* by John Hiden (Longman, 1977)

*France and the Coming of the Second World War* by Anthony Adamthwaite (Cass, 1977)

*Italian Foreign Policy, 1870–1940* by C.J. Lowe and F. Marzari (Routledge & Kegan Paul, 1975)

*The Origins of the Second World War Reconsidered: The A.J.P. Taylor Debate after Twenty-Five Years* edited by Gordon Martel (Routledge, 1986)

*The Origins of the Second World War* by A.J.P. Taylor (Penguin, 1964) and *Hitler: a Study in Tyranny* by Alan Bullock (Penguin, 1962) remain classic studies of this subject.

# 4 The Second World War

## Key Issues

- Why did the Second World War expand into a global conflict?

- What economic and racial policies did the Nazis pursue in the territories that they occupied?

- Why did the resistance of the Axis powers collapse in 1944–1945?

**4.1** Why was the German war effort so successful in 1939–1940?

**4.2** How and why did the conflict expand in 1940–1942?

**4.3** Why did the German offensive against the Soviet Union fail?

**4.4** In what respects had the challenges facing Nazi Germany changed by the end of 1942?

**4.5** By what methods and with what success did Nazi Germany govern the territories that it conquered?

**4.6** Why did the Nazis pursue a 'Final Solution to the Jewish Question' in the war years?

**4.7** Historical interpretation: Did the resistance movements in occupied Europe play any significant role in the defeat of Nazi Germany?

**4.8** Why did the Axis collapse in 1944–1945?

**4.9** What plans had the allies made for a peace settlement?

**4.10** What were the immediate consequences of the conflict?

## Framework of Events

| | |
|---|---|
| **1939** | September: German invasion of Poland. Britain and France declare war on Germany |
| | November: Beginning of 'Winter War' between USSR and Finland |
| **1940** | Russian annexation of Baltic states |
| | April: German invasion of Norway and Denmark |
| | May: German invasion of Holland, Belgium and France |
| | June: Dunkirk evacuation and fall of France |
| | July–September: Battle of Britain |
| **1941** | March: 'Lend–Lease' agreement between Britain and USA |
| | June: Germany launches 'Operation Barbarossa', the invasion of the USSR |
| | September: Britain and USA sign 'Atlantic Charter' |
| | December: Japanese attack upon Pearl Harbor. American entry into war |
| **1942** | August: German assault on Stalingrad |
| | October: German defeat in North Africa at El Alamein |
| **1943** | January: German defeat at Stalingrad |
| | July: German defeat at Kursk. Allied invasion of Italy. Mussolini falls from power |
| **1944** | June: British and American forces launch D-Day landings in Normandy. Fall of Rome to allied forces |
| **1945** | January: Fall of Warsaw to Soviet troops |
| | February: Allied conference at Yalta. Allied forces cross the Rhine |
| | April: Russian forces enter Berlin |
| | May: Unconditional surrender of German forces |
| | August: Atomic bombs dropped on Hiroshima and Nagasaki |
| | September: Unconditional surrender of Japanese forces. Allied conference at Potsdam. |

## Overview

*Blitzkrieg* (German – 'lightning war'): A form of warfare in which victory is won by rapid, devastating and decisive offensives, rather than by protracted campaigns.

ALTHOUGH the Second World War was different in many respects from the war of 1914–18, it too began with a misconception. Hitler did not anticipate a global conflict of long duration, but had planned a series of limited, rapid campaigns that would achieve strictly defined objectives in a manner that would not stretch German economic resources. The first of these crushed Poland in a matter of weeks (September 1939) and another, the following year, destroyed French resistance almost as rapidly. Subsequently, however, Hitler's calculations began to go wrong. Britain did not immediately give in once its French ally had been defeated, nor did Hitler's third *Blitzkrieg*, launched from the air, succeed in bringing it to its knees. Instead, Britain gained material assistance from the United States of America and, within a year, could count the USA as a direct ally after Japanese aggression had brought them into the war. Nevertheless, Hitler's political and racial beliefs led him to believe that his next projected offensive, against the Soviet Union, must also succeed.

Germany owed its impressive successes in 1939–41 to the fact that its military commanders had perfected this art of *Blitzkrieg*. They had appreciated before any of their contemporaries the impact of large tank forces, supported from the air by superior forces of rapid fighter planes and dive-bombers. When this strategy failed a second time, however, and the Soviet Union survived the massive blow struck against it, it became clear that the Second World War would actually be decided in the same manner as the first. It would be won by those who possessed the greatest industrial resources and who could bring them most effectively to bear. By 1942 Hitler and his allies were involved in a great struggle that stretched from one end of Europe to the other, from the Channel coast to the Caspian Sea. It was linked with another struggle on the other side of the globe, for Japan's leaders had also miscalculated, underestimating America's aerial and naval power, failing similarly to achieve a quick 'knock-out' blow, and becoming locked in a desperate battle for survival in the Pacific. Britain's colonial interests in Canada, Australasia, South Africa and India drew those regions, too, into what was now a truly global war.

In effect, by the end of 1942, this was a war that Germany and its allies could not win. Germany in particular, however, adapted its war effort impressively in an attempt to stave off defeat. This involved the mobilisation of Germany's domestic economy to meet the demands of 'total war', and only from 1942 did the Nazis realise the country's potential for making war. It also meant the most ruthless exploitation of the resources available to Germany in the territories that it had occupied. Enormous efforts were made to seize material resources and to mobilise foreign labour to work in German industry, either by force or by more subtle inducements. One of the most remarkable features of this stage of the war was the willingness with which some elements within the occupied states, especially in western Europe, co-operated and collaborated with the invaders. This ruthless exploitation also stimulated resistance to the Germans, and in eastern Europe in particular, this put further obstacles in the path of Germany's war effort. At the same time, the Nazi leadership placed additional obstacles in its own path by judging that the time was now ripe for a 'final solution' to the 'problem' of Europe's Jewish population. Even as the war was being lost, human resources, transport and the like were being used for ferrying Jews to the concentration camps where genocide was to take place.

Great though the scope of the war was by 1942, its focus was the German campaign against the Soviet Union, and the decisive battles of the whole world war were those fought around Moscow, Leningrad and Stalingrad. There, once the invaders had lost the element of surprise, their forces were steadily ground down by the geography and climate of the region, and by the vast resources that the Soviet Union could mobilise. In the meantime, the American economy attained the highest levels of industrial production that the world had ever witnessed, and its military resources were steadily concentrated in Britain and in North Africa. In the course of 1944 Germany found itself fighting on three fronts. Whereas the First World War ended without a single foreign soldier on German soil, the Second World War drew to a close with the wholesale destruction of German cities, with Soviet troops in the heart of Berlin, and with the arrest and condemnation of many of Germany's political leaders. The year 1945 marked the most comprehensive military and political defeat that any modern state had ever experienced.

Six years of bitter conflict had serious implications for the political and economic balance of Europe and of the world at large. To say that they brought about the destruction of the German state, the downfall of the political regimes of several other European states, the end of Europe's international supremacy, and a new political balance between two world superpowers, is only to list some of the war's results. Some historians argue that the two world wars must be viewed together, the second completing some of the unfinished business of the first. Looked at in this way it might be possible to conclude that the extreme nationalist movements of the 1920s and the 1930s were only makeshift expedients to fill the gaps left by the collapse of the aristocratic empires of pre-1914 Europe. The defeat of such movements left supremacy in Europe to be disputed between the liberal democracies that were already well developed by 1914, and the vast socialist power of the Soviet Union that had achieved such apparent permanency under the rule of Joseph Stalin.

## 4.1 Why was the German war effort so successful in 1939–1940?

### Military and tactical superiority

The table on page 84 gives some indication of the relative strengths of the major European powers in 1939, yet such figures do not tell the whole story. As the lessons of the 1914–18 war should have taught, the importance of the 'big battalions' was now outweighed by technical and tactical superiority. In these respects, German leadership was indisputable. Under the influence of such commanders as Heinz Guderian and Erwin Rommel, the **Wehrmacht** had adopted the principles of mechanised warfare – of

*Wehrmacht*: German armed forces other than *Waffen SS.*

| **Heinz Guderian (1888–1954)** | | **Erwin Rommel (1891–1944)** | |
| --- | --- | --- | --- |
| An important pre-war theorist of tank warfare; one of the architects of the German *Panzer* divisions. | Commanded *Panzer* forces in Poland (1939), France and Russia (1940). Inspector General of tanks (1943). Chief of Staff of the *Wehrmacht* (1944). | Commander of the Afrika Korps (1941–43). Commander of German forces in northern Italy | (1943). Commander of forces in France (1943–44). Implicated in the army plot to assassinate Hitler, Rommel was arrested and committed suicide. |

rapid thrusts against a slow-moving enemy to cut its lines of supply and of retreat – far more effectively than Germany's opponents. Germany enjoyed a distinct advantage in the areas vital to this 'lightning war', in the design and deployment of its tanks and the use of aerial support. It had turned its enforced disarmament of 1919 to its advantage, building modern weapons while its opponents laboured under the weight of obsolete equipment. The modern planes of the *Luftwaffe* were faster and more manoeuvrable than anything possessed by the French or the Poles.

Also, although Germany's 3,200 tanks did not represent a numerical superiority, models such as the PkwIII and the PkwIV were superior to their counterparts. The *Wehrmacht* also used these new weapons more effectively. Despite the entreaties in the early 1930s of a young tank officer, Colonel Charles de Gaulle, French military commanders continued to think of the tank as a form of mechanised horse, supporting the all-important infantry advances. Neither they nor their allies appreciated the value of the weapon used in massed formations. Their plans and their armies proceeded at the pace of the foot soldier in a military world dominated by the internal combustion engine. Most ominous of all for the allies' immediate prospects in the autumn of 1939 was the weakness of the Polish armed forces, largely unchanged since their successes against the Russians 20 years before.

---

### The military balance of power in Europe, 1939

|  | Army divisions | No. of aircraft | Capital ships | Submarines |
|---|---|---|---|---|
| Germany | 125 | 4,210 | 5 | 65 |
| Italy | 73 | 1,531 | 4 | 104 |
| USSR | 125 | 3,361 | 3 | 18 |
| France | 86 | 1,234 | 7 | 78 |
| Great Britain | 4 | 1,750 | 15 | 57 |
| Poland | 40 | 500 | – | – |

Source: A. Adamthwaite, *The Making of the Second World War* (1977)

---

### Action in the east, inaction in the west

The historian A.J.P. Taylor wrote that 'although Hitler blundered in supposing that the two western powers would not go to war at all, his expectation that they would not go to war seriously turned out to be correct.' Poland received no material support from its allies and the tactics of all three powers contrasted starkly with those of the invaders. Poland became the first victim of the *Blitzkrieg* perfected by the German forces. Pitching armoured columns and overwhelming aerial superiority against an army that continued to trust in the mobility of large cavalry forces, the *Wehrmacht* made rapid progress eastwards, encircling the defending forces in a **pincer movement**. On 17 September the fate of Poland was sealed when Soviet forces began their occupation of its eastern regions. Within ten days the German and Soviet forces had reached the line agreed in the Ribbentrop–Molotov Pact, and the Polish state ceased to exist.

In the west, meanwhile, a different kind of war was being waged. The contemporary military historian, Sir Basil Liddell Hart, believed that the allies, with 86 French divisions alone, could have taken effective action against the 42 divisions that guarded the German frontier, without tanks, aircraft or substantial supplies. Yet nothing positive was done. This was

**Pincer movement**: Splitting your forces and moving them round either side of the enemy.

largely due to the outmoded thinking of the French commanders, still wedded to the defensive strategy of the previous war. It was also due to the hesitation of political leaders who had still not overcome the appeasement mentality of the last decade. Thus, when allied bombers did fly over German industrial towns, they dropped propaganda leaflets rather than bombs. This curious state of suspended hostility was christened the 'phoney war'. To the Germans it became the 'sitting-down war' (*Sitzkrieg*) in ironic contrast to the more effective tactics of the Eastern Front.

Illogically, the attention of allied strategists during this 'phoney war' turned towards Scandinavia. There, in the mines of Sweden and Norway, lay the source of 51% of Germany's supplies of iron ore. This might explain the allies' attempts to entice Norway and Sweden into the war on their side. However, with the opening of the Soviet Union's 'Winter War' with Finland (November 1939–March 1940), it is hard to resist the conclusion that the allied governments continued to be as much concerned with the Soviet threat as with that posed by Germany. Similarly, French actions in the Middle East against Hitler's Caspian oil supplies were as much anti-Soviet in conception as anti-German. In both cases, allied action proved hesitant and half-hearted. While they debated the mining of neutral Norwegian waters to prevent the passage of ore to Germany, Hitler ordered the extension of operations to Scandinavia to safeguard his supplies. The invasion of Denmark (April 1940), necessary for the purposes of communication, was an immediate success, but the simultaneous assault on Norway encountered stiffer resistance. By the end of June, however, all allied forces had been forced to withdraw, leaving Norway in German hands.

## The fall of France

The 'phoney war' ended abruptly on 10 May 1940 with the launching of the German offensive into France and the **Low Countries**. Despite the months that had been available for preparation, the defending forces were taken largely unaware, not only by the speed and power of the German attack, but also by its strategy. Expecting an offensive like that of 1914, based upon a drive through central Belgium, allied strategists envisaged an advance into Belgium to check the enemy's right wing short of the French frontier while the rest of his forces dashed themselves against the defences of the Maginot Line. Indeed, until January 1940, Belgium had played a leading role in *Wehrmacht* plans. Only then had a daring new strategy been introduced. German commanders were aware that the allies regarded the hilly, wooded region of the Ardennes, beyond the flank of the Maginot Line, as virtually impassable, and that it was thus only lightly defended. General von Manstein therefore proposed an armoured attack across the river Meuse, into this weakest sector of the allied line.

In the event, the German offensive combined both strategies. For the first ten days Holland and Belgium suffered heavy aerial bombardment and assault by infantry, artillery and airborne troops. In particular, the bombing of Rotterdam, where nearly 1,000 civilians died within a few minutes, was unprecedented in European experience and created a deep psychological impression. The Dutch government surrendered on 15 May. British and French forces were drawn into Belgium to check the German advance and were threatened with encirclement when (12 May) a massive armoured force under General von Kleist broke through the Ardennes and breached the French line near Sedan. This breakthrough effectively decided the outcome of the battle for France. Faced with the alternatives of evacuation or annihilation, the British forces, with some 10,000 French troops, retreated to the Channel at Dunkirk. Here, by a combination of heroism,

**Low Countries**: The region forming the Kingdoms of Holland and Belgium, and the grand duchy of Luxembourg.

**Ewald von Kleist (1881–1954)**
Commanded German forces in the Caucasus, the Crimea and the Ukraine (1942–43). Relieved of his command by Hitler after ordering retreat on the Eastern Front. Died in captivity in the Soviet Union.

'The withdrawal from Dunkirk', June 1940, by Charles Cundall

good fortune and puzzling German tactics, they were transported back to Britain by a fleet of 860 assorted vessels hastily assembled for the task (26 May – 4 June). The operation owed much, perhaps everything, to Hitler's curious decision to hold back tanks and aircraft that could have destroyed the allied forces and their rescuers on the beaches. Variously explained as a temporary loss of nerve, or as evidence of a continuing hope that Britain would still conclude a separate peace, Hitler's decision allowed an escape which, in subsequent British propaganda, did something to obscure the magnitude of the allied defeat.

The new French line, along the rivers Aisne and Somme, broke three days later, and the government abandoned Paris for the safety of the south (9 June). Any remaining hope of national survival vanished the following day when Mussolini judged the moment ripe for Italy, too, to declare war on France. From their retreat near Bordeaux the French government, now led by the hero of the First World War, Marshal Philippe Pétain, rejected the option of flight to Africa and requested Germany's terms for an armistice. In 46 days of fighting, France had lost 84,000 men dead, 120,000 injured and 1,500,000 taken prisoner. Considering the extent of this defeat the terms dictated at Rethondes (21 June), in the same railway carriage used for the German surrender in 1918, were moderate.

- With the exception of strategic areas in the north and along the Atlantic coast, French officials retained responsibility for civil administration.

- The French government retained complete sovereignty over the southern 40% of the country free from German military occupation.

- No territory was earmarked for annexation by Germany, although Italy claimed the return of Nice and Savoy.

- France kept control of its fleet and of its Empire.

- The fact remained, as the future would show, that with total military domination, Hitler could take what he did not now claim whenever he felt the need.

### What were the causes and significance of the French defeat?

**Mohacs in 1526**: Victory in the Battle of Mohacs allowed Turkish forces under Sultan Suleiman the Magnificent to overrun and destroy the Kingdom of Hungary. This seemed to contemporaries to represent the collapse of the outer defences of Christendom.

**1. What were the main reasons for the rapid victory gained by German forces on the Western Front in 1940?**

**2. To what extent were Hitler's successes in 1939 and 1940 due to the weaknesses and mistakes of Germany's opponents?**

The astonishing collapse of France had many causes. Among these the confused foreign policy of the last two decades, the deep domestic divisions of recent years, and the extraordinary incompetence of commanders who neglected air power, mechanised forces and modern communications, are prominent. Although the transformation of this European conflict into a true world war was eventually to reverse the outcome of 1940, the significance of the German victory in purely European terms must not be underestimated. A nation that had held the first place in the affairs of the continent for three centuries had been rendered impotent within five weeks, and the rise of German power, checked at great cost in 1918, seemed after all to have reached its logical conclusion. The historians Peter Calvocoressi and Guy Wint, in *Total War* (1970), have summarised the impact of these events in his judgement that 'the fall of France opened an abyss of uncertainty for the whole continent and shook the imagination as perhaps nothing had shaken it since the victory of the Turks at **Mohacs in 1526**'.

## 4.2 How and why did the conflict expand in 1940–1942?

**Winston Churchill (1874–1965)**
British politician in Parliament from 1900 (as a Liberal until 1923). He held a number of ministerial offices, including First Lord of the Admiralty (1911–15) and Chancellor of the Exchequer (1924–29). Absent from the Cabinet in the 1930s, he returned in September 1939 to lead a coalition government (1940–45). Typifying resistance to the threat of Germany, he was also successful in forging the alliance with the USA and the USSR that led to Germany's unconditional surrender in 1945. Prime Minister again 1951–55. In 1953 Churchill received the Nobel Prize for Literature and was made Knight of the Garter.

This stage of the European conflict could scarcely have continued, let alone expanded, had not some basis survived for resistance against Nazi Germany. At first, the collapse of France seemed likely to end the war in western Europe. Britain's chances of continuing the struggle seemed hopeless. Its land forces, although extricated from Dunkirk, had lost most of their equipment, and the defence of 3,000 kilometres of coastline posed enormous problems. Yet, stiffened by the extraordinary leadership and resolution of the new Prime Minister, Winston Churchill, Britain did not sue for peace. Instead, Churchill announced his determination that 'we shall fight on the beaches, we shall fight on the landing grounds, we shall fight in the hills; we shall never surrender'. Hitler's response to this decision seems to have been conditioned by three factors.

1. Although it is unlikely that Britain could have resisted an invasion, no definite plans had been prepared for one, so sure was the German High Command that the fall of France would end the western campaign.

2. Hitler professed a persistent reluctance to treat a 'Germanic' civilisation in the same way that he had treated the Poles.

3. If Britain still needed to be prodded towards peace, the commander of the *Luftwaffe*, Hermann Goering, was determined that his forces should be allowed to demonstrate their effectiveness.

### The Battle of Britain

Unlike the Battle of France, the Battle of Britain took the form of a concentrated aerial attack, firstly upon Britain's airfields, to gain total air supremacy, and then upon London and other centres to break the resistance of the civilian population. Neither effort was successful. The numerical superiority of the *Luftwaffe* – about 1,200 bombers and 1,000 fighters to some 900 British fighters – was offset by several other factors. The relatively light German bombers such as the Heinkel 111 and the Dornier 215 were vulnerable without substantial fighter support, and the range of such fighters as the Messerschmitt 109E was only sufficient to give them a few minutes of combat over British targets. On the British side, the Spitfire and Hurricane fighters were formidable weapons – fast, manoeuvrable, heavily armed, and with the advantage of fighting over their own territory. The rapid development of radar and its establishment along the southern and eastern coasts of Britain provided valuable early warning of the German bombers' approach.

Thus, in the main phase of the engagement (early August–late September 1940), the *Luftwaffe* lost over 1,100 aircraft, against a British loss of 650. Hitler, half-hearted in his campaign from the outset, and impatient to turn against his 'real' enemy in the east, suspended the plan for invasion on 17 September, and reduced *Luftwaffe* operations over Britain at the end of the month. Although the struggle was decided as much by German errors and miscalculations as by British strengths, the Battle of Britain represented a first checking of Germany's triumphant military progress, and the beginning of that over-stretching of its military resources that was to be its downfall.

## The Mediterranean and the Balkans

In mid-1940, the conflict was a strictly limited one, tightly confined to areas of western and northern Europe. The failure of Germany in that summer to eliminate British opposition began a process of proliferation that transformed this into a truly global war. Firstly, after the failure of aerial warfare, the Atlantic Ocean became the major theatre of Anglo–German conflict. The German navy sought, with submarines, surface raiders and mines, to cut British supply lines. Secondly, the entry of Italy into the war inevitably spread the conflict to those areas that Mussolini considered to be his sphere of influence: the Balkans, the Mediterranean, and North Africa.

Two factors led to German involvement in these regions. The failure of Italian forces to sustain their offensive against Greece (October 1940) and the British decision to send aid to the Greeks seriously threatened interests that Germany had carefully built up in that region. By a mixture of bullying and diplomacy, Hitler had ensured that Hungary, Romania and Yugoslavia would remain sympathetic to German ambitions in eastern Europe, the source of valuable strategic supplies and potential assembly areas for anti-Soviet forces.

The hope that General Franco might repay his debt from the Spanish Civil War by supporting **Axis** interests in the Mediterranean had collapsed by the end of 1940. In a series of discussions in October and November the Spanish leader made it clear that his priority was domestic consolidation and reconstruction. Thus, with Italian forces checked in Greece and later in North Africa, and with the pro-German government of Yugoslavia overthrown by a *coup d'état* (March 1941), Hitler found himself forced into large-scale intervention. The military campaign was successful, with Greece cleared of hostile troops by late April and the island of Crete captured in May. Yet the commitment of 28 divisions to the Balkans and of several mechanised divisions to North Africa forced a postponement of the planned Russian offensive and the establishment of a costly and lasting 'sideshow' for the Germans.

**Axis**: The name given to the alliance between Germany, Italy and Japan during the Second World War.

> **Francisco Franco (1892–1975)**
> He was a general at 41. Commandant of the Military Academy at Saragossa, closed as part of the Republican Army reforms. After the Popular Front's victory of 1936 Franco was regarded as a threat to the Republic and was sent to the Canary Islands. From there he flew to Morocco and was soon the leader of the Nationalists. He was dictator ('El Caudillo') of Spain until his death.

# The entry of the United States of America

**Franklin D. Roosevelt (1882–1945)**
Democrat senator for New York State (1910); Secretary for the Navy (1910); Governor of New York (1929); President of the USA (1932–45). In peacetime, his greatest achievements were those connected with the New Deal, to restore economic prosperity after the Great Depression. Roosevelt's foreign policy moved steadily away from isolationism, and he showed great sympathy for British resistance to Nazi Germany. The Japanese attack upon Pearl Harbor finally gave him the opportunity to lead the USA into the war.

Of far greater significance was the gradual involvement of the United States of America in the conflict. American isolationism, re-established by the Senate's refusal to ratify the Versailles Treaty, and confirmed by three Neutrality Acts (1935, 1936, 1937), was only slowly eroded by the influence of Churchill's close personal relationship with President Franklin D. Roosevelt. Public opinion in the USA also took time to realise that world events were beginning to pose a direct threat to American interests. The fall of France, for instance, presented the prospect of an Atlantic Ocean dominated by hostile fleets at the same time as Japanese influence spread in the Pacific Ocean. The Battle of the Atlantic, with its extensive German submarine action, not only confirmed this prospect, but posed a definite danger to American shipping. By September 1940, there was sufficient support in the USA for the 'Destroyer Deal', which transferred 50 older ships into British hands. This was followed by the more important 'Lend–Lease' agreement (March 1941), by which purchase of war materials from American companies was financed by the American government regardless of Britain's current dollar reserves. By late 1941, largely due to the influence of Roosevelt himself, the USA had taken up an ambiguous position – clearly sympathetic to Germany's opponents, but not openly committed to war.

This position changed dramatically on 7 December 1941 with the Japanese air attack upon the American Pacific fleet at Pearl Harbor. The American declaration of war upon Japan was followed almost immediately (11 December) by Hitler's declaration of war upon the USA. Many have since followed the historian Alan Bullock in regarding this declaration as 'the greatest single mistake of his career'. On the other hand, some have interpreted Hitler's declaration of war as a simple acceptance of American hostility to Germany. Where Hitler certainly did commit a serious error was in grossly underestimating the strength of his new enemy. Applying his racial views to the USA, he refused to believe that a country 'half Judaised and the other half negrified' could effectively challenge Germany. Only slowly, in the phrase of historian Michael Burleigh (*The Third Reich: A New History*, 2000) did Hitler realise 'the creative, economic, intellectual and military potentialities he had stirred against himself, like a man surprised at the effects of poking a stick into a large beehive.'

## The invasion of the USSR

The most far-reaching escalation of the European conflict came with Hitler's decision to launch his attack upon the Soviet Union. Although increasingly committed to secondary theatres of war, he would not postpone this major element in his policy beyond June 1941. The assault was dictated by long-term hostility to Bolshevism and by theories of *Lebensraum*, but there were also logical, short-term factors that determined its timing. An attack now upon the Soviet Union would leave Britain with no prospect of future support in Europe, and would leave Japan without any distraction in its impending confrontation with the USA. Besides, Hitler was convinced that his successes in eastern Europe would, sooner or later, cause Stalin to take action to redress the balance. It made no sense to delay until the Soviet Army had time to fortify the territories occupied in 1939. On 22 June 121 divisions of the *Wehrmacht*, with massive aerial support, were launched across the frontier. Dismissing his generals' insistence upon a direct assault on Moscow, Hitler made the Soviet capital only one of three objectives for his army. An attack upon Leningrad would secure his Baltic flank with Finnish aid, while a thrust into the Ukraine would secure valuable industrial and agricultural resources.

**1. What factors enabled Britain to avoid invasion and defeat by Germany in 1940?**

**2. Why had Hitler decided by 1941 to go to war with both the USA and the Soviet Union?**

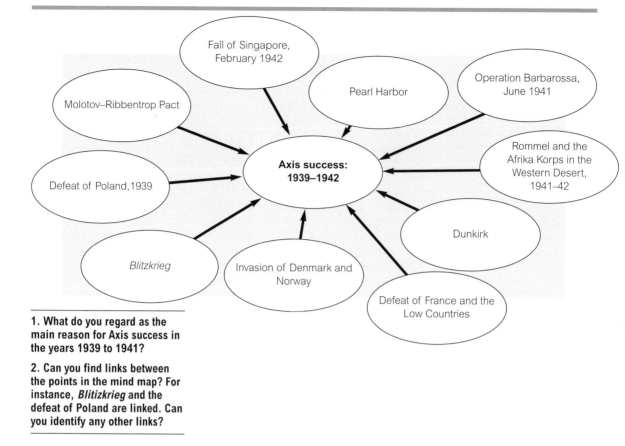

1. **What do you regard as the main reason for Axis success in the years 1939 to 1941?**

2. **Can you find links between the points in the mind map? For instance, *Blitizkrieg* and the defeat of Poland are linked. Can you identify any other links?**

## 4.3 Why did the German offensive against the Soviet Union fail?

At the time of the German offensive the Red Army had more men, more tanks, and more aircraft, yet the invaders enjoyed several advantages. They had the element of surprise, for Soviet propaganda had allowed no word to escape of worsening German–Soviet relations. They attacked an army which, although it had learned much from the difficult war with Finland a year earlier, had not yet had time to implement the necessary improvements in command and materials. The Red Army, uncertain which enemy posed the greater threat, still divided its forces between its frontier with the Germans and that in the east with Japan. Thus, the initial success of the German offensive was staggering. Soviet resistance was brave, but it lacked the co-ordination to contain the enemy advance for any period. In the north, Leningrad found itself surrounded and besieged by September. In the south, a Soviet force of 600,000 was surrounded and the key Ukrainian city of Kiev fell in the same month. By mid-October the *Wehrmacht* had pushed over 650 kilometres into central Russia and was within 80 kilometres of the Soviet capital. Soviet losses were huge; some three million men and 18,000 tanks in three months. Ominously, German casualties – some 750,000 of them – were also far higher than in any previous campaign.

### Soviet recovery and resistance

Great as German successes were, none of the objectives of the invasion had been completely secured by the beginning of the autumn, and there were signs that the tide was turning. The first factor in the Soviet recovery was the weather. Heavy rain in October blocked the German advance with seas of mud, and heavy frosts in November exposed them to all the horrors of a winter campaign in Russia. Frostbite claimed 100,000 victims. Aircraft, tanks, lorries and guns could not operate for want of antifreeze, and men were reduced to stuffing their uniforms with paper to keep out temperatures as low as 40 degrees below freezing.

The German forces also encountered astonishing resistance from military and civilians alike. Although reinforced by fear of retribution from their own side from the NKVD, this resistance came mainly from patriotism, as a reaction to ill-advised German behaviour in the territories they occupied, and from an awareness of the nature of the German threat. In his first wartime address to the nation, Stalin played upon this awareness in his declaration that the enemy was 'out to seize our lands watered by the sweat of our brows, to seize our grain and oil, secured by the labour of our hands, to restore the rule of the landlords'.

It is also possible to argue that German resources were less suited to their task than is often supposed. In *The German Economy at War* (1965), historian Alan Milward is highly critical of German preparation for this vast undertaking. If the Nazi economy was deliberately geared for war, Milward argued, it was geared inadequately. Just as Hitler failed to defeat Britain because he had not built an air force adequate for the task, so he failed against the Soviet Union because he had not built a sufficient tank force. His failure to secure a quick victory in the east then forced him to strike at the resources of southern Russia where his army, insufficiently mobile for the task that he had set it, encountered its decisive defeat.

## Leningrad and Stalingrad

In the north, German plans were narrowly frustrated. Of the seven Soviet cities awarded the title 'Hero City' after the war, none deserved it more than Leningrad. The **siege**, a product of Hitler's determination to destroy the cradle of Bolshevism, lasted from September 1941 to January 1944. Desperately short of food and precariously supplied by routes built over the ice of Lake Ladoga and by rail routes open to constant German attack, the inhabitants suffered constant bombardment and the threat of starvation. It is possible that the total casualty figures for the siege may have been as high as 1.5 million, most of them civilians. That Leningrad never fell was due to the heroism of the inhabitants, and to the shrewd defensive organisation of Marshal Georgi Zhukov. It also owed much to the eventual need of the *Wehrmacht* to divert substantial resources of men and material to the south-west of the USSR.

The key theatre of the European war in 1942 lay in Stalingrad. Given the industrial potential of the world's largest state and the failure of the 1941 campaign to crush its resistance, time was against Hitler. It was essential that Germany should complete the conquest of the oil-rich regions between the Black Sea and the Caspian as quickly as possible. In a fateful strategic decision, Hitler resolved to divide his southern forces between a drive against the Caucasian oilfields to the south and an assault upon the important communications centre of Stalingrad, on the Volga river, to the east. The personal links between Stalin and the city that bore his name gave the ensuing battle special significance for both sides. From September 1942 until January 1943, the streets, houses and factories of the city were the scene of constant and bitter fighting. This continued until the German Sixth Army, surrounded since November, but forbidden to retreat by Hitler, finally submitted. The battle cost the Germans 70,000 casualties, over 100,000 prisoners and vast quantities of guns and vehicles. The Soviet victory forced the retreat of those German forces further south that now faced the danger of being cut off. Worst of all, the invincible reputation of the *Wehrmacht* and the impetus of two years of *Blitzkrieg* campaigns in the east also died.

**Siege**: A military operation in which an army tries to capture a town by surrounding it and preventing food or help from reaching the people inside.

---

**Georgi Zhukov (1896–1974)**
Commanded the Red Army in actions against the Japanese in the Far East (1939). Chief of Soviet General Staff (1941). Commanded forces in the defence of Leningrad (1941), the defence of Stalingrad (1942), the campaigns in the Ukraine (1943–44), and the invasion of Germany (1944–45). Zhukov was the first commander of Soviet occupation forces in Germany.

---

1. What were the consequences of Hitler's decision to attack the Soviet Union in 1941?

2. How would you explain (a) the initial weakness of the Soviet response to the German invasion and (b) the later success of Soviet resistance?

3. Why was the German war effort so much more successful in 1939–41 than in 1942–43?

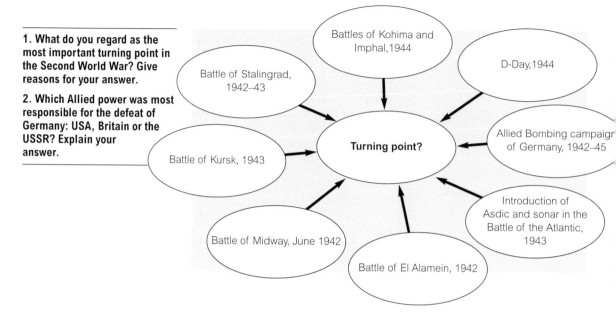

1. What do you regard as the most important turning point in the Second World War? Give reasons for your answer.

2. Which Allied power was most responsible for the defeat of Germany: USA, Britain or the USSR? Explain your answer.

## 4.4 In what respects had the challenges facing Nazi Germany changed by the end of 1942?

This was now a transformed war, in which Germany and its allies no longer faced an Anglo-French alliance, but a coalition that included the world's two largest states. The balance of industrial and economic forces would now only admit one eventual outcome.

### The Soviet war effort

**Kremlin**: Location of the Soviet central government in Moscow.

The Soviet Union brought to the conflict enormous industrial resources and a centralised political authority uniquely capable of mobilising and directing them. In the **Kremlin**, some of the government's firmest pre-war principles were now revised in the interests of national unity. The Orthodox Church was rehabilitated, and the privileges of higher military ranks were restored to ensure the army's undivided loyalty in the struggle. Industrially, on the other hand, the Soviet Union had lost much in the early months of the war, including some 60% of its coal and iron production and as much as 25% of its workforce.

The process of industrial re-organisation had already begun before the war, when the third Five-Year Plan had established many new industrial concentrations in the Ural mountains and in Siberia. These plants were beyond the reach of German attacks. Now they were supplemented at remarkable speed by the transfer of factories from the vulnerable western regions. In 1942 1,360 factories moved eastwards, and 2,250 new units of production arose there between 1942 and 1944. The astonishing nature of this achievement is conveyed by this description by the historian Peter Calvocoressi:

'At the new sites wooden structures were thrown up to house machinery, but there was often neither time nor materials to build houses for the workers. They slept on the floor by their machines. Mortality was high, output poor. The wonder is that they were not worse.'

Eventually, results were outstanding in regions old and new. The Moscow coalfield, reduced to an output of 590 tons per day in January 1942, was back to its pre-war norm of 35,000 tons per day by the following October. The trans-Ural regions, at their peak, were producing at 2.5 times the rate of the whole of Soviet industry in 1940. Russian military production overhauled that of Germany to reach a peak of 30,000 tanks and 40,000 aircraft in 1943.

## The contribution of the United States of America

A glance at the industrial capacity of the USA suffices to show the vital role that nation played in the outcome of the Second World War. American increases in armament production in the war years were amazing – from 6,000 aircraft in 1940 to 96,000 in 1945, from under a thousand tanks in 1940 to 21,000 in 1943. Much of this went to fight the war in the Pacific, but the American contribution to the European theatre of war remained invaluable. On D-Day (6 June 1944) the British army operated 3,300 Sherman tanks and 86,000 American motor vehicles. Some 20% of the Royal Air Force's strength in 1943–45 was also made up of American planes. The USSR benefited from 'Lend–Lease' agreements (October 1941 and June 1942), similar to that negotiated with Britain. These agreements provided 2,000 tanks and 1,300 planes by mid-1942, at the height of the Soviet crisis.

## British war production

**Empire and Dominions**: Although countries such as Australia, Canada, New Zealand and South Africa had become self-governing Dominions (legally independent in all internal and external matters, though economic and other ties remained), Britain still had a large Empire. Almost all the Dominions joined Britain to fight during the Second World War.

Although Great Britain could not match these figures, its contribution was considerable. Like the Soviet Union, Britain had won time to mobilise its resources and it did so effectively. From four divisions ready for combat in 1939, it could count on 60 by mid-1941, 20 of them from the **Empire and Dominions**. Domestic resources were also fully exploited. In 1940–42 British aircraft production was actually higher than that of Germany, and by the time Germany regained the lead in 1944, American and Soviet production had already put the issue of industrial supremacy beyond doubt.

## The German war effort from 1942

**Fritz Todt (1891–1942)**
Inspector of German Highways (1932–42). Founder and Head of the Organisation Todt, and in charge of construction projects under the Four-Year Plan (1938–42). Minister for Armaments and Munitions (1940–42), until his death in a plane crash.

Against these overwhelming forces, the German economy performed miracles, but laboured under a variety of obstacles. It had never been geared for a long war, only for the production of materials for *Blitzkrieg*, and Germany needed to undergo a miniature 'industrial revolution' to meet its new crisis. Central figures in this process were Fritz Todt, Minister of Armaments and Munitions until his death in February 1942, and his successor, Albert Speer. As a relatively civilised and realistic figure surrounded by Nazi extremists, Speer has since received lenient treatment both from the Nuremberg judges and, until recently, from historians. His role in equipping Germany to fight the war in 1942–45 was of great importance. Aircraft production reached a peak of 25,285 in 1944, as against 3,744 in 1940. The rebuilding of factories to protect them from air raids was so effective that 5,000 new aircraft were produced in the first four months of 1945 even as the allies were over-running Germany.

Speer could not, however, overcome Germany's severe political and geographical disadvantages. It was subjected to bombing from two sides

**Albert Speer (1905–1981)**
Architect, who directed many of Hitler's projects for the redevelopment of Berlin. Minister for Armaments and Munitions (1942–45). Speer was tried at Nuremberg and imprisoned. The memoirs that he wrote whilst in Spandau Prison are an important source of information on the government of Nazi Germany.

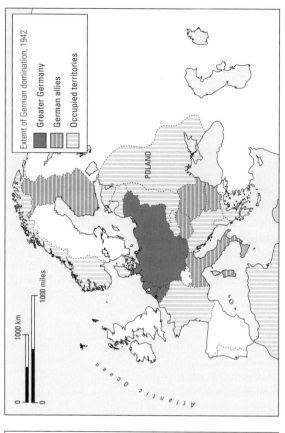

Extent of German domination, 1942

- Greater Germany
- German allies
- Occupied territories

POLAND

1000 km
1000 miles

Atlantic Ocean

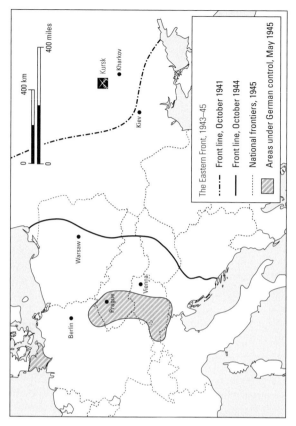

The Eastern Front, 1943–45

- Front line, October 1941
- Front line, October 1944
- National frontiers, 1945
- Areas under German control, May 1945

400 km
400 miles

Kursk
Kharkov
Kiev
Warsaw
Vienna
Prague
Berlin

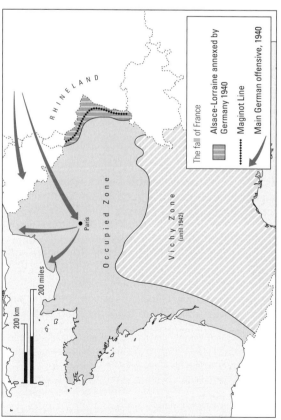

The fall of France

- Alsace-Lorraine annexed by Germany 1940
- Maginot Line
- Main German offensive, 1940

R H I N E L A N D

Occupied Zone

Vichy Zone
(until 1942)

Paris

200 km
200 miles

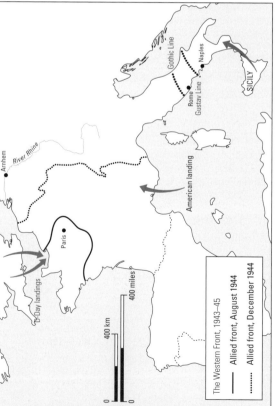

The Western Front, 1943–45

- Allied front, August 1944
- Allied front, December 1944

Gothic Line
Naples
Rome
Gustav Line
SICILY

American landing

Arnhem
River Rhine

Paris

D-Day landings

400 km
400 miles

The Second World War in Europe, 1939–45

*Gauleiters*: Senior Nazi officials, responsible for the administration of a *Gau* (province of the Reich).

**1. What disadvantages did Nazi Germany suffer from 1942 onwards in terms of the production of military material?**

**2. How convincing is the argument that Germany had the capacity to win the Second World War had it not been for the entry of the USA into the conflict?**

while American and Siberian factories lay beyond the reach of its own aircraft. There was no central authority in Germany to co-ordinate production. While Hitler specialised in oratory, Speer had frequently to struggle against the influence of Goering, the chiefs of various state agencies, and the local jealousies of the *Gauleiters*, over questions of policy and resources. In the latter stages of the war, resources such as the coal and iron of the Ruhr and of Silesia shrank as allied forces advanced.

## 4.5 By what methods and with what success did Nazi Germany govern the territories that it conquered?

'Puppet' governments: Governments which appear, and pretend, to be independent, but which are in fact controlled by a foreign government (i.e. someone else is 'pulling the strings').

For four years, Nazi Germany dominated the mainland of Europe more completely than it had ever been dominated before. In the west, in France, Norway and Denmark, 'puppet' governments were installed, checked at every turn by German military commanders and representatives of the security forces, to ensure that German interests were served. '**Puppet' governments** also operated in the Balkans, Greece, Yugoslavia and Romania. In eastern Europe, where the 'inferior' Slavs could not be afforded even this limited freedom, direct German government was the rule. Poland was placed under the arbitrary authority of a German Governor-General (Hans Frank), and Bohemia and Moravia under that of a protector (first Constantine von Neurath, then Reinhard Heydrich, then Wilhelm Frick). The territories of Ostland and the Ukraine, created from captured Soviet territory, came under the authority of the *Reichsminister* for the East, the fanatical Nazi theorist, Alfred Rosenberg.

### The Nazi 'New Order': appearance and reality

The 'new order' that these regimes advertised and imposed had a dual nature. In Nazi propaganda, especially in western Europe, it took the form of a gigantic union of European states to combat the alien menace of Judaism and its political offshoot, Bolshevism. It was a highly successful interpretation which found a living expression in the many international units, such as the French 'Legion of Volunteers Against Bolshevism' and the Belgian 'Flemish Legion', recruited in occupied countries to join the *Wehrmacht* on the Eastern Front.

In reality, the 'new order' took the form of a plundering of European resources for the exclusive benefit of Germany. This could be explained as a necessity imposed by the continuing war, but in large part it arose from the long-term plans of Nazi theorists. Hitler's aims in the Soviet Union were not merely to defeat its communist leadership, but to 'Germanise the country by the settlement of Germans and treat the natives as **redskins**'. Germany would provide the industrial heartland of this new Europe, and would in turn be fed by the less developed, largely agricultural territories that surrounded it.

'Redskins': A derogatory term used in America to refer to native Americans. In other words, Hitler planned to place the native populations in these areas upon 'reservations', as Americans had done with 'Red Indians', while German immigrants enjoyed the best resources.

Occupation administrations were assigned two main tasks: the economic exploitation of the conquered territories in the interests of the war effort, and the breaking of local political and intellectual structures. The first function was dominated by two central figures, Hermann

**Fritz Sauckel (1894–1946)**
An adherent to Nazism, Sauckel held high administrative office within the movement from an early date. He was party chief in Thuringia from 1927, and subsequently administered that province as *Gauleiter* (see opposite) and as Governor (*Reichstatthalter*) 1933–45. In March 1942, Sauckel was given overall responsibility for the recruitment of foreign labour to serve the German economy. For his role in the exploitation of forced labour, he was tried at Nuremberg and executed.

**Summary execution**: Execution carried out on the spot, without any legal process.

**Collaboration**: The act of working with the enemy army or government which has taken control of your country by force. The collaborators give help to the enemy.

Goering, as Commissioner of the Five-Year Plan, and Fritz Sauckel, the official responsible for the supply of labour to German industries. It took a number of forms, including the exploitation of local resources, such as the coal deposits of Silesia, the adaptation of local plant to German requirements, the transfer of some of that plant to German factories, and the recruitment of foreign labour for service in Germany. In the west, this last task was often tackled by subtle enticements, such as the promise of higher wages or the placing of obstacles in the way of local employment, but in eastern Europe physical force was the norm. Seven million foreign workers had been transferred to German factories by 1944, not more than 200,000 of them as volunteers, and foreign resources in the same year supplied some 20%–25% of the rations consumed by German civilians.

Although the system was effective in terms of quantity, it had its drawbacks. Forced labour was bound to be unreliable, especially in more skilled jobs, and the system provided tremendous problems for a transport network also committed to supplying troops on several fronts. As the historian Norman Rich points out, in *Hitler's War Aims* (1974), the two tasks of the occupation administrations frequently clashed with each other, when the military advantages of a friendly local population were sacrificed to the economic and ideological demands for suppression and exploitation.

Terror was a standard feature of the 'new order'. Sometimes it was deliberately applied as a matter of policy, as by the special SS squads (*Einsatzgruppen*) whose specific task in some eastern areas was to purge undesirable groups. The 33,000 Jews murdered at Babi Yar in the Ukraine (September 1941) were some of the victims of these groups. Sometimes atrocities were a means of reprisal following local opposition or resistance. Proclaiming that 'wars are not won by the methods of the Salvation Army', Hitler fully approved of General Keitel's 'Night and Mist' (*Nacht und Nebel*) order (December 1941) which prescribed death as the automatic punishment for any act of sabotage or resistance, and advised **summary execution**. Most occupied territories suffered some example of the German tactic of destroying whole communities, often at random, as reprisals for attacks upon German personnel. The deaths of nearly 200 innocent civilians at Lidice in Czechoslovakia (May 1942) and of 642 at Oradour sur Glane in France (July 1944) are the most notorious examples. To this list could be added Palmiry (near Warsaw), Televaag (Norway), Boves (Italy) and Putten (Netherlands).

### How and why did politicians in the occupied territories collaborate with the Nazis?

Resistance to this Nazi 'new order', especially in the first two years of the war, remained the prerogative of a brave, but small, minority. The apparent finality of the German victories up to the end of 1941 made it seem that the main problem of the conquered was how to live with the conquerors. In general, as the historian Norman Rich concludes, 'the response of the European peoples to Nazi dominion reflects an instinct of people everywhere to cling to life and to seek physical and economic security for themselves and their families'.

**Collaboration** was especially evident in France where Pierre Laval, Foreign Minister from October 1940 and Prime Minister from April 1942, showed particular enthusiasm for co-operation with Germany. Although this made him the special butt of allied propaganda and led to his execution in 1945, Laval's fault was an inability to appreciate the international extent of the conflict, rather than any true sympathy with Nazi aims. Laval's motives were, indeed, simple. They were to save France from the fate of Poland, from dismemberment and disintegration. To do this it was necessary to co-operate with the new masters of Europe. Others had more positive motives, springing from an actual sympathy with the aims of Nazism, sometimes anti-semitic, sometimes anti-British, often anti-Communist. Thirdly, many collaborated simply because the Germans were the winners, with the money, the resources, business contracts and influence that people still sought in war as in peace.

France provided a rare example of an established government, staffed by credible, pre-war politicians, collaborating enthusiastically with the Germans. Yet western Europe provided many other examples of 'puppet' administrations and national Fascist bodies willing to co-operate for opportunist or ideological reasons. The Netherlands had a Nazi party, under A.A. Mussert, which claimed a membership of 50,000 during the war. Belgium had its Flemish nationalists under Staf de Clercq, who saw collaboration with the Germans as a means of breaking the power of the French-speaking **Walloons**. Not to be outdone, the Walloons produced enthusiastic collaborators of their own, in the form of the Rexist movement, led by Leon Degrelle. In Norway, the government of Vidkun Quisling, whose name gave a new word to the English language to describe such collaborators, enthusiastically supported the ideology of Nazism, but generally failed to convince the Norwegian people of its value. In all of these cases, the relationship with Germany ended in frustration as it became clear that Hitler sought, not ideological support, but unconditional domination.

### Collaboration in eastern Europe

If open collaboration was rarer in eastern Europe, it was because Nazi theory generally forbade co-operation with the 'sub-human' Slavs. Some such co-operation, however, still existed. Even in the USSR racial minorities such as Tartars and Chechens sought German aid against Soviet oppression, and a Russian Liberation Army under General A.A. Vlasov numbered 50,000 men by the end of the war. Similarly, the anti-communist attitudes of Dmitri Mihailovic and his Chetnik force, and of Ante Pavelic in Yugoslavia offered possibilities for the German and Italian occupiers, which were generally thrown away because of the brutal and callous attitudes of Nazism towards the Slavs.

## What did collaboration achieve?

The benefits of collaboration varied from case to case. In France, Laval's policy bore little fruit. It did not greatly hasten the return of prisoners-of-war, did not prevent a 50% rise in the mortality rate due largely to cases of malnutrition, and did not save France from total occupation when German interests demanded it (November 1942). On the other hand, it served the Germans well:

● 37% of all German materials and finances from foreign sources came from France, and tanks and army trucks rolled off the production lines of Renault and Berliet.

● 45,000 Frenchmen joined the *Milice*.

Elsewhere, the results were sometimes better. Slovakia was spared a German occupation by the co-operation of Joseph Tiso's government, while Admiral Horthy ensured that Hungary escaped lightly. Denmark succeeded in preserving its monarchy, part of its army, and even most of its Jews, all 7,000 of whom were smuggled into neutral Sweden. In short, it was sometimes possible after the war to justify collaboration in terms of short-term local successes. In the wider context of Nazi inhumanity, the policy was always much harder to justify.

---

**Walloons**: The term used to describe the French-speaking natives of the Walloon provinces of Belgium.

---

**Vidkun Quisling (1887–1945)**
Leader from 1933 of the Norwegian Fascist Party. He aided the Nazis invasion of Norway in 1940 by delaying mobilisation of troops and by urging non-resistance. Quisling was made premier by Hitler (1942), but was arrested and shot as a traitor by the Norwegians three years later. His name (Quisling) became a generic term in the English language for a traitor who aids an occupying force.

---

**Milice**: A French paramilitary force that combated the resistance and attempted to maintain domestic stability in the last years of the occupation.

---

1. What were the main aims of the Nazi 'new order' (a) as portrayed in German propaganda and (b) in reality?

2. How effectively was the German war effort served by the Nazi authorities in the occupied territories?

3. Who benefited most from policies of collaboration, the Nazis or the populations of the territories that they occupied?

# 4.6 Why did the Nazis pursue a 'Final Solution to the Jewish Question' in the war years?

'Final Solution' (*Endlösung*): This was the euphemism (polite expression) employed in German administration to describe the strategy of mass genocide by which German Jews and those in territories under German occupation would be systematically murdered in extermination camps or elsewhere. The implementation of this strategy is now more commonly referred to as 'the Holocaust'.

## The prelude to the 'final solution'

The unprecedented domination that the Nazis enjoyed over the continent of Europe also provided them with the opportunity to implement the obsessive anti-semitism that was a prominent principle of their movement. Like his foreign policy, Hitler's anti-semitism was a mixture of unswerving principle and uncertain means. For all his hostility towards them, Hitler had little clear idea in 1939 what he intended to do with the Jews. The most likely official plan was that which called for the shipment of European Jews to the island of Madagascar in the Indian Ocean, which would be demanded from France for that purpose after that nation's defeat. The first two years of warfare, however, caused the rethinking of this plan. Firstly, although France was defeated, the continuing hostility of Britain made regular sea access to Madagascar difficult. Secondly, the fall of Poland enlarged the Jewish 'problem' dramatically. Whereas the Reich in 1939 had a Jewish population of about 357,000, the large number of Polish Jews meant that there were ten times that number in the Greater Reich in 1940.

Prior to and during the war, the Nazis maintained concentration camps, principally for containing Jews and Soviet prisoners of war, but also political prisoners, gypsies, homosexuals, people with disabilities and the mentally ill. Many camps were located in occupied Poland, allowing the Nazis to transport German Jews outside of the German main territory. Meanwhile, Polish Jews were also being systematically moved into ever more crowded ghettoes. These tightly packed, specially designated areas of Eastern European cities were rife with starvation, illness, and consequently, high mortality rates. The Warsaw Ghetto was the largest of these ghettos, with 380,000 people (30% of the population forced to live in an area covering 2.4% of the city). The ghettos were walled off, and any Jew discovered leaving them was shot. In January 1942 after continued Soviet resistance had ruled out the interim plan of dumping the Jews in Siberia, it was officially resolved that the 'final solution to the Jewish question' was to consist of wholesale and systematic extermination.

Although millions of prisoners died in concentration camps through mistreatment, disease, starvation, and overwork, or were executed as unfit for labour, Holocaust scholars make a point of drawing a distinction between concentration camps and extermination (or death) camps. Extermination camps were purpose-built during a later phase of the program of annihilation in occupied Poland and Belarus at Chelmno, Treblinka, Sobibor and Belzec. Auschwitz II was actually part of a pre-existing labour camp complex. In the earlier years of the Holocaust, Jews were primarily sent to concentration camps or the ghettos, but from 1942 onward they were mostly deported to the extermination camps where most died in the gas chambers as soon as they arrived. Almost 300,000 people were deported from the Warsaw Ghetto to Treblinka in less than eight weeks.

## The scale of the 'final solution'

Between 1941 and 1944, technological refinements – such as the special Cyclon-B gas and specially designed ovens for incineration – allowed the 'final solution' to proceed with awful efficiency. Treblinka amassed up to 6,000 victims a day at its peak, while Auschwitz was responsible for the murder of some three million people in the course of three years.

The German government declared in November 1943, although it was not entirely correct, that there were no Jews left in the Greater Reich. By the end of the war, 50% of Belgian Jews, 66% of Romanian Jews and 75% of the Dutch community were dead. The best records for the protection of Jews were those of Denmark and of France, although in the latter case the government only preserved the lives of French Jews by assisting the capture and deportation of those who were not French citizens. Lucy Dawidowicz, in *The War Against the Jews, 1933–1945* (1990), has settled upon a figure of 5.93 million as the final toll of Jewish victims, estimating that it embraces 67% of occupied Europe's pre-war Jewish population. Nor should it be forgotten that some three million non-Jews, mainly Slavs and political opponents of Nazism, also died in extermination camps. These camps were responsible for the destruction, in the most horrible circumstances, of some 7.5 million human lives. Such is the monument to the 'new order' of Nazism.

### The 'final solution' in the context of the war

**1. What was Hitler's 'final solution' to the 'Jewish problem'?**

**2. How effective was the Nazis' implementation of the 'final solution'?**

The insane intensity of this anti-semitism is illustrated by the fact that, while locked in an increasingly unsuccessful war, the German government still saw fit to devote substantial resources of manpower, communications and technology to this horrible task. In the midst of the eastern campaigns in 1942, trainloads of Jews from France, Belgium and the Netherlands were being shipped the length of Europe to the eastern camps. In 1943 and 1944, the SS was still expanding its programme to deal with Greek and Hungarian Jews. Only in October 1944, with the Red Army threatening to overrun the camps, did Himmler give the order for them to cease their dreadful routine.

## 4.7 Did the resistance movements in occupied Europe play any significant role in the defeat of Nazi Germany?
### A CASE STUDY IN HISTORICAL INTERPRETATION

The German victories in the early stages of the war seemed to be so definitive that resistance to the Nazi 'new order' appeared useless. Only a small, but highly honourable minority chose to resist. Writing of the French resistance movements after 1941, in *France 1940–55* (1957), Alexander Werth identified simple national pride as the basis of other motives:

> 'they resisted because it was a matter of ordinary self respect to do so. They were unwilling to accept that while London was "taking it", or that while the Red Army was fighting the Battle of Stalingrad, France was doing nothing.'

Secondly, the brutality of German policy in the occupied territories convinced many of the need for resistance. This was especially true in the eastern territories, where the recruitment of forced labour made resistance the surer means towards survival. In France, too, it was the recruitment of labour that drove many young men into the countryside, where their groups took their names from the shrub-like bushes (*maquis*) that gave them shelter.

The entry into the war of the Soviet Union also stimulated resistance, setting the Communist parties of the occupied countries, previously nonplussed by the Russo–German Pact of 1939, in opposition to the invaders. In September 1941, General Keitel, as Chief of Staff, ordered that all acts of resistance or sabotage should be ascribed to Communists and that batches of alleged Communists should be executed as reprisals. Communists thus had little to lose by active resistance.

## How effective was this resistance?

In many countries at the end of the war, national commentators attached great importance to the role that resistance had played in the defeat of Nazism. The official history of the French resistance movements ran to four volumes, and the title of the relevant volume in Henri Amouroux's comprehensive history of the occupation (*History of the French under the Occupation*, 1979), 'The People Awake', summarises the image that such writers wished to convey. Historians surveying the part played by resistance movements in the allied victory as a whole have generally been less impressed. Alan Milward, in *The German Economy at War* (1965), puts forward the view that in no case did a resistance movement seriously defeat German military intentions. The crushing of the Warsaw Rising (August 1944) and the heavy losses of the French resistance at Vercors (June 1944) showed the relative impotence of resistance forces when not backed by allied troops. The assassination of Reinhard Heydrich, 'Protector' of Bohemia and Moravia, was paid for with 1,500 Czech lives and the destruction of the villages of Lidice and Lezaky. The price exacted by the Germans in reprisals leads Alan Milward to his conclusion that resistance 'seems to have been seldom effective, sometimes stultifying, frequently dangerous, and almost always too costly'. Referring to France in particular, the historian John Keegan in *The Battle for History: Re-fighting the Second World War* (1995) reaches similar conclusions, stating that the resistance movement was 'a nuisance rather than an impediment to German operations'.

The impact of resistance must, in any case, be measured against the benefits that the occupiers gained from economic collaboration. Of all French exports, 82% went to Germany in 1943, and 84% of all Dutch exports. The expansion of the German army in the years of 'total war' would have been impossible without the industrial labour that was recruited from the occupied states. By 1944, this amounted to seven million workers, roughly 20% of the total labour force within Germany. In 1944, 10% of the French adult male population between 18 and 50 years of age was thus employed in Germany. It is impossible to resist the conclusion, therefore, that the support that the German war effort gained from the occupied territories of western Europe far outweighed any damage that the resistance movements could do to it.

It is important, however, to distinguish between the slight effect of resistance in western Europe, and the very different role that it played in eastern Europe. There, in John Keegan's words, 'it caused the occupiers considerable trouble, ranging in scale from chronic insecurity to outright civil war'. Although this can be explained in large part by the savage racial attitudes that the Nazis adopted towards local populations in the east, Keegan also links it to historical traditions of peasant opposition to national governments and, in the Balkans, to long traditions of local opposition to Turkish rule. In Greece and in Yugoslavia, resistance amounted effectively to lesser wars within the greater war. In Yugoslavia, Tito's **partisan movement** fought not only against the Germans, but equally against domestic elements, such as Bosnian Muslims, who viewed German occupation as a means of escaping Serbian domination. Thus the struggle against the Germans and their supporters effectively made Yugoslavia ungovernable, but at an enormous price. The war years probably claimed as many as 1.6 million lives, about 10% of the pre-war population. Similarly, in the Soviet Union, partisan groups played an important role in areas under German occupation. By mid-1942 there were an estimated 150,000 partisan fighters operating behind German lines in the Soviet Union, disrupting communications and tying down large numbers of regular troops.

**Partisan movement**: An official organisation, made up of armed fighters, that is formed in a country occupied by enemy soldiers. The intention of the movement is to disrupt the occupying force as much as possible, usually by fighting.

In both western and eastern Europe, resistance groups achieved their greatest military impact when the German war effort was weakening and they could co-operate directly with advancing allied forces. In the west, resistance actions delayed and weakened important German units moving to combat the Normandy landings. The French FFI (*Forces Françaises de l'Intérieur*) also played a significant role in the liberation of several French cities and in the final thrust into Germany. Sixty thousand Czech partisans fought with the Soviet Army, and local partisan forces played a major part in the liberation of Belgrade, and of many of the cities of northern Italy.

If it is difficult to argue that local resistance fighters changed the course of the war in general, it is possible to detect cases in which local initiatives did much to obstruct specific elements of Nazi policy. A prime example is that of Denmark. Overall, that country was controlled quite comfortably by the Nazis, and its political life showed a remarkable degree of continuity. When the occupying authorities attempted to implement the 'final solution', however, it received no co-operation from the Danes. In *The Rescue of the Danish Jews: Moral Courage under Stress* (1987), historian Leo Goldberger has shown how the entire Danish Jewish community was smuggled to safety in neutral Sweden. In the military context of the war, the Norwegian resistance also made an extremely important contribution through its co-operation with British intelligence agents to deny Germany the supplies that it needed to advance its atomic programme.

Most forms of non-violent resistance were of largely local significance. Norway provided a fine example of passive resistance when its bishops and high court judges resigned *en masse*. The dissemination of war news and propaganda was another important, but more dangerous, function. In Belgium alone some 300 illegal journals were published, and over 1,000 such papers appeared in France between 1940 and 1944. Belgium was also the centre of a complex network of groups specialising in the sheltering of allied airmen shot down over Europe, and in smuggling them back to home bases. Similar networks in Poland and in Czechoslovakia did valuable work by providing intelligence on German troop movements to allied forces. Considering such examples as these, the historian M.R.D. Foot in *Resistance* (1978) draws the important conclusion that 'the greatest good that resistance did lay in the hearts of the people who took part in it'. The greatest contribution of resistance lay not so much in what it achieved during the war, as in the contribution that it made after the war to the re-establishment of national self-confidence and self-respect. This was particularly true in France, where the traumatic shock of defeat and occupation had been devastating, and where its scars still exist.

**1. What different conclusions have historians drawn about the importance of resistance movements during the Second World War?**

**2. In what respects, and for what reasons, have historians disagreed about the importance of resistance movements in the history of the Second World War as a whole?**

---

## Source-based questions: Collaboration in France during the Second World War

**Study the following source material and then answer the questions which follow.**

### SOURCE A

It is with honour and to maintain ten centuries of French unity within the context of the new European order that I enter today upon the path of collaboration. This collaboration must be sincere. It must involve patient and confident effort. The present armistice is not a peace settlement. France is bound by many obligations with regard to her conqueror, but at least she retains her sovereignty.

From Marshal Pétain's radio broadcast to the French people, 30 October 1940. Pétain was the leader of the Vichy government in France 1940–42.

---

**Source-based questions: Collaboration in France during the Second World War**

## SOURCE B

My desire is to re-establish normal and trusting relations with Germany and with Italy. A new Europe will inevitably arise from this war, and I wish for a German victory because, without it, Bolshevism will establish itself everywhere. When I say that this policy is the only one that can ensure the status of France and guarantee her development in the peace to come, you must believe me and follow me. This war is a revolution from which a new world will spring. A younger Republic, stronger and more humane, will be born.

From a speech by Pierre Laval, Prime Minister of the Vichy government, 22 June 1942

## SOURCE C

As far as the case of France is concerned, the main point is to ensure that a French government continues to function on French soil. This will be much preferable to the situation that would arise if the French government refused to accept German terms, and fled abroad, to London, to continue the war. Apart from the problems that would arise with regard to the administration of the occupied territory, an understanding with the French government would be equally advantageous because of the French fleet. If that fleet were placed at the disposition of the British, in some categories of ships, British naval strength would be doubled.

Adolf Hitler explains to Mussolini his policy towards France, 18 June 1940.

---

**(a) Use Source A and your own knowledge.**

**Explain briefly why Pétain refers to a 'new order' in European affairs.**

**(b) Use Sources A and B and your own knowledge.**

**Explain how the motives for collaboration with Germany expressed in Source B differ from those expressed in Source A.**

**(c) Use Sources A, B and C and your own knowledge.**

**How far does your knowledge of wartime collaboration, and the evidence contained in these sources, support the view that the Nazi regime always gained more from collaboration than the governments that collaborated with it?**

---

**Source-based questions: The Holocaust**

**Study the following four passages and answer both of the sub-questions which follow.**

## SOURCE A

To supplement the task that was assigned to you on 24 January 1939, which dealt with the solution of the Jewish problem by emigration and evacuation in the most suitable way: I hereby charge you with making all necessary preparations with regard to organisational, technical and material matters for bringing about a complete solution of the Jewish question within the German sphere of influence in Europe. Whatever other government agencies are involved, these are to co-operate with you. I request you further to send me, in the near future, an overall plan covering the organisational, technical and material measures necessary for the accomplishment of the final solution of the Jewish question, which we desire.

An order signed by Herman Goering and dispatched to senior SS officers in July 1941

## SOURCE B

The criminal mass destruction of the Jews must not be seen simply as the continuation of the legal discrimination against the Jews after 1933. Procedurally this was in fact a break with former practices and in that respect had a different quality. All the same, the previous laws and decrees which step by step had further discriminated against the Jews in Germany, had subjected them to emergency laws and had condemned them to a social ghetto, paved the way for the 'Final Solution'.

From Martin Broszat, *The Hitler State*, published in 1981. This historian argues that the 'Final Solution' was an escalation of earlier German anti-semitic policies, and separate from them.

## SOURCE C

Anti-semitism was the core of Hitler's system of beliefs and the central motivation of his policies. He believed himself to be the saviour who would bring redemption to the German people through the annihilation of the Jews, the people who embodied, in his eyes, the Satanic hosts. From the moment he made his entrance upon the historical stage until his death in a Berlin bunker, the sense of messianic mission never departed from him, nor could any appeal to reason deflect him from pursuing his murderous purpose.

From Lucy Dawidowicz, *The War against the Jews 1933–45*, published in 1975. This historian argues that violent anti-semitism was always central to Nazi policy and that the 'Final Solution' was its logical culmination.

## SOURCE D

The genocide was the outgrowth not of Hitler's moods, not of local initiatives, not of the impersonal hand of structural obstacles, but of Hitler's idea to eliminate all Jewish power, an idea that was broadly shared in Germany. Rarely has a national leader so openly, frequently and emphatically announced an apocalyptic intention – in this case, to destroy Jewish power and even the Jews themselves – and made good on his promise. It is almost inexplicable that interpreters today could construe Hitler's oft stated intention to destroy the Jews to have been meant but metaphorically, or to have been but meaningless verbiage. The will to kill the Jews was not infused into Hitler and his followers by external conditions. Racial anti-semitism was the motive force of the eliminationist programme, pushing it to its logical genocidal conclusion once German military prowess succeeded in creating appropriate conditions.

From Daniel Goldhagen, *Hitler's Willing Executioners*, published in 1996. This historian argues that the Holocaust was always the intended outcome of Hitler's anti-semitic philosophy, and that it was only delayed because Germany lacked the practical means to implement it.

**(a)** Compare the conclusions reached in passages B and D about the degree of continuity that existed in Nazi anti-semitic policy.

**(b)** Using these four passages and your own knowledge, explain how and why historians disagree about the development of the Final Solution in Nazi anti-semitic policy.

# 4.8 Why did the Axis collapse in 1944–1945?

### The assault on Italy and the collapse of the Fascist government

The clearance of German and Italian troops from North Africa by combined British and American forces by May 1943 left the southern flank of Fascist Europe exposed. The daunting task of renewing the offensive against 'Fortress Europe' began (10 July 1943) with an allied assault upon Sicily, at the southern tip of Italy. It was not strongly resisted by the Axis forces and within six weeks the island was in allied hands. The decision to proceed from Sicily to the Italian mainland was unpopular with Stalin, who preferred an attack upon German forces in France, to relieve pressure upon the Soviet Union. However, it was based upon sound strategic sense. Italy was clearly the weakest point of the Axis, and by its elimination from the war the Mediterranean could be secured, and bases could be won for a future assault upon Germany.

The capture of Sicily caused the final crisis for the Italian Fascist government and transformed Italy's position in the war. Having joined Hitler's war effort when success seemed certain, Mussolini now faced an invasion of Italian territory, deprived of the services of 200,000 troops killed or captured in North Africa, and of a further million committed to distant theatres of war. Resistance to the allies could only be maintained by turning the country over to the Germans, clearly a terrible price to pay, and a rejection of all that Fascist nationalism stood for. Mussolini's failure to extricate himself from the

**1. Even if it were not dated, what elements in the cartoon indicate that it was published in the latter stages of the war?**

**2. Why would the Soviet government have been unlikely to publish this form of anti-German propaganda in 1941 or 1942?**

A Soviet cartoon published in 1944. The original caption read: 'The general from the Eastern Front seeks orders, and the Führer deliberates.'

**Cost-of-living index**: A list of the prices charged for goods and services. It is updated on a regular basis and shows how much prices are rising or falling.

disastrous German alliance caused the collapse of his political position which was wrecked by strikes and demonstrations, by the withdrawal of the support of the Fascist Grand Council (24 July 1943), and by his dismissal as Prime Minister by the King (25 July). Briefly, the Fascist government survived under the leadership of Marshal Badoglio. He had two primary aims: to maintain the credibility of Fascism, and to lead Italy into the allied camp without substantial German reprisals. On both counts he failed. While anti-Fascist partisan forces reduced parts of Italy to a state of civil war, and Italian forces disintegrated in the confusion, the German High Command took the decision to defend as much of the country as possible from the allied forces now on the mainland (9 September 1943).

Defending first the Gustav Line, midway between Naples and Rome, then the Gothic Line 190 kilometres further north, the *Wehrmacht* ensured that the allies would have to fight for every metre of Italian soil. Mussolini, sensationally rescued from imprisonment and installed as head of the 'Italian Social Republic' in the north, found himself reduced to the 'puppet' status of many of Germany's would-be allies. It was perhaps the logical outcome of his 'savage friendship' with Hitler. Rome was not occupied by the allies until 4 June 1944, and German troops continued to resist in Milan and other northern cities long after allied troops had crossed the Rhine.

The price paid by the allies for the 18 months of warfare in Italy was high, but for Italy itself that period constituted the final disaster of Fascism. A further 100,000 Italians died in military action, and bombing raids caused great damage to the cultural heritage of the nation. The destruction of the Benedictine monastery of Monte Cassino was only the worst example of many. Inflation and the **cost-of-living index** soared, the latter from a base of 100 in 1938 to 5,313 in October 1947. On top of this came political collapse. Badoglio's government disintegrated in June 1944 and King Victor Emmanuel III abdicated in May 1946. Forty-three days later a referendum in favour of a republic ended 85 years of Italian monarchy. Mussolini did not live to see all this. Captured by partisans as he tried to flee into Switzerland, he was shot without trial, and his body hanged from a meat hook in a Milan square (28–29 April 1945).

## The Western Front

By the beginning of 1944 British and American commanders were able to concentrate men and materials for their greatest undertaking, the re-invasion of France. The technical difficulties facing 'Operation Overlord' were enormous, including the laying of oil pipelines across the Channel, and the designing of artificial 'Mulberry' harbours to provide anchorages for subsequent supply ships. German hopes of resisting the invasion depended entirely on checking it on the landing beaches. That the High Command failed to do so owed much to the element of surprise, for they had judged an invasion more likely in the region of Calais, rather than in Normandy, and much to the enormous air superiority of the allies.

On D-Day (6 July 1944), the allies began to land 326,000 men along an 80-kilometre stretch of beach. Within a month, a million men had landed, suffering only 9,000 fatal casualties. Stiff German resistance around Caen and Falaise could not be sustained after a further American landing in the south (15 August). The collapse of German control in France was subsequently rapid. Paris was liberated, appropriately by Free French forces, on 24 August. Brussels and Antwerp were freed in the first week of September.

Dresden in ruins, 1945

By the onset of autumn, German forces were manning the defences of the Siegfried Line on their own frontiers.

The German war effort, however, was not quite exhausted. Contemporary historian Sir Basil Liddell Hart has stressed the decision of the allies to demand unconditional surrender, and the importance of this decision in encouraging last-ditch German resistance. In the last days of 1944 the *Wehrmacht* enjoyed its last successes on the Western Front. It defeated an allied attempt to outflank the Siegfried Line at Arnhem (17–24 September), and temporarily regained ground in the Ardennes by the counter-attack known as the 'Battle of the Bulge' (16 December 1944 – 13 January 1945). The first months of 1945, however, saw its steady disintegration. The *Wehrmacht* had to make good its losses by the conscription of raw teenagers, fuel supplies were on the brink of exhaustion, and the *Luftwaffe* had finally lost the struggle for air supremacy. Brilliant new weapons, such as the Messerschmitt 262 jet fighter and the V1 and V2 rockets, came too late to save the Reich.

### The last stages of the German collapse

The surviving German units proved quite insufficient to prevent an allied crossing of the Rhine (7–23 March 1945). Thereafter the main cities of Germany fell regularly to the advancing allied forces until advanced American units made contact with the Soviet army at Torgau in Saxony (25 April 1945). Hitler's vision of a defeated Germany destroying itself in a Wagnerian 'Twilight of the Gods' came to nothing. Civilian morale was severely strained by the 'Thousand Bomber' raids on Dresden (13–14 February). Also the planned yard-by-yard resistance of the German 'Home Guard' (*Volkssturm*) failed to materialise, and local and central officials at last showed open defiance of Hitler's will by disobeying orders to destroy strategic buildings and important industrial plant.

## The Eastern Front

The rapid allied successes in the west owed much to the heavy German commitment on the Russian front. There, the campaigns of 1943 continued to be fought deep into Soviet territory, but with the Soviet army steadily developing numerical and technical superiority. A German counter-attack at Kharkov (February 1943) achieved considerable success, but could not be sustained, and an attempt to drive back Soviet forces at Kursk (July 1943) was thwarted in the biggest tank battle of the war. In the south, the Soviet army's own counter-attacks after the Battle of Kursk drove the German forces back to the river Dnieper and cut off those units occupying the Crimea.

In 1944 it was the turn of the northern units of the *Wehrmacht* to feel the weight of the Soviet offensive. In 1943 they had held a defensive line from Orel to Leningrad relatively comfortably, an illustration of the error of Hitler's offensive strategy in the south. Now, a series of massive Soviet campaigns finally broke the encirclement of Leningrad (January 1944), re-occupied Minsk in White Russia (July), and drove into Poland and the Baltic territories (August), capturing 30 German divisions in the process. Then offensives in the south cleared Soviet soil of German troops and caused the surrender of Germany's Romanian (August) and Bulgarian (September) allies.

### The Soviet thrust into Germany

In the east, as in the west, the beginning of 1945 saw allied troops poised for the final thrust into the Greater German Reich. Although more heavily manned and equipped on the Eastern Front, Germany was similarly in no shape to resist. Hitler himself was now ravaged by nervous disease. As historian Alan Bullock describes him, in *Hitler: A Study in Tyranny* (1962), 'his orders became wilder and more contradictory, his demands more impossible, his decisions more arbitrary. His answer to every proposal was: no withdrawal.' In addition, Hitler had shattered his own High Command, dismissing such able generals as Erich von Manstein and Gerd von Rundstedt for their failures to carry out impossible tasks. Gunther von Kluge and Erwin Rommel had both committed suicide when their roles in a plot to murder Hitler and set the war upon a sounder footing (July 1944) were discovered.

The final assault, by four armies on a front from the Baltic to the Carpathian mountains, made rapid progress. In March, Soviet forces crossed the Oder river, driving beyond Berlin to ensure that it was their forces, and not those of their allies, that occupied the German capital. Although he has been criticised for it since, the commander of the western forces, General Eisenhower, kept strictly to the spheres of influence agreed by the political leaders and there was no race for Berlin.

The week from 30 April to 7 May 1945 witnessed the last days of the Third Reich. Raging against the incompetence of his generals, and repeating his doctrines of anti-semitism and of the German need for *Lebensraum*, Hitler killed himself on 30 April and had his body burned to ensure that it could not be treated as that of Mussolini had been. On 7 May, after several unsuccessful attempts to negotiate separate peace treaties and so to divide the allies, the German government ended the war in Europe by surrendering unconditionally to the combined allied forces.

1. What were the main military blows that the allies struck at German control of mainland Europe between 1943 and 1945?

2. To what extent do you agree with the claim that 'the success of the D-Day landings was the crucial factor in the defeat of Germany'?

## 4.9  What plans had the allies made for a peace settlement?

Although Germany and its allies entered the war with complex but quite well defined aims, its opponents, especially Britain and the Soviet Union, fought originally for no other reason than that war was forced upon them by German aggression. At first, their war aims were simple and largely negative; to survive, and to destroy Nazism as a means to survival.

Only in 1942 did it become practical to consider in detail the settlement that the allies should pursue in the event of their victory. In the diplomatic discussions that followed, three main European issues were at stake:

● the treatment of Germany after its defeat

● the fate of eastern European states

● the means of ensuring future stability.

General principles 'for common action to preserve peace and resist aggression in the post-war period' had been laid down in an Anglo–Russian treaty of May 1942, and by British agreements with America. Only in November 1943 did the allied leaders, Churchill, Roosevelt and Stalin, meet at Tehran in Iran, to define details. Although the Tehran meeting was preoccupied with military strategy against Germany, it contained the seeds of the post-war settlement and gave early indications of Soviet ambitions. Roosevelt suggested that post-war Germany be divided into five sectors, with its industrial heartlands of the Ruhr, the Saar, Hamburg and the Kiel Canal placed under international control. Stalin, determined that the Soviet Union would no longer be threatened by the instability of its immediate European neighbours, produced a 'shopping list'. This list stipulated future Soviet influence in East Prussia, and in most of those territories gained as a result of the 1939 pact with Germany.

The next meeting of the allied leaders was over a year later, at Yalta in the Crimea (4 February 1945). By then, German resistance was on the verge of collapse, and much of eastern Europe was in the hands of the Soviet Army. Roosevelt and Churchill have since incurred criticism for their apparent acquiescence in the establishment of a substantial Soviet sphere of influence, but practical circumstances left them with little choice. Only by force could eastern Europe be wrested from Soviet control, and even then it seems unlikely that forceful tactics could have succeeded.

Thus, Stalin emerged from Yalta with confirmation of his dominance in Romania, Bulgaria, Hungary and Poland. There was to be a lesser degree of Soviet influence in Yugoslavia, and none in Greece, because the Mediterranean location of those states made them as much subject to Anglo–American sea power as to Soviet land power. In return for this agreement, to which the Soviet Union stuck closely, Stalin agreed wholesale to American proposals for a four-zone occupation of Germany, with a zone allocated to the French, and for the establishment of a **United Nations organisation**. The last great **tripartite** meeting, at Potsdam (July 1945), was mainly concerned with the detailed implementation of the Yalta agreements.

The broad concept of a 'world organisation' to replace the League of Nations had arisen at Tehran, and at a separate meeting of foreign ministers in Moscow (November 1943). Its specific format was thrashed out at an inter-allied conference at Dumbarton Oaks, Washington, in August–October 1944. Among other decisions, it was agreed that the major powers sitting permanently on the central council of the organisation could employ a veto over any measure that displeased them. Between April and June 1945 delegates of 50 nations met in San Francisco to draft what has become the United Nations Charter. The decision that the seat of the United Nations Organisation should be in New York was perhaps symbolic of the fact that Europe was no longer the focal point of world politics.

**United Nations organisation**: Formed after the Second World War. It tries to encourage international peace, co-operation and friendship.

**Tripartite**: Discussions or agreements involving three people, three groups or three countries.

## 4.10 What were the immediate consequences of the conflict?

### What was the cost of the war?

The impact of the Second World War upon the next generation of Europeans was two-fold: unparalleled physical and economic destruction, and revolutionary political change. The table on page 108, including non-European powers for purposes of comparison, shows the enormous cost of the war.

The human losses of the USSR alone in 1941–45 were equal to the total casualty toll of the First World War, and German losses were double those of the earlier conflict. The nature of the warfare in the Second World War

**Costs of the Second World War**

| | Probable military casualties | Probable civilian casualties | Probable cost (£ million) |
|---|---|---|---|
| USSR | 13,600,000 | 7,700,000 | 23,253 |
| Germany | 3,480,000 | 3,890,000 | 53,084 |
| Japan | 1,700,000 | 360,000 | 10,317 |
| Great Britain | 452,000 | 60,000 | 12,446 |
| Italy | 330,000 | 85,000 | 5,267 |
| USA | 295,000 | – | 62,560 |
| France | 250,000 | 360,000 | 27,818 |
| Poland | 120,000 | 5,300,000 | not known |

Why did the USSR lose so many soldiers and Poland so many civilians during the Second World War?

meant that British and French losses were lighter than in 1914–18, but the devastation of those areas that saw the bulk of the fighting exceeded all precedents. Again, the Soviet Union and Germany suffered most. In the USSR between half and three-quarters of all living quarters in the theatre of war were destroyed. In addition to its casualties, Europe faced the problem between 1939 and 1947 of some 16 million refugees rendered homeless by the fighting.

## What was the political impact upon Europe?

Although the war made no such impact upon the map of Europe as the Napoleonic Wars and the First World War had done, its effect upon the political balance of the continent was revolutionary. Fascism and Nazism, proclaimed by Mussolini and Hitler as the dominant doctrines of the next millennium, vanished and have made no significant reappearance. Even more remarkable was that Germany, the central feature of the last century of European history, also vanished. When, eventually, two states emerged from the post-war chaos, both were closely tied to one of the two power blocs that now dominated world politics. The dominance that Germany had long aspired to and had briefly enjoyed now passed to the Soviet Union. Although not dominating the eastern European states in the same fashion as Germany had done, its military and economic superiority over the socialist republics that arose with Soviet assistance in Czechoslovakia, Poland, Hungary, Bulgaria and Romania, survived intact for over 40 years with only two serious challenges. Although Yugoslavia avoided such direct influence from Moscow, its socialist philosophy affiliated it to this formidable eastern bloc.

Indeed, the Soviet Union could claim to have emerged from the war, not only as the main European power, but perhaps as the only European power of world stature. European global dominance was one of the major casualties of the last great European war. The intercontinental empires of Britain, France, Italy, Belgium and the Netherlands were racked with difficulties before 1939. The defeats of these powers, or the vast economic strain of their eventual victories, meant that the post-war history of their empires was one of steady liquidation. As a result, the whole nature of political confrontation in the world changed. It no longer centred around the economic and political ambitions of a few European states, but around the different conceptions of human freedom and democracy represented by the two great world powers – one created by refugees from Europe, the other as much Asian as European in its culture and history.

The war also contributed to the emergence of the other superpower. The enormous impact of the United States of America upon the war was matched by the impact of the war upon the USA. In 1940 a large proportion of America's economic potential remained unused, and the war played a crucial role in unleashing the full power of the world's greatest industrial economy.

The nature of the confrontation between these two great powers was determined by another major product of the Second World War. The nuclear arms race dated from the dropping by the USA of the first atomic bomb on the Japanese city of Hiroshima (6 August 1945), the culmination of the increasing sophistication of weaponry during the war. In this, as in many other respects, a new era of European and world history began in 1945.

**What changes did the Second World War bring about in the balance of political power in Europe?**

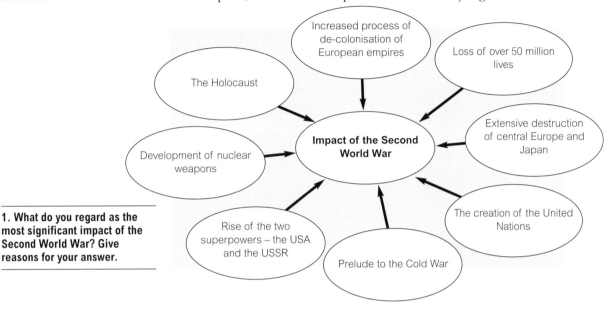

**1. What do you regard as the most significant impact of the Second World War? Give reasons for your answer.**

## Further Reading

### Texts designed for AS and A2 Level students

Many of the books on the national histories of the states that took part in the war contain details of the country's role in the Second World War. Little has been produced so far specifically for Sixth Form students that summarises the economic and social impacts of the war.

### More advanced reading

*Second World War* by Sir Martin Gilbert (Fontana, 1990)

*Total War: Causes and Courses of the Second World War* by Peter Calvocoressi and Guy Wint (Pelican, 1974)

*The Second World War* by John Keegan (Pimlico, 1989)

*The Road to Stalingrad* by John Erickson (Weidenfeld & Nicolson, 1975) and *The Road to Berlin* by John Erickson (Weidenfeld & Nicolson, 1983) form the definitive work on the war on the Eastern Front.

*Hitler's War Aims: The Establishment of the New Order* by Norman Rich (André Deutsch, 1974)

*Resistance* by M.R.D. Foot (Paladin, 1978)

*Life with the Enemy* by Werner Rings (Doubleday, 1982) deals with the balance between resistance and collaboration in the occupied territories.

*War, Economy and Society 1939–1945* by Alan Milward (Allen Lane, 1977) is the classic work on the economics and the economic implications of the war.

*The Battle for History: Re-Fighting the Second World War* by John Keegan (Hutchinson, 1995) provides a concise summary of historical debates on this subject.

# 5 The Cold War in Europe, 1945–1991

## Key Issues

- To what extent was the Cold War a global rather than a European problem?

- How did the division between East and West affect Europe during the Cold War?

- Why did the Cold War come to an end in 1991?

5.1 Historical interpretation: Why did a Cold War develop in Europe between 1945 and 1949?

5.2 How did the USSR establish control over eastern Europe 1945–1949?

5.3 Why was Germany a central issue during the Cold War?

5.4 Why was it difficult for the USSR to maintain control of eastern Europe between 1949 and 1989?

5.5 Why did the Cold War come to an end in 1991?

## Framework of Events

| | |
|---|---|
| 1945 | February: Yalta Conference between USSR, USA and Britain |
| | May: Germany surrenders |
| | July/August: Potsdam Conferences between USSR, USA and Britain |
| | August: Nuclear attacks on Hiroshima and Nagasaki |
| 1946 | Churchill's Iron Curtain Speech |
| | Kennan's Long Telegram |
| 1947 | Truman Doctrine |
| | Marshall Plan |
| | USA takes over from Britain in Greece and Turkey |
| 1948 | Czechoslovak coup |
| | Berlin Airlift Crisis |
| 1949 | End of Berlin airlift; formation of West Germany and East Germany |
| | Creation of NATO |
| | USSR explodes 'A' bomb |
| 1950 | Korean War begins |
| 1953 | Stalin dies |
| | Ceasefire in Korea |
| 1955 | Austrian State Treaty |
| | West Germany joins NATO |
| | Warsaw Pact formed |
| 1956 | 20th Party Congress of CPSU denounces Stalin |
| | Hungarian Uprising |
| | Poznan Rising in Poland |
| 1958 | Berlin Crisis begins |
| 1961 | Berlin Wall Crisis |
| 1968 | Prague Spring in Czechoslovakia |
| | Warsaw Pact invasion of Czechoslovakia |
| 1972 | *Détente* between USA and USSR |
| | SALT I treaty |
| 1975 | Helsinki Agreement |
| 1978 | John Paul II becomes Pope |

| 1979 | SALT II treaty |
|------|----------------|
|      | Pope visits Poland |
| 1980 | Solidarity movement begins in Poland |
| 1981 | Martial Law in Poland |
| 1985 | Mikhail Gorbachev becomes Soviet leader |
| 1988 | INF Treaty between USSR and USA |
| 1989 | Velvet Revolution in Czechoslovakia |
|      | Political change in Poland |
|      | Berlin Wall comes down |
| 1990 | Ceauçescu overthrown in Romania |
|      | East and West Germany unite into one country |
| 1991 | Anti-Gorbachev communist takeover prevented |
|      | Gorbachev replaced by Boris Yeltsin |
|      | Soviet Union collapses. |

| US Presidents 1945–1991 | Chancellors of West Germany, 1949–1998 | Soviet leaders 1945–1991 |
|---|---|---|
| 1945–1953 Harry S. Truman | | 1945–1953 Joseph Stalin |
| 1953–1961 Dwight D. Eisenhower | 1949–1963 Konrad Adenauer (Christian Democrat) | 1953–1955 Georgi Malenkov |
| 1961–1963 John F. Kennedy | | 1955–1958 Nikolai Bulganin and Nikita Khrushchev |
| 1963–1969 Lyndon B. Johnson | 1963–1966 Ludwig Erhard (Christian Democrat) | |
| 1969–1974 Richard M. Nixon | | 1958–1964 Nikita Khrushchev |
| 1974–1977 Gerald R. Ford | 1966–1969 Kurt Kiesinger (Christian Democrat) | 1964–1968 Alexander Kosygin and Leonid Brezhnev |
| 1977–1981 James E. Carter | | |
| 1981–1989 Ronald W. Reagan | 1969–1974 Willi Brandt (Social Democrat) | 1968–1982 Leonid Brezhnev |
| 1989–1993 George H. Bush | | 1982–1984 Yuri Andropov |
| | 1974–1982 Helmut Schmidt (Social Democrat) | 1984–1985 Konstantin Chernenko |
| | | 1985–1991 Mikhail Gorbachev |
| | 1982–1998 Helmut Kohl (Christian Democrat) | |

# Overview

**Bi-polar**: Division of the world into two major power blocs.

**Economic warfare**: Using trade and the world economy to undermine the opposition. It could involve placing tariffs (taxes) on opponents' goods, banning trade with, or buying goods from, the opposition.

FOR nearly 45 years after the Second World War Europe was divided by the Cold War. In the **bi-polar** world of the two superpowers, the USSR and the USA, Europe was one of the most important areas of political and military tension.

The Cold War describes the period of tension between the USSR and the USA. It began in 1945, although tension between the two powers had existed since the Bolshevik Revolution of 1917. The Cold War involved conflict short of direct war between the two superpowers. It saw both sides constantly prepared for war. This situation was supported by a propaganda war where each side adopted a strong ideological position. The USA regarded itself as leader of the Free World against godless Communism. The USSR was the leader of the socialist world against a capitalist system that exploited the world. Spying and **economic warfare** were part of the conflict. The Cold War was not limited to Europe. Following the

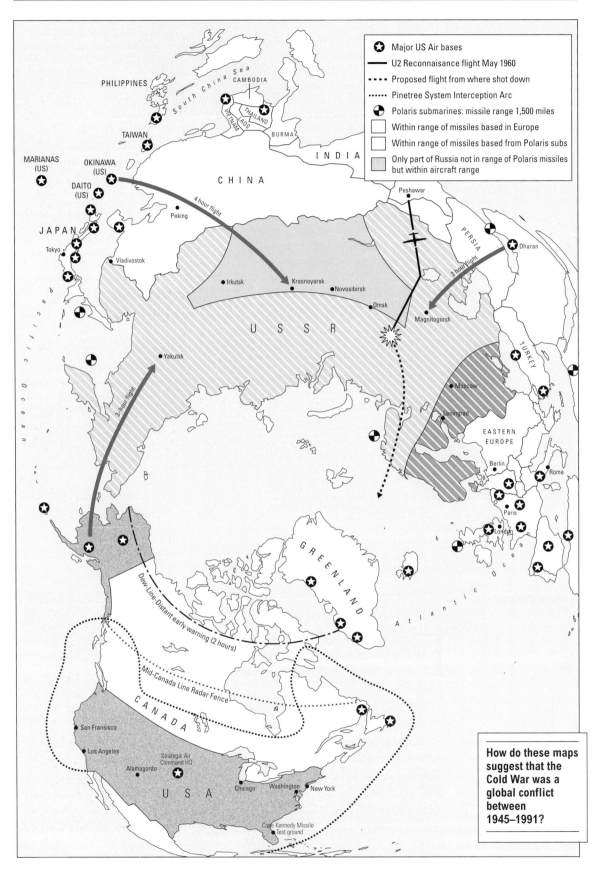

American preparedness in 1960

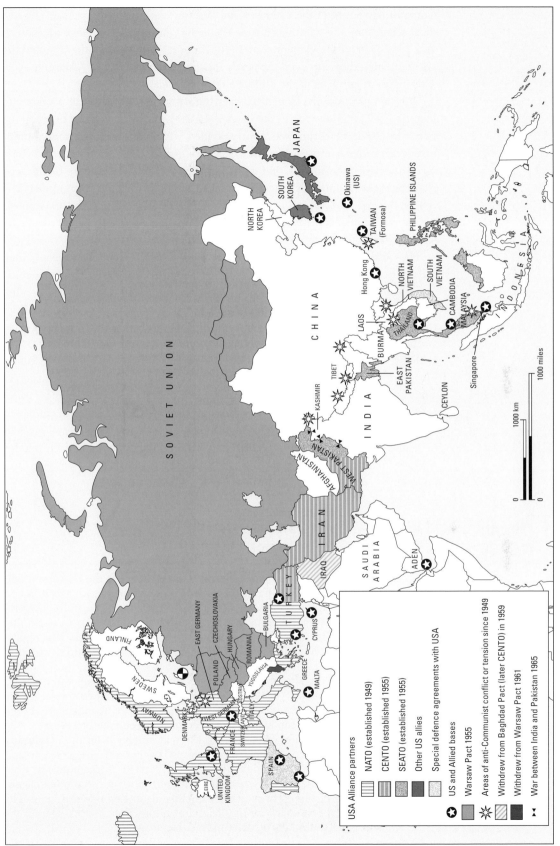

European and Asian alliances 1949–1965

**USA Alliance partners**

| | |
|---|---|
| ▥ | NATO (established 1949) |
| ▨ | CENTO (established 1955) |
| ▦ | SEATO (established 1955) |
| ▓ | Other US allies |
| ▩ | Special defence agreements with USA |
| ✪ | US and Allied bases |
| ▬ | Warsaw Pact 1955 |
| ✺ | Areas of anti-Communist conflict or tension since 1949 |
| ▨ | Withdrew from Baghdad Pact (later CENTO) in 1959 |
| ▬ | Withdrew from Warsaw Pact 1961 |
| ⤸ | War between India and Pakistan 1965 |

Communist victory in the Chinese Civil War, in 1949, it spread to Asia. The two most serious military conflicts during the Cold War occurred in Asia: the Korean War 1950–53 and the Vietnam War 1946–75. Furthermore, both the USA and the USSR attempted to 'win over' the newly independent countries of Africa and Asia. This involved conflicts in the Middle East and Africa.

Why a Cold War developed between two wartime allies is still a matter of historical debate. However, in the years 1945–49 Europe was divided between the two sides. By 1949 Europe was clearly divided into communist and non-communist sectors. In eastern Europe the USSR established communist regimes which owed allegiance to Moscow. Throughout the period 1949–1980, the USSR faced challenges to its control of eastern Europe. This ranged from anti-communist riots in East Berlin (1953) to full-scale revolution in Hungary (1956). By 1989 opposition to communist control of eastern Europe was so widespread that all the Soviet **satellite states** disappeared in a matter of months.

**Satellite states**: Countries which are under the influence of a larger and more powerful neighbouring country.

The Cold War's front line was Germany. Since 1945 Germany had been divided into military zones of occupation. Throughout the period Germany remained under military occupation. Within Germany Berlin epitomised the conflict between East and West. In 1961 all-out nuclear war seemed possible as a result of the erection of the Berlin Wall. Up to 1989 the border between East and West Germany remained one of the most heavily defended in the world.

The Cold War ended during the late 1980s for a variety of reasons: the failure of the Soviet economy to match the armaments spending of the USA; the succession of Mikhail Gorbachev to the Soviet leadership. His twin policies of *Glasnost* (openness) and *Perestroika* (restructuring) undermined Soviet political control in Eastern Europe.

With remarkable suddenness the Iron Curtain which had divided Europe for over a generation had disappeared by the end of December 1989. Two years later communist rule came to an end in the USSR.

## 5.1 Why did a Cold War develop in Europe between 1945 and 1949?
A CASE STUDY IN HISTORICAL INTERPRETATION

Ever since the break-up of the Grand Alliance between the USA, the USSR and the British Empire took place at the end of the Second World War, a debate has taken place among historians to explain the creation of the bi-polar world. Some historians have regarded the Cold War as beginning with the Bolshevik Revolution in Russia (1917). This created a new regime that had as its programme the conversion of the whole world to communism. The international dimension of Soviet Communism meant that it was seen as a threat to non-communist states such as Britain and the USA. As a result, hostility between East and West had occurred long before 1945. In fact, the Grand Alliance was a 'marriage of convenience' between states, which had been mutually hostile to each other before 1941.

This interpretation of events places great emphasis on the ideological differences between the Soviet communist system and the western capitalist system. Both sides highlighted this difference throughout the Cold War. The USSR saw itself as the defender of the world's exploited classes against 'Big Business' in western capitalist countries like the USA. The USA, in turn, saw itself as the defender of the 'Free World' against the international ambitions of a communist dictatorship.

However, rather than seeing the origins of the Cold War as a clash of different ideologies some historians have highlighted other factors. One of these is the Soviet desire for security. By 1945 the USSR had suffered considerable human and material damage. Around 27 million Soviet citizens had died in the Second World War. In addition, a large part of the western USSR had suffered economic devastation. From 1945 Stalin was determined to prevent any further invasions of the Soviet Union from Europe. He therefore aimed to create Soviet-style regimes in neighbouring countries which would be natural allies of the USSR. As a result, in the years 1945–49 the USSR helped to establish communist regimes in all the countries under its sphere of influence in eastern Europe.

To support this, Stalin did little to support the communist side in the Greek Civil War (1945–49). He also did little to encourage the large communist parties that existed in France and Italy. Stalin is seen as a practical politician interested in protecting the USSR rather than someone who wanted to spread communism throughout Europe and the world.

Both these views have one thing in common. They both regard the Soviet Union as the main cause of the Cold War. However, from the 1960s, a group of western historians began to regard the USA as being at least partly responsible for the origins of the Cold War. This interpretation of events was given support by President Truman's recollection of the years after 1945, which were made in a series of memoirs (published in 1955–56). Truman's views were supported in *Present at the Creation* by Truman's Secretary of State, Dean Acheson. However, this 'orthodox' view was still supported in 1979 when Vojtech Mastny, in *Russia's Road to the Cold War*, saw the USSR's attempt to gain more influence in Europe as the main cause of the conflict.

American and western policy makers took this view because they interpreted Soviet actions in post-war Europe as threatening and provocative. In addition, in 1946, 'The Long Telegram' from the US ambassador in the USSR, George Kennan, to Washington DC suggested that the only way to prevent the growth of the Soviet Union was openly to prevent further Soviet aggression. This view reinforced the belief in the USA that the Second World War in Europe was caused by the **appeasement** of Hitler. It became the basis of the policy of **containment** in the form of the Truman Doctrine, announced in March 1947.

The belief that the Soviet Union and, in particular, Stalin, were mainly responsible for the breakdown of the Grand Alliance was challenged by a group of historians who offered a historical explanation different from the accepted, or orthodox, view. Known as 'revisionist historians', they believed that the USA was partly to blame for the post-1945 Cold War. In 1959 William Appleman, in *Tragedy of American Diplomacy*, was one of the first historians to claim that the USA, not the USSR, was to blame for the Cold War.

This view became popular in the 1960s as opposition to US involvement in the Vietnam War began to grow. This war ruined the USA's reputation as the defender of freedom and the opponent of **tyranny**. Two notable studies were *From Yalta to Vietnam* by David Horowitz (1967) and *The Rise to Globalism: a study of US foreign policy from 1938–1970* by Stephen Ambrose (1971).

The USA was responsible for causing the breakdown of the Grand Alliance for several reasons:

● During the presidency of Franklin D. Roosevelt, relations between the USA and USSR were kept on a reasonably friendly level. This was shown at the Yalta Conference of February 1945. However, this relationship changed when Roosevelt died in April 1945. His

---

**Harry S. Truman (1894–1972)**
US President (1945–53). Possessed little knowledge of foreign affairs when he became president on Franklin Roosevelt's death in 1945. Truman was responsible for taking a hard line against Communism. He supported Churchill's **Iron Curtain speech**. It was President Truman who introduced containment policy. He stood up to the USSR over Berlin in 1948–49 but was accused by opponents of losing China to Communism by 1949.

**Iron Curtain speech**: Speech made by Winston Churchill at Fulton, Missouri, in 1946. It increased tension with the USSR by claiming that the eastern half of Europe was under tyranny (see page 116).

**Appeasement**: A policy of making concessions to a potentially hostile power in order to secure peace. Example: the 1938 Munich settlement, under which the German-speaking part of Czechoslovakia (the Sudetenland) was transferred to Hitler's Germany.

**Containment**: US policy for much of the Cold War. Put forward by President Truman in April 1947 as the Truman Doctrine. The aim of the policy was to limit the spread of world communism.

**Tyranny**: Cruel and unjust rule by a person or small group of people who have absolute power over everyone else in their country.

## The start of the Cold War 1945–1949: who was responsible?

**1945**

4–12 February: Yalta Summit Conference takes place in the Crimea, in southern USSR. Stalin, Roosevelt and Churchill discuss the post-war political organisation of Europe. Roosevelt and Churchill are suspicious of Soviet plans for eastern Europe. In particular, they are concerned about the political future of Poland.

12 April: Roosevelt dies and is replaced by Vice-President Truman.

23 April: Truman confronts Molotov, Soviet Foreign Minister, over Soviet plans for eastern Europe.

17 July–2 August: Britain, the USA and USSR meet at Potsdam, Germany, in which the post-war borders of Europe are finalised. Germany and Austria are divided into four military zones of occupation. Truman informs Stalin that the USA possesses a new powerful weapon (he means the atomic bomb).

August: USA explodes 'A' bombs at Hiroshima and Nagasaki.

11 September–2 October: London Conference between USA, USSR, Britain, China and France. Major disagreements take place with USSR.

**1946**

5 March: Churchill makes 'Iron Curtain' speech in Fulton, Missouri, with Truman present. He criticises increased Communist controls over Soviet-occupied eastern Europe.

5 June: US plan for the control of atomic weapons (the Baruch Plan) openly criticised by USSR who dislike US monopoly over nuclear weapons technology.

10 September: Communists start civil war in Greece.

2 December: Bizonia created by joining US and British zones in Germany. USSR suspicious that the western Allies are trying to reunite Germany.

**1947**

12 March: Truman Doctrine announced in US Congress. US pledge aid to Greece and Turkey in their attempts to resist communism. Truman Doctrine aims to 'contain' the spread of communism in Europe and Asia.

5 June: European Recovery or Marshall Plan launched. USA to give massive economic aid to Europe. $13.2 billion given in aid.

10 July: the USSR forces Czechoslovakia and Poland to reject Marshall Aid.

**1948**

19–25 February: Communists take over Czechoslovakia. Means all eastern Europe (Romania, Albania, Bulgaria, Poland, Hungary) have communist-controlled governments.

24 June: USSR blocks all land routes to west Berlin. Start of Berlin airlift. Major confrontation between USSR and the western powers.

**1949**

22 January: Chinese Communists capture Beijing and are victorious in Chinese Civil War.

4 April: creation of North Atlantic Treaty Organisation (NATO) to defend Europe against Communist aggression.

8 May: creation of West Germany from US, British and French zones of occupation.

12 May: USSR ends blockade of West Berlin.

30 May: USSR sets up state of East Germany.

29 August: USSR successfully explodes an atomic bomb. The US atomic monopoly ends.

21 September: People's Republic of China created.

successor was Harry Truman. Truman had very little knowledge of foreign affairs. He also had an abrasive and direct style when dealing with representatives of the Soviet government such as Molotov, the Soviet Foreign Minister. As a result, Truman must take personal responsibility for the breakdown in US–Soviet relations.

● There were important economic advantages for the USA in starting a cold war. US policymakers feared another economic depression once the Second World War was over. To prevent this from taking place the US government hoped to keep high levels of military and government expenditure. As a result, the USSR was portrayed as aggressive and threatening. To prevent the spread of Communism to western Europe, the US government launched the European Recovery Programme in 1947. Known as **Marshall Aid**, billions of US dollars were used to bring economic recovery to western Europe as the best means of limiting communist influence. Truman was responsible for creating the military-industrial complex where big business in the USA supported the conflict with the USSR in order to keep high levels of military spending.

● The USA contributed to the start of the Cold War because of Truman's use of **atomic diplomacy**. Some revisionist historians, such as Gar Alperovitz in *Atomic Diplomacy* (1965), believe that the use of atomic weapons against Japan was to display American military power to the Soviet Union.

**Marshall Aid**: Proposed by US Secretary of State, George Marshall in June 1947. It was produced because of US concern about growing support for communism in Europe and fear that Europe would not recover as a trading partner. The aid was offered to all European states, including the USSR. Although Czechoslovakia originally applied for aid they were forced to withdraw under Soviet pressure. Between 1947 and 1952, $17 billion were given in aid.

**Atomic diplomacy**: The use of the threat of atomic weapons to force other nations to stop doing something, or to threaten them into submission. Example: in 1946, Truman threatened Stalin with nuclear weapons to force the Soviet military withdrawal from northern Iran.

However, other views have played down US policy in causing the Cold War. Historians such as John Lewis Gaddis, in *The United States and the Origins of the Cold War, 1941–1947*, believe the USA did not follow a consistent policy after 1945. Instead, the USA had to adjust to a rapidly changing European scene. This was due to a number of reasons:

● The weakness of Britain and France after 1945 forced the USA into taking a more active role in European affairs. France was economically exhausted and badly damaged by 1945. Although Britain tried to play an active role in European affairs after 1945, by 1947 it was clear that Britain was too weak. The British decision to stop aiding Greece and Turkey in that year demonstrates this point.

● The economic weakness of Europe after 1945 also forced a US response. The European Recovery, or Marshall Plan, of 1947–48 can be seen as a real attempt by the USA to help post-war reconstruction. It was offered to all European states including the USSR. Fortunately for the USA, the USSR refused to accept aid and also forced its eastern European satellite states to refuse. In its place the USSR established **Comecon**.

**Comecom**: Council for Mutual Economic Aid (1949–91). Mainly a Soviet reaction to the Marshall Plan, it was dominated by the USSR. However, attempts were made to broaden its work. In 1971, a Complex Programme was introduced, leading to joint economic projects between states. In 1972, an investment bank was created. However, Comecon was partially undermined by Romania's desire to be more independent. Later it was broadened to include other communist states, such as Cuba who joined in 1972 and Vietnam in 1978.

As mentioned by historian Derrick Murphy in 'The Cold War 1945–1949' in *Modern History Review*:

'It seems clear that some form of tension between the USA and USSR would have sprung up following the end of the Second World War. The two new superpowers were competing for influence in a new international order. Germany and Japan had been defeated and had suffered considerable economic damage. France and Italy had also suffered economically. The British Empire was in rapid decline as a world power.'

However, it was the speed of the collapse of the wartime Grand Alliance which shocked contemporaries and has captured the interests of historians. Roosevelt's untimely death, and his replacement by Truman, helped to speed up the collapse of the Alliance. The crude means used in creating

Soviet regimes in Eastern Europe gave rise to much suspicion in the West. In the end, the creation of mutual suspicions, bolstered by fierce ideological rivalry, gave the Cold War its intensity and its potential for future military conflict.

---

**1. In what ways have historians differed in their views of which country was most responsible for the outbreak of the Cold War after 1945?**

**2. Why, do you think, historians have differed in their interpretations of who was responsible for the Cold War?**

**3. On the basis of the information in this section, who do you think was most responsible for the Cold War, the USA or USSR? Explain your answer.**

---

**1. Which of the reasons in the mind map would be regarded as most important in causing the Cold War by (a) a traditionalist historian; (b) a revisionist historian; and (c) A post-revisionist historian? Give reasons for your answer.**

**2. Can you find links between the different causes of the Cold War in Europe?**

**For instance, Yalta and Potsdam and Stalin's policies in eastern Europe are linked. Can you identify any other links?**

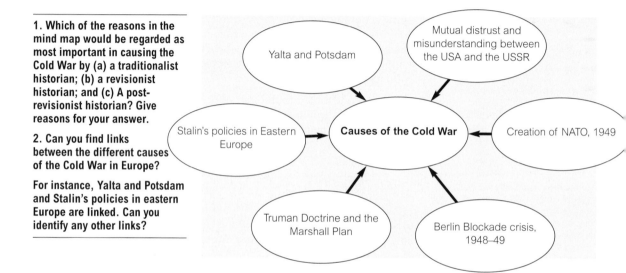

Yalta and Potsdam

Mutual distrust and misunderstanding between the USA and the USSR

Stalin's policies in Eastern Europe → Causes of the Cold War ← Creation of NATO, 1949

Truman Doctrine and the Marshall Plan

Berlin Blockade crisis, 1948–49

## 5.2 How did the USSR establish control over eastern Europe 1945–1949?

**Josef Broz, alias Tito (1892–1980)**
Communist leader in Yugoslavia from 1937. During the Second World War Tito led the communist partisan army against the German, Italian and Croat and Serb nationalists. He was able to form a Yugoslav communist government in 1945, after liberating his own country from German control. A dispute with Stalin led to Yugoslavia's expulsion from Cominform (see page 120) in 1948. After that date, Tito led independent, neutral communist Yugoslavia until his death. Yugoslavia became a leading state in the non-aligned movement of countries not linked to NATO or the Soviet bloc.

An important cause of the Cold War was the way in which the USSR established communist control over eastern Europe from the end of the Second World War until 1949. To critics of the USSR this was evidence that Stalin had broken the agreements he had made at Yalta. It helped President Truman to ensure that his Doctrine became the basis of US foreign policy from March 1947. It also helped the Truman administration to get the Marshall Plan accepted by Congress.

Although eastern Europe had been 'liberated' by the Soviet Army, it did not have a strong tradition of support for Communism. Much of the area was agricultural. What little industry that had existed was all but destroyed by 1945. What had not been destroyed was usually removed to the Soviet Union as reparations. In particular, this was true of East Germany.

In two areas local communists did play an important role in creating communist regimes. In Yugoslavia Joseph Broz, known as 'Tito', led the Yugoslav resistance to the Nazis during the war. In Albania local communists overthrew King Zog to create a communist state in 1945.

Also parts of eastern Europe were taken over by the USSR. These were the former states of Latvia, Lithuania and Estonia. It also included the eastern part of Poland, Ruthenia (from Czechoslovakia) and Moldovia from Romania. Communist regimes were not established immediately on the arrival of the Soviet army. It took until February 1948 for a communist government to be established in Czechoslovakia.

## So how did the USSR establish Soviet-style regimes in eastern Europe?

### Poland

Before the end of the Second World War, Stalin had already laid the groundwork for the creation of a communist regime. In 1940 most of the officers of the Polish Army, captured by the Soviet army, had been murdered in captivity. In the summer of 1944 the Warsaw Uprising by anti-communist Poles was not supported by the Soviet Army. As a result, the Polish 'Home Army' was badly defeated by the Nazis. Once the Soviet Army had entered eastern Poland, in 1944, a pro-Communist regime was established at Lublin.

In June 1945, a government containing socialists, communists, Catholics and peasants was formed under the socialist Osobka. Under his government, the new boundaries of Poland were implemented. A major cause in the move towards communist control came from the unlikely quarter of the leader of the Peasant Party, Stanislaw Mikolajczyk. The Peasant Party performed well in a referendum held in June 1946. However, Mikolajczyk's demand for a large share in government and his conservative views forced the socialists into close partnership with the communists (Polish United Workers' Party). Eventually, these two groups merged and in January 1947 'rigged' the election to ensure a communist victory which then established a one-party state.

### Romania

Romania had been a close ally of Nazi Germany during the Second World War. In August 1944, King Michael was successful in removing the pro-Nazi government. However, a communist-controlled government was achieved through a variety of means. Firstly, like Poland, communists were encouraged to join a government of national unity with non-communist parties known as the National Democratic Bloc government. Secondly, encouraged by Moscow, the Romanian communists, under Gherghiu-Dej, took part in demonstrations to disrupt the government, beginning in January 1945. Finally, in March 1945, the Soviet Army intervened. It disarmed the Romanian army in the capital, Bucharest, and forced the King to appoint a government dominated by the communists under Groza.

Eventually, by November 1946, the communist and socialist parties had merged and dominated Romanian politics. In the elections of that month, they gained 80% of the vote. The communists provided opposition to traditional political parties which had been associated with military defeat. They also supported economic and social reform.

### Hungary

Like Romania, Hungary had also been an ally of Hitler. In a predominantly rural country, the Smallholders' Party was popular after the war. They received 50% of the vote in the November 1945 election. However, as in Poland and Romania, the communists joined forces with the socialists offering a radical electoral package of social and economic reform in a country experiencing major economic crisis. In addition, the communists made sure they controlled the Ministry of the Interior. They used this control to good effect in 1947 by arresting the leader of the Smallholders' Party, Kovacs, for 'offences against the State'. The Prime Minister, Imre Nagy, was forced to resign. In a general election, in August 1947, the

---

**Imre Nagy (1896–1958)**

A Hungarian Communist who criticised Stalin's political and economic policies. He was Prime Minister of Hungary (1953–55), following Stalin's death. He tried to introduce more liberal reforms but was replaced by Matyos Rakosi in 1955. In the Hungarian Uprising (October 1956), Nagy was returned to power. He supported Hungary's withdrawal from the Warsaw Pact (see page 123). Captured by Soviet troops and executed in 1958.

communists and their allies made sure they would win a large share of the vote (45%). By June 1948 the socialists had merged with the communist-dominated Hungarian Workers' Party.

### Czechoslovakia

Of all the countries in Soviet-occupied Europe only Czechoslovakia had a pre-war tradition of democracy. During the latter stages of the Second World War, communist partisans had participated in the Slovak National Uprising. Czechoslovakia was also an industrialised state with a large working class. Therefore, unlike other Eastern Europe states, its Communist Party had sizeable support.

As in other eastern European countries, a multi-party government of national unity was formed at the end of the war. The Prime Minister, from May 1946, was Klement Gottwald. He allowed the communists to control the police and armed forces. In 1947 he was forced, by pressure from the USSR, to reject Marshall Aid.

However, the move towards communist control, like Poland, was forced by non-communists who wanted the President Edvard Beneš to follow a non-communist policy. To achieve this, all non-communist members of the government resigned in February 1948. Instead, the communists were able to portray this act as an attempt to create a reactionary, conservative government. Beneš supported the communists who had created 'action committees' to oppose a possible conservative government.

### East Germany

At the end of the war Germany was divided into four military zones of occupation. The Soviet zone became East Germany (The German Democratic Republic) in 1949. It could be argued that the creation of a communist regime in East Germany was a direct result of actions by Britain and the USA. In their attempt to bring economic recovery to Germany, they had merged their zones, in 1946, to form **Bizonia**. By 1948 the three non-Soviet zones had created a new currency, the Deutschmark.

Stalin's response made matters worse. The Berlin Airlift Crisis of 1948–49 provided positive proof for the Truman Doctrine. It also portrayed the USSR as aggressive and threatening. The failure to force the western allies to abandon West Berlin was a major Soviet failure. It led directly to the creation of both **NATO** and West Germany. In retaliation, the Soviets created a Soviet-style regime in their German zone.

## Summary

Soviet policy towards eastern Europe did not follow a carefully worked out plan. Stalin wanted friendly governments in these states for security reasons. However, there were some common features. In each of the states, communists joined forces with other parties to form governments of national unity. They used this position to gain control of the security system of each state. They were also aided by major political miscalculations by their opponents, most noticeably in Poland and Czechoslovakia.

Apart from Czechoslovakia, none of these states had traditions of democratic government. The dictatorship by the Communists merely replaced a tradition of dictatorship by other political groups. However, the Soviet Union did establish two institutions which helped bring some unity to Eastern Europe:

- **Cominform** helped bring co-ordination to most of the communist-controlled governments of eastern Europe. It led to a split between the USSR and the Communist government of Yugoslavia under Tito. The Yugoslav leader wanted to adopt a political line that was independent from Moscow. This split meant that although Yugoslavia remained

**Bizonia**: Name for the two military zones of Germany merged by the USA and Britain in 1946.

**NATO**: Stands for North Atlantic Treaty Organisation.

**Cominform**: Communist Information Bureau (1947–56). It was created as part of the Soviet response to Marshall Aid, an attempt to unite all communist parties in one organisation in order to co-ordinate political activity. It was seen by the West as a new version of Comintern (Communist International) which had been dissolved by Stalin in 1943. The aim of Cominform was to spread communist ideas. It was limited to communist parties in Europe, such as the Eastern bloc and France and Italy. Cominform remained the main organisation for co-operation between Eastern bloc countries until Khrushchev dissolved it in 1956. He hoped this move could lead to better relations with Tito's Yugoslavia which had been expelled from the organisation in 1948.

communist-controlled it adopted a neutral position in foreign policy during the Cold War.

**1. What common features were there in the establishment of communist governments in eastern Europe after 1945?**

**2. How easy was it for the USSR to impose communist government in eastern Europe after 1945?**

● Comecon was an economic organisation that aimed to bring all the eastern European economies into closer union with the USSR.

By the end of 1949 the pattern of political and economic development of eastern Europe was established. Communist government, based on the Soviet model, was created in all the states. Close links and guidance from Moscow were the norm. In addition, the economies of Eastern Europe now looked to the USSR rather than to the west as its main market. The 'Iron Curtain', which Churchill described in 1946, was now fully in place.

# 5.3  Why was Germany a central issue during the Cold War?

The tearing down of the Berlin Wall in 1989 was the symbolic end of the Cold War. From 1945 the position of Germany within Europe was a central issue. This was due to several reasons.

● When Germany was defeated, the Great Powers (the USSR, Britain and the USA) met at Potsdam, near Berlin, to decide on the future of Germany. As a result of the two Potsdam conferences, Germany and Austria were divided into four military zones of occupation. The USSR, the USA, Britain and France each controlled a zone. In addition, the two capital cities – Berlin and Vienna – were divided into four military zones. Through accident of geography both capital cities were within the Soviet zone of occupation. Therefore, the three western powers (Britain, the USA and France) could only have access to their zones by crossing Soviet-controlled territory. The problems caused by these arrangements increased tension between East and West.

● Secondly, although the allies met at the end of the war to consider the organisation of the post-war world, no formal peace treaty was signed. As a result, the futures of Germany and Austria were not decided. Throughout the post-1945 period attempts were made to deal with the German and Austrian problems. The Austrian State Treaty of 1955 solved the latter. The four occupying powers agreed to leave Austria. As a result, Austria became a democratic but neutral state.

### What impact did the Berlin Airlift Crisis (1948–1949) have on the Cold War?

The first major international crisis involving Germany came in 1948. In response to western attempts to create a single economic zone from their military zones, Stalin ordered the land blockade of West Berlin. Stalin's actions were prompted by the belief that the West wanted to reunite and remilitarise Germany. As a result, Soviet actions could be seen as defensive and based on security concerns. However, the West regarded Soviet action as aggressive and expansionist.

The Berlin Airlift Crisis greatly increased East–West tension. It led directly to the formation, in 1949, of two German states:

● West Germany, or the German Federal Republic, was pro-western and democratic.

● East Germany, or the German Democratic Republic, became a communist state.

Unfortunately, West Berlin was technically not part of this new West

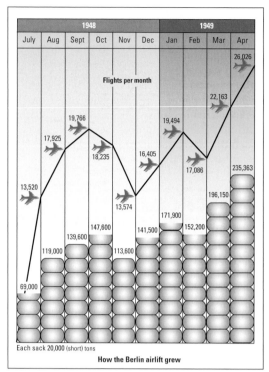

How the Berlin airlift grew

| Airlifts statistics, 28 June 1948 – 11 May 1949 | | | |
|---|---|---|---|
| | USAF | RAF | Civil |
| Flights to Berlin and back | 131,378 | 49,733 | 13,879 |
| Miles flown | 69,257,475 | 18,205,284 | 4,866,093 |
| Tonnage flown in (short tons) | 1,214,339 | 281,727 | 87,619 |

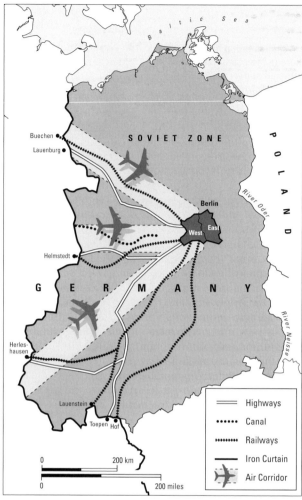

The Berlin Airlift

---

**Dwight Eisenhower
(1890–1969)**
US President 1953–61.
Supported New Look foreign
policy that aimed to roll back
the advance of Communism.
However, this foreign policy
was a little different to Truman's
'containment' policy.
Eisenhower did nothing to aid
the Hungarians in 1956. His
presidency is also associated
with the idea of 'brinkmanship'
where Secretary of State John
F. Dulles threatened the use of
nuclear war as a diplomatic
weapon.

---

**Conventional forces**: Armed forces
which did not use nuclear, biological
or chemical weapons.

German state. It remained as three western military zones well within East
Germany.

The crisis stands out as one of the major tests for the US foreign policy
explained by President Truman to the US Congress in March 1947. This
was the policy of containment.

## Why was German re-armament a major issue in the early 1950s?

During the first half of the 1950s, German re-armament was a central issue
in the European part of the Cold War. With the outbreak of the Korean
War, US forces had to be spread across the globe in their attempt to contain
the spread of communism. In addition, from 1953, the new US President,
Dwight Eisenhower, planned to reduce the US **conventional forces**. The
idea that West Germany would have a powerful armed force was viewed
with suspicion by the USSR and France. Both nations had been the victims
of German armed might during the first half of the century.

The French solution to the issue of German re-armament was the
Pleven Plan, named after the French Prime Minister. In 1951, Rene Pleven
suggested that West Germany should only have an armed force as part of a
European army. In May 1952, as part of this process, the European Defence
Community (EDC) was created involving West Germany, Italy, France,
Belgium, Luxembourg and Holland.

The EDC failed to develop into a European army. This was due, in part, to opposition within France. More importantly, it was linked to a threatened withdrawal of US troops from Europe. In May 1955, with the French bowing to American pressure, West Germany became a member of NATO.

The USSR was bitterly opposed to German re-armament. They believed it broke the Potsdam Agreement of 1945. In 1955 the new Soviet leadership of Nikita Khrushchev and Nikolai Bulganin reacted to German re-armament by creating the **Warsaw Pact**, a military alliance of Eastern Bloc countries. From 1955 Europe was divided into two hostile military alliances, similar to the position before the First World War.

**Warsaw Pact**: The military alliance of eastern bloc states created in 1955. It was created one week after West Germany was allowed to join NATO.

### How serious was the issue of Berlin in the Cold War between 1958 and 1961?

The German question turned into one of the most serious crises in the Cold War. At issue was the status of Berlin. The Soviet leader created the crisis in 1958 by threatening to hand over the Soviet military zone in Berlin to East Germany. However, the crisis reached its height in 1961 with the building of the Berlin Wall.

Berlin was a key issue in East–West relations for several reasons. Firstly, West Berlin was a western military outpost well within the Communist bloc. Secondly, Berlin was the only gap in the 'Iron Curtain' where free travel between East and West could take place.

Ever since 1949 large numbers of East Germans had fled to the West through this 'gap'. By 1961 the East German state's existence was becoming undermined by this development. In the first six months of 1961 around 100,000 fled to West Berlin. In August alone 30,000 fled from East to West. In order to save East Germany and close the last gap in the Iron Curtain, the Warsaw Pact countries decided on 3 August to erect the Berlin Wall. On 12–13 August a temporary barrier was built, and eventually the Wall itself. The crisis was seen at the time as a major confrontation between East and West. On 26 October 1961, Soviet and US tanks collided briefly with each other, at Checkpoint Charlie. The erection of the wall closed the last gap in the Iron Curtain and stopped the flood of refugees from East Germany. It also confirmed the division of Germany into two states. Even though the USSR tried to interfere with convoys travelling from the West to Berlin in 1962 and 1963, it also confirmed the permanence of the western military presence in West Berlin. As the historian John W. Mason states in *The Cold War 1945 to 1991* (1996):

> 'The Wall solved the refugee problem at a stroke, but at the same time it became a symbol all over the world of repression in the Soviet sphere. Khrushchev withdrew his threat to make a separate peace treaty with East Germany and the Berlin crisis came to an end. He had failed to dislodge the West from Berlin and had come under fierce criticism from China for capitulating [giving in] to the capitalist powers.'

**Détente**: Relaxation of tension between countries; also characterised by increased economic co-operation and cultural exchanges, such as tours of the West by Soviet athletes and ballet companies.

**SALT** (Strategic Arms Limitation Treaty): The aim was to limit the increase in nuclear weapons. The first treaty, SALT I, was aimed at preventing the development of ABMs (Anti-Ballistic Missile systems).

### How did the German question affect the creation of *détente* between East and West after 1962?

During the remainder of the 1960s, the main areas of confrontation in the Cold War were outside Europe. The most serious crisis occurred in October 1962 over Cuba. Later in the decade, conflict was centred on Vietnam. By the early 1970s a new era of the Cold War began: *détente*, a relaxation of tension between the two superpowers. This was highlighted in May 1972 when President Richard Nixon of the USA and Leonid Brezhnev of the USSR signed the **SALT** I treaty. This was the first major

Annexed to USSR
Satellite States
1938 Frontiers

FINLAND

NORWAY

SWEDEN

Oslo

Stockholm

Helsinki
Porkkala
(Russia 1945–56)

Viborg

Leningrad

ESTONIA

Novgorod

North Sea

DENMARK

Copenhagen

Baltic Sea

Riga

LATVIA

Smolensk

LITHUANIA

USSR

Lübeck

EAST
GERMANY

Gdansk

Hamburg

Bremen

NETHERLANDS

Berlin
(4 power control)

Warsaw

POLAND

Brest-Litovsk

WEST GERMANY

Leipzig

BELGIUM

Bonn

LUX

Prague

CZECHOSLOVAKIA

Krak

Lvov

Kiev

Paris

Munich

Vienna

Bratislava

FRANCE

Liechtenstein

AUSTRIA
(Neutralised)

Budapest

HUNGARY

BESSARABIA

Odessa

SWITZERLAND

Zagreb

Lyons

Milan

Trieste
Fiume

ROMANIA

ITALY

YUGOSLAVIA
(Independent communist state)

Belgrade

Bucharest

Black Sea

Marseilles

Monaco

Sarajevo

Sofia

BULGARIA

CORSICA
(France)

Rome

ALBANIA

Istanbul

SARDINIA
(Italy)

Salonika

GREECE
(Communist revolt
suppressed)

CORFU

TURKEY

Mediterranean Sea

SICILY

Athens

CRETE

0        400 km

0        400 miles

Central Europe 1955

**Willi Brandt (1913–1992)**
Adopted name of Karl Herbert Frahm, a German socialist politician. As mayor of West Berlin (1957–66), Brandt became internationally known during the Berlin Wall crisis. Federal chancellor (premier) of West Germany (1969–74). Played a key role in the remoulding of the Social Democratic Party (SPD). He was awarded the Nobel Peace Prize in 1971.

**Ostpolitik** (German – 'Eastern policy'): German policy towards eastern Europe, associated mainly with the Federal Republic of Germany's cultivation of good relations with the German Democratic Republic and the rest of the Communist bloc in the 1960s.

**Non-proliferation treaty**: To prevent the spread of nuclear weapons to new countries.

**'Oder–Neisse Line'**: Border between East Germany and Poland in 1945. The rivers Oder and Neisse formed a natural barrier (see map on page 124).

**What message does each photograph give of the Berlin Wall?**

international treaty that attempted to limit the increase in strategic (nuclear) weapons.

During this period, West German leaders embarked on a new foreign policy which aimed to relax tension between the two German states: *Ostpolitik*. This led, eventually, to the Basic Treaty (December 1972). The main force behind *Ostpolitik* was the West German Social Democrat Willi Brandt.

Brandt's decision to increase links between the two Germanies was developed separately from the US desire to improve relations with the USSR. At times Brandt's plans were kept from the USA. As the historian Simon J. Ball notes in *The Cold War 1947 to 1991* (1998) '*détente* and *Ostpolitik* had quite different roots in different perceived national interest'. However, at no time did Brandt wish to cause a rift between West Germany and the rest of NATO. Nevertheless, Brandt wanted to ease East–West tension in central Europe mainly because Germany would be the main battlefield in any conflict. By the mid-1960s the two Germanies were host to large armed forces of both NATO and the Warsaw Pact. By improving relations with the East, Brandt hoped to create a '*Mitteleuropa*' (Middle Europe) area.

The Basic Treaty with East Germany was preceded by treaties, in 1970, with the USSR and Poland. In the Moscow Treaty with the USSR, West Germany promised to sign a nuclear **non-proliferation treaty** and would support the idea of a European security conference. In the Warsaw Treaty with Poland, Brandt accepted the **'Oder–Neisse Line'** as the permanent frontier between Poland and East Germany. This confirmed the acquisition by Poland of a large area of the former German state in 1945.

The 1972 Basic Treaty accepted the division of Germany into two states. However, it did not rule out the possibility of future unification. The treaty also allowed for closer economic links. The USSR supported the treaty because it gave international recognition to East Germany. It eventually led to both East and West Germany joining the United Nations (September 1973).

(Left) Berlin Wall, 7 September 1962. East German policemen lift the body of Peter Fechter, who was shot down while trying to escape to the West.

(Right) Celebrations at the Berlin Wall after unification, 1989.

Brandt's *Ostpolitik* may have had different origins to *détente* but it helped to relax international tension in central Europe. Both policies led to the Helsinki Accords of August 1975. This was the high-water mark of *détente* in Europe. Thirty-five countries, including the two Germanies, signed these accords. The agreements included acceptance that all European borders were inviolable (permanent). They also suggested greater economic co-operation between East and West. Finally, the Accords required the signatories to respect human rights across Europe. This proved to be the most controversial aspect of the Accords and one which the Eastern bloc countries were criticised by the West for not implementing.

### Why did Germany become the centre of a new crisis between East and West between 1979 and 1985?

The end of the 1970s saw a major deterioration in relations between East and West. In December 1979 the USSR invaded Afghanistan. In retaliation, the US Senate refused to ratify the SALT II treaty that had been negotiated by President Jimmy Carter. Carter then refused to allow US athletes to compete in the 1980 Moscow Olympic Games. In Eastern Europe martial law was declared in Poland (1981), as part of a campaign to suppress the independent trade union movement, **Solidarity**.

Germany and Europe, in general, became a centre for this increased conflict over the issue of nuclear weapons. By the late 1970s the main issue in the nuclear conflict between East and West were **INF (Intermediate Range Nuclear Forces)**. The deployment of these new nuclear weapons by the USA caused considerable protests in western Europe. A women's camp of anti-nuclear protesters was created at RAF Greenham Common, in the UK, against the deployment of Cruise missiles.

These developments increased tension with the USSR. This occurred for several reasons. Between 1979 and 1985 the USSR faced a major leadership crisis. Leonid Brezhnev was an ageing and ill leader by 1980. After his death, in 1982, he was followed, in succession, by Yuri Andropov and Konstantin Chernenko, both elderly and ill. Not until 1985 was the USSR led by a relatively young, dynamic leader, Mikhail Gorbachev.

Secondly, from 1981, the USA was led by Ronald Reagan. During his presidency he greatly increased military spending. In particular, he launched his 'Star Wars' or **'Strategic Defence Initiative'** (SDI) in March 1983. This initiative, if successfully introduced, would have made Soviet nuclear missiles ineffective.

The combination of these factors meant that Germany again became the centre of renewed military conflict between the USA and the USSR. Fortunately, the SDI proposal was never implemented and both Gorbachev and Reagan began, in 1985, to negotiate seriously about the reduction of nuclear weapons – and with them, international tension.

**Solidarity**: Independent trade union movement in Poland.

**INF (Intermediate Range Nuclear Forces)**: These were nuclear weapons based in and aimed at other parts of Europe. In the USSR these took the form of the mobile SS20 missile. The USA countered by basing Pershing I and II and Lance missiles in Germany and Cruise missiles in Britain.

---

**Leonid Brezhnev (1906–1982)**
In 1964 he helped overthrow Khrushchev. Then became joint leader with Kosygin until 1967. Responsible for Brezhnev Doctrine of 1968 and détente with the West from 1971. Economic policies at home led to lack of economic growth. Final years affected by Soviet decision to invade Afghanistan that led to New Cold War.

---

**'Strategic Defence Initiative'**: The US plan to develop satellite-based laser weapons which could destroy Soviet ICBMs (intercontinental ballistic missiles) in the outer atmosphere.

---

**Mikhail Gorbachev (1931– )**
Soviet President (1985–91). Was a member of the Politburo from 1980. As general secretary of the Communist Party (CPSU) 1985–91 and president of the Supreme Soviet 1988–91, he introduced liberal reforms at home (*perestroika* and *glasnost*), proposed the introduction of multi-party democracy, and attempted to halt the arms race abroad. Nobel Peace Prize winner in 1990.

**Ronald Reagan (1911–2004 )**
US President (1981–89). Republican with strong anti-communist views. He described the USSR as an 'evil empire'. During the 1980s he launched the biggest peacetime military build-up in US history. Reagan was a supporter of the Star Wars initiative. However, from 1985 he negotiated with Soviet leader Gorbachev towards reducing nuclear arsenals in START (strategic arms reduction talks).

1. In what ways was Germany the centre of Cold War confrontation in Europe 1945–1989?

2. Why did disputes over Germany not lead to war between the USA and the USSR between 1945 and 1989?

3. 'In the period 1945–1989 Germans had virtually no control over their own affairs.' Assess the validity of this statement.

## Summary

Throughout most of the Cold War in Europe, Germany was a major issue. This was due both to the legacy of the Second World War and to Germany's geographical location in the centre. The division of Germany into two states was a major symbol of the division of the world between East and West. When the Berlin Wall was finally torn down, in 1989, it was seen as the beginning of the end of the Cold War in Europe.

# 5.4 Why was it difficult for the USSR to maintain control of eastern Europe between 1949 and 1989?

By 1949 the Cold War division of Europe had occurred. The Iron Curtain had divided the continent into two distinct political and economic systems. In the East, the USSR dominated the region militarily. It had also imposed on the eastern European states a communist form of government and a communist economic system. Both looked to Moscow for leadership and guidance. As a result, Stalin had achieved one of his major post-war aims in Europe: he had created a security zone of friendly, dependent states on his western frontier.

However, in spite of the USSR's overwhelming military might, control of eastern Europe proved to be a problem for Soviet leaders. In the period 1949–81 the USSR faced a series of crises which tried either to change or remove Soviet influence in eastern Europe. Eventually, by 1989, Soviet control of eastern Europe disappeared almost overnight. In most countries this was achieved without bloodshed. Only in Romania was violent revolution part of this change.

### What problems did the USSR face in trying to maintain control over eastern Europe?

*Nationalism*
One major problem faced by the USSR throughout this period was the issue of **nationalism**. In inter-war Europe (1919–39) Communism had never achieved majority support in any country outside the USSR. Even before 1948 the issue of nationalism and national independence had affected Soviet control. In mid-1948, Communist Yugoslavia was expelled from Cominform. From 1948 to the 1990s, Yugoslavia remained a communist state independent of the USSR. Under Tito, the Yugoslavs adopted a neutral position in the Cold War. Only after Tito's death (1980), did national tensions within Yugoslavia become a destabilising influence. These led eventually to the disintegration of Yugoslavia in the 1990s.

Nationalism also affected Soviet control in other countries. In Poland resentment against Soviet control centred on two episodes in the Second World War.

**Nationalism**: The desire of individual racial groups to form their own state.

● In 1943, the bodies of thousands of Polish army officers were uncovered by the Germans at Katyn in the USSR. The USSR was accused of the massacre.

● In 1944, the Soviet Army failed to aid the Polish Home Army in the Warsaw Uprising.

In Czechoslovakia resentment centred on the communist-led take-over of February 1948 which saw the murder or suicide of the Czech Foreign Minister, Jan Masaryk. In Hungary, which had fought as Hitler's ally on the Eastern Front (1941–44), the desire to re-assert national independence was also an issue.

Even within the Soviet Union national feeling had the potential to disrupt the state. By 1945 the USSR had absorbed formerly independent states such as Latvia, Lithuania and Estonia. Nationalist groups also existed in Georgia and the Ukraine.

*Economic hardship*
Unlike the rest of Europe, the Eastern bloc did not benefit from the billions of dollars in American aid under the European Recovery or Marshall Plan. The area had also suffered considerable economic damage as a result of the Second World War. The USSR had lost 27 million dead and Poland 25% of its population (6 million). In addition, large parts of eastern Europe had always been based on agriculture, with limited industry.

The introduction of Soviet-style central economic planning and collectivised agriculture meant that eastern Europe followed a completely different economic course to the western world. Shortages of food and raw material, and the lack of economic freedom were important causes of resentment. The contrast between East and West was most apparent in Berlin. Before 1961, East Berliners could travel freely to West Berlin. The attraction of greater wealth and political freedom resulted in 2.7 million East Germans fleeing to West Berlin by the time the Berlin Wall was erected.

*Lack of political and religious freedom*
Like the USSR under Stalin, a Stalinist political system was established in all Eastern bloc states by 1949. Except for Czechoslovakia, eastern Europe did not have a strong tradition of democracy. A desire for a relaxation in the rigid control of the Communist Party was always apparent in almost every Eastern bloc state. This was most noticeable in the relations between communist governments and the Roman Catholic Church. Communist control over education and its support for **atheism** meant that conflict was inevitable. Catholic support for anti-communist groups occurred in Hungary, in 1956, with Cardinal Mindsentzy. It was most significant in Poland, the most Catholic of Eastern bloc states. The Catholic Church supported the free trade union movement, Solidarity. In 1978 the Catholic Church in the Eastern bloc received a considerable boost with the election of Cardinal Karol Wojtyla of Poland as Pope John Paul II. This led to a resurgence in Polish Catholicism which helped undermine communist rule.

**Atheism**: The belief that there is no God.

### How serious were the crises which faced the USSR in eastern Europe after 1949?

*Hungary and Poland, 1956*
Soviet control over eastern Europe was affected by political change within the Soviet Union, and relations between the USSR and the West. The combination of these two developments helped to undermine Soviet control in 1956.

Following Stalin's death in March 1953, a power struggle ensued. By 1955 Nikita Khrushchev emerged as the new Soviet leader. In 1956, at the 20th Party Congress of the Communist Party of the Soviet Union,

Khrushchev denounced Stalin. The new Soviet leader criticised the barbarity of Stalin's rule and the growth of what Khrushchev called 'the cult of personality'. A new, less repressive regime was to be developed within the USSR.

On the international stage, relations between East and West seemed to be improving in 1955. In that year the USSR and the western powers signed the Austrian State Treaty. Soviet forces left eastern Austria. Austria was declared a united, neutral state. Hopes were high that this treaty would be followed by a similar one on Germany.

Partly as a result of these developments Soviet control faced major challenges in Poland and Hungary. In Poland on 28 June 1956, Polish workers began a series of political strikes aimed against Soviet-type rule and poor working conditions. Although the 'Poznan Rising' was put down by the Polish Army it did lead to a change in government. Wladyslaw Gomulka was recalled as Communist Party leader because of his close association with Polish nationalism.

More serious for the USSR was the Hungarian Uprising of October/November. A popular movement developed which clashed with Soviet military forces in Budapest. This resulted in four days of street fighting at the end of October. The result was the creation of a multi-party government and the decision by Hungary to leave the Warsaw Pact. The Soviet reaction was to invade Hungary and quell the uprising by force. In the ensuing fighting, 3,000 Hungarians were killed and 200,000 fled the country.

Considerable controversy surrounds the actions of Hungarian communist Imre Nagy. To many Hungarians, he was a patriot who wanted to relax Soviet control. Like several other eastern European communists in the period, he believed that the Soviet Union would allow greater political freedom within their zone of influence. The Soviet Union executed Nagy for his part in the Uprising.

Developments in Poland and Hungary had several common characteristics. The relaxation of Stalinist control in the USSR led to demands for greater political freedom elsewhere. Both states also faced economic hardships that caused resentment. Finally, in neither state did the western powers wish to intervene. President Eisenhower (1953–61) had stated that his 'New Look' foreign policy planned to roll back communist influence around the world. However, the USA did not aid the Poles or the Hungarians. Britain and France did not intervene either. This was, in part, due to their military dependence on the USA through NATO. It was also due to their involvement in the **Suez Crisis** in October/November 1956.

### Czechoslovakia, 1968

The 'Prague Spring' of 1968 was a major attempt by an Eastern bloc country to introduce a new liberal version of communist rule under the leadership of Alexander Dubček. In some ways Dubček's views were similar to those of Imre Nagy in Hungary in 1955–56. In the Action Programme of 10 April 1968 Dubček wanted to build 'a new profoundly democratic model of Czechoslovak socialism conforming to Czechoslovak conditions'. He wanted to broaden the basis of communist rule by including other organisations such as the trade unions. In this sense he was trying to recreate the National Front of 1945.

The rise of Dubček, and support for his ideas, had a number of causes. According to the historians G. and N. Swain, in *Eastern Europe since 1945* (1993), the liberals within the Slovak Communist Party had gradually increased their influence since the 12th Party Congress of the Czechoslovak Communist Party in December 1962, when Stalinism was denounced.

The increasing influence of liberal communists was combined with a decline in support for the Czech President Antonin Novotny because of

**Wladyslaw Gomulka (1905–1982)**
Polish Communist. Came to power following Poznan Uprising of 1956 by posing as a Polish nationalist. He brought agricultural collectivisation to an end. In turn, he was ousted from power after strikes in 1970 following failure of his economic policies to bring improvements to the standard of living. He was replaced by Edouard Gierek.

**Suez Crisis**: Occurred following the decision by President Nasser of Egypt to nationalise the Suez Canal. The British and French, in league with the Israelis, invaded Egypt to take control of the canal. Britain and France were forced into a humiliating withdrawal because of Soviet and American opposition.

**Alexander Dubček (1921–1992 )**
Czechoslovak leader who tried to introduce liberal reforms in the 'Prague Spring' of 1968. Overthrown by Warsaw Pact invasion; demoted to ambassador to Turkey in 1969; and then expelled from Communist Party (1970). Dubček re-emerged as a national figure during the Velvet Revolution of November 1989 when he became president of the Czechoslovak parliament.

**Brezhnev Doctrine**: The western name given to the policy put forward by the Soviet leader in 1968, Leonid Brezhnev, claiming that the USSR had the right to intervene in any communist state (i.e. any country in the 'Eastern bloc' where 'socialism' was under threat. This policy was abandoned by Gorbachev when he withdrew from Afghanistan.

**Iranian Revolution in 1979**: The Shah (Emperor) of Iran was overthrown in a revolution led by fundamentalist (extreme) Muslims. He was replaced by the religious leader, the Ayatollah Khomeini.

> **Lech Wałęsa (1943– )**
> As an electrician in Lenin shipyard, Gdansk, Wałęsa became leader of Solidarity, the free trade union movement in Poland, in 1980. A powerful orator and clever negotiator, he became well known worldwide due to intense media coverage of Polish affairs. Wałęsa was placed under 'house arrest' in December 1981 when **martial law** was introduced. He was awarded the Nobel Peace Prize in 1983 and had a private audience with the Polish Pope John Paul II in the Vatican. Wałęsa was elected President of Poland in 1990 but was defeated in the 1995 presidential election.

**Martial law**: Military law when applied to civilians. Normal civil rights are suspended, allowing the government to arrest individuals and detain them without trial. Suspects could be tried by military court (without a jury) and given the death penalty if found guilty.

major failings in the economy during the 1960s. This led to the abandonment of the five-year economic plan in 1962.

Dubček's liberal communism led to the creation of political groups outside the Communist Party, such as the Social Democrats in June 1968. Unlike the Hungarians in 1956, the Czechoslovaks made no attempt to leave the Warsaw Pact. Indeed, Czech leaders had agreed with the USSR by 1 August 1968 to suppress the Social Democrats and had re-affirmed Czechoslovakia's support for the Warsaw Pact and Comecon. Nevertheless, Warsaw Pact forces invaded Czechoslovakia on the night of 20–21 August. Unlike Hungary in 1956, they faced no armed resistance.

The Warsaw Pact invasion reinforced the Cold War split in Europe. Before the invasion, President Johnson had informed the Soviet leader Brezhnev that the USA would not intervene if the USSR took military action. The invasion also acted as an example of the **Brezhnev Doctrine**. As the historian S.J. Ball states in *The Cold War 1947 to 1991* (1998), 'there was a fear among (Soviet) Politburo members that the reformist spirit might affect the Ukraine and thus spread to the Soviet Union itself'.

## Poland, 1980–1981

By 1980 the USA and the USSR entered a new, tense phase of the Cold War brought on by the Soviet invasion of Afghanistan and the issue of INF in Europe. This period also saw a major economic crisis affecting eastern Europe. There was a major oil crisis in 1973 and another following the **Iranian Revolution in 1979**. The poor economic performance of the Polish economy was made worse by a large international debt. In 1980–81 the USSR had to give Poland $3 billion in western currency to avoid economic collapse.

The economic crisis forced the Polish government to increase the prices of basic foodstuffs. This acted as the catalyst for a number of strikes which began at the Lenin shipyard in the northern port of Gdansk (formally Danzig). The strikes eventually developed into an independent trade union movement called Solidarity. Led by a shipyard electrician, Lech Wałęsa, Solidarity had the support of political liberals and the Catholic Church, as well as disgruntled workers.

The Solidarity movement did have some success. Its rise led to the fall of Polish Communist leader Edouard Gierek. The union was recognised formally by Gierek's successor, Kania, in November 1980. Lech Wałęsa was hailed as a leader of a democratic movement fighting depression.

However, as in Hungary and Czechoslovakia, an independent organisation such as Solidarity threatened Soviet control. Instead of a Soviet military invasion the Polish Prime Minister, General Jaruzelski, introduced **martial law** in December 1981 and banned Solidarity. Wałęsa was placed under 'house arrest' for a year.

## The collapse of Soviet influence in eastern Europe, 1989

The fall of all the communist regimes of eastern Europe within the space of a year and with little bloodshed was one of the more remarkable events of 20th-century Europe. It had some similarity to the Year of Revolutions of 1848. Unlike 1848, the revolutions of 1989 were successful.

Like the unrest that affected Poland and Hungary in 1956, the revolutions of 1989 had their origins within the USSR. The appointment of Mikhail Gorbachev as Soviet leader in 1985 began a process that was to lead directly to the events of 1989. His attempts to modernise the USSR led to the call for *glasnost* (openness) and *perestroika* (restructuring).

Gorbachev's new programme was the result of poor economic growth in the USSR and with it Soviet difficulties in keeping up with the USA in the arms race (see tables). However, the lessening of central political and economic control undermined the authority of the Communist Party in the USSR and in the Eastern bloc. Economic problems were not limited to the USSR. By 1989 Poland still had a foreign debt of $40 billion. Other Eastern bloc countries faced similar problems.

Within the space of a few short months in 1989, Jaruzelski in Poland began talks with Solidarity, Hungary opened its borders with the West and finally the Berlin Wall was opened.

---

**How does the data contained here help to explain why the USSR faced financial problems caused by military spending?**

---

**Strategic bombers**

|      | 1956 | 1960 | 1965 | 1970 | 1975 | 1979 |
|------|------|------|------|------|------|------|
| USA  | 560  | 550  | 630  | 405  | 330  | 316  |
| USSR | 60   | 175  | 200  | 190  | 140  | 140  |

**Inter-continental ballistic missiles (ICBMs)**

|      | 1960 | 1962 | 1966 | 1968  | 1970  | 1972  | 1974  | 1979  |
|------|------|------|------|-------|-------|-------|-------|-------|
| USA  | 295  | 835  | 900  | 1,054 | 1,054 | 1,054 | 1,054 | 1,054 |
| USSR | 75   | 200  | 300  | 800   | 1,300 | 1,527 | 1,587 | 1,398 |

**Submarine-launched ballistic missiles (SLBMs)**

|      | 1962 | 1965 | 1968 | 1972 | 1975 | 1979 |
|------|------|------|------|------|------|------|
| USA  | 145  | 500  | 656  | 656  | 656  | 656  |
| USSR | 45   | 125  | 130  | 497  | 740  | 989  |

---

**1. What problems did the USSR face in trying to keep control over eastern Europe from 1949 to 1989?**

**2. Why was the USSR able to keep control over eastern Europe between 1949 and 1989?**

**3. To what extent was nationalism the cause of anti-Soviet feeling in eastern Europe between 1949 and 1989?**

---

The main reason why the revolutions of 1989 succeeded was the unwillingness of the Soviet Union to implement the Brezhnev Doctrine. By 1989 the USSR was no longer in a position to put down widespread unrest in eastern Europe. The Soviet involvement in Afghanistan (1979–1989) had a similar impact on the USSR as the Vietnam War had on the USA. The political and economic crisis within the Soviet Union forced it to relinquish control over eastern Europe.

The revolution of 1989 also reflected another aspect of the Cold War. Throughout the Cold War period western propaganda claimed that communism had little support in eastern Europe. It was maintained only through Soviet military might. The events of 1989 seem to confirm that view.

---

## Political revolution in eastern Europe, 1989

11 January: Hungary legalises independent political parties.
6 February: open discussion between Polish Communist Party and Solidarity.
15 February: Soviet forces complete withdrawal from Afghanistan.
25 April: Soviet Army begins withdrawal from Hungary.
4 June: Solidarity achieve success in Polish elections.
24 August: end of Communist rule in Poland. Tadeusz Mazowiecki becomes Prime Minister.
10 September: Hungarian government allows thousands of East German 'holiday-makers' to cross the border into Austria.
1 October: Thousands of East Germans allowed to leave for West through West German embassies in Warsaw and Prague.
18 October: East German leader Erich Honecker resigns; replaced by Egon Krenz.
10 November: Berlin Wall opened.
November: Bulgarian Communist leader Topol Zhivkov overthrown.
17–27 November: Velvet Revolution in Czechoslovakia. Communism overthrown.
21 December: Armed revolution begins in Romania.
25 December: Romanian Communist leader Nicolae Ceauçescu executed.
28 December: Prague Spring leader Alexander Dubček elected leader of Czech parliament.

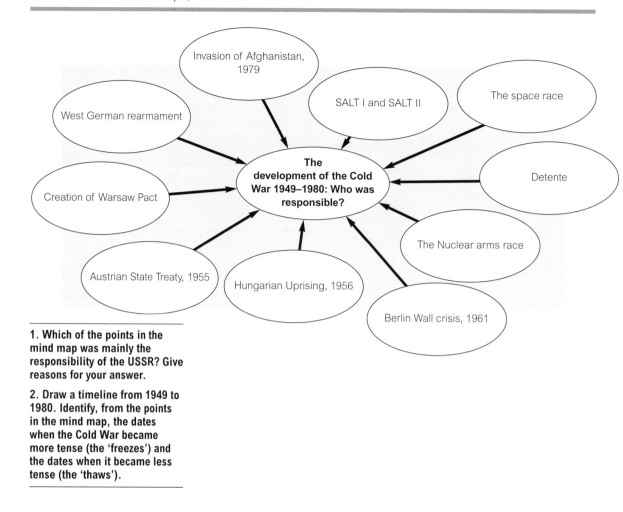

1. **Which of the points in the mind map was mainly the responsibility of the USSR? Give reasons for your answer.**

2. **Draw a timeline from 1949 to 1980. Identify, from the points in the mind map, the dates when the Cold War became more tense (the 'freezes') and the dates when it became less tense (the 'thaws').**

## 5.5 Why did the Cold War come to an end in 1991?

According to the historian Martin McCauley in *Russia, America and the Cold War 1949 to 1991* (1998): 'The Cold War came to an end because it was impossible for two powers to divide and rule the world. The will power had drained away. The burden was so great that the Soviet Union buckled and then disintegrated. By 1991 the United States was no longer able to intervene at will and was immensely relieved when the need to do so, the communist threat, melted away.'

Another historian, Simon Ball, in *The Cold War 1947 to 1991* (1998), takes a similar view. He states that 'there is little doubt that the Cold War came to an end as a result of Soviet economic failure. This failure led in turn to a failure of nerve amongst the Soviet governing elite.'

Both historians point to the fact that by the late 1980s the USSR was no longer in a position to maintain the military forces necessary for super-power status. Few western observers were able to predict the rapid collapse of Soviet power in eastern Europe in 1989 and the end of the USSR in 1991. However, the *Economist* journal, in the 1980s, described the USSR as 'Upper Volta [now Burkina Faso] with missiles'. This suggested that the Soviet economy was of Third World standard. Also, Richard Perle, national security adviser to Ronald Reagan, had predicted in 1991 that any increase in the arms race between the superpowers would eventually lead to the bankruptcy of the Soviet Union.

**Boris Yeltsin (1931– 2007)** Communist reformer and subsequently President of the Russian Federation. In 1985 he became communist mayor of Moscow as part of Gorbachev's plans to liberalise Soviet politics. Yeltsin was expelled from the Politburo (Cabinet) in October 1987 as part of a reaction against Gorbachev's liberal reforms. In 1991, though, he was a major figure in stopping traditional communist take-over. He replaced Gorbachev as leader of the Russian state (December 1991). Twice elected President of the Russian Federation. His second term was badly affected by his ill health. He stood down in January 2000.

Gorbachev's attempts to modernise the USSR were too little too late. The origins of the USSR's failure to control eastern Europe could be traced back to the years of stagnation in economic development under Brezhnev. In *Rise and Fall of the Great Powers* (1989), the historian Paul Kennedy states that a common cause of great power decline was over-commitment of military forces. Although a great Eurasian power, the Soviet Union simply did not possess the economic power to sustain a global conflict against the USA. Support for regimes such as Cuba, Angola, Vietnam and eastern Europe proved too demanding. The Soviet invasion of Afghanistan and a protracted war in that country lasting ten years was one military burden too many for the state.

Once Soviet military power weakened, the disruptive forces of nationalism took hold. The desire for national independence undermined Soviet influence in eastern Europe. It also undermined the USSR from within. By 1990 the Baltic states of Latvia, Lithuania and Estonia all sought independence from the USSR. In the Caucasus region, Georgia, Azerbaijan and Armenia followed suit. By 1991 the old USSR had fragmented into 15 separate states.

The failure of Gorbachev's attempts to modernise the USSR through *glasnost* and *perestroika* produced a backlash. Traditional communist leaders, such as Yegor Ligachev, had opposed Gorbachev's policies from the start. By August 1991 opposition within the Communist Party of the Soviet Union had become so great that an attempt was made to 'turn the clock back' by staging a take-over of the Soviet government. Soviet troops were sent to Moscow. Gorbachev and his family were placed under 'house arrest' while on holiday in the Crimea. The attempted coup failed completely. The soldiers mingled with civilians. Former Moscow mayor Boris Yeltsin persuaded the soldiers to lay down their arms. The USSR, like so many Eastern bloc countries in 1989, faced a peaceful revolution in government. The traditional communists were disgraced, Gorbachev was discredited. By the end of 1991 Yeltsin had replaced Gorbachev as leader. The USSR was replaced with the Commonwealth of Independent States made up of 11 of the former 15 republics of the USSR. In turn, this confederation collapsed leaving the Russian Federation merely one of 15 new independent states.

1. What was the main reason for the end of the Cold War in 1991? Explain your answer.

2. To what extent was Mikhail Gorbachev responsible for the end of the Cold War?

3. Using information in this chapter, was the collapse of Soviet control in eastern Europe, and the USSR itself, inevitable?

## Source-based questions: Gorbachev and the Cold War

**Study Sources 1–5 and answer questions (a) and (b) which follow.**

### SOURCE 1

The accession of Gorbachev to power in March 1985 marked the beginning of the end of the cold war – indeed, he set out deliberately to end it. Arms control lay at the heart of the search for a political accommodation with the United States. Gorbachev and Reagan met in four summit meetings between 1985 and 1988 and transformed the chilly relationship between their countries into one of trust and conciliation by the end of the decade.

At their first summit meeting in Geneva in November 1985 no concrete results were achieved, but the two leaders agreed that 'a nuclear war cannot be won and must not be fought'. This statement represented a significant shift in Soviet thinking and pointed to the possibility that the Soviet Union might consider reducing its ICBM force. But Soviet opposition to SDI proved to be the main stumbling block to any practical agreement in arms control.

The second summit meeting between Reagan and Gorbachev was held at a reputedly haunted house in Reykjavik, Iceland, in October 1986. It was to prove the most bizarre meeting in the history of nuclear diplomacy. Contrary to each country's expectations, the agenda at Reykjavik turned out to be not arms control, not even arms reduction, but the most implausible theme of the nuclear age – complete disarmament. In the final session Reagan called for the elimination of all ballistic missiles within ten years. Gorbachev insisted that US research on SDI must be confined to the 'laboratory'. Reagan would make no concessions over SDI and the summit ended in failure.

*From The Cold War 1945–1991 by John Mason,*
*Routledge, 1996 pages 64–65*

### SOURCE 2

The Geneva Summit (of 1985) was a watershed in relations. Gorbachev's attitude to Reagan was that he was more than a conservative, he was a political dinosaur. The American President reciprocated by viewing the Soviet Union as (Burkina Faso) with missiles, but potentially a threat to the free world. He despised everything about communism. Reagan's dislike of Russia and Russians was abstract – he had never visited the country. However, the few Russians he had met, such as Dobrynin and Gromyko, he liked. Geneva was regarded as a success by both sides. The personal chemistry worked. One of the reasons for this was that Gorbachev noticed that Reagan did not like detail. Reagan was keen to get across the message that a nuclear war could not be won, so should not be fought. The Russian proposed that the two superpowers should issue a statement that neither would be the first to launch a nuclear war. The US objected to this as it precluded an American nuclear response to a Soviet conventional invasion of western Europe. The compromise reached was to agree to prevent any war between them, whether nuclear or conventional.

*From Russia, America and the Cold War 1949–1991*
*by Martin McCauley, 1998*

### SOURCE 3

We realised it was vitally necessary to correct the distorted ideas we had about other nations. These misconceptions had made us oppose the rest of the world for many decades, which had negative effects on our economy. We understand that in today's world of mutual interdependence, progress is unthinkable for any society which is fenced off from the world by impenetrable state frontiers and ideological barriers. A country can develop its full potential by interacting with other societies, yet without giving up its own identity.

We realised that we could not ensure our country's security without reckoning with the interests of other countries, and that, in our nuclear age, you could not build a safe security system based solely on military means. This prompted us to propose an entirely new concept of global security, which included all aspects of international relations.

*From Mikhail Gorbachev: Memoirs, 1996, commenting on the*
*USSR's new foreign policy of 1986*

## SOURCE 4

In 1985 global military expenditure was $940 billion (more than the entire income of the poorer half of the world). The two superpowers were each devoting over $250 billion annually to defence. Their leaders were hard-pressed to find ways of carrying through the three essential functions of maintaining military security, satisfying the socio-economic needs of their citizens and ensuring sustaining economic growth.

*From The Cold War by Hugh Higgins, 1993*

## SOURCE 5

Gorbachev: We have to alter our views on the measures connected to the latest hostile behaviour of the American administration. The turn of events in Reykjavik reveals that our 'friends' in the USA lack any positive programme and are doing everything to increase pressure on us. And … with extreme brutality, and are conducting themselves like true bandits. We have to keep on applying pressure on the American administration by explaining our positions to the public and demonstrate that the responsibility for the failure to agree on the limitation and liquidation of nuclear armaments rests fairly and squarely with the Americans.

*From a meeting of the Soviet Politburo (cabinet) on 22 October 1986. From Judgement in Moscow: A Dissident in the Kremlin Archives by Vladimir Boukovsky, 1995*

**Answer both questions (a) and (b).**

**(a) Using your own knowledge and the evidence in Sources, 1, 2 and 4 what do you consider to be the main reasons for the ending of the Cold War between the USA and USSR in the years 1985–1989?**

**(b) 'The Cold War in Europe came to an end mainly because of the efforts of Mikhail Gorbachev.'**

**Using your own knowledge and the evidence from all five sources, explain how far you agree with this interpretation.**

# Further Reading

### Texts designed for AS and A2 Level students

*The Cold War 1945–1965* by Joseph Smith (Blackwell, Historical Association Studies, 1989)

*The Origins of the Cold War 1941–1949* by Martin McCauley (Longman, Seminar Studies series, 2nd edition, 1995)

*Russia, America and the Cold War 1949–1991* by Martin McCauley (Longman, Seminar Studies series, 1998)

*The USA and the Cold War* by Oliver Edwards (Hodder, Access to History series, 1997)

*The Cold War 1945–1991* by John W. Mason (Routledge, Lancaster Pamphlets, 1996)

*The Cold War* by Hugh Higgins (Heinemann, 3rd edition, 1993)

### More advanced reading

*The Cold War 1947–1991* by Simon Ball (Hodder Headline, 1998)

*Cold War Europe 1945–1989* by John W. Young (Edward Arnold, 1991)

*Eastern Europe since 1945* by G. and N. Swain (Macmillan, 1993)

*Western Europe since 1945* by D.W. Urwin (Longman, 4th edition, 1991)

*Britain and the Cold War 1945–1991* by S. Greenwood (Macmillan, 2000)

*The Cold War, the Great Powers and their Allies* by J.P.D. Dunbabin (Longman, 1994)

# 6 The USA and the Cold War in Asia, 1945–1973

## Key Issues

- Why did the Cold War spread to Asia after 1945?

- With what success did the USA contain the spread of communism in Asia, 1945–1975?

- How far did US policy towards Asia change, 1945–1975?

6.1 How successful were US policies towards Japan, 1945–1952?

6.2 Why did the United States fail to prevent a Communist victory in China?

6.3 How and with what consequences for foreign policy in Asia did the USA get involved in war in Korea?

6.4 Historical interpretation: Why did the Korean War take place?

6.5 What problems did China/Taiwanese relations pose for the United States after 1949?

6.6 Why did the USA become increasingly involved in South East Asia, 1945–1965?

6.7 A study in depth: Who was more responsible for US involvement in Vietnam: JFK or LBJ?

6.8 Why did the USA fail to defeat communism in South East Asia, 1965–1973?

6.9 What impact did the Nixon presidency have on US policy towards Asia?

## Framework of Events

| | |
|---|---|
| 1945 | US occupation of Japan begins |
| 1946 | Truce in Chinese Civil War |
| 1948 | China Aid Act |
| | Two separate governments set up in North and South Korea |
| 1949 | Communist victory in Chinese Civil War |
| 1950 | USSR and China sign mutual defence pact |
| | June: Outbreak of war in Korea |
| 1951 | US–Japanese treaty |
| | US treaty with the Philippines |
| 1952 | US occupation of Japan ends |
| 1953 | End of Korean War |
| 1954 | Fall of Dien Bien Phu |
| | Geneva Accords on French Indo-China |
| | Defence Pact between USA and Taiwan/Formosa |
| | September: Signing of SEATO |
| 1955 | First Formosa/Taiwan Crisis |
| 1958 | Second Formosa/Taiwan Crisis |
| 1962 | Neutrality of Laos agreed in Geneva |
| 1963 | 2 November: Assassination of President Diem of South Vietnam |
| | 22 November: Assassination of President Kennedy |
| 1964 | August: Gulf of Tonkin Incident |
| 1965 | February: Attack on US military base at Pleiku |
| | March: Marines land at Da Nang in South Vietnam |
| | Anti-war protests by Students for a Democratic Society |

| 1968 | January: Tet Offensive in South Vietnam |
| | 16 March: My Lai Massacre |
| 1969 | May: Paris peace talks begin |
| | 15 October: March Against Death |
| 1970 | 30 April: Invasion of Cambodia |
| | 4 May: Students killed in protest at Kent State University |
| 1972 | Linebacker bombing campaigns |
| | 22 February: Nixon visits China |
| 1973 | 27 January: Paris Peace Agreement |
| | March: Americans withdraw from South Vietnam |
| 1975 | April: Fall of Saigon. |

## Overview

WHILE President Truman focused his attention on Europe after the end of the Second World War, there were those in government who argued that equal attention needed to be paid to the East. After all, it was the attack on Pearl Harbor by the Japanese that had brought the Americans into the War and the USA had a long history of friendship with the Chinese going back to the 1890s. As America also got rubber and oil from the East and had bases in the Pacific, the Far East was also strategically important. These 'Asia-firsters' argued that Europeans could take care of themselves and that the government should pay more attention to the East. But as the chief adversary in the Cold War was the Soviet Union, Europe tended to play a larger role in American foreign policy. At times, events in Asia forced themselves to the forefront.

At the end of the Second World War, the Americans took on the role of main occupiers in Japan, hoping to turn it into a democratic and peaceful power. It was to be weakened so that it would never again threaten America's interests in the Pacific. Events in China forced a change of attitude. When China 'fell' to communism in 1949, Japan was turned into the United States' foremost ally in the region and was built up to be a balance against communist expansion in Asia. By 1951, the Americans had a formal alliance with their recent enemy.

The threat of the world's most populous nation falling to communism led to the extension of the Truman Doctrine to the Far East. However, geographical, as well as political, realities prevented the USA from helping the Nationalist forces in China to halt the advance of Mao's Communists. By continuing to back Chiang Kai-Shek and the Nationalists, the Americans found themselves on the verge of war with China in 1955, and again in 1958. The disagreements were over the fate of the islands of Formosa (now known as Taiwan), to which the Nationalists had fled in 1949. Disputes over the islands have continued to damage American relations with China ever since.

The policy of containment, embodied in the Truman Doctrine in 1947, could be said to have prevented war in Europe for 40 years, yet that same policy found the Americans getting into a war in the Far East in 1950. At the end of the Second World War, Korea had been divided into a Communist North and a Democratic South, led by Kim Il Sung and Syngman Rhee respectively, who both wanted to re-unify their nation. In 1950, the North Koreans invaded the South to do just that.

President Truman, supported by the United Nations, decided to take a stand. An army from 16 countries went to Korea to throw out the invaders. Rather than achieving a quick and easy victory, American arrogance led to the Chinese entering the war and a two-year stalemate resulted. The war finally ended in 1953, with Korea still divided.

Even more damaging was the American involvement in Vietnam. When the former French colony of Indo-China attempted to gain its independence, in 1945, they hoped the Americans, as former colonials themselves, would help. Instead the Americans chose to back their NATO ally in their unsuccessful attempt to hold on to power. After the French defeat at Dien Bien Phu, Indo-China was divided into four areas, with Vietnam divided, like Korea, into a communist North and a non-communist South. Unlike Korea, however, there was widespread support in Vietnam – North and South – for the Communist leader Ho Chi Minh. As in Korea, the Americans tried to enforce containment. The so-called 'Domino Theory' convinced them that, if South Vietnam were allowed to fall to communism, then the rest of Asia would follow.

Over the next two decades, American involvement in South Vietnam was gradually increased. By 1965, combat troops landed at Da Nang, the first marines sent abroad to fight since Korea: America was again at war. This time though they were fighting a jungle war, with no clear enemy in a different uniform, and they were fighting without the support of the majority of the population or of their allies. The conduct of the war in Vietnam and American losses led to an anti-war movement at home which actively opposed the governments of Johnson and Nixon. The war divided American society like no other since the Civil War. It was a war which the country was not winning. Finally, in 1973, a peace treaty was agreed and the United States pulled its troops out of Vietnam. The 'fall' which they had tried so hard to prevent happened just two years later with a North Vietnamese invasion followed by the unification of the country under Communist leadership.

American conduct of the Cold War in Asia was far less successful than its policy in Europe. In many ways, containment was an inappropriate response to events in the Far East. It assumed that the Soviet Union was behind all communist movements and, when China became communist, it was assumed the two powers acted as one. In both these assumptions, the Americans were wrong. The Soviet Union was undoubtedly involved in the spread of communism to Asia, and it did sometimes work hand in hand with China. More often the rise of communism was the result of local conditions. Revolutionary groups such as the Vietcong were frequently more nationalist than communist. This failure to understand the Far East was affected by the McCarthyism of the 1940s, which saw the removal of many experts from the State Department because of accusations of communist sympathies. It was also due to seeing policies work in Europe and falsely believing that they could be applied elsewhere. Some argue it was also due to American racism going back to the 19th century which underestimated Asian peoples. The USA did have some successes in the Far East, in fact they achieved their aims much of the time. It was the disaster in Vietnam which was the major weakness in US policy in the Far East during the Cold War.

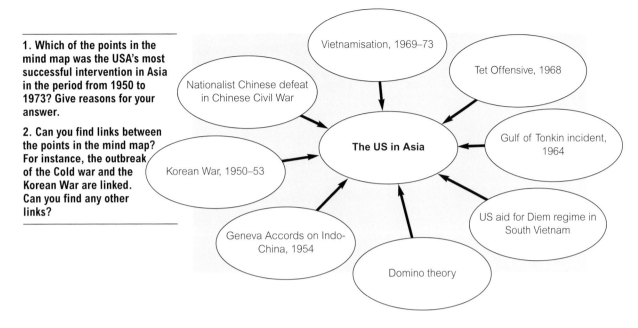

1. Which of the points in the mind map was the USA's most successful intervention in Asia in the period from 1950 to 1973? Give reasons for your answer.

2. Can you find links between the points in the mind map? For instance, the outbreak of the Cold war and the Korean War are linked. Can you find any other links?

Mind map labels: Vietnamisation, 1969–73; Tet Offensive, 1968; Nationalist Chinese defeat in Chinese Civil War; The US in Asia; Gulf of Tonkin incident, 1964; Korean War, 1950–53; US aid for Diem regime in South Vietnam; Geneva Accords on Indo-China, 1954; Domino theory

## 6.1 How successful were US policies towards Japan, 1945–1952?

**Douglas MacArthur (1880–1964)**
Professional soldier who served in France during the First World War and in the Philippines in the 1930s. He commanded US forces in the Pacific during the Second World War and after a retreat from the Philippine Islands he organised the 'island hopping' campaign which helped to recapture the Pacific. He was in command of UN forces in Korea until removed by Truman.

**Feudalism:** A system of organising society based on land ownership and obligation. In return for protection and being able to farm the land, the peasant gives obedience and service to the landowner. This system had been widespread in Europe but had died out in the 18th and 19th centuries. A type of feudalism had continued in Japan, and the Americans believed it held Japan back from developing democratic institutions. Also, because it emphasised obedience, it had allowed the military to lead Japan into war. The Americans hoped that abolishing it would speed up Japan's modernisation.

After the surrender in August 1945, the United States occupied Japan in order to establish a new, democratic government. As in Germany, there was a council of the four powers to discuss Japanese issues, but only US troops occupied the country. The USA also took control of several Pacific islands including the Marshall Islands, the Marianas and the Carolinas. They also occupied the islands of Okinawa and Iwo Jima which they had fought so hard to capture during the War. This American dominance angered the Soviets but, as they had entered the war against Japan so late, they could do little more than protest. In respect for their contribution to the war and for their strategic concerns in Asia, they were given a role in the occupation of Korea instead. The USA did as much as possible to limit Soviet and, therefore, communist influence in the Far Eastern settlement.

General MacArthur, the American commander in Japan, was given almost dictatorial power to turn Japan from a militaristic state into a democratic one. Communists were banned from government posts, the military was drastically reduced and **feudalism** was ended. MacArthur encouraged reform with votes for women, legalisation of trade unions, a democratic constitution that outlawed war, and a democratically elected government. The kind of democracy the Americans wished to create in Japan between 1945 and 1952 was very much in their own image. Communists were banned from government positions or from posts in the universities where they might influence future leaders, and restrictions were placed on trade unions. While trade links with other Asian states were encouraged, the Americans did not wish to see Japan regain its former position. It would be taught by the USA to be democratic and peaceful and content within its own islands.

### Why did American policy towards Japan change?

Originally, the USA had seen China as its main trading and military partner in the Far East, but 1949 changed that. When the communists won the civil war in China, it became important to build Japan back up as a strong

Chinese troops march through Beijing in 1949. The soldiers on the lorry are holding up a photograph of Mao Ze-dong and a propaganda poster.

power to counter-balance 'Red' China. Building up the Japanese economy would also have the added benefit of providing a market for US goods now that much of the former trade with China was lost. Also, as in Europe, there was the fear that if Japan remained a poor country it would be more susceptible to communism itself. All these factors turned American policy towards Japan around. It would continue to be developed as a democratic nation, but from 1950 onwards there would be help and support for its rapid economic redevelopment. The occupying forces did much to rebuild Japanese industry and Congress gave $500 million in aid. America's allies in the East – Thailand, the Philippines and Indonesia, for example – were encouraged to trade with Japan and open up their markets to Japanese exports. The Americans were determined that as the old colonial powers lost their influence in Asia, America would not lose its and it would not see communism take over. In the words of historian Richard Crockatt, in *The United States and the Cold War 1941–1953* (1989), 'Japan became the keystone of containment in Asia.'

The decision to strengthen Japan was given added urgency in 1950 when war broke out in Korea between the communist North and the western-backed South. Japan could now be useful as a base from which to run operations in Korea and as a place for 'R and R' (rest and recuperation away from the war) for American soldiers. To reinforce the new friendship a treaty was signed, in 1951, formally ending the war between the USA and Japan. The occupation ended on 28 April 1952. Also, in September 1951, a Mutual Security Treaty was signed allowing the USA to maintain military bases and troops on Japanese territory. Japan was allowed to develop an army of 110,000 men for its own defence.

Although they had been part of the war against Japan, the Soviets refused to sign the treaty. Relations between the USA and the Soviet Union had deteriorated badly in Europe since 1945 and conflicts in the East made things worse. Understandably, they took differing positions with regard to the revolution in China and the war in Korea. The USSR also resented the way it had been edged out of all decisions relating to Japan. The Soviets felt that they had a valid interest in the area. (Japan and Russia had fought a war, 1905–06, and had several historical disputes over territory.) They knew that Japan was being built up as part of American containment policy and, to the USSR, it looked as if they were being encircled.

The Soviets were not the only ones less than happy with these developments. Those countries which had suffered Japanese attack during the War were very uneasy and, within Japan itself, there were several demonstrations against the American bases. In 1954, anti-American riots forced Eisenhower to cancel a proposed visit to Japan.

In spite of the concerns, Japan quickly became economically powerful and was one of America's strongest allies in the East. Continued support and aid built Japan up from a defeated nation to one that was competing economically with the United States itself by the 1960s. The constitution which the USA had given it meant that they never supplied military help to the Americans in places such as Korea or Vietnam but, ironically, this also meant that they spent their money on economic growth not war. The thriving capitalist economy was a stronger protection against communist infiltration than any number of US bases.

**1. In what ways was the political system of Japan changed under the Allied occupation?**

**2. Why was the USSR excluded from the Japanese settlement?**

**3. Why and how did American policy towards Japan change?**

# 6.2 Why did the United States fail to prevent a Communist victory in China?

* Chinese names can be spelled a number of ways. Chiang Kai-Shek is sometimes seen as Jiang Jei-shi and Mao Ze-dong as Mao Tse-Tung.

## What was American policy towards the Chinese Civil War, 1945–1949?

In 1927 a civil war broke out in China between the Nationalists, led by Chiang Kai-Shek* and the Communists, led by Mao Ze-dong. The USA had ties of trade and immigration with China going back into the 19th

**Chiang Kai-Shek (1887–1975)**
The son of a middle-class family who became a professional soldier in 1906. While in the military he became a republican and revolutionary. When the empire fell apart, Chiang joined Sun Yat-sen's Nationalists who were trying to re-unite China. Jiang went to Moscow in 1923 to study the Soviet system, but in 1927 he threw the communists out of the Nationalist Party. In 1928, he established a government in Nanking, but it was in conflict with the communists and then the Japanese. When Chiang lost the civil war in 1949 he took his forces to Taiwan where, with the backing of the USA, he established an economically successful state.

**Mao Ze-dong (1883–1976)**
Born into a peasant family, he studied at Beijing University and worked for a while as a primary teacher. Mao was a founding member of the Chinese Communist Party (CCP) in 1921. He worked on labour organisations. Unlike most communists, who said that the urban working classes were the foundation of the revolution, Mao argued that the peasants were also potential revolutionaries. When Chiang threw the communists out of the Nationalist Party (1927), Mao and his followers began to organise the peasants in the countryside. In 1934, he led the 'Long March' during which his followers fled 6,000 miles across China to escape attack by the Nationalists. Under Mao's leadership, the CCP grew to over a million strong by 1945. During the 1950s, Mao attempted to modernise China with the 'Great Leap Forward' programmes of industrialisation and **collectivisation** of agriculture, but they produced much hardship for the Chinese people. As rivalry for the leadership of world communism intensified, Chinese relations with the USSR deteriorated in the 1960s, while in the 1970s friendship with the USA grew.

**Collectivisation**: The bringing under state ownership and control of farms and factories. The usual method is to combine a number of small firms or factories into one larger one.

century and China was therefore seen as culturally and economically important to the USA. Their isolationist policies of the 1920s meant they watched with interest but took no real part in events. When the Japanese attacked China in 1937, the various groups in the civil war put aside their differences to fight the invader. At Yalta, Roosevelt had persuaded Stalin to support Chiang and to keep Mao under control so that they could focus on defeating Japan. However, conflict broke out again in 1945.

Clearly, the Americans did not want the Communists to win. A communist victory, they felt, would endanger the 'open door' trade policy which they had fought so hard to establish in China decades before. There was also a danger of communism spreading to Japan, where the USA was working hard to establish a democratic government. On the other hand, State Department officials warned Truman of the danger of identifying the Americans too closely with Chiang who was both corrupt and unpopular. Ideally, what Truman wanted was a negotiated peace which would allow the Nationalists a part in government, as well as remove the need for US intervention. An American-backed conference between Chiang and Mao, in 1945, failed to find a solution. Chiang refused to make concessions, particularly over the industrialised area of Manchuria, which both sides wished to control. Truman sent 50,000 US troops to try to help Chiang establish control once the Soviets had pulled out. This encouraged Chiang to believe that he would have American support for whatever policies he chose.

The following year, President Truman sent George Marshall to try and find a solution. He managed to negotiate a truce in January 1946, but it fell apart within three months when Chiang's forces attacked Manchuria after the Soviets had pulled out leaving Mao in control of the area. American support failed to help the Nationalists take the province and as popular resentment against Chiang grew, it was also turned against the United States. In 1946, the Americans started to withdraw.

In the USA, Truman was criticised, especially by the Republicans, for not applying the principles of containment to Asia. General Wedemeyer advised giving further financial support to the Nationalists and, in 1948, the China Aid Act gave $400 million to Chiang, bringing to $3 billion the amount of aid given by the US since 1945. However, the aid was having little effect. Even as the Act was being passed, the Communists were moving towards victory. The outbreak of the crisis in Berlin meant that American attention was focused firmly on events in Germany. By October 1949, the Communists had won and Chiang Kai-Shek and and his two million followers had fled to the island of Formosa/Taiwan. The Americans refused to recognise the communist government of the People's Republic of China. Instead they continued to refer to Taiwan and its government as Nationalist China.

**Albert Coady Wedemeyer (1897–1989)**

A professional soldier, Wedemeyer served in China and Germany between the wars and spoke Mandarin Chinese. During the Second World War he worked with General Marshall and helped to plan the Normandy landings. In 1944, he was sent again to the Far East and advised support for the Nationalists in China. He retired in 1951.

## Why did the USA not intervene in China?

When General Wedemeyer gave his advice to President Truman, he said that the USA should send another 10,000 troops to help Chiang, but Truman refused. Secretary of State, Dean Acheson, pointed out that sending advisors or military chiefs would lead to more troops being sent and America had neither the men nor the desire to get into a land war in China. The defeat was also happening at the same time as problems were increasing in Berlin, so the government did not want to tie up troops in the Far East when they might be needed in Europe.

Acheson also had to admit that it was largely Chiang's own fault that he had lost. The Nationalist leader was corrupt and undemocratic, so support for Mao was strong among the poor in China. The Nationalists refused to support land reform and therefore failed to gain the support of the peasants, who made up 80% of the population. They even lost middle-class support by letting inflation run at 700%, wiping out people's savings and businesses. In 1945, Chiang had an army of 2½ million, outnumbering the Communists five to one but, by 1949, the Nationalist forces had halved through defections to the Communist side.

**China lobby**: Politicians, businessmen and others who tried to pressure the government over their policy on China. They were usually the 'Asia-firsters' (see page 147) but included others who wanted the government to do more for China.

American political sympathies might have been with the Nationalists, but nothing either Truman or the **China lobby** could say or do would alter the realities of the situation. The USA simply could not send tens of thousands of men across an ocean to face an enemy of several millions, or do this in support of a government which was unpopular among many of its own people. As Acheson wrote, in the so-called 'China White Paper' published in 1949, 'Nothing this country did or could have done within the reasonable limits of its capabilities would have changed the result [of the civil war].'

The geographical and political realities did not stop Truman's critics from accusing him of 'losing' China. To many Americans, it seemed that communism was indeed spreading. The signing of a mutual defence pact between China and the USSR, in 1950, confirmed the belief that the Soviet Union was bent on world domination and had now added the world's most populous country to its sphere of influence. Together the USSR and China formed a massive bloc, cutting off a huge market for US trade and spreading communist dominance into the Far East.

## What was the effect of the 'loss' of China on US policy?

John Dulles called it 'the worst defeat the United States has suffered in its history'. In many ways the United States over-reacted to the events in China. Firstly, for all the politicians might argue, China had not been America's to 'lose' – as many historians have pointed out. Acheson was right when he acknowledged that there was nothing the USA could have done to affect the outcome of the Civil War. It was a fight over which they had no control and which was about China, not about the Cold War as they believed (a lesson America might well have learned before Vietnam). The Americans also overestimated the strength of the bonds between China and the USSR. They might have signed an alliance, but there were deep-seated rivalries over territory in Manchuria and over the nature and leadership of worldwide communism. The USA assumed that the two communist states acted together, and in this they were frequently wrong. However, the 'loss' was very damaging for Truman and did affect both foreign and domestic policy.

The Republicans blamed Truman for the fall of China to communism. It helped to fuel the rise in McCarthyism as they accused spies in the State Department of being responsible. Their accusation of spies in the government was given added weight when the Soviet Union exploded its own atom bomb the same year that China fell. This not only cost many State Department officials their jobs, losing valuable expertise on far Eastern affairs, but also meant that Truman had to respond to the criticism by being seen to be equally tough on communism – which fuelled the anti-communist hysteria still further.

In spite of an early attempt by Mao Ze-dong to build a relationship with the United States, the Truman Administration refused to see Communist China as anything other than a Soviet puppet. Internationally, they tried to weaken Mao's position. They blocked the entry of the People's Republic into the United Nations and tried, largely unsuccessfully, to persuade their allies not to recognise Mao's government. They continued to give financial

**1. In what ways did President Truman support the Nationalist Chinese?**

**2. How successful was American policy towards China in the years 1945 to 1949?**

and moral support to the Nationalists in Taiwan. This support was to cause continuing problems for Eisenhower in the 1950s.

American policy in Asia was deeply affected by the loss of China. It led to a complete turn around in its conduct towards the Japanese, who now became the United States' most valued ally in the region. It also meant that, when Truman was faced with further communist aggression in Korea, he could not afford to back down.

## 6.3 How and with what consequences for foreign policy in Asia did the USA get involved in war in Korea?

**Syngman Rhee (1875–1965)**
Korean nationalist who was imprisoned by the government in his youth for his political activities. He studied in the USA, returning briefly to Korea before Japan occupied it in 1912. He returned to the USA to campaign for Korean independence. He was elected president of South Korea four times between 1948 and 1960. Although in theory South Korea was a democracy, Rhee's rule was very dictatorial. Student-led protests in 1960 led to his resignation and exile.

**Kim Il Sung (1912–1994)**
As a young man he fought in the guerrilla movements against Japanese occupation. In the 1930s, he went to train in the USSR and during the Second World War he served in a Korean unit in the Red Army. He became the Soviet-backed leader of North Korea in 1948. After the war he made North Korea into a one-party dictatorship. Even after the fall of communism in Europe in 1989, North Korea remained firmly **Stalinist**. He remained leader of the country until his death in 1994, when his son succeeded him.

**Stalinist**: A political system based on the type of communism developed by Stalin in the USSR 1929–53. It is highly centralised, the leader has great authority, and there is widespread use of terror.

During the Second World War, Korea had been occupied by the Japanese. As a result of agreements at Potsdam, the Soviet Union had joined the war against Japan and helped to liberate Korea. Consequently, the country was divided at the end of the war into two zones, occupied by the Americans and the Soviets, with the border being the 38th Parallel (see map on page 148). As in Germany, the division was meant to be temporary and elections were to be held to unify the country. However, when the Americans submitted the issue to the United Nations in 1947, the USSR refused to go along with it. The Americans decided to go ahead and hold elections in their zone the next year. The two superpowers then pulled their troops out, leaving a divided Korea with Syngman Rhee leader of a democratic South and a communist-backed North under Kim Il Sung.

The Soviets had opposed the elections, as they believed Korea would vote to be a capitalist democracy. The USSR wanted to extend their power into the Far East, so a united, non-communist Korea was not in their interests. With China about to fall under communist control, Korea would add to the strength of communism in the area and extend Soviet influence. For similar reasons, the Americans did not want a united Korea if it were under communism. So, when the Soviet Union refused to go along with the elections, the Americans just held elections in their own zone. Though they wanted free elections they were not prepared to fight the USSR over the issue, especially when Berlin and China were of more immediate concern.

### How did the war break out?

On 25 June 1950, North Korean troops invaded the South. Almost 100,000 men, equipped with Soviet-made tanks and aircraft, poured into the South capturing Seoul (the southern capital) and most of the country down to Pusan. The attack came without warning and was totally unexpected by the USA. In fact, diplomats heard the news first from journalists and refused to believe it. The South Koreans turned to America for help.

Truman felt he had no choice but to take a stand. Morally, the South Koreans had suffered an unprovoked attack and deserved aid from their allies. On a domestic political level, he had to take action. He was low in the opinion polls and there were mid-term elections coming in November. Truman had already been heavily criticised by McCarthy and by the Republicans for 'losing' China: he could not afford to lose Korea too. He also believed in the need for containment. He was convinced that the Soviet Union was behind the attack and, if the United States did not stop them in Korea, they would 'swallow up one piece of Asia after another'.

Two days after the attack, Truman ordered military supplies to be sent to South Korea from the American bases in Japan and ordered US planes and ships to the area. The 7th Fleet was sent to the China Sea to ensure the Chinese did not take advantage of the situation and attack Taiwan. Truman had decided that America would fight but, to avoid lengthy debate in

Congress, he went to the United Nations for support for his action. He asked the UN Secretary General for a meeting of the Security Council. The UN Charter said that all the members would support any fellow member who suffered an unprovoked attack. It seemed that South Korea was in that position so the United Nations authorised the USA to organise and coordinate military action by 16 member nations against the North Koreans to get them out of the South.

Of the 11 members of the Security Council, only Communist Yugoslavia voted against the Korean operation. The Soviets could have exercised their veto in the Security Council to prevent the action, but the USSR was boycotting the UN at the time in protest at America blocking Communist China's entry to the organisation, so the vote passed. They did not make this mistake again.

### How effectively did the UN pursue the war?

In July 1950, the first American troops landed in Korea. The counter-attack began in September when UN troops under General Douglas MacArthur landed at Inchon, behind the North Korean lines. The invasion quickly collapsed and by 8 October they had forced the North Koreans back behind the 38th Parallel. At this point, the Americans had achieved containment. They had done what the UN had authorised them to do (i.e. get the invaders out of South Korea). Instead of calling a ceasefire, the American-led forces invaded the North and, by October, had captured the northern capital, Pyongyang. With victory seeming so easy, the Americans decided to try and retake the initiative in the Cold War and regain some territory from the Communists.

An invasion of North Korea would be seen by the Chinese as a threat to their security. Urged on by Stalin, they warned the Americans not to invade North Korea. Neither the Americans nor their allies took the warning seriously. As American troops neared the Yalu River, the border between Korea and China, the Chinese invaded. On 19 October, 250,000 Chinese troops poured over the border. The UN forces were completely overwhelmed and

---

**The United Nations**
Set up in 1945 in San Francisco to remove sources of conflict and to preserve peace.

**The General Assembly**
Each member state has a representative. It meets once a year and debates issues and allocates the budget.

**The Security Council**
It has five permanent members – Britain, USA, USSR, France and China – and originally had six non-permanent members. These are elected for two years by the Assembly, and the number has increased as the UN has grown. The permanent members have a veto over Council decisions.

**The Secretariat**
This is the UN civil service and does the day-to-day work. In charge of it is the Secretary General, elected for five years by the Assembly. He (there has been no female Secretary General yet) is the face of the UN and can bring any matter to its attention.

The UN also has many agencies which deal with specific issues, such as the UNHCR for refugees, UNESCO for education and culture, WHO for health etc.

The UN has only twice organised peace enforcement operations: Korea in 1950–53 and the Gulf War in 1992.

within four months they had been pushed back and Seoul was once again in Communist hands. The Americans and the UN forces stood their ground and pushed northwards once again and, by late spring, the fighting settled around the 38th Parallel and got bogged down – almost like First World War trench warfare.

### How was the war brought to an end?

Neither power wanted the war to spread to an all-out fight between America and China, nor did they want to involve the Soviets. Yet neither side wanted to back down. The Chinese knew the Americans would continue to support Chiang in Taiwan and that if they also controlled the Korean peninsula it would threaten Chinese security. While the Americans would not pull out of Korea, leaving it all in communist hands, containment meant they had to protect the South. Two years of attrition was the result.

To break the deadlock, General MacArthur wanted Truman to 'unleash Chiang' (i.e. to support an attack on the People's Republic by Nationalist forces from Taiwan). The British urged the Americans to be cautious about extending the boundaries of the war. Any direct attack on Chinese territory ran the risk of bringing the Soviet Union in to protect China. The danger was a third world war, and the British knew full well that the Soviets would probably launch an attack in Europe. The United Nations had only given them a mandate to remove the invaders from South Korea; they had not given permission for an attack on Communist China. President Truman knew that at home the people were growing tired of a war which had seemed to promise a short and easy victory, but had so far dragged on for over a year with no end in sight.

MacArthur, however, continued to press his arguments and even suggested that Truman use the atom bomb on China. In the spring of 1951, when Truman refused to see things his way, MacArthur complained to Joseph Martin, a Republican Congressman. Martin then went to the press and made public the disagreement over policies. In spite of the popularity of MacArthur, Truman had no choice but to sack him. A military commander could not be allowed to flout the will of the President and dispute his orders in public. MacArthur was replaced. The Joint Chiefs of Staff fully supported Truman's decision, but MacArthur was welcomed home as a hero. His dismissal did nothing for Truman's falling popularity.

It was obvious, even before 1951 was out, that the war was not going to be over quickly. Negotiations for an armistice began in Panmunjon but they dragged on for two years, while the fighting continued to claim lives from each side and from among the Korean civilian population. Then, in 1953, world circumstances changed, allowing for progress in the war. Stalin died and Eisenhower became President of the USA. During the election, 'Ike' had promised to end the war. Stalin's death meant the Soviet Union also had an excuse to improve relations with the USA and with a new government which genuinely wanted the war to end.

During the 1952 presidential election campaign, 'Ike' had promised to go to Korea personally to end the war. The death of Stalin meant that there was a more sympathetic attitude in the Soviet Union and a willingness to put pressure on China for a settlement. The negotiations, however, were not smooth. Twice nuclear war was threatened by US Secretary of State John Dulles who wanted to ensure the Chinese knew America was serious about ending the war one way or another. He threatened a second time when China stalled the talks because Syngman Rhee had released 25,000 prisoners when it had been agreed that the UN would do all prisoner repatriation. In order to get negotiations going again, Dulles threatened China with nuclear weapons, and they backed down.

A ceasefire was finally agreed in 1953, with the border being the 38th Parallel, where it remains today between communist North Korea and democratic South Korea. A de-militarised zone keeps the two sides apart.

The three-year war had ended with the situation pretty much as it had been before the war started. With the new border, the South Koreans gained 1,500 square miles of land. The cost of those 1,500 square miles was two million lives. During the course of the Korean War, 54,246 American soldiers died – only 4,000 fewer than in the 12-year conflict in Vietnam – and another 106,000 were wounded. The financial cost has been estimated as, at least, $20 billion. Containment in Asia was proving to be very expensive.

## What were the effects of the Korean War on US policy?

Apart from the millions of dead and wounded, as well as the damage done to the villages and people of Korea, the war had important domestic and foreign policy effects on the United States.

**Bipartisan**: Supported by both parties. The parties put aside their differences for a while (e.g. in a war or over a piece of legislation on which they both agree).

Initially, the war had **bipartisan** support in Congress, but it quickly turned to criticism of Truman. The dragging out of the war after 1951 began to raise serious questions at home, which once again fuelled McCarthyism. The United States was the most powerful nation in the world and it was fighting, along with 15 other nations, a small Asian state. Why had they not won easily? Even when the Chinese entered the war, many Americans still could not understand their failure to secure victory against a country far less developed than theirs. Rather than look for real causes in the nature of the fighting or in the fact that a country of two billion people could absorb massive losses in battle, they looked for a scapegoat. Many found it by continuing to believe that traitors in the State Department and in government were to blame.

Many Republicans also blamed Truman for the war happening in the first place. The 'Asia-firsters' maintained that, if he had shown more resolve over China, Communist expansion would have been halted before it even reached Korea. They were still assuming that the Democratic Administration could have affected the Chinese civil war. Since Truman had proclaimed his Doctrine, the USA had been faced with having to decide whether or not to enforce it in Berlin, in China and in Korea. In the first it had succeeded, in the second it had not really been attempted, and in the third situation it had in fact succeeded by getting the North Koreans and the Chinese out of South Korea. But, as far as many Republicans were concerned, Truman's containment policy was failing in Asia.

When President Truman bypassed Congress and went to the United Nations to get support for a military operation in Korea, he was not going beyond his powers. As a member of the UN and signatory to the Charter, the USA could be expected to help a fellow member. As Commander-in-Chief of the US armed forces, Truman could send soldiers to fight abroad. Taking military action without fully consulting Congress was a further growth in Presidential power which began under Roosevelt and was to develop still further under Kennedy and Johnson with regard to Vietnam – and with more dire consequences.

The Korean War also had a serious impact on foreign policy. Korea had shown Truman the necessity of strengthening America's military position in the Far East. Truman set about forming treaties to put this right. Two defence treaties were signed in 1951, with Japan and with the Philippines. The same year, a defence pact was signed between Australia, New Zealand and the USA – the ANZUS Pact. This meant the USA was now more closely

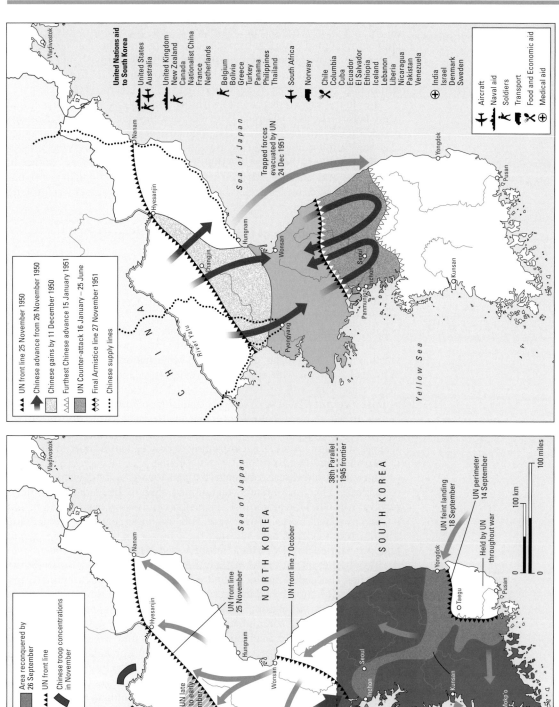

The Korean War: (left) June–November 1950; (right) November 1950–November 1951

involved in Asian affairs. The Truman Doctrine, it seemed, was going to be applied to the East as well as to Europe. Although to Truman himself, Europe would always be more important, America built up bases and friendships in the East. Both military and economic aid was sent to its allies in Japan, the Philippines and Thailand.

The experience of the Korean War led the United States to be more active in its pursuit of containment in Asia. Not only did America build a system of alliances throughout the region, but there was a much firmer approach to crises in the area. When emergencies arose in Taiwan and when the French found themselves facing communist-led rebellion in Indo-China, the American position was firm. It seemed that military action was no longer ruled out. In fact, the military was deployed more frequently in Asia during the Cold War than in Europe.

President Truman not only strengthened America's military position in the Asia, he also strengthened NATO and built bases in North Africa. Eisenhower extended the system of treaties and bases creating the South East Asian Treaty Organisation (SEATO) and the Baghdad Pact in 1954. According to historian Stephen Ambrose, in *Rise to Globalism* (1997), 'Truman extended American bases around the world, hemming in both China and Russia.' The result of this containment was massive military spending. The defence budget, in 1953, was $52.6 billion. Kennan had thought of containment in primarily political and economic terms, but it was now firmly a military policy.

**1. Why did the Korean War last three years?**

**2. General Omar Bradley famously said of MacArthur's plan to attack China that it would be 'the wrong war, in the wrong place, at the wrong time, against the wrong enemy'. How valid is this view when applied to US involvement in the Korean War?**

## 6.4 Why did the Korean War take place?
### A CASE STUDY IN HISTORICAL INTERPRETATION

The Korean War is often referred to by veterans as the 'forgotten war'. Sandwiched between the slaughter of the Second World War and the nightmare of Vietnam, its importance and its costs are often overlooked. In some ways, it is a simple war to explain: the North launched an unprovoked attack on the South; the UN came to the defence of the South and threw out the armies of the North. The intervention of the Chinese was a mistake. Unfortunately, it meant the war took longer than it should have.

The issues of the Korean War are much more complex than that. Whose fault was the war? Some blame Truman for not backing the South more forcefully, while others blame the South because there were many border incidents caused by the South which could have led to war. The North Koreans invaded, but would Kim Il Sung have dared to start a war without consulting Stalin?

Coming as it did just after the 'fall' of China, many people at the time saw the Korean War in the context of the Cold War in Asia. Many on the right, such as the 'Asia-firsters', blamed Truman for the war, arguing that his policies encouraged it. Firstly, they argued that by removing American troops in 1948 he had left South Korea defenceless against the Communists. Secondly, they pointed out that Secretary of State, Dean Acheson, had made a speech in January 1951 saying that Korea was outside the US 'defence perimeter' (i.e. the parts of Asia important to US defence). This encouraged the North Koreans and the Soviet Union to believe that South Korea was not important to America and it would not fight to defend it: a belief encouraged by America's unwillingness to fight in China.

The historian Stephen Ambrose also blames Truman, but for very different reasons. He is critical of American foreign policy and argues strongly that Truman wanted to 'sell' NSC-68 to the people and to Congress, and the Korean War was perfect. Ambrose also maintains that the President wanted to increase US involvement in Asia and that his rapid reaction to events was evidence of this policy.

James Patterson, in *America in the Twentieth Century* (1994), is much more sympathetic to the US government. He points out that Truman's military advisors, including MacArthur, had recommended removing troops from Korea. It had little strategic value and the military needed the resources being used in Korea to strengthen NATO. If Truman had conveyed the message that South Korea did not matter to the USA it was certainly not his intention and he should not take the blame for a war. Patterson also argues that although the military might suggest higher spending through NSC-68 they would hardly want a war to get it. The war did, in fact, enable a massive build-up in the US military with spending rising from $14 billion in 1949 to $52.6 billion in 1953 – 60% of the federal budget. (Though this fell again after the war.) Patterson also points out the obvious fact that it was the North who invaded the South. Therefore, whatever else might be said, they had started the war.

Gary Reichard, in *Politics as Usual: the Age of Truman and Eisenhower* (1988), looks at the personalities of the men involved as well as their policies. He agrees that Truman did react quickly when the invasion occurred, but says that this rapid reaction was simply typical of his quick, and even unthinking, response to crises.

The Americans themselves clearly believed that the Soviets were behind the attack. Kim Il Sung had visited Moscow in April 1950 and it now seems clear from the Soviet archives which have been opened recently to western historians, that Stalin did give his backing for the invasion. In May and June, the Soviets sent military supplies to North Korea, including 150 T-34 tanks. As has been pointed out – see Thomas G. Paterson et al, *American Foreign Relations: A History Since 1920* (2000) – the Soviet support was half-hearted, particularly once the war had started. It seems likely that the USSR gave its support to Kim Il Sung hoping for a quick victory in Asia after the failure in Berlin. Once the Americans made their position clear and the war began, the Soviets backed off. They were not willing to go to war with the United States in order to fulfil Kim's dream of a united Korea.

Perhaps some of the blame should go to Syngman Rhee, the South Korean leader. It may be argued that he was aggressive in his behaviour and attitude to the North, and he made no secret of the fact that he wanted to unite Korea. He encouraged border incidents hoping to bring about a war so that the USA would come to his defence and unite Korea under his leadership.

Peter Lowe's study, *The Origins of the Korean War* (1997), looks at how all the major players had an influence in the events leading to the war. He analyses each one of them in turn. Both the Americans and the Soviets played their roles. Lowe points out that Korea needs to be seen in the international context of the Cold War. In other words, the USA, the USSR and China each hoped to improve their international position by the stand they took in Korea. However, Lowe points out that what must not be forgotten is the Korean context. As well as a Cold War conflict, Korea was also a civil war and, at its heart, were the desires of Kim Il Sung and Syngman Rhee.

Although the UN investigation just after the war found that Rhee was not to blame for the invasion, it was only looking at immediate events. There was a history of border skirmishes, harassment and **inflammatory rhetoric**. Rhee had constantly looked to the United States for aid and support, and believed that he had it. Though he might not have started the war, he did welcome it.

**Inflammatory rhetoric**: Speeches and statements made deliberately to annoy and anger, in this case, the North Koreans.

1. What would have been the advantages to the USSR of supporting Kim Il Sung in the invasion of South Korea?

2. How far and for what reasons do historians differ on their interpretations of the causes of the Korean War?

Both Lowe and Paterson agree on the central role of Kim Il Sung in events. Like Rhee, he also wanted to unite the two Koreas, but he is the one who did something about it. The visit to Moscow, in 1950, was to secure Soviet support for his plans. Kim misled Stalin over how easy the victory would be to ensure his backing and to get the necessary supplies. If Stalin had refused, he would have gone to Mao to try and secure the backing of the Communist Chinese. As Paterson puts it: 'The initiative, and probably the timing, of the war came from Pyongyang not from Moscow or Beijing.'

## 6.5 What problems did China/Taiwanese relations pose for the United States after 1949?

When Eisenhower became President in 1953, the Nationalist Chinese still held Taiwan, as well as the neighbouring islands of Quemoy, Matsu and Tachen. American support for the Nationalists had continued after 1949, and had been increased after the Korean War as the USA put more emphasis on its Asian alliances. Aid to Taiwan was averaging $250 million per year. The US 7th fleet, sent by Truman in 1950, was still blockading Taiwan in order to keep the peace between the Nationalists and the Communist Chinese. In 1954, Secretary of State John Dulles signed a treaty promising US protection to defend Taiwan and its islands.

At home, 'Ike' was under great pressure from the 'Grand Old Party' (as the Republican Party was nicknamed) to continue to support Chiang and not recognise communist China. The Republicans and the 'Asia-firsters' did not want another victory for Mao. Partly because of this pressure and partly because of the need to force China to negotiate over the Korean armistice, 'Ike' removed the fleet in 1953 to 'unleash Chiang'. Nationalists raided the coast of China, so in retaliation the Chinese bombarded Quemoy and Matsu and invaded the Tachen islands. Nationalist raids on the coast of China were a common occurrence and the Communists used this opportunity to retaliate. They were also keen to test how strong the defence treaty of 1954 was.

In fact, the Republican Administration in America saw Quemoy as crucial to the defence of Taiwan, and Taiwan as crucial to US security in

### Timeline of Sino(Chinese)–USA relations

**1949**   US Ambassador in China refuses invitation to meet Chinese Communist Party (CCP) leaders in Beijing

**1950**   USA pledges itself to defend Taiwan against the CCP and recognises Guomindang (GMD) in Taiwan as official Chinese government
Chinese attack US troops on North Korean border

**1950s**   USA and China on very bad terms: supported opposite sides during Korean War (1950–53); US citizens forbidden to buy anything from China

**1960s**   Relationship still very poor: worsened by Vietnam War (1965–73) – support opposite sides again

**1964**   China tests first nuclear weapon; alarms the USA

**1971**   US advisor secretly visits Beijing
Communist China allowed into the United Nations

**1972**   President Nixon visits China
USA allows China to purchase a wide range of non-military goods.

Asia. So, in January 1955, 'Ike' got approval from Congress to deploy troops to the area as he saw fit under the 'Formosa Resolution'. This was the first 'area resolution' which gave the President almost unlimited authority to use US forces in a certain area of the world. It passed both Houses of Congress with healthy majorities of 83–3 in the Senate and 410–3 in the House of Representatives. This was a very important extension of presidential power. As Dulles pointed out, at least 'Ike' was getting Congressional approval for his actions, unlike Truman in Korea.

As Eisenhower was now operating the 'New Look' policy with its doctrine of massive retaliation, the Americans threatened to use the atom bomb if China continued the bombardment. He also got the USSR to put additional pressure on China, and it finally backed down. As historian Stephen Ambrose says, '**Brinkmanship** held the line. In the process, however, it scared the wits out of people around the globe.' The United States was again enforcing containment and standing by its alliances. If Mao had been testing the defence treaty he had been given his answer.

**Brinkmanship**: This means taking arguments to the very brink to convince opponents you are serious, hence brinkmanship. Part of the problem with massive retaliation as a policy was that the enemy had to believe you were serious about using atomic weapons.

### Why did problems between China and Taiwan arise again in 1958?

In 1958, a crisis over Quemoy rose again. Chiang had increased the Nationalist army on the islands to 100,000 men, which the Chinese saw as provocative. Once again China commenced a bombardment and, once again, Chiang turned to the Americans for help. Eisenhower sent ships to the area to escort Nationalist ships in safety, but he resisted pressure from Republicans at home and from Chiang to use nuclear weapons. Dulles made it clear to the Communists that Chiang still had American support. He also made it clear to Chiang that the USA was under no obligation to help him every time he chose to provoke Mao. The USA would have fought for Taiwan itself, but did not want to get dragged into a war over Quemoy. Once again, timing was important.

In the same year, another crisis arose over Berlin. Khrushchev was paying a visit to the United States so the added problem of conflict in Asia was to be avoided. In October 1958, Chiang removed some of the troops and China ceased the bombardment.

What Taiwan showed, as did events in Korea and Indo-China, were the limitations on brinkmanship. It also showed how the USA was losing patience with Chiang who seemed to think the Americans would automatically help out no matter what he did. Eisenhower and Dulles had no intention of getting into a war with China for Chiang's sake. Like Truman, they also realised the growing importance of Asia as a Cold War arena and the need to build up American strength in the area.

The South East Asia Treaty Organisation (SEATO) was set up in September 1954. This organisation laid down that:

● all parties would consult if they felt threatened;

● they would act against aggressors if all agreed;

● and a separate protocol would guarantee the freedom of Cambodia, Laos and South Vietnam (the former French colony of Indo-China).

The USA, Britain, Australia, New Zealand, France, Thailand, Pakistan and the Philippines signed SEATO. It was different from NATO in that it was only a promise to consult, not a promise to act. Unlike NATO, SEATO had no permanent organisation or military force. Yet, although Dulles assured Congress that SEATO was only about consultation, at the same time he told the Cabinet that the USA would act in Asia if necessary to protect American interests, even if that meant acting alone. The USA was committing itself to containment in Asia under Eisenhower just as much as it had under Truman.

**1. In what ways did Eisenhower use American military power in his policy towards the Far East?**

**2. How effective was Dulles' policy of brinkmanship?**

# 6.6  Why did the USA become increasingly involved in South East Asia, 1945–1965?

**Ho Chi Minh (1890–1969)**
As a young man he travelled and worked in Europe. A strong nationalist, he campaigned unsuccessfully for Vietnamese independence at the Paris Peace Conference in 1919. He joined the Communist Party and trained in Moscow. Before returning to Vietnam, Ho worked in the USSR and China. He led the Vietminh to success against the French but then as leader of North Vietnam he fought against the Americans and the South Vietnamese for the rest of his life, never living to see an independent Vietnam.

The area of South East Asia which now covers Vietnam, Cambodia and Laos was taken over by the French Empire in the 19th century. In 1930, Ho Chi Minh formed the Indo-Chinese Communist Party, the Vietminh, to fight for independence from France. During the Second World War, the Vietminh, helped by the Allies, fought against Japan. When the war ended, they resumed their fight against France. As they had helped America against the Japanese, and since America was anti-colonial, Ho Chi Minh hoped the Americans would help them to get independence for Vietnam, but that did not happen.

## Why did America support the French in Indo-China?

Even though the USA was anti-imperialist, Truman supported France financially, spending $2 billion which, at its peak, was 78% of France's costs. He also gave $50 billion in economic aid to the region. Truman saw the conflict in Vietnam in Cold War terms. He believed the Vietminh were taking orders from Stalin, so supporting France was enforcing containment and the Truman Doctrine. This was especially important to Truman after 1949 as he was still being criticised for the 'loss' of China and did not want another communist country in the East. He had to show he was still tough on communism.

Many State Department officials pointed out that Ho was more of a nationalist than a communist. There were many Vietnamese who were not communists, but nevertheless supported Ho Chi Minh. Dean Acheson said this was irrelevant. However, by ignoring the fact that Ho was fighting for his country's independence, the Americans always continued to see Vietnam in Cold War terms – meaning that they dangerously misunderstood the nature of the war.

Historian Vivienne Sanders, in *The USA and Vietnam, 1945–1975* (1998), quotes a far-sighted Defence Department official, who said in 1950 about Truman's continued support for the French:

> 'We are gradually increasing our stake in the outcome of the struggle … we are dangerously close to the point of being so deeply committed that we may find ourselves completely committed to direct intervention. These situations, unfortunately, have a way of snowballing.'

Even though Truman gave financial aid to the French, he did not want military involvement or to send troops to South East Asia. He was more concerned with European affairs in the 1940s and Korea in the 1950s.

## How did American involvement increase under Eisenhower?

By 1953, the Vietminh had 250,000 regular soldiers and a militia of nearly two million. Also, their promises of education, healthcare and land did much to win over the ordinary people. They were also getting supplies from the Chinese. The Vietminh were numerous, popular and well-supplied.

By 1954, France was losing the battle at Dien Bien Phu where the Vietminh surrounded their forces. There was debate in the US government about what to do and whether Vietnam mattered to US security. Dulles and Vice-President Nixon wanted to bomb the Vietminh, but 'Ike' refused. He had been elected partly on his promise to end the war in Korea, so the American public would not stand for US troops being sent to another war in Asia so soon after the ceasefire. Congress made it clear they would not support involvement and, when 'Ike' sounded out America's allies, he found that they also refused to back the idea of intervention.

Eisenhower, though, worried that if Indo-China fell to communism the surrounding countries would also fall, like a row of dominoes. He believed the USA had to give some support to the French. Therefore, he continued Truman's policy of financial support but he also sent 300 US personnel to help France as the Military Assistance Advisory Group. This put the first American personnel in South East Asia.

In spite of American help, in May 1954 the French surrendered with 7,200 dead and 11,000 taken prisoner. A peace settlement was agreed between the involved powers at Geneva. Under the Geneva Accords 1954, Indo-China was split into four: Laos, Cambodia, and North and South Vietnam, which were divided along the 17th Parallel.

It was intended to hold elections in all four countries in 1956 and to reunite the two Vietnams, but the USA was afraid if they held elections Ho Chi Minh would win. 'Ike' admitted in his diary that Ho Chi Minh would probably get 80% of the vote. Therefore, the USA refused to sign the Accords and backed Ngo Dinh Diem as leader of South Vietnam, with North Vietnam being led by Ho Chi Minh. The USA invited South Vietnam to join SEATO and stepped up the amount of aid to $500 million a year. More advisors were sent, in contravention of the Geneva Accords. By 1960, there were more than 1,500 US personnel in South East Asia. As the anonymous diplomat had warned, the USA was gradually increasing its stake in Vietnam.

Diem was not a popular Prime Minister and even the USA admitted he was only the best of a bad bunch. He was Catholic in a country of Buddhists and gave jobs to his family. He made no attempt to win peasant support, as Ho did. Corruption and torture of prisoners became routine. 'Ike' urged Diem to introduce land reform to gain the support of the people, but Diem ignored him.

Many people in South Vietnam demanded the elections they had been promised and actively opposed the government of Diem. The opposition to Diem consisted of many groups and was known as the National Front for the Liberation of South Vietnam, or NLF. The Communists largely formed the military wing of the NLF, as they were the strongest group. These South Vietnamese communists were known as the Vietcong (VC). They were supported and equipped by Ho Chi Minh who, in turn, received support and help from the Chinese and the Soviet Union.

This communist backing convinced Eisenhower that this was, indeed, a Cold War conflict. His belief in the Domino Theory persuaded him that it was necessary to support Diem. Above all, Ho and the NLF were Vietnamese nationalists. They had not fought the French and the Japanese, and the French again, simply to come under American control. This misunderstanding of the nationalist nature of the Vietnam conflict was fatal for Eisenhower and his successors.

**Ngo Dinh Diem (1901–1963)**
Aristocratic and catholic politician who served in the French-backed governments until 1933. He rejoined politics in 1954 as Prime Minister. In 1955, he declared himself President but refused to hold the elections as proposed at Geneva. His American-backed government was corrupt and dominated by his family. His failure to reform led to his assassination in 1963.

### Why was the involvement in South East Asia intensified under Kennedy?

Under President Kennedy, foreign policy was very much controlled from the White House. He was more interested in foreign than domestic affairs. Military spending grew dramatically and Kennedy believed he also had to take a firm stand in South East Asia, for both foreign and domestic reasons. Having made Republican 'weakness' an election issue, he could hardly do less than they had, but his own views on the Cold War led him to increase American involvement.

Like Eisenhower, Kennedy also believed in the Domino Theory, especially in places like Vietnam. He believed that Third World areas were where the Cold War would now be fought. He was a strong supporter of the policy of containment, having entered Congress in 1946 and voted in support of the Truman Doctrine in his first days as a politician. In his own inauguration speech, in January 1963, he promised to 'bear any burden, support any friend and oppose any foe' to ensure liberty: Vietnam was an arena to put this into practice. JFK's advisors also encouraged further involvement in Vietnam. Robert McNamara, Secretary of Defence, was convinced that US military superiority would win and he advised sending 40,000 troops. Dean Rusk, Kennedy's Secretary of State, and National Security Advisor McGeorge Bundy also felt the USA should stand up to communism in South East Asia, as did the Joint Chiefs of Staff. No one was seriously suggesting to Kennedy that he might pull back from Eisenhower's position.

Like Eisenhower, Kennedy did not want to get the USA militarily involved in Vietnam, so he refused even though he was under pressure from the army to send troops. More money and more advisors were sent to help Diem so that, by 1963, 23,000 US personnel were in the country. Simply by being there it meant the US personnel were likely to get more involved.

Kennedy initially found himself involved in the affairs of Laos, where a civil war had also broken out, partly due to American backing for anti-government forces in the country. Kennedy sent some military supplies through Thailand, and sent advisors to Laos itself. An agreement, reached at Geneva in 1962, established a neutral government in Laos, but the USA continued to send arms and supplies as they felt that strengthening anti-Communist forces in Laos would improve their position in Vietnam.

### How did military strategy increase involvement?

One of the difficulties preventing success against the NLF and VC was that the Army of the Republic of Vietnam (ARVN) and their American advisors were fighting a war against guerrillas. To combat the terrorist tactics used by the NLF and the VC, Kennedy wanted a policy of 'flexible response'. This entailed using several different methods of fighting, not just one, with particular emphasis on Special Forces such as the Green Berets. They were to train the South Vietnamese in counter-insurgency (i.e. how to defeat terrorists).

One policy used was 'strategic hamlets'. This entailed rounding people up and putting them into villages fortified and protected by the military to isolate them from the VC. However, this created resentment against the government and these hamlets could be infiltrated or taken over by VC guerrillas without the ARVN being aware.

Bombers and helicopters were sent to help, but the American crews often ended up doing the fighting.

The policies being pursued by the ARVN and the Americans were not very effective in military terms or in terms of gaining support from the people of South Vietnam. The VC, on the other hand, treated the people well, paying them for any supplies they took. Like Eisenhower, Kennedy failed to get Diem to appreciate the need to win the support of the people. In May 1963, there were widespread protests against Diem, including one by a Buddhist priest who set himself alight to show his opposition to the Diem regime.

In the same year, a plot to assassinate Diem was hatched by men within his own government. The CIA knew the plan, as did the American ambassador in Saigon, but they saw him as a liability so did not stop it. Diem was murdered just a few weeks before Kennedy himself was assassinated in Dallas. General Westmoreland, the American military commander in Vietnam, said that this involvement in assassination made the USA morally obliged to stay in the country to sort out the mess.

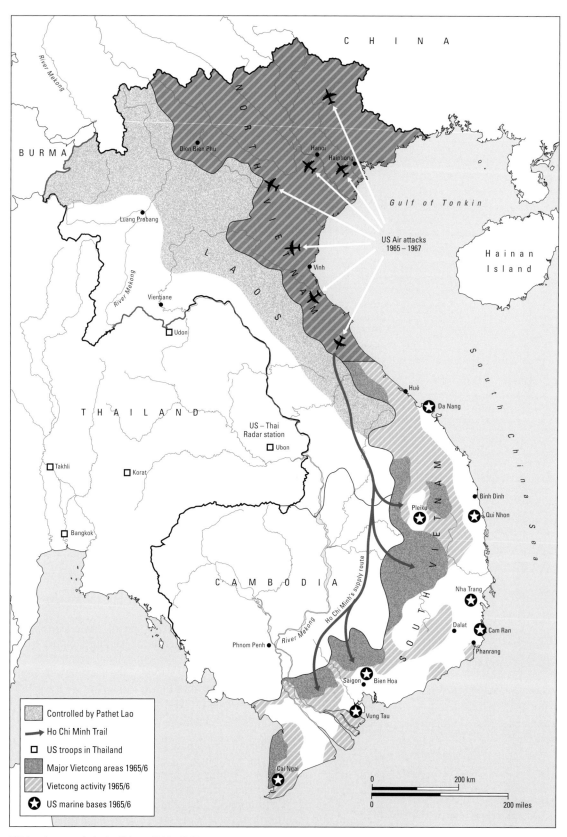

US involvement in Indo-China, 1965–1967

By 1963, there were 16,700 Special Forces troops and advisors in South Vietnam. There were American helicopters, planes and boats. The number of US personnel killed in 1963 was 489. Step by step, three presidents had increased American involvement in the war in South Vietnam.

### Why did Vietnam become a military conflict under President Johnson?

The death of Kennedy provided a perfect opportunity for America to withdraw from the conflict. Instead, the new president, Lyndon Johnson (LBJ), immediately increased the number of personnel in South Vietnam by 30%. Why?

The attitude of the Johnson Administration towards the growing involvement in Vietnam was made clear when Secretary of State, Robert McNamara, said: 'We want an independent, non-communist Vietnam.' To a strongly-held belief in the Domino Theory, Johnson added the belief that the USA had to stand by its allies such as South Vietnam because, if it did not, no one would trust it again. A retreat from Vietnam would send a signal to the world of American retreat elsewhere.

Johnson's own interest was really in domestic policy and the creation of the 'Great Society'. He believed that the United States could free South Vietnam from the Communist threat and then reform it just as he was reforming America. The reality, on the ground, was that the Vietcong controlled 40% of the Vietnamese countryside and they were not going to give this up without a fight.

Having inherited Kennedy's Cabinet, Johnson also inherited Kennedy's advisors. They continued to support a military solution to the problem of South East Asia. Even when some cabinet members started to have second thoughts in the mid-1960s about American policy, LBJ's personality discouraged opposition. They were afraid to tell him the truth or disagree when he said he did not want to be 'the first president to lose a war'.

### What was the impact of the Tonkin Incident on US policy in Vietnam?

At first, Johnson continued JFK's policies of sending aid and advisors, although the numbers increased greatly. In 1964, things changed. On 2 August, North Vietnamese patrol boats fired on the 'USS Maddox' while it was on patrol in the Gulf of Tonkin, but planes from the carrier 'Ticonderoga' drove them off. Two days later, the 'Maddox' and the 'C. Turner Joy' were again patrolling (a **euphemism** for spying on North Vietnamese coastal installations) when they reported being fired on by the North Vietnamese. They returned fire, but later investigations were unclear whether they had been attacked or had been mistaken. The incident gave Johnson the perfect opportunity he had been waiting for to escalate American involvement in the war.

In response to his request, Congress passed an area resolution. The Tonkin Resolution allowed LBJ to take 'all necessary steps including the use of military force' in South East Asia to protect US interests. It also allowed him to take the war to the North Vietnamese who were supplying the VC. By Johnson emphasising the attack and not the provocative patrols, the resolution easily passed both Houses (416–0 and 88–2).

The war now began to escalate dramatically. A US base at Pleiku was attacked, in February 1965, killing eight American servicemen and leading to air strikes on North Vietnam. In March 1965, US marines, the first combat troops sent to Vietnam, landed at Da Nang. The USA was slowly but surely taking over the fighting from the South Vietnamese. (By the end of 1965, there were 184,000 US military personnel in Vietnam.)

**Euphemism**: A polite word or expression which you can use instead of one that might offend or upset people (e.g. 'to pass on' is a euphemism for 'to die').

---

**1.** Why did Truman and Eisenhower support the French in Indo-China?

**2.** According to the 'Quagmire Theory', the USA got sucked into the conflict in Vietnam almost without realising it was happening. How far would you agree with this explanation of Kennedy and Johnson's increasing involvement in Vietnam 1961–1965?

# 6.7 A study in depth: Who was more responsible for US involvement in Vietnam: JFK or LBJ?

■ To what extent did Kennedy commit the US to involvement in Vietnam?

■ Did Johnson merely follow Kennedy's policies on Vietnam?

## Framework of Events

| | |
|---|---|
| 1954 | Geneva Peace Accords; temporary division of French Indo-China into four states |
| 1956 | Supported by the US, anti-communist Ngo Dinh Diem becomes leader of South Vietnam |
| 1960 | National Liberation Front (NFL) of South Vietnam is born; beginning of communist attempt to overthrow South Vietnam Government |
| 1961 | JFK increases number of US military advisers to South Vietnam |
| 1962 | International agreement of Laos, which declares that country 'neutral' |
| | Strategic Hamlets Programme begins |
| 1963 | Assassination of Ngo Dinh Diem |
| | Assassination of Kennedy three weeks later |
| | LBJ takes over US presidency |
| 1964 | Gulf of Tonkin incident and resolution |
| 1965 | Operation Rolling Thunder begins |
| | US ground troops sent to South Vietnam |
| 1968 | Communist Tet Offensive in South Vietnam |
| | US troop level reaches 565,000 |
| | LBJ announces he will not seek re-election as president |
| | LBJ begins negotiations with North Vietnam |

THE Vietnam War bitterly divided the USA in a way no other conflict had done since the Civil War of 1861–5. Over two and a half million Americans served in Vietnam. Fifty-eight thousand were killed. It was the first time in US history that America had lost a war.

Why did the USA become involved in a conflict 10,000 miles from the USA? Ever since the 1960s, contemporaries and historians have debated who was responsible for US military involvement. Did JFK lay the foundations for involvement? Had JFK lived would the involvement of US ground troops have been avoided? Was it really Lyndon Johnson's war?

Dependent upon whom you believe, Vietnam destroyed the presidencies of both men. The plot of Oliver Stone's film, *JFK*, suggests that Kennedy was assassinated because he wanted to pull out of Vietnam. Johnson's presidency was clearly adversely affected. His decision not to seek re-election as president in 1968 was directly due to Vietnam.

# To what extent did Kennedy commit the US to involvement in Vietnam?

### Kennedy and Indo-China in 1961

In his inaugural address as US president, made on 20 January 1961, JFK stated:

> 'Let every nation know ... that we shall pay any price, bear any burden, meet any hardship, support any friend, oppose any foe, in order to assure the survival and success of liberty.'

## Indo-China

This map shows Indo-China in 1954, after the Geneva Accords.

- Indo-China is a region of South East Asia, once ruled by France until 1954. Between 1946 and 1954, France fought a major war against Vietnamese nationalists who wanted independence from France. By 1954, France had lost 78,000 people in the war.
- In 1954, in Geneva, Switzerland, an agreement was made between the USA, USSR, China, Britain and France about the future of Indo-China.
- Indo-China was divided into four states. Two states became monarchies: Laos and Cambodia. However, from the late 1950s, communist forces attempted to take over eastern Laos.
- Vietnam was divided into two states. North Vietnam was communist and ruled by Ho Chi Minh. South Vietnam was non-communist. It was ruled by Ngo Dinh Diem, who acted as a dictator.
- The Geneva Peace Accords (Agreement) planned to have elections throughout Vietnam in 1956 to decide its future. Under US pressure, Diem cancelled the elections. President Eisenhower feared Ho Chi Minh would win and create a united, communist Vietnam.
- In 1960, communists in the South created the NLF, National Liberation Front. The USA called them Viet Cong (VC). They planned a guerrilla war, with Northern assistance, to unite Vietnam as a communist state.

**John Fitzgerald Kennedy (1917–1963)**
35th President of the USA (1961–63), the first Roman Catholic and the youngest person to be elected US President at 43 years old. 'JFK' made his name as a supporter of civil rights' legislation and as a prominent internationalist. He was the symbol of the new changes many American wanted to see. Perhaps most controversially , he involved the USA in the military defence of South Vietnam. In foreign affairs he had a great triumph in the Cuban Missile Crisis of October 1962 when Soviet missiles were withdrawn from Cuba. However, he also had many failures. In April 1961, a C.I.A. plot to invade Cuba, named the Bay of Pigs fiasco, failed badly. On 22 November 1963, JFK was assassinated in Dallas, his death causing worldwide grief. It is difficult to know whether JFK would have succeeded in foreign affairs had he lived.

**Lyndon Baines Johnson (1908–1973)**
He served as vice president until Kennedy's death, when he assumed the presidency (1963–69). In many ways Johnson's presidency was a continuation of JFK's. 'LBJ' became the most reformist president since the New Deal of the 1930s. He was also able to do more for African-American rights than any president had done since the US Civil War. LBJ's most controversial act was the commitment of ground troops to South Vietnam. So great was the financial cost of engagement in a vicious guerrilla ground war and the opposition to the war in the USA that, in 1968, LBJ decided not to seek re-election as president.

To understand JFK's view towards Vietnam one must remember that he became president at the height of the Cold War. It was widely believed by decision makers in Washington DC at the time that the USA faced a communist conspiracy to extend communism across the globe. In this endeavour, the USSR, Communist China and North Vietnam all acted together. Opposing communism in Indo-China was part of a worldwide conflict.

The importance of the USA in the global conflict against communism was made clear by the outgoing President Dwight Eisenhower. In 1954, Eisenhower had stated:

> 'You have a row of dominoes set up, you knock over the first one, and what will happen to the last one is the certainty that it will go over very quickly … When we come to a possible sequence of events, the loss of Indo-China, of Burma [Myanmar], of Thailand, of Malaya and Indonesia following.'

In addition, when Eisenhower briefed Kennedy on foreign policy in 1961, he stated that the most important issue facing the USA in the conflict with communism at that time was the communist attempt to take over Laos. In fact, for most of his presidency, Kennedy spent more time dealing with Laos than South Vietnam. It was only in 1963 that Vietnam became a more dominant problem.

### The case against holding Kennedy responsible for US military involvement in Vietnam

Ever since JFK's assassination, speculation has developed about exactly what he was willing to do to protect South Vietnam from a communist takeover.

Robert F. Kennedy, JFK's younger brother, who was attorney general between 1961 and 1963, said in a conversation in 1967:

> 'We saw the position the French were in [in 1954] and my brother was determined early that we would never get into that position.'

General Maxwell Taylor, who led several US missions to South Vietnam between 1961 and 1963, made a similar comment regarding JFK. After Taylor requested that the USA send 8000 ground troops to aid South Vietnam in 1961, he stated:

> 'I don't recall anyone strongly against this plan except one man, the President. It was really the President's personal conviction that US ground troops shouldn't go in.'

Some historians also believe that JFK was unwilling to make a large military commitment. Arthur M. Schlesinger, in *Robert Kennedy and His Times* (1978), believes JFK occupied a middle position between two opposing groups of advisers on Vietnam. On the one hand, there were 'hawks' such as the head of the **Joint Chiefs of Staff**, General Lyman Lemnitzer. He wanted strong military support for South Vietnam. On the other hand, there were those like US Ambassador to India J.K. Galbraith, who wanted a phased withdrawal of US support for Vietnam. This group tended to support a solution similar to that achieved over Laos in 1962. In that year US envoy, William Averell Harriman, was able to get an agreement with the USSR. Both sides agreed on the 'neutralisation' of Laos. This meant the creation of a coalition government that contained communist and non-communist elements. According to Arthur Schlesinger, Kennedy wanted a solution to the problem in South Vietnam that would avoid a large military commitment by the USA. He wanted to support the South Vietnamese Government in defeating the communist guerrillas.

**General Maxwell Taylor (1901–87)**
Taylor was a Second-World-War general who led the 101st Airborne Brigade at the Battle of Arnhem. Between 1961 and 1965, he was a personal military adviser on Vietnam. He made several fact-finding missions to South Vietnam to appraise the situation. In the autumn of 1961, Taylor, with economic adviser Walt Rostow, visited Saigon and reported on the chaotic situation in South Vietnam. Taylor suggested sending ground troops. His wish was finally granted by LBJ in March 1965.

**Joint Chiefs of Staff**: the leading generals and admirals of the US armed forces.

**Third World**: a term used during the Cold War. The First World was the West, including the USA, Japan and Western Europe; the Second World was the communist world. The rest of the globe was termed the Third World. It included Southern Asia, Africa and Latin America.

On JFK's accession to presidency, there were 800 military advisers in South Vietnam. He increased this number to 3000 by December 1961, to 10,000 in 1962 and to 16,000 by the time of his assassination. Advisers included a contingent of Green Berets – an elite group of special forces trained to fight guerrilla war. JFK hoped that such forces could help defeat communism in **Third World** countries while avoiding a direct military confrontation with the USSR. In addition, JFK increased military aid to the South Vietnamese army (ARVN). In many ways, JFK was buying time. In 1961 and 1962, Vietnam was still a sideshow in US foreign policy. Crises over Berlin and Cuba absorbed much more attention.

According to historian Lawrence Freedman in his book *Kennedy's Wars* (2000), JFK planned to withdraw US advisers once he had won the 1964 presidential election. Senator Mike Mansfield remembers JFK saying, 'I can't depart until 1965 – after I'm re-elected.' When asked by his aide Ken O'Donnell how the USA would be able to withdraw from South Vietnam, JFK stated, 'Easy, put a government in there that will ask us to leave.'

Throughout 1961 and 1962, the Kennedy administration consistently stated that Ngo Dinh Diem was the strong man of Vietnam, who had to be supported in order to defeat the communist uprising. However, by 1963, Diem's regime had become very unpopular. He was a Roman Catholic in charge of a predominantly Buddhist country. His government was dominated by Catholics and was noted for corruption. Instead of using US aid to fight the communists, he used it to gain support for his own government.

**Strategic Hamlets Programme**: villagers in rural areas were rounded up and put in hamlets to isolate them from communist influences.

In 1962, the US suggested the creation of the **Strategic Hamlets Programme**. A similar programme had been used by the British in Malaya, where they successfully defeated a communist uprising in the 1950s. However, Diem and his brother Ngo Dinh Nhu did not create hamlets in areas threatened by communists but in areas where they could gain more political support. They believed the USA would always back them, no matter what they did, because the alternative was a communist victory.

By the spring of 1963, JFK's advisers were suggesting that Diem was in fact the cause of growing communist influence rather than the solution.

In November 1963, generals of ARVN, with CIA help, overthrew Diem, killing him and his brother in the process. This was part of JFK's plan to find a strong South Vietnamese Government that would allow the US to eventually withdraw.

In assessing what JFK might have done had he lived beyond 22 November 1963, several historians have passed comment. Lawrence Freedman, in *Kennedy's Wars* (2000), believes that JFK's advisers were badly divided about what to do in South Vietnam and that Kennedy's policy was aimed at healing rifts among them. Hugh Brogan, in *Kennedy* (1996), states:

> All that can be said is that Kennedy would have been more reluctant than Johnson in accepting a [military commitment] and might well have looked sooner, harder and more successfully for an alternative.

In *The Imperial Presidency* (1973), Arthur Schlesinger helps to explain why. In sending 16,000 advisers, JFK had merely followed actions taken by previous presidents in foreign policy. Also, by November 1963, only 100 US servicemen had been killed in South Vietnam. To most Americans, Vietnam was still a little-known sideshow.

### The case for holding Kennedy responsible for US involvement in Vietnam

JFK fervently believed that the US faced a global communist threat. He accepted Eisenhower's 'domino theory'. JFK was faced with a communist uprising in a 'friendly country' and could not afford defeat. US prestige

## JFK/LBJ advisers on Vietnam

The title 'The best and the brightest' was given to the members of the JFK/LBJ administrations because they were recruited from top universities and large businesses.

**Dean Rusk: Secretary of State**
- Rusk was a highly intelligent man, who had studied for three years at Oxford University before joining the State Department during President Truman's administration (1945–53).
- He was former Under Secretary of State whom JFK chose because he thought he would be a good second-in-command. JFK wanted to be his own Secretary of State. During the Kennedy years, Rusk was sidelined as JFK tended to get advice from his brother, Robert F. Kennedy. Rusk was given more freedom to operate under LBJ, but he was never in the position where he could have offered independent advice. In the debates on Vietnam, he was overshadowed first by Robert Kennedy and later by McGeorge Bundy.

**Robert McNamara: Secretary of Defense**
- McNamara had attended the University of California at Berkeley and also Harvard University. After one month as chief executive of the Ford Motor Company, he left his post, in January 1961, to become Defense Secretary. He became JFK's and LBJ's major adviser on Vietnam.
- With a razor-sharp mind and strong personality, McNamara became a central figure in developing US policy on Vietnam. Kept in the post by Johnson, he virtually ran US policy on Vietnam until August 1968 when he resigned to become president of the World Bank. He was described as aggressive and as being characterised by toughness, quickness, fluency, competence, incorruptibility and a force of personality.

**McGeorge Bundy: National Security Adviser**
- Bundy came from a very wealthy family in Boston, Massachusetts. He attended the best private schools: the Dexter School (where JFK also attended) and Groton (where Franklin D. Roosevelt had been a pupil). He then studied at Yale University. At 30 years old, he became a lecturer in Government at Harvard University.
- Although Bundy was a supporter of the Republican Party, he was strongly attracted to JFK's policies and willing to join his government. He was appointed National Security Adviser from 1961 to 1966, when he resigned to become president of the Ford Foundation. As National Security Adviser, he usually worked a 12—hour day and played a central role in all JFK's foreign policy decisions over Berlin, Cuba and Vietnam. His brother, William P. Bundy, Assistant Secretary of State for Far Eastern Affairs, led the Working Group in 1965 that advised LBJ to begin bombing North Vietnam.

across the world was at stake. Only in this global context can JFK's actions be understood.

Even in 'neutral' Laos, JFK used the CIA to support anti-communist forces. Supplies were flown in, by CIA-owned 'Air America', from Thailand. In addition, US B52 bombers attacked communist positions in central and eastern Laos between 1962 and 1963. These actions were done secretly without Congressional approval.

Kennedy was determined to use South Vietnam as a testing ground for new theories on how to combat communist aggression. He placed great hope in counter-insurgency forces, which would fight guerrilla forces on their own terms. The Green Berets were the force that would be used across the globe for this purpose. According to historian Stephen E. Ambrose, in *Rise to Globalism: American Foreign Policy Since 1938* (1971), 'Kennedy was prepared to do anything to prevent a Viet Cong victory.'

The main strategy of the Kennedy administration until 1963 was to support Ngo Dinh Diem at all costs. He was believed to be the strong man, capable of defeating communism. Unfortunately, such a policy backfired. Diem was immensely unpopular. His leadership was in many ways the reason why the Viet Cong (VC) gained influence in 1961 and 1962. Diem feared a military coup against him by ARVN generals and was very suspicious of any general who won military victories. Instead of fighting the VC, ARVN generals tried to avoid conflict at all costs. A spectacular example was the Battle of Ap Bac in January 1963 when 2000 ARVN troops with US helicopter support were ordered not to move forward and attack 350 lightly armed VC. Instead they were ordered to change their mission to one of blocking positions – a decision that had serious consequences.

Within the USA, opposition to Diem's regime came from journalists such as Neil Sheehan of *United Press International* and David Halberstam of *The New York Times*. The latter noted:

> [Diem] became more convinced than ever that it had its ally [USA] in a corner, that it could do anything it wanted, that continued support would be guaranteed because of the communist threat [and that] the US could not suddenly admit that it had made a vast mistake.

It was Halberstam who first put forward the 'quagmire theory' – the idea that the USA, without forethought, had been sucked into giving military support to Diem.

A key turning point came in August 1963 with the appointment of Henry Cabot Lodge as US Ambassador to South Vietnam. Lodge had been defeated by JFK in the Senate election of 1952. He had also been Nixon's vice-presidential candidate in 1960. From the moment Lodge arrived in Saigon, on 22 August 1963, he was convinced Diem had to be removed. Nationwide protests by Buddhists had brought the country to the point of revolt. From late August to November, Lodge worked with ARVN generals to remove Diem. On 1 November 1963, Diem was overthrown.

Diem's fall, however, led to increased instability in the Southern Government. Diem was first replaced by General Minh and then, in February 1964, by General Khahn. They both formed weak governments. Instead of improving the situation, JFK's policy had made matters worse.

When JFK was assassinated three weeks later, his Vietnam policy was in a mess. Although JFK had ruled out military action against North Vietnam in 1963, Lawrence Freedman in *Kennedy's Wars* (2000) suggests that, in 1964, he might have been forced to change his mind as the military situation deteriorated in the South. This is also the view held by several of today's historians. Historian William H. Chafe notes, in *The Unfinished Journey: America Since World War II* (1999):

> Kennedy and his advisers had charted a course that step-by-step involved the United States inextricably deeper in the Vietnam tragedy. As Ambassador Maxwell Taylor later recalled, 'Diem's overthrow set in motion a sequence of crises, political and military, over the next two years which eventually forced President Johnson in 1965 to choose between accepting defeat or introducing US combat troops.'

Historian James N. Giglio states, in *The Presidency of John F. Kennedy* (1991):

> Given what we know of President Kennedy, it is difficult to conceive of his pulling out of Vietnam without a reasonable honourable settlement.

So was Lyndon Johnson put in an impossible position over Vietnam when he became president on 22 November 1963?

## Did Johnson merely follow Kennedy's policies on Vietnam?

When LBJ became president he did possess some knowledge of Vietnam. As vice president, he had visited South Vietnam during a tour of Asia. However, the situation was still regarded as a sideshow in the early months of Johnson's presidency and he concentrated on enacting domestic reform such as the Civil Rights Act and the Great Society Programme.

Nevertheless, it was difficult for LBJ to change Kennedy's policies on Vietnam. He had, after all, inherited Kennedy's foreign policy advisers. On 26 November 1963, a National Security Action Memorandum (NSAM) stated:

> The central object of the US to South Vietnam [is] to assist the people and government of that country to win their contest against the externally directed and supported communist conspiracy.

So, from November 1963 to the summer of 1964, US policy followed the line of offering financial and military aid to the South Vietnamese Government. Johnson openly stated that he would carry on JFK's work. He said:

> 'I swore to myself that I would carry on. When I took over I often felt as if President Kennedy was sitting in the room looking at me.'

However, by the time Johnson decided not to seek re-election, on 31 March 1968, the situation was transformed. There were 565,000 US ground troops stationed in South Vietnam. The US air force flew bombing missions against targets in North Vietnam. General Westmoreland, US commander in Vietnam, was requesting 200,000 extra troops. The war was costing the US $60 million a day and the USA was bitterly divided about supporting a war that had cost over 35,000 lives and wounded 175,000.

There is considerable evidence to suggest that LBJ would commit the USA to a major war in Vietnam. Historian William H. Chafe, in *The Unfinished Journey: America Since World War II* (1999), suggests that Johnson's Texan background made him determined not to be the first president to lose a war.

By mid-1964, the military and political situation in South Vietnam had deteriorated so much that LBJ's advisers feared the state might collapse. The USA could not afford to lose South Vietnam to communism at the height of the Cold War.

Like JFK, Johnson was a firm believer in the 'domino theory' and the need to stand up to communist aggression. On 27 April 1965, he made the comment:

> 'We are resisting aggression, and as long as aggressors attack, we shall stay there [Vietnam] and resist them – whether we make friends or lose friends.'

Yet, as late as 12 August 1964, Johnson was telling the American Bar Association:

> 'They [the South Vietnamese] call upon us to supply American boys to do the job that Asian boys should do. They ask us to take reckless actions which might risk the lives of millions. Moreover, such action would offer no solution at all to the real problems of Vietnam.'

## Why did Johnson decide to escalate the war, between February 1964 and March 1965?

There are a number of differing interpretations as to why Johnson decided to escalate the war. One interpretation involves the presidential election of 1964 when Johnson faced an extreme anti-communist opponent in the Republican candidate Barry Goldwater.

At the height of the campaign, between 2 August and 4 August, an incident occurred in the Gulf of Tonkin, off the coast of North Vietnam. On 2 August, two US destroyers, the USS Maddox and the USS C. Turner Joy were allegedly attacked by North Vietnamese torpedo boats. A second, alleged attack occurred on 4 August. There is considerable confusion even today about what actually happened. In the confidential Department of Defense documents, the **Pentagon Papers**, released in 1971, there is a strong suggestion that no actual attacks took place. Johnson, however, used the incident to intervene directly in the Vietnam War. For most of the period since 1963, Secretary of Defense Robert McNamara had run the war. Johnson used the incident to get Congress to pass the South East Asia (or Gulf of Tonkin) Resolution. As historian Arthur M. Schlesinger notes, in *The Imperial Presidency* (1973), this was 'rushed through Congress in a stampede of misinformation and misconception, if not of deliberate deception'. Schlesinger and others such as journalist Neil Sheehan, whose book on Vietnam is called *A Bright Shining Lie: John Paul Vann and America in Vietnam* (1989), see Johnson as deliberately misleading Congress and the US public into escalating the war in Vietnam.

The Gulf of Tonkin Resolution gave the US President powers to wage limited war abroad. Initially, Johnson authorised air attacks against specific targets in North Vietnam. In February 1965, this policy was broadened into Operation Rolling Thunder. This was a systematic attempt to bomb North Vietnam and supply lines through Laos known as the Ho Chi Minh trail. Some historians believe that this was the turning point. Rowland Evans and Robert Novak state in their book *Lyndon Johnson and the Exercise of Power* (1966):

> From that moment the war that had been impersonal, distant and secondary became for Lyndon Johnson the consuming passion of his presidency. It became, more than any other war in the 20th century for any other president, a personal war.

On 8 March 1965, following a Viet Cong attack on a US air base at Pleiku, South Vietnam, Johnson committed ground troops for the first time. Three and a half thousand US Marines landed at Da Nang. By April, the numbers had risen to 18,000. On 28 July 1965, Johnson announced that troop levels would rise to 125,000. They had reached 200,000 by the end of the year.

## Should Johnson be blamed personally for direct US military involvement?

To an extent, LBJ was a victim of circumstance. In his biography of Johnson, entitled *Big Daddy from the Pedernales* (1986), historian Paul K. Conkin notes:

> Johnson's policies flowed consistently from a series of decisions made by three earlier presidents [Truman, Eisenhower, Kennedy]. Continuity, not new departures, marked his choices, not because of a lack of experience on his part but because of his own belief and values. He wanted above all else to contain the Vietnam conflict.

It must be remembered that it took LBJ 18 months before he eventually committed ground troops to South Vietnam. In the period from November

**The Pentagon Papers, 1971:** These were government documents on the Vietnam War, compiled under the instruction of Secretary of Defense Robert McNamara. They contained records from the State and Defense Departments and from CIA files. They also contained papers prepared for the Joint Chiefs of Staff and communications between the State Department and the US Embassy in Saigon. The documents go as far back as 1945, but have detailed coverage of the 1963–5 period. The papers were released to The New York Times by Defense Department employee Dr Daniel Ellsberg. President Nixon tried to prevent their publication and took his case to the US Supreme Court but lost. He also tried to discredit Ellsberg by attempting to steal his personal records from his psychiatrist. The Pentagon Papers revealed the depth of secret activity undertaken by the US Government in South East Asia. In particular, they highlighted the deception surrounding the Gulf of Tonkin Resolution.

Defense Secretary Robert McNamara and President Johnson after receiving information of new problems in Vietnam in 1964.

1963 to March 1965, considerable debate took place among his advisers about what to do. Throughout this critical period, Johnson received pessimistic reports about the quality of ARVN and its inability to prevent communist infiltration of South Vietnam.

Johnson set up a Working Group to study possible options in South Vietnam. It was chaired by McGeorge Bundy's brother, William P. Bundy, and contained members from the Department of Defense, the Central Intelligence Agency, the State Department and the Joint Chiefs of Staff. William Bundy reported the findings of the Working Group to LBJ. He explained that the South Vietnamese Government was very weak. He advocated bombing the North as a way of taking pressure off the South Vietnamese Government. In 'The War in Vietnam' in *The Johnson Years* (1981), historian George C. Herring notes:

> The United States [was] primarily responsible for escalating the war [as a] desperate attempt to stave off the collapse of South Vietnam from within.

What Johnson and his major advisers failed to comprehend was the limited impact superior US military technology would have on an enemy determined to unite their own country.

The only dissenting voice from among the inner circle of advisers came from Under Secretary of State George Ball. He thought the commitment of US ground troops would be disastrous. He concluded that once the US was committed to militarily defending South Vietnam they were there for the long haul. His suggestion that up to 500,000 troops would have to be deployed was met with astonishment by the other advisers. However, historians Leslie K. Gelb and Richard H. Betts, in *The Irony of Vietnam: The System Worked* (1979), claim that LBJ and his advisers knew exactly what they were getting into when they escalated the war in February and March 1965.

In retrospect, it is perhaps easy to see the folly of the decision of Johnson and his advisers. However, as historian George Herring states, in 'The War in Vietnam', in *The Johnson Years* (1981):

> It must be stressed that the situation he inherited in Vietnam lent itself to no easy solution – perhaps no solution at all. Those who argue that a more decisive use of military power and a deeper commitment to negotiations would have brought the desired results conveniently overlook the harsh realities of the conflict: (1) a determined, fanatical

enemy (2) the threat of Soviet and Chinese intervention (3) a weak ally (4) domestic consensus which wanted success in Vietnam without paying a high price.

Johnson and his administration are often criticised for having made crucial decisions on escalation without notifying Congress. The escalation into a major conflict, involving US troops, was done in an atmosphere of misinformation about what was actually happening. Only after the publication of the Pentagon Papers in 1971, did the degree of deception and misinformation become apparent. On this point, LBJ and his advisers should be held accountable.

## Who was responsible?

Whether you believe the US stumbled into the quagmire of a land war in Vietnam or consciously and deliberately chose to do so depends upon the historical evidence available. However, the context of the 1960s needs to be taken into consideration when making your final decision. The USA was involved in a global struggle against communism. It was widely believed that Ho Chi Minh in Hanoi worked closely with Chairman Mao in China and the Soviet leadership. Any failure to stand up to communism in Vietnam would have worldwide consequences. The USA had already stood up to communist aggression in Europe in the late 1940s over Berlin. It had also done so in Asia in the Korean War. The war in Vietnam was a continuation of the same policy.

The arrogance of American power at the time also needs to be borne in mind. The USA, with its vastly superior military equipment, thought it could easily defeat an economically backward South East Asian state in North Vietnam. The USA greatly underestimated the nature of guerrilla warfare where lightly-armed troops could be very effective against US forces.

American soldiers fighting a guerrilla attack on a US artillery-infantry base, 1967.

**Conscript**: a person forced to do compulsory military service.

If US military involvement had been kept to aerial bombing, public opinion may have supported the war longer. By committing **conscript** ground troops, the loss of American lives in Vietnam helped turn public opinion against the war by early 1968.

President Johnson later assessed what had gone wrong. Historian Vaughn Davis Bornet, in *The Presidency of Lyndon B. Johnson* (1983), notes:

> President Johnson admitted that two 'key mistakes' had been made on Vietnam. 'Kennedy should have had more than 16,000 military advisers there in the early 1960s. And then I made the situation worse by waiting 18 months before putting more men in. By then the war was lost.'

This would suggest that, rather than showing reluctance in going to war, Johnson believed that more effective military action earlier would have succeeded.

---

## Who was more responsible for US involvement in Vietnam: JFK or LBJ?

**1. Read the following extract and answer the question.**

Johnson and his advisers insisted that by intervening in Vietnam they were defending vital interests of the United States. It resurrected the 'domino theory' first publicised by Eisenhower in 1954, warning that the fall of South Vietnam would cause the loss of all South East Asia with disastrous economic, political, and strategic consequences for the United States. Johnson and his Secretary of State, Dean Rusk, repeatedly emphasised that the failure to stand up to aggression would encourage further aggression, upsetting the international order the United States had established since World War II and perhaps provoking a third world war.

(Adapted from G.C. Herring, 'The War in Vietnam', in *The Johnson Years: Foreign Policy, the Great Society, and the White House*, edited by Robert A. Divine, University of Texas Press, 1981, p 28.)

**Using the information in the extract above, and from this section, explain why the USA increased its military commitment in Vietnam between 1961 and 1965.**

**2. 'Johnson, not Kennedy, was responsible for US military involvement in Vietnam by 1965.' How far do you agree with this statement?**

---

## 6.8 Why did the USA fail to defeat communism in South East Asia, 1965–1973?

The number of American soldiers in Vietnam rose steadily from 200,000 in 1965 to 543,000 by 1969. Even though America largely took over the fighting from the ARVN, the war did not go any better. In fact, the way in which the war itself was fought often meant even greater involvement: if a policy failed they had to do more to make up losses. Therefore the intensity of the war increased. The desire to close down the Ho Chi Minh Trail, along which supplies were fed from North to South, led to Operation Rolling Thunder, a bombing campaign against North Vietnam. Although between 1965 and 1968 more bombs were dropped on North Vietnam than all the bombs dropped in the Second World War, they failed to have a significant effect. In the cities of North Vietnam production was moved out of Hanoi and spread around the country so that the raids did minimal damage. On the Trail, the North Vietnamese and Vietcong simply built another road in another part of the jungle.

Free-fire zones were designated, in which anyone could be a target. New technologies were brought into the fighting. For example, **defoliants** such as Agent Orange were sprayed to try and destroy the jungle cover of the VC, and **napalm** was used in raids. There was a policy of 'pacification' which meant that, where a village was suspected of helping the VC, it was destroyed. Because they were not fighting an easily identifiable enemy, success began to be measured by 'body count' and 'kill ratio'. A dead Vietnamese was presumed to be a dead VC, whether they were or not.

Understandably, rather than winning the 'hearts and minds' of the Vietnamese peasants, these kind of policies turned many of them against the Americans and pushed them into support for the Vietcong. Young American soldiers, drafted into the war, could not understand how they were not welcomed as liberating heroes as their fathers had been in Europe. Morale in the American army worsened, with drug taking and desertions becoming serious problems. Violence against civilians worsened most horrifically at My Lai in 1968 where 347 unarmed men, women and children were killed by American soldiers (see panel).

Yet all the time the generals were telling the President, and the President was telling the public, that they were winning the war and that victory was just around the corner. This fiction was dramatically exposed in January 1968, when the North Vietnamese Army (NVA) and the Vietcong launched the Tet Offensive.

NVA troops and the VC mounted a coordinated attack in 36 of the 44 provincial capitals throughout the South, hoping to spark off a mass uprising against Saigon. It was the largest engagement of the war. The

**Defoliants**: Chemicals used on trees and plants that make all their leaves fall off. This made it harder for guerrilla fighters to hide in the forests.

**Napalm**: A type of petroleum jelly which is used to make bombs that burn and destroy people and plants.

## The My Lai Massacre

On 16 March 1968, soldiers from the 11th Infantry brigade entered the village of My Lai as part of a search and destroy mission in Vietcong-held territory. During the raid, the men of 'C' company killed over 300 men, women and children, including 70 who were gathered into a pit and shot. Soldiers shot or bayoneted children as young as two years old. For over a year, the army covered up the massacre. Then it was leaked to the 'New York Times' and an investigation and trial were launched. Thirteen soldiers were charged with war crimes, but only the platoon commander, Lieutenant William Calley, was convicted. He served three years of a ten-year sentence, then he was pardoned.

The average age of the American soldiers in Vietnam was just 19. One soldier spoke of the war 'wearing us down, driving us mad, killing us'. In spite of this and in spite of the fact that the majority of soldiers did not commit atrocities, the My Lai Massacre had a

profound effect on the war at home. American people were revolted by it and thought the sentences were far too lenient. Many were angry at the military cover-up. Others saw it as simply part of the madness of the war. It contributed significantly to the growing divisions in the United States over the war in Vietnam.

Murdered women and children at My Lai, 1968

death toll consisted of 58,400 Communists, 4,000 US troops, more than 2,000 ARVN and 14,300 civilians. The US Embassy itself was attacked. Four embassy staff were killed. It took three weeks to re-take Saigon. In military terms, Tet was a failure for the NVA. Their losses were massive, far more devastating than the Americans realised, and they had failed to launch an uprising against the South Vietnamese government. However, psychologically, it was a turning point for the Americans. Seeing the television pictures of VC in the embassy compound brought home to the public that, in spite of what the government was telling them, they were not winning the Vietnam War.

Despite their superior technology and money, it seemed the United States could not win this war. The Americans were still backing an unpopular corrupt government that lacked the support of the majority of the people. With the help of the peasants, the VC and NVA could use the jungle and the country villages to hide out and continue their guerrilla warfare. Many military men at the time and since have argued that part of the problem was that the wrong approach was used to meet this challenge. After Tet, the army asked for a further 206,000 men. To defeat the Communists, the American government had to commit itself to total war and fully use the resources of the world's most powerful nation, as they had in the Second World War. But Johnson was not prepared to do this. Vietnam was already taking finance away from his beloved Great Society programmes and by 1968 the government was $25.3 billion in debt. There were already half a million men in Vietnam and it is doubtful if the American public would have allowed him to raise the money and manpower necessary to achieve a complete military victory. In fact, the American public was increasingly turning against the war, especially after the 1968 Tet Offensive.

While the majority of Americans had supported government policy throughout the war, an increasing number were questioning why they were in Vietnam. It was among students that the anti-war movement started, with the first 'teach-in' at the University of Michigan in 1965. The anti-war movement then spread among students, organised by Students for a Democratic Society (SDS). Their protest was about the morality of the war as much as its effectiveness. It was taking money away from Johnson's poverty programmes. In their view, the United States had no right to tell other countries how to run their governments. The students organised protest marches, burned draft cards, held debates, broke up classes etc. During the March Against Death in 1969, 300,000 filed past the White House in silence for 40 hours each carrying the name of a dead soldier or a destroyed village. At Kent State University, in 1970, four students were killed and 11 injured when National Guardsmen opened fire on a protest against Nixon's invasion of Cambodia.

Opposition was not just from students. The growing 'credibility gap' between what the government was telling people about the war and what was actually happening concerned many Americans. Among liberals especially, hostility to the war increased in the 1960s. President Kennedy's brother, Robert Kennedy, came out against the war in 1968 when he decided to run for the Democratic presidential nomination against another anti-war candidate, Eugene McCarthy. The architect of containment himself, George Kennan, was also a critic of the war. There were also protests in other countries and much criticism of US policy. Whether the anti-war movement had any real impact on the conduct of the war is an area of current debate. It is doubtful that the protests in themselves forced the government to make peace but, in a democracy, no government can ignore totally the protests of a large and growing section of the population.

There had been a halt in bombing as early as 1965 in order to explore peace talks, but the USA would not accept any Communists as part of the government of Vietnam so they failed. By 1968, President Johnson realised that the war had to end. Opposition was increasing at home and abroad, the war was costing billions of dollars and thousands of lives, and Tet had shown them they were not winning. The opposition and failure to make any headway in the war led Johnson to announce on television to the American public that the USA would be seeking peace talks. He also made the surprise announcement that he would not be seeking re-election in 1968. Peace talks began in May 1968 in Paris. Nothing was agreed before Johnson left office.

### Why did Nixon take action between 1969–1973 to end the war?

When Nixon came to office, in 1969, he wanted to end the war for the same reasons as Johnson. But Nixon also had other foreign policy aims, especially building friendship with China, which demanded peace in Vietnam. He formulated the so-called 'Nixon Doctrine': the USA would give aid to countries facing internal revolt but not ground troops. This meant withdrawal from South East Asia and no more Vietnams. Nixon felt that he could not just pull out, as this would look like a defeat. He wanted 'peace with honour'. Nixon hoped for a Korean-style solution with Thieu in charge of South Vietnam. In the meantime, while negotiations were going on, US troops had to be removed without South Vietnam collapsing. The solution was the policy of Vietnamisation (i.e. getting the ARVN to take back the responsibility for the fighting).

Historian Stephen Ambrose says that this 'proved to be a disastrous choice, one of the worst decisions ever made by a Cold War president'. The policy bought the Americans time for negotiation and withdrawal, but it worsened the situation on the ground. The US troops saw little point in fighting when it was clear they were going to leave and the ARVN felt betrayed. Desertions increased in both armies. At the same time, the USA had to pour more supplies into Vietnam in order to equip them to fight the NVA; so the costs of the war increased.

**Nguyen Van Thieu (1923–2001 )**

A soldier who for a while fought with the Vietminh but then sided with the French. He served under Diem and then under his successor Nguyen Cao Ky. Thieu was involved in Diem's assassination in 1963. He was elected President in 1967, a post he held until the fall of South Vietnam in 1975. His rule, like Diem's, was undemocratic and corrupt.

**Look at the picture here, the photograph on pages 169 and Source B on page 177. How do these events help to explain why so many people in the USA opposed US involvement in South East Asia?**

A student screams in horror. Soldiers shot dead four students at Kent State University who were part of a protest against the Vietnam War in 1970.

**1. What message is this cartoon making about Nixon's policy?**

**2. Do you think the cartoonist believed that Nixon's Vietnam policy was likely to be successful? Explain your answer.**

Cartoon by Nicholas Garland, which appeared in 'Daily Telegraph' on 3 April 1970, entitled 'The good samaritan …'.

**TNT**: Abbreviation for the most famous high explosive: trinitrotoluene.

**Khmer Rouge**: Communist guerrilla forces in Cambodia whose leader was Pol Pot, a man of mystery who fought in jungles for five years before 1975 without making any clear statement of his political intentions. For more on the actions of the Khmer Rouge and Pol Pot see page 174.

To put more pressure on North Vietnam in the peace talks, and to cover the withdrawal of US troops, the bombing intensified. For example, Operation Linebacker I dropped 155,000 tons of **TNT** on North Vietnam in 1972. Nixon's bombing campaigns were part of his 'mad man' strategy: he wanted North Vietnam to believe he was mad enough to use an atom bomb if they did not negotiate. In 1969, the secret and illegal bombing of neighbouring Laos and Cambodia began, followed in April 1970 by an invasion to try and destroy the Ho Chi Minh Trail and communist bases in these countries.

When the 'New York Times' leaked the story about Cambodia, there were forceful protests at home and abroad. Congress reacted by repealing the Tonkin Resolution and passing the Cooper–Church Amendment cutting off any military aid that was being used against Cambodia. Nixon backed off, but the damage to Cambodia was immeasurable. The destabilisation of the country allowed the **Khmer Rouge** to seize power in 1975. The murderous regime, led by Pol Pot, wiped out a quarter of the entire population before it was stopped in 1979, by the Vietnamese.

Throughout 1968–1972, negotiations took place, but with little success. The USA wanted North Vietnam to accept Thieu in the South, but it refused. As the negotiations dragged on so, therefore, did the war. An attack by the North Vietnamese, in March 1972, led Nixon to launch Linebacker II – a ten-day bombing raid so fierce that the Swedish Prime Minister likened it to the crimes of the Nazi death camp at Treblinka.

In the end the negotiation, the continued fighting and pressure from the

Soviet Union and China, who also wanted an end to the war, finally worked. The peace treaty was signed in Paris on 27 January 1973. Under its terms, the USA would withdraw from South Vietnam, all prisoners of war were to be returned, and there were to be negotiations to decide the future of North and South Vietnam. A Committee of National Reconciliation was to organise free elections, which included representatives of the South Vietnamese, the Communists and neutrals. In effect, Nixon had got a treaty which he could have had in 1968. Each side had made compromises but, in the intervening four years, 20,553 more Americans and half a million more Vietnamese had died.

---

**Paris Peace Agreement, 27 January 1973**
- US troops to be withdrawn from Vietnam, Laos and Cambodia.
- Establishment of a National Council for Reconciliation in South Vietnam which would include the Communists and which would organise free elections in the South.
- An international commission to oversee the ceasefire.
- Full exchange of prisoners.

---

The USA continued to give aid to the government of South Vietnam after 1973. They had withdrawn their troops, but had not given up hope of seeing South Vietnam remain non-communist. CIA advisors, as well as military personnel, remained behind. In 1974, Congress voted $700 million in aid for Thieu's government. But the North Vietnamese had no more intention of abiding by the ceasefire agreement than the Americans. In 1975, they launched an attack which quickly over-ran the country. The ARVN collapsed, with thousands deserting or changing sides. Thieu's government fell and, in April, Saigon was captured. Vietnam was united under communist leadership.

## What were the effects of the Vietnam War on the USA and on South East Asia?

The social and psychological costs of the Vietnam War were enormous, as were the costs in people and material. The USA had spent at least $150 billion on the war, taking badly needed resources away from social policies at home. Eighty thousand Americans and at least two million Vietnamese were killed. Added to this were hundreds of thousands wounded and disabled in the USA and in Asia. The social problems of veterans returning home having lost a war they were expected to win were ignored for decades.

More bombs were dropped on Vietnam, Laos and Cambodia during the war than had been dropped in the entire history of the world. The physical damage to these countries caused suffering for many years afterwards. Thousands were disabled, thousands more developed cancer from the defoliants used by the Americans. The rebuilding of the economies and infrastructures of South East Asia would take years.

The American government and its political system were also affected badly by the war. The politicians were shown to have consistently lied to the public (e.g. over troop numbers and over the bombing of Cambodia). After the war there was a lack of faith in government. (This was made much worse by the Watergate scandal happening shortly after.)

Congress was also very concerned about the way they, too, had been misled. They also worried about the way succeeding presidents had increased America's commitments in Vietnam largely through their own office rather than through consulting Congress. JFK had used executive power to send Green Berets; LBJ also did the same and lied about the numbers of soldiers sent. The Tonkin Resolution extended presidential power in South East Asia, and Nixon illegally bombed and invaded Cambodia. To reassert its authority, Congress passed the War Powers Act in 1973 requiring that it be consulted before the President sends US forces into a war or consulted within 48 hours in an emergency. The President also had to get Congress' approval for continuance of a war beyond 60 days. In fact, the War Powers Act has never been invoked, but it symbolised how far Congress thought the Executive had sidelined them during the war.

There was disillusionment with the United States' world role among both the public and politicians, at home and abroad. The Americans were no longer the 'good guys' in the Cold War. Their role as 'world's policeman' was questioned and their willingness to act militarily was severely undermined in case it became 'another Vietnam'.

Truman had extended the policy of containment from Europe to Asia. Eisenhower's belief in the domino theory had convinced him to follow Truman's lead. Kennedy and Johnson had increased American involvement to the level that it became an all-out war to determine the political future of Vietnam. What the Americans never understood was that Vietnam was not about the Cold War: it was a nationalist war about Vietnam finally getting its independence from colonial or occupying powers in order to determine its own future. The Americans also consistently underestimated how much punishment the Vietnamese were willing to take to get that independence. When they did finally realise in 1968 that they could not win, they got out. But their determination to try not to make it look like the defeat it was kept the war going for an unnecessary five more years, at immense cost to both sides.

**1. In what ways did the fighting intensify between 1968–1973?**

**2. Why were the Americans unable to win the 'hearts and minds' of the Vietnamese people?**

**3. How successful was Nixon's policy of Vietnamisation?**

# 6.9 What impact did the Nixon presidency have on US policy towards Asia?

### What was the impact on Laos and Cambodia?

As well as presiding over the American withdrawal from Vietnam, the military policies pursued by the Nixon government affected the states bordering Vietnam. The NVA sent supplies to the South through Laos and Cambodia. They had bases in both countries from which they operated. To destroy these lines of communication, both countries were bombed and invaded. In Laos, the ARVN was put into the field and it performed very poorly, being defeated by Laotian troops. The bombing of the country, however, caused much damage and cost many lives.

The effects in Cambodia were much more serious. In March 1969, the Cambodian ruler, Prince Norodom Sihanouk, was toppled in a **coup** by military leader Lon Nol. Sihanouk had tried to maintain neutrality in the war in Vietnam in spite of the Ho Chi Minh Trail passing through Cambodian territory. Nixon saw the coup as an opportunity. The Cambodian government had its own problems with the Khmer Rouge. Nixon believed that he could join with Lon Nol in the crusade against communism and that the Cambodians would, in turn, close down Vietnamese operations in Cambodia. The American invasion, however, destabilised the country and when the USA pulled out of South East Asia they also pulled out of Cambodia, allowing the Khmer Rouge to take power in 1975.

Under the leadership of dictator Pol Pot, the Khmer Rouge set about building a new society in the renamed country of Kampuchea. This involved wiping out all opposition, all intellectuals, all those corrupted by western influences etc. Over the four years of the Khmer Rouge terror, a

**Coup**: An attempt by a group of people, often army officers, to get rid of the ruler or government of a country and to seize power for themselves.

quarter of the Cambodian people were killed, including almost all the country's doctors, nurses, teachers and engineers. In 1979, the Vietnamese army invaded and removed Pol Pot, setting up a pro-Vietnamese government. The Americans were not to blame for the genocide of the Khmer Rouge but their interference in Cambodia, while it tried to stay out of the war, was a major factor in creating the conditions which allowed the Khmer Rouge to take over. What was just as damaging was that the American vote in the United Nations stopped UN aid going to Cambodia for many years because it had a Vietnamese-backed government. In many ways, the suffering of Cambodia was worse than that of Vietnam.

### How did Nixon and Kissinger attempt to improve relations with China?

In July 1971, President Nixon shocked the American public by announcing his intention to visit the People's Republic of China. Henry Kissinger had arranged the visit secretly a few months before and it turned out to be a tremendous success.

Nixon had decided, on taking office, that he would modify US policy towards China. He would be able to do this in a way no Democrat could, because as a Republican and with his background of support for McCarthy no one could accuse him of being soft on communism. He could count on the support of his Republican colleagues while, at the same time, getting the endorsement of Democrats who desired better relations with China. That this would gain him votes in the 1972 presidential election was certainly a factor in his policy. He ensured that the television coverage of the visit was extensive and extremely favourable.

However, the election was only one factor in Nixon's change of strategy. A major factor was the war in Vietnam. Better relations with China might encourage the Chinese to reduce their aid to the North Vietnamese. In this he was unsuccessful as communist aid continued to flow into Vietnam. Though when peace talks started, they did have more support from the Chinese than they might otherwise have had.

A visit to China would also have the added advantage of worrying the Soviets. Where Truman had seen communism as **monolithic**, in fact relations between the USSR and China had always been tense. By 1969, the split had come out into the open. Nixon believed he could play the two states off against each other. Both would fear the other making an alliance with the United States, leaving them isolated. The longer he could keep them guessing, the stronger America's position would be. It would also make them each more likely to cooperate with his policy of *détente*. For China and Russia the advantage of friendship with the US was obvious, as it would strengthen their position against the other.

In the early 1970s, Nixon pursued a policy of *détente* towards the USSR, by which Nixon and Kissinger were able to build much better relations with the Soviet government. This led to a visit by the President to Moscow, in 1972, and to the signing of the Strategic Arms Limitation Treaty (SALT). Through the policy of *détente* and 'triangular diplomacy' between the USA, USSR and China, President Nixon was able to achieve two things. Firstly, he was reducing the amount of support available to the North Vietnamese. The Soviet Union would not stop supporting its ally altogether, but the new relationship with the USA would encourage it to limit that support. For example, when Nixon launched the Linebacker operations the Soviets did not respond directly as they did not want to damage *détente*. Secondly, Nixon was able to play the Soviets and the Chinese off against each other. Each was fearful of isolation. That also gave Nixon more support and freedom of action in Vietnam.

**Monolithic**: Like a single, large block.

**What impact did demonstrations like the one shown in this photograph have on US policy towards Vietnam?**

From the film 'Born on the Fourth of July', starring Tom Cruise as Vietnam veteran Ron Kovik.

**Recession**: A temporary decline or setback in economic activity or prosperity.

The state of the economy was also a factor in Nixon's calculations. In the early 1970s, the world was entering a deep **recession**. As it had for a century, China promised new markets for American goods.

The Americans made steps towards improved relations early on in the Administration with the lifting of restrictions on trade and travel to China. Nixon also gave permission for the American table tennis team to visit the People's Republic. Although this led to many jokes about 'ping-pong diplomacy', it was an important step in improving relations. The actual visit lasted seven days and was a great success. There were meetings between Nixon, Kissinger, Mao and the Chinese premier Zhou En-lai. There were banquets and visits to the Great Wall – all broadcast throughout the world.

The visit produced only a slight change in policy in Vietnam, notably pressure from China on the North Vietnamese delegation in Paris to come to an agreement. It was another six years before the Chinese and Americans resumed full diplomatic relations, but it did have some important effects. Trade between China and the USA increased to $700 million by 1973 and, just after Nixon's visit, the People's Republic was granted the Chinese seat in the United Nations. Both Japan and Taiwan were concerned by the growing friendship between the USA and the Communists so, to ensure that they were not left behind, both countries made their own efforts to build closer ties with Communist China. The problems had not gone away. Taiwan's fate remained a problem for the two countries and the two political systems were still opposed, but Nixon's trip had done much to increase understanding between the two nations and to ease some of the tensions of the Cold War.

## Source-based questions: Opposition to the Vietnam War

### SOURCE A

A poster entitled 'Cooperation in battle. Shoot down any enemy aircraft in order to launch the offensive.' It was produced in North Vietnam in 1972

### SOURCE B

Newspaper picture of 8 June 1972. The nine-year-old South Vietnamese girl, Kim Phuc, was the victim of a napalm attack.

### SOURCE C

Generally … the media were instinctively pro-war and only shifted when sharp elite divisions had already become apparent. Undoubtedly, the famous photographs and film footage of napalm and bomb damage did have an impact. Analysis of television and press coverage, however, does not support Nixon's charges of anti-war bias. White House communication failures … were more damaging to the Administration cause than any activities of crusading journalists.

From *Vietnam: American Involvement at Home and Abroad* by John Dumbrell, 1992

### SOURCE D

By the end of February [1968], the most respected figures of American journalism had placed themselves on record in opposition to the administration policy, creating in the process [approval for opposition to] the war that would ultimately compel the government to reassess its position.

From *The Unfinished Journey* by William H. Chafe, 1986

---

**Source-based questions: Opposition to the Vietnam War**

## SOURCE E

Traditional history portrays the end of wars as coming from the initiative of leaders – negotiations in Paris or Brussels or Geneva or Versailles – just as it often finds the coming of war a response to the demand of 'the people'. The Vietnam war gave clear evidence that at least for that war (making one wonder about the others) the political leaders were the last to take steps to end the war – 'the people' were far ahead. The President was always far behind.

*From A People's History of the United States by Howard Zinn, 1980*

## SOURCE F

I remember sitting on this wretched outpost one day with a couple of my sergeants … This one sergeant of mine, Prior was his name, said, 'You know Lieutenant, I don't see how we're ever going to win this.' And I said, 'Well Sarge, I'm not supposed to say this to you as your officer – but I don't either.'

*Philip Caputo, quoted in Cold War by Jeremy Isaacs and Taylor Downing, 1998*

**1. Study Source A.**

Explain what is meant by the term 'propaganda'.

How might this photograph be used as propaganda?

**2. Study Source B.**

What impact did images such as this have on the anti-war movement?

**3. Study Sources C and D.**

How far do they agree on press support for the war?

**4. Using all the sources and your own knowledge, assess the importance of domestic opposition on America's withdrawal from the Vietnam War.**

---

## Further Reading

### Texts designed for AS Level students

*The Enduring Vision* by Paul Boyer and others (D.C. Heath and Co., 1993) – easy to read and well-illustrated narrative.

*The USA and Vietnam, 1945–1975* by Vivienne Sanders (Hodder and Stoughton, Access to History series, 1999).

*The Cold War* by Bradley Lightbody (Routledge, 1999) – good, clear chapters covering whole period with lots of source questions.

### Texts for A2 and advanced study

*Rise to Globalism* by Stephen Ambrose and Douglas Brinkley (Penguin, 1997) – fascinating and detailed account of post-war policy; quite critical of the USA.

*Vietnam* by John Dumbrell (British Association for American Studies, 1992) – an easy-to-read pamphlet covering the war 1945–1975 at home and abroad.

*A Noble Cause? America and Vietnam* by Gerard de Groot (Longman, 1999) – covers the military, strategic, political and cultural aspects of the war as well as looking at the legacy for both countries.

*Dispatches* by Michael Herr (Picador, 1991) – a journalist's account of the war from talking to soldiers that truly brings home the nightmare quality of Vietnam.

*America's Longest War* by George Herring (McGraw-Hill, 1996) – detailed analysis of American policy from the 1950s onwards in Indo-China.

*Vietnam: A History* by Stanley Karnow (Pimlico, 1991) – detailed and comprehensive analysis of the war.

*The Korean War* by Peter Lowe (Longman, Origins of Modern Wars series, 1997) – looks at the war from the perspective of all the countries involved.

*The Limits of Liberty* by Maldwyn Jones (Oxford University Press, 1995) – clear narrative account.

*American Foreign Relations: A History Since 1920* edited by Thomas G. Paterson, J. Garry Clifford, Kenneth J. Hagan (Houghton Mifflin, 2000) – detailed narrative, well illustrated.

### Television and video

'The Cold War' – CNN production shown on the BBC (1999–2000).

'Vietnam: A Television History' – 13-part series produced by PBS shown on Channel Four in 1982.

'Truman' – a video written and produced by David Grubin for 'The American Experience' series (1994). It is divided into three one-hour episodes: the first covers Truman's political rise and the dropping of the atom bomb on Japan in 1945; the second episode covers Truman's Administration in domestic and foreign affairs up to 1949; the third episode concentrates on the Korean War.

### Websites

The Cold War in Asia has hundreds of websites. The following are just a few.

http://www.gwu.edu/~nsaarchiv – the US National Security Archive containing lots of sources and their international Cold War history project.

http://www.eagle3.american.edu/~mm5860a/origins – description of the Cold War but also lots of links.

http://www.cnn.com/specials/cold.war – site for CNN televison series, but has interesting photographs and bits of information including some animated summaries.

http://hometown.aol.com/veterans/warlib6k – websites for the Korean War.

http://hometown.aol.com/veterans/warlib6v – websites for the Vietnam War.

www.yale.edu/lawweb/avalon/coldwar.htm – a site for primary documents on the Cold War in Asia.

http://www.lbjlib.utexas.edu/shwv/shwvhome.html – internet project on Vietnam with images and links.

www.pbs.org/wgbh/pages/amex/vietnam/- – website for 13—part series 'Vietnam: A Television History' containing the scripts of each one-hour episode.

# 7 Crisis in the Middle East, the state of Israel and Arab nationalism, 1945–2004

## Key Issues

- Why was the Middle East a region of political instability, 1945–2004?

- Why did the world's major powers become involved in the Middle East, 1945–2004?

- How did the Middle East affect international relations from 1945 to 2004?

**7.1** Why was the state of Israel created in 1948?

**7.2** What were the causes and consequences of the Arab–Israeli wars of 1948–1973?

**7.3** What impact did Nasser have on the Arab world?

**7.4** How has the 'Palestinian problem' affected the Middle East?

**7.5** How did the Iranian Revolution of 1979 affect the Middle East?

**7.6** To what extent was Iraq responsible for the crises in the Middle East from 1990 to 2004?

## Framework of Events

| | |
|---|---|
| 1945 | End of Second World War |
| | Lebanon independent from France |
| 1946 | Syria independent from France |
| 1947 | UN announces end of British mandate over Palestine |
| 1948 | British Mandates end |
| | Proclamation of Israeli independence |
| | First Arab–Israeli War begins |
| 1949 | End of First Arab–Israeli War |
| | Large numbers of Palestinian Arab refugees in Arab countries adjacent to Israel |
| 1953 | Nasser takes power in Egypt |
| 1956 | Second Arab–Israeli War |
| | Suez Crisis |
| 1967 | Six Day War |
| 1973 | Yom Kippur War |
| 1978 | Camp David Agreement signed between USA, Egypt and Israel |
| 1979 | Iranian Revolution. Shah is overthrown and replaced by Ayatollah Khomeini. |
| 1980 | Start of Iraq–Iran War which lasts until 1988 |
| 1981 | Assassination of Sadat |
| 1982 | Israeli invasion of Lebanon |
| 1990 | Iraq invasion of Kuwait |
| 1991 | Gulf War. US-led coalition forces liberate Kuwait |
| 1993 | Oslo Accords |
| 2000 | Camp David Meeting – 'Road Map to Peace' |
| 2001 | 9/11 attack by al-Qaeda on USA |
| 2003 | US-led invasion of Iraq. Fall of Saddam Hussein |
| 2004 | Insurgency against coalition forces in Iraq |
| | Deadlock in Palestinian–Israeli relations |

## Overview

THE Middle East – which covers the area between the Eastern Mediterranean Sea and the Persian Gulf – has been at the forefront of international relations from 1945 to 2004.

One of the problems facing the area after 1945 was the withdrawal of European administration. In 1945–46 France left Lebanon and Syria. Britain withdrew its administration from Palestine and Jordan from 1947. In the 1960s Britain was forced to withdraw from Aden, following a brief war. Finally, in the 1970s, Britain gave up its 'international protection' of Kuwait, Bahrain and the Emirates. The most serious crisis involving the withdrawal of western administration was the Suez Crisis of 1956. When Egypt took over the Canal Zone and **nationalised** the Suez Canal, Britain and France invaded Egypt. The humiliating withdrawal of British and French troops from the Suez area following US and Soviet opposition marked a turning-point in Anglo-French influence in the region.

**Nationalised**: Taken into government ownership.

Another major issue in the Middle East was the impact of the creation of Israel. Following British withdrawal from Palestine, the state of Israel was declared in 1948. This sparked off a series of wars between Israel and its Arab neighbours. These wars – in 1948–49, 1956, 1967, 1973 and 1982 – dominated Middle Eastern affairs. For most of the period since 1948 most Arab states refused to recognise Israel as an independent state. From 1979 Iran also adopted this view. As a result, ever since its creation Israel has been on a permanent war footing.

Linked to the Arab–Israeli problem has been the Palestinian refugee problem. The Israeli victories in the 1948–49 and 1967 wars forced hundreds of thousands of Palestinian Arabs to flee their homeland. They took up residence in refugee camps in neighbouring Arab states such as Lebanon and Jordan. This caused political instability in these states, and then led to the creation of Palestinian organisations which aimed to attack Israel. From the 1970s onwards, numerous attempts have been made to resolve the Palestinian issue. The world's major powers have attempted to find a solution involving the creation of some form of Palestinian state, in peace with Israel.

However, the involvement of the world's major powers has not always brought political stability to the region. By the 1960s the Middle East had become a region associated with the Cold War between the USA and the USSR. From the 1960s the USA has been Israel's major international supporter. From the late 1950s to the 1970s the USSR was the main international supporter of the Arab states, such as Egypt and Syria.

US involvement in the region also involved the overthrow of the nationalist Prime Minister of Iran, Mosaddeq, in 1953. This raised another issue central to Middle Eastern affairs: oil. Oil is the essential energy resource for the world economy, and the Middle East has the world's greatest reserves. Britain and the USA have long attempted to maintain close links with oil-producing states, including Saudi Arabia, Kuwait, the Emirates, Iraq and Iran.

In 1979 the Iranian Revolution proved to be a major blow to western influence in the region. In 1990, Saddam Hussein's invasion of Kuwait and his threat to Saudi Arabia forced an immediate US response: the Gulf War. Finally, a major motive for the Iraq War of 2003 was the acquisition of Iraq's oil reserves.

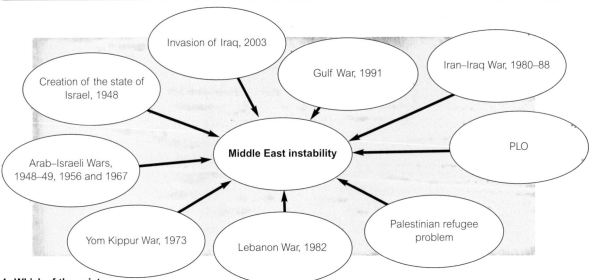

**1. Which of the points in the mind map was the most important reason in explaining instability in the Middle East from 1945 to 2003? Give reasons for your answer.**

**2. Which of the points involved intervention by the Western powers?**

**Shi'ite** and **Sunni Muslims**: Shi'ite Islam is a branch of the Muslim faith centred on Iran. However, there are sizeable Shi'ite minorities in other Muslim states such as Iraq, Syria and Lebanon. Shi'ite Islam believes in the succession of Ali, the Prophet Muhammad's cousin as true source of Islamic teaching. Sunni Islam is the largest group within the Muslim world. Sunnis accept the Caliphs, beginning with Abu Bakr as true line of Islamic teaching. Until 1924 the Caliphate was held by the Sultan of the Ottoman Empire. Both groups have been involved in conflict, in particular in Iraq since 2003.

An important theme in the period 1945 to 2004 has been the leadership of the Arab world. Arabs are the dominant ethnic group in the region, and an 'Arab League' exists to defend their interests. However, the Arab states have never been united. Some, like Saudi Arabia, are monarchies, where the ruler has almost absolute power. Others are secular republics, such as Iraq was under Saddam Hussein. Since 1945, attempts had been made to bring greater Arab unity. In the 1960s, Nasser of Egypt created the 'United Arab Republic' with Syria, but this was short-lived. From 1948 to 2004 there was only one issue that seemed to unite the Arab states – their opposition to Israel.

Since the Iranian Revolution of 1979 a new issue has begun to dominate the Middle East, the rise of Islamic fundamentalism. Since 1979, Iran has been an Islamic Republic, and it has sponsored Islamic groups in other Middle Eastern countries, such as Lebanon. This development has highlighted a potential split within the Middle East between **Shi'ite Muslims** and **Sunni Muslims**. The most important area affected by this split has been Iraq, especially since 2003.

**Saddam Hussein (1937–2006)**
Leader of Iraq from 1970 to 2003. Leader of Ba'ath Party. Responsible for outbreak of the Iran–Iraq War (1980–88) when he attempted to acquire Iran's oil-rich province of Khuzistan. Also responsible for invasion of Kuwait in 1990. Overthrown in Iraq War of 2003 by US-led coalition forces.

**Gamal Abdel Nasser (1918–1970)**
Ruler of Egypt from 1954 to 1970. Overthrew General Naguib in 1954 and became President of Egypt in 1956. Aimed to be leader of Arab nationalism. Created the United Arab Republic with . Syria from 1958 to 1961. Modernised the Egyptian economy. Led the Arab coalition against Israel in 1967. The defeat by Israel in the Six Day War badly damaged his reputation. Died in 1970 and was replaced as Egyptian leader by his Deputy, Anwar Sadat.

**1. What do you regard as the major problems in the Middle East since 1945?**

**2. Was the Arab–Israeli conflict the most important problem in the Middle East since 1945? Explain your answer.**

As an area of almost unending political instability and an area of enormous economic importance to the global economy, the Middle East, since 1945, has been one of the most, if not *the* most significant problem in international relations.

# 7.1 Why was the state of Israel created in 1948?

## The declaration of independence

> **David Ben-Gurion (1886–1973)**
> First Prime Minister of Israel. Born in Russian Poland. He emigrated to Palestine in 1906. Joined the British Army in 1918 as part of the Jewish Legion but returned to Palestine after the First World War. He created the Zionist Labour Movement in 1919. Made the Israeli declaration of independence in May 1948. He also oversaw Israeli military operations in the Israeli War of Independence, 1948–49. Prime Minister from 1948 to 1953 and 1954 to 1963. Oversaw the early development of the Israeli state. Regarded as the 'father' of the state of Israel.

On Friday 14 May 1948, in Tel Aviv, David Ben-Gurion, the leader of Palestine's Jewish community, read out a 1027-word declaration of Israeli independence.

That day, the British **mandate** over Palestine came to an end. The creation of Israel was one of the most important events in the history of the Middle East since 1945. For the first time since the Roman Empire Jewish people had a recognised homeland. But it was also an event which began a protracted period of conflict and warfare between Israel and its Arab neighbours. So why was Israel proclaimed as an independent state?

## The development of Zionism

The desire to create a Jewish homeland was linked directly to the development of the Zionist Movement at the end of the nineteenth century. Under the leadership of Theodore Herzl, many European Jews joined a movement which aimed to find a permanent home for the millions of Jews who lived across the globe. From the time of the Roman Empire (AD 70) Jews had been forced to live outside Palestine – across Europe and the Middle East, mostly, though by 1900 there was also a sizeable population of Jews in the United States.

In the 1890s, Uganda was considered as a possible homeland. However, by 1900, the Zionist Movement aimed to create a Jewish state, Israel, in the ancient homeland of the Jewish people, Palestine.

**Mandate**: After the First World War former territories were handed over to the new international organisation, the League of Nations. The League of Nations then gave Allied powers, such as Britain and France, the task of administering these territories on their behalf.

## The impact of the First World War

Before 1920, Palestine was part of the Ottoman Empire. This was a Turkish-dominated empire which stretched across the Middle East and was centred on Constantinople (modern-day Istanbul). The Empire was dominated by Muslims. Palestine possessed a minority of Jews, but most of the population were Arabs. In the First World War the Ottoman Empire went to war with Britain, but by 1918 British forces based in Egypt had defeated the Ottoman forces and had occupied Palestine. At the height of this war the British government sought assistance from various groups. One was the Arabs, and Britain supported an Arab revolt against the Ottoman Turks. Another group were the Jews. To gain Jewish financial support for the British war effort a commitment was made by the British to support the proposed Zionist state in Palestine. On 2 November 1917 the Balfour Declaration stated that: 'His Majesty's Government view with favour the establishment in Palestine of a national home for the Jewish people.'

> **Theodore Herzl (1860–1904)**
> A journalist who founded the Zionist Movement. Born in Budapest, then part of the Austro-Hungarian Empire. Helped create the first Zionist Congress which met in Basle, Switzerland in 1897.

Palestine under the British
Mandate of 1923–48

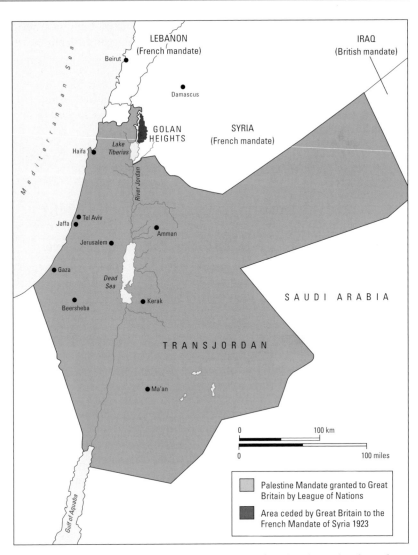

But no timetable was set for the creation for this homeland, and no precise borders were mentioned. This lack of clarity created major problems for the British after the First World War.

## The British mandate

In the Paris Peace Settlement of 1919–20 Britain was given the administration of large parts of the former Ottoman Empire – it had mandate control of Palestine, Transjordan and Iraq. France was given similar control over Lebanon and Syria. These mandates received official recognition from the League of Nations in 1923. Under the arrangement, Britain recognised the 'historical connection of the Jewish people to Palestine'.

From 1923 to 1939 Britain steadfastly hoped to be able to accommodate both the Jewish and the Palestinian Arab populations. However, from 1923 to 1939 the number of Jews emigrating to Palestine increased considerably. From 1919–1923 there were 35,000 immigrants. From 1924 to 1932 the numbers rose to 60,000. In the period after 1932 the numbers rose dramatically to over 200,000. Jews emigrated to Palestine partly to fulfil the Zionist hope of a Jewish homeland. But in the 1930s most fled to Palestine to avoid persecution, in particular after the rise of Hitler to power in 1933.

The wave of Jewish immigration sparked off Arab resistance. Initially it was in the forms of riots, then in 1936 the Arabs called a general strike. This was the beginning of the Arab Revolt. In response, the British set up the Peel Commission in 1937, which recommended the partition of Palestine into separate Jewish and Arab entities. However, the League of Nations and a subsequent British commission report, the Woodhead Commission of 1938, rejected partition. Instead, on the eve of the Second World War, a White Paper suggested severe restrictions on Jewish immigration.

## The impact of the Second World War

The Second World War changed everything. The Holocaust resulted in the extermination of 6 million European Jews. This increased greatly the Jewish desire to establish their own state in Palestine. Also, during the war Zionist leaders such as Chaim Weizmann obtained support for their plans from the US government at the Biltmore Conference of 1942, in the USA. At the end of the war, Britain was virtually bankrupt, and its commitment to defend its vast empire put severe strains on the British government. In the Middle East, Britain faced major problems of law and order, and Jewish groups in Palestine were now more determined than ever to create an independent state.

## The fight for independence

There were three main Jewish groups aiming to force the British out of Palestine, as a prelude to creating a Jewish state. They were the Hagganah, the Irgun and the Stern Gang. The Hagganah were a secret military force created in 1920 to protect the Jewish population of Palestine and, in particular, its community government, known as the Yishuv. It was later disbanded, but re-formed following the outbreak of the Arab Revolt of 1936. By 1939 it numbered 14,500 – approx 5 per cent of the adult Jewish population. From 1945 to 1948 it remained the largest Jewish military force. Eventually, after independence, it formed the basis of the Israeli Defence Force, under the control of David Ben-Gurion.

The Irgun – short for Irgun Zvai Leumi (National Military Organisation) – was formed in 1929. It was created in response to anti-Jewish riots by the Arabs.

It attracted those who felt that the Hagganah did not do enough to defend the Jewish population from Arab attack. But after the publication of the British White Paper of 1939, restricting Jewish immigration, it turned its attention to attacking the British. From 1943 to 1948 it was led by Menachem Begin, the future Prime Minister of Israel.

The most extreme Jewish military group was the Stern Gang (also known as the Lehi or Fighters for the Freedom of Israel). They split from the Irgun in 1940, and for much the Second World War they fought a hit-and-run war against the British authorities.

After 1945, the British maintained strict limits on Jewish immigration. This led to a union of the three Jewish military groups into the Jewish United Resistance Movement. From 1945 to 1948 this movement engaged in war against the British authorities, defended Jewish settlements and attacked Palestinian Arabs. The most significant act in this war was the blowing up, by the Irgun, of a wing of the King David Hotel, in Jerusalem on 22 July 1946. The Hotel was the centre of the British administration in Palestine, and 91 civilians – including 15 Jews – were killed. The British reaction was Operation Shark, a major military operation which arrested 787 leading Jewish radicals.

Britain's policy of immigration restriction united the Jewish population across Europe and the USA. It also brought Britain into conflict with the

**Chaim Weizmann**
**(1874–1952)** First President of Israel, elected in 1949. Born in the Russian Empire, he later worked for the British Navy as a chemist. Broke with Herzl in 1902 to found the Democratic Zionist Party. In 1904 became Professor of Chemistry at University of Manchester in England. From 1920 he was recognised as the leader of the world Zionist Movement. In 1948 he helped persuade US President Truman to recognise the state of Israel.

United Nations partition plan, 1947

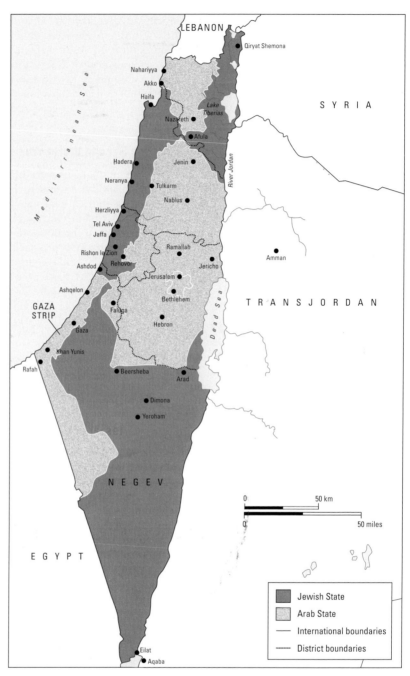

US government. The USA wanted to end the major refugee problem facing its administration in Europe, and favoured the emigration of Jewish refugees to Palestine. Throughout the period 1945 to 1948 Zionist groups in Europe organised illegal emigration to Palestine. The most famous example of this plan was the activity of the ship *Exodus 1947*, which contained 4500 illegal Jewish refugees. It attempted to break a British naval blockade of the Palestine coast but was captured, and the refugees were forced back to its port of embarkation in southern France. The incident caused considerable international opposition. It also helped persuade the United Nations Special Committee on Palestine (UNSCOP) to recommend an end to the British mandate.

The British were also keen to leave Palestine. Their military commitments across the globe were becoming increasingly difficult to meet. In 1947 Britain announced it could no longer assist Greece and Turkey militarily. In the same year Britain withdrew from India and Pakistan. In Palestine, Britain was faced with a situation it found difficult to control – the increasing likelihood of a civil war between Arabs and Jews. Therefore, Britain supported the UNSCOP recommendation.

On 29 November 1947 the General Assembly of the United Nations accepted UNSCOP's report that the British mandate should end. It also recommended that Palestine be partitioned into separate Jewish and Arab areas. Hailed as a triumph by the Yishuv and the Zionist Movement, it was opposed by Palestinian Arabs. Under the leadership of the Arab Higher Committee they organised strikes against partition, beginning on 11 December 1947. In that month, 39 Jews were killed by Arabs, in Haifa. On 9 April 1948, 110 Arabs were massacred in Deir Yassin by Jewish fighters, in retaliation for the murder of 77 Jewish doctors and nurses in Jerusalem. This was the beginning of a civil war between Jews and Arabs that led to the first Arab–Israeli War.

The decision to end the British mandate and to partition Palestine into Jewish and Arab areas opened the way for the creation of the state of Israel. In his declaration of 14 May 1948, Ben-Gurion stated that:

**Eretz-Israel**: The Land of Israel

> We, members of the People's Council, representatives of the Jewish community of **Eretz-Israel** and of the Zionist Movement … hereby declare the establishment of a Jewish state in Eretz-Israel, to be known as the state of Israel.
>
> The state of Israel will be open for Jewish immigration. It will be based on freedom, justice and peace, as envisaged by the prophets of Israel, and it will ensure complete equality of social and political rights to all its inhabitants irrespective of religion, race or sex.

This declaration raised many important issues. Was Israel to be a Jewish state for the Jewish people? Or would it be a multi-racial, multi-religious state?

---

### Prime Ministers of Israel 1948–2004

(Party affiliation in brackets. Likud is a centre-right political group.)

| | |
|---|---|
| 1948–1953 | David Ben-Gurion (Labour) |
| 1953–1955 | Moshe Sharett (Labour) |
| 1955–1963 | David Ben-Gurion (Labour) |
| 1963–1969 | Levi Eshkol (Labour) |
| 1969–1974 | Golda Meir (Labour) |
| 1974–1977 | Yitzhak Rabin (Labour) |
| 1977–1983 | Menachem Begin (Likud) |
| 1983–1984 | Yitzhak Shamir (Likud) |
| 1984–1986 | Shimon Peres (Labour) |
| 1986–1992 | Yitzhak Shamir (Likud) |
| 1992–1995 | Yitzhak Rabin (Labour) |
| 1995–1996 | Shimon Peres (Labour) |
| 1996–1999 | Benjamin Netanyahu (Likud) |
| 1999–2001 | Ehud Barak (Labour) |
| 2001–2004 | Ariel Sharon (Likud) |

**1. Who or what was the most important reason why Israel was created as a state in 1948?**

## 7.2 What were the causes and consequences of the Arab–Israeli Wars of 1948–1973?

A recurrent theme of the history of Israel has been its almost continual conflict with its Arab neighbours. As soon as the state of Israel was declared on 14 May 1948, the armies of five Arab states prepared for an invasion of the new country.

The mere existence of the state of Israel in an area claimed as part of the Arab world was the underlying cause of all the Arab–Israeli Wars.

### The war of 1948–49 – the War of Independence

The War of Independence saw a small, newly created state, Israel, fight and defeat the might of the armies of the combined Arab states. On 15 May 1948, its first day as a new state, Israel was invaded by armies from Lebanon, Syria, Iraq, Transjordan and Egypt. These five armies were supported by units from Saudi Arabia. At face value it would seem Israel was doomed to defeat. However, Israel was able to triumph – for various reasons.

First, Israel received international recognition. On 15 May, the USA recognised Israel, followed by the USSR. On 17 May, the USA introduced a UN Security Council resolution that the Arab invasion of Palestine was a breach of the peace. When Britain tried to stop this resolution, pro-Israeli groups in the USA pressured the US government to stop the US loan to Britain. As a result, Britain ended all arms shipments to the Arab states. On 29 May, the Security Council called for a ceasefire. This came into effect on 11 June, beginning a month-long truce. These developments greatly assisted the early survival of Israel.

Secondly, on 28 May the Israeli Defence Force (IDF) was created out of Hagganah and Irgun units. Throughout the 1948–49 war the IDF fought as an effective military force which exploited differences between the Arab states.

Thirdly, Israel was effective in acquiring arms during the truce. These came mainly from Czechoslovakia and included ex-German air force ME 109 fighters. At the same time, Israel was able to thwart UN plans for a union between Israel and the Arab kingdom of Jordan which were made in June/July 1948.

Finally, when the truce between Israel and the Arab states ended on 8 July the IDF took the opportunity to widen its area of control around Jerusalem and in Lower Galilee (see map on page 189).

The War of Independence came to an end in 1949, following an Israeli withdrawal from the Sinai peninsula in Egypt. There was no formal end to the war, only an armistice – a series of ceasefires agreed between Israel and the individual Arab states during the months February to July. (Only Iraq refused an armistice.)

Technically, Israel was still at war with its Arab neighbours. However, four de-militarised zones were now created on Israel's borders, as an attempt to stop future fighting. These were on the borders with Syria and Egypt and two in the Jerusalem area between Israel and Transjordan.

As a consequence of the war, Israel had not only survived – it had increased its territory beyond the area of the UN partition plan (see map on page 186). But the war had also created a major refugee problem. Approximately 500,000 Palestinian Arabs had fled their homes, which were now located within Israel. By 1949 only 160,000 Palestinian Arabs still lived in the Israeli part of Palestine. The majority of Palestinian refugee camps were located in Lebanon and in Transjordan. A United Nations Relief and Works Agency (UNRWA) was created to assist the

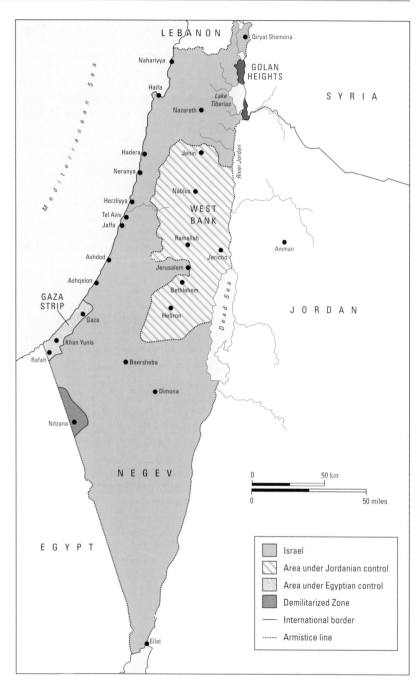

Armistice lines, 1949–1967

Palestinian refugees. But the refugee problem was not easily solved and it continued to plague Arab–Israeli relations into the twenty-first century.

The war created the myth that little Israel saw off the armies of far larger states. It is true that the combined populations of Israel's opponents were 40 times that of Israel. However, the armed forces of both sides were roughly equal – Israel having an army of 26,000 against the 23,000 of the combined Arab armies.

## The Suez War of 1956

The war of 1956 was part of a wider conflict between Egypt on one side, and Britain and France on the other. The immediate cause of the war was the decision by the Egyptian leader, Nasser, to nationalise the Suez Canal in 1956. Up until that date the Canal was owned by a company made up mainly of British and French shareholders.

In an attempt to topple Nasser from power and recover control of the Canal, the British and French secretly persuaded the Israelis to invade Egypt, cross the Sinai Peninsula and attack the Suez Canal. The British and French would then enter the canal area, apparently to separate Egyptian and Israeli forces.

Israel was willing to support this plan as a way of ending cross-border attacks on Israel from Egypt. The culprits were mainly Palestinian Arab guerrillas, known as the fedayeen, whose attacks reached an all-time high in October 1956.

In that month Israeli forces, under Moshe Dayan, were successful in overrunning the Sinai Peninsula and getting within 50 miles of the Suez Canal. Britain and France intervened, as planned, but the war ended in disgrace for them. Although successful militarily, they were forced to withdraw from the Canal because of opposition from both the USA and USSR.

There were several consequences of the war. Israel returned to its pre-war frontier with Egypt, but now the border was monitored by a UN peacekeeping force – the United Nations Emergency Force (UNEF). UNEF was also used to demilitarise the Gaza Strip, the Palestinian enclave in Egypt. Egypt committed itself to ending the fedayeen raids, but this was never implemented. Finally, the Straits of Tiran were opened to Israeli shipping, allowing them to develop their port at Eilat in the Gulf of Aqaba.

## The Six Day War of 1967

The Six Day War began in similar circumstances to the 1956 war. Syrian–Israeli relations deteriorated because Syria had allowed armed Palestinian units to attacks northern Israel from Syrian territory. There was also a dispute between Israel and Syria over water supplies from the River Jordan. The main cause of the 1967 war However was the desire by the Egyptian leader, Nasser, to unite the Arab world under his leadership.

Nasser had become leader of Egypt in 1954, following a military coup in 1952, and he won widespread acclaim from the Arab world when he nationalised the Suez Canal in 1956. The withdrawal of British and French troops during the Suez Crisis made Nasser a major figure in the Arab world. In 1958 he announced the creation of the United Arab Republic, a union of Egypt and Syria, which lasted until 1961. This was followed in November 1966 by a mutual defence pact between Egypt and Syria, which posed a major military threat to Israel.

On 13 May 1967 Soviet intelligence warned Syria of a build-up of Israeli troops along her border. Syria expected an Israeli attack. In support of Syria, Nasser ordered the mobilisation of his troops along Egypt's border with Israel, ordering the UN forces (UNEF) to leave Egyptian soil. He also began diplomatic activity with other Arab states, such as Jordan, in an attempt to create an anti-Israeli coalition.

The immediate cause of the war was the Egyptian decision on 23 May to block the Straits of Tiran to Israeli shipping. Israel was now faced with the possibility of attack from three Arab states, but mainly from Egypt. In the last week of May the Israeli Foreign Minister attempted to get diplomatic support from both the USA and France to stop the possibility of an Arab attack – but this failed. In order to prevent a possible defeat, therefore, the Israeli government decided on a pre-emptive attack.

At 7.45 am on 5 June, Israel launched Operation Moked, and what became known as the 'Six Day War' began. Beginning with a surprise air attack on the Egyptian air force, Israel knocked out the opposing Arab air

**Moshe Dayan (1915–1981)**
Born in Galilee in northern Palestine. Joined Hagganah in the Second World War and later worked closely with the British Army. Chief of Staff of the Israeli Defence Force (1953–58). From 1959 to 1964 he was Minister of Agriculture in the Labour government. Israeli military leader in the Six Day War of 1967. Heavily involved in planning Israeli strategy in Yom Kippur War of 1973. In 1977 he joined the Likud government as Foreign Minister. Played a major role in the Camp David Accords of 1978. Left Likud and formed his own political party, Telem, in 1981. Party won only two seats in the Knesset (Israeli parliament).

Israel and its occupied territories, 1967

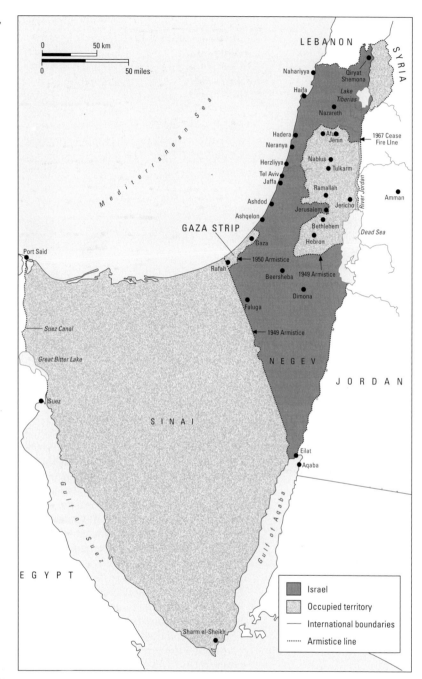

forces within 36 hours. This was followed by a lightning Israeli attack on Egypt in the Sinai peninsula. With five days Israeli forces had reached the Suez Canal. At the same time Israeli forces captured Arab East Jerusalem and the entire West Bank of the River Jordan from Jordan. Finally, Israeli forces captured the Golan Heights from Syria. It was all over in six days. This was a spectacular victory, and a hammer blow to Nasser's prestige, which never recovered. The war was a turning-point in the post-war history of the Middle East.

The war had a dramatic effect on Israel. It raised Israeli morale –no longer did Israel fear attacks by Arab states or Arab terrorists. The war also helped transform the Israeli economy. It sparked off an economic boom, with

Capture of the old town of Jerusalem by the Israeli army. Paratroopers at the Dome of the Rock during the Six Day War.

tourism now becoming a major source of income. In terms of territorial size the war transformed Israel (see map on page 191). Israeli-controlled territory now included the entire Sinai peninsula as far as the Suez Canal, the whole of the former mandate of Palestine and the Golan Heights.

In military terms, the war completely changed the balance of power. Israel was now the dominant military force within the Middle East – a position it was to hold into the twenty-first century. But victory in war also brought with it problems. The capture of the West Bank meant that large numbers of Palestinian Arabs were now under Israeli military occupation, and the decision to annex all Jerusalem to Israel enraged Arab opinion.

Like the previous two wars, this war ended with a ceasefire and no permanent political agreement. At the Arab League Conference in August/September 1967 it was declared that there could be: 'no peace with Israel, no recognition of Israel and no negotiation with Israel'. On 22 November 1967, the UN Security Council passed Resolution 242, which called on both Israel and the Arab states to make peace. It also called on Israel to withdraw from all the territory it occupied. This Resolution was never implemented.

Another feature of the war was the involvement of the two superpowers. By 1967 the USA had become Israel's major international supporter, and the USSR had become the major supporter and military supplier to Egypt and Syria. The Arab–Israeli conflict had become a Cold War conflict.

## The Yom Kippur War of 1973

From 1967 to 1973 an undeclared war existed between Israel and the Arabs, with cross-border incidents occurring with Egypt and Syria. However, a new player had appeared on the scene – the Palestinian Liberation Organisation (PLO). Founded in 1964, this organisation began a major terrorist campaign against Israel from 1967. In September 1970 a faction of the PLO – Black September – began hijacking civilian airliners.

A Palestinian terrorist during Black September as Israeli athletes are held hostage at the Munich Olympic Village, 1972.

**Anwar Sadat (1918–1981)**
Third President of Egyptian Republic following death of Nasser in 1970. Born to a poor family in Egypt, his father was Egyptian and his mother was from Sudan. Following Nasser's death Sadat introduced a multi-party political system in Egypt. Responsible for launching the Yom Kippur War against Israel in 1973. Made the historic decision to be first Arab leader to visit Israel in 1977. Signed the Camp David Accords and the Treaty of Washington with Israel in 1978–79. First Arab leader to make peace with Israel and to recognise the Israeli state. Assassinated in 1981 by Arab extremists in the Egyptian army.

1. **Why was Israel so successful in its wars with Arab states in the period 1948 to 1973?**

In 1972 this group achieved its biggest success when it captured and subsequently murdered Israeli athletes at the Munich Olympic Games.

However, the person most responsible for the outbreak of the war of 1973 was the Egyptian leader, Anwar Sadat (who had taken over in September 1970 when Nasser died). Using Soviet military equipment, both Egypt and Syria completely rearmed after the 1967 war, and by 1973 they were ready to launch another attack on Israel.

Sadat's motives for going to war again were complex. He wanted to win back prestige for Egypt. He also wanted to reopen the Suez Canal, which had been blocked since the 1967 war, with Israeli troops occupying its eastern bank.

However, Sadat also had the long-term goal of making peace with Israel. Even if Egypt lost the war he hoped that the crisis created would force the USA and the USSR to somehow bring about a lasting Israeli–Egyptian peace.

As in 1967, Israel was aware of a build-up of Egyptian forces along the west bank of the Suez Canal. However, unlike 1967, Israel did not strike first. On 6 October 1973, on one of the most holy days in the Jewish calendar, Yom Kippur (the Day of Atonement) the Egyptians attacked across the Suez Canal. This was followed by a Syrian tank attack on the Golan Heights. Israel suffered heavy losses, in particular in aircraft. The Egyptians also succeeded in crossing the Suez Canal. However, after a week the Israelis regrouped, helped by a massive airlift of military equipment from the USA. Egypt and Syria received similar shipments from the USSR. On 22 October a ceasefire came into effect. By that stage Israeli forces had crossed the Suez Canal and were heading towards Cairo. Israeli forces had also recaptured the Golan Heights and were heading towards Damascus.

The return to peace was a triumph of US diplomacy. In Paris, the US Secretary of State, Henry Kissinger, got all the sides to agree to end the war. On 21 December 1973, a peace agreement was signed by the USA, USSR, Israel, Egypt and Jordan – but not Syria. It was announced that this was a step towards peace. Prisoners were exchanged and Israel agreed to return to the pre-war borders. Israel had losses of 2500 dead and over 7000 wounded, and the war had cost Israel $7 billion. It also brought to an end the idea of Israeli invincibility.

# 7.3 What impact did Nasser have on the Arab world?

Gamal Abdel Nasser was ruler of Egypt from 1953 until his death in 1970. During that time he transformed Egypt. He was also seen as the leading Arab nationalist, attempting to bring greater unity to the Arab world. Internationally, he was most closely associated with the Suez Crisis of 1956 and the Six Day War of 1967. In many ways, by the end of his life, Nasser saw himself as a failure. He had made, however, a major impact on the politics of the Middle East.

## Nasser's rise to power

On 23 July 1952, Nasser was one of a group of young Egyptian army officers, known as the Free Officers, who overthrew their ruler, King Farouk I. Farouk was replaced by General Naguib, who became president of an Egyptian Republic in 1953. Egypt had been under British control from 1882 to 1922, and even after the British administration came to an end British troops were stationed in the country. During the Second World War Egypt was a major British and Commonwealth base. After 1945, the influence of Europe continued in the country, the most visible sign being its control of the Suez Canal. The area around the Canal was occupied by British troops until 1956, and the profits from the Canal went to the Suez Canal Company, not the Egyptian government.

King Farouk I ran a corrupt, inefficient government, and he seemed to spend more time enjoying life than ruling Egypt. As a result, the 'revolution' of 1952 was seen by many as inevitable.

Although Naguib had been the leader of the revolution, by 1954 street demonstrations in Cairo demanded his replacement. Nasser used these demonstrations and his influence on the Revolutionary Command Council to force Naguib to resign on 23 February 1954.

## Political and economic change

When Nasser became leader he embarked on radical political and economic change. He introduced a new constitution, which allowed for free, democratic elections and individual freedom. However, in reality, Egypt became a one-party state – under Nasser's party, the National Union. Old political parties were banned, new political parties were prohibited from forming. The Minister of the Interior could arrest and imprison anyone suspected of 'counter-revolutionary' activity. Nasser used referendums to gain support for the constitution – and they were supported by 99% of the voters!

Nasser also made efforts to modernise the Egyptian economy, bringing in greater state control of economic development, along socialist lines. Initially efforts were centred on increasing electricity generation and industry. Egypt's main cash crop, cotton, also saw big increases in output during Nasser's early years in power. But not all Nasser's economic projects were successful. His plan to build a large steel plant at Helwan, for example, fell way behind schedule.

The most radical aspect of Nasser's reforms affected agriculture. Large farms were taken over by the government and distributed to poorer peasants – greatly increasing Nasser's popularity among the poor. Another of Nasser's aims was to improve the quality of the armed forces, and by 1955 spending on the armed forces had risen 25% above 1953 levels.

## Nasser, the Aswan High Dam and the Suez Crisis

The most prestigious economic project undertaken by Nasser was the decision to build the Aswan High Dam on the River Nile. This would generate

**King Farouk I (1920–1965)**
King of Egypt 1936 to 1952. Weak, ineffectual ruler under the influence of western countries, in particular Britain. Overthrown in the Free Officers coup of 1952.

**General Muhammad Naguib (1901–1984)**
First President of the Egyptian Republic 1953–1954.

large amounts of hydro-electric power, create a vast lake which would be used for irrigation, and control flooding on the River Nile, a major problem facing Egyptian agriculture.

Nasser initially hoped to finance the construction of the Aswan High Dam from western sources, such as the USA. But his decision to purchase large amounts of military equipment from communist countries such as Czechoslovakia caused major strains with the USA, which feared increasing communist influence in Egypt. A turning-point came in July 1956 when the USA and other western countries withdrew their offers of financing the Aswan High Dam. To meet the shortfall in finance, Nasser decided to take the Suez Canal into the public ownership of the Egyptian government, as from 26 July 1956. This was the immediate cause of the Suez Crisis of October 1956.

To the British Prime Minister, Anthony Eden, Nasser was an Arab dictator who planned to remove British influence from the Middle East. Eden felt immediate action had to be take to stop Nasser, so from August to October 1956 the British and French governments developed a secret plan to topple him. They contacted Israel and planned to use an Israeli attack on Egypt as a pretext to launch a military occupation of the Suez Canal. This would then lead to the overthrow of Nasser. The Israeli invasion began on 29 October 1956 and two days later British and French forces occupied the area around the Suez Canal, as planned.

Neither the USA nor the USSR were aware of the plan. The USA was facing a presidential election in early November. President Eisenhower reacted angrily to the attack and demanded immediate British and French withdrawal. On 5 November 1956 the USSR issued an ultimatum, demanding the withdrawal of all military forces from Egypt, which was backed by the United Nations. Britain, France and Israel were forced to withdraw. The British invasion had caused uproar in Britain, and by early 1957 Eden had resigned as Prime Minister.

In Egypt, meanwhile, Nasser was hailed as a hero. He had nationalised the Suez Canal and 'defeated' Britain and France. And from 1956 onwards he became increasingly linked with the Soviet bloc. The USSR provided the finance and the engineering skill to construct the Aswan High Dam, which was built between 1960 and 1970.

> **Anthony Eden (1897–1977)**
> British Prime Minister
> 1955–1957.

> **President Eisenhower (1890–1969)**
> US President 1953–1961.

## Nasser and the Arab world

When Nasser took power in Egypt, in 1954, most Arab countries were ruled by monarchies, which had complete political power. Having created a socialist republic in Egypt, Nasser planned to export his version of Arab nationalism to other parts of the Arab world. In 1957 he began to intervene in Yemen, where he planned to overthrow the Yemeni monarchy. In 1962 he even sent Egyptian troops to support the pro-Nasser Yemeni rebels, and by 1965 50,000 Egyptian troops were deployed there, at great cost.

In 1958 Nasser took another step in his quest for Arab unity, under his leadership. In that year Syria and Egypt agreed to merge into one Arab state, the United Arab Republic. Unfortunately, the plan was short lived – the union was dissolved in 1961. However, both countries worked closely with each other in military matters.

The issue that was to be a major move towards Nasser's leadership of the Arab world was his confrontation with Israel. Opposition to Israel was the one issue on which all Arab states agreed. In 1967 Nasser successfully built a coalition of Arab states which aimed to defeat Israel. But before they could even start, Israel won a spectacular victory in the Six Day War. This was the greatest humiliation suffered by Nasser – and he never recovered.

President Nasser on the cover of Time Magazine, 1963.

---

**1. Why was Nasser regarded as an important Arab leader, in the years 1954 to 1970?**

**2. What do you regard as Nasser's greatest success? Explain your answer.**

---

### Nasser's impact

Nasser made major changes within Egypt. He freed the country from western economic influence, and he made major strides towards modernising the Egyptian economy, his lasting monument being the Aswan High Dam. Nasser's popularity with ordinary Egyptians was ensured through his land reform and his support for Arab nationalism.

Beyond Egypt, Nasser's attempts to export his version of Arab nationalism met with very limited success – a pro-Nasser government was established in Yemen, and secular republics existed in Syria and Iraq, after 1958. But the Arab world was as disunited in 1970 as it had been in 1954, when Nasser took power. His long-term dream of a United Arab Republic lasted only from 1958 to 1961.

It took Nasser's successor, Anwar Sadat to make an important lasting impact on Middle East affairs. Sadat partially restored Egyptian prestige when he launched the Yom Kippur War against Israel in 1973. Although Egypt did not win the war, Egyptian forces had performed well for much of it. Sadat's greatest contribution came in 1977 when he announced he would visit Israel to discuss peace. He was the first Arab leader to visit Israel. In the following year he signed the Camp David Accords with Israel. He brought an end to the war that had existed between Israel and Egypt since 1948, and in return Egypt acquired the Sinai Peninsula lost to Israel since the 1967 war. This also allowed the reopening of the Suez Canal, a major source of revenue for Egypt.

Unfortunately, Sadat isolated himself from other Arab leaders by his actions, and in 1981 he was assassinated by Egyptian troops opposed to his policy of peace with Israel.

## 7.4  How has the 'Palestinian problem' affected the Middle East?

The most enduring problem facing the Middle East from 1948 to 2004 has been the issue of Palestinian Arabs. In the Israel War of Independence, 1948–1949, thousands of Palestinians fled their homes to take up residence in refugee camps in neighbouring Arab countries, such as Lebanon and Jordan. These camps still exist today. In 1967 the Palestinian problem became greater as Israel occupied the whole West Bank, thereby taking control over the whole of Palestine.

Why was the Palestinian problem so important and why has it been so difficult to find a solution? A number of issues have prevented a lasting peace:

● The Israeli desire for security

● The Palestinian Arabs' claim to their own state

● Jewish settlements in Palestinian Arab areas

● The rise of radical Arab and Islamic groups.

**Hamas**: A Palestinian militant movement, founded in 1987, which aims to create an Islamic state in Palestine and to destroy Israel.

**Hezbollah**: A Shi'ite militant group, founded in the early 1980s and based in Lebanon. Hezbollah (Party of God) aims to create an Islamic state in Lebanon and to destroy Israel.

---

**Menachem Begin (1913–1992)**

Born in the Russian Empire at Brest-Litovsk. In 1940 he was arrested and imprisoned by Soviet secret police. In 1942 he joined Polish Free Army and then moved to Palestine the same year. Leader of the Irgun terrorist group from 1943 to 1948. Irgun was responsible for the King David Hotel attack of 1946. In 1948 he founded the Herut Party. In 1977 he won the Israeli General Election, in which Herut was part of a centre-right coalition called Likud. Prime Minister of Israel 1977–1981. Signed the Camp David Accords with Egypt, for which he was awarded the Nobel Peace Prize.

---

**Yitzhak Rabin (1922–1995)**

Born in Jerusalem. Israeli Chief of Staff from 1964. Under his command Israel won the Six Day War. Twice Israeli Prime Minister, 1974–77 and 1992–95. Won Nobel Peace Prize in 1994 for his work in the Oslo Accords of 1993. Assassinated by an Israeli extremist who was opposed to Rabin's policies towards the PLO.

---

Ever since the creation of the state of Israel, security has been a central issue. For most of Israel's existence, neighbouring Arab states refused to recognise its existence. From 1978 onwards, starting with Egypt, several Arab states and the PLO have recognised Israel's right to exist. However, in 2004 Israel still faced the issue of recognition. Iran and radical Islamic groups such as **Hamas** in Palestine and **Hezbollah** still opposed Israel.

Therefore, Israel has made several attempts to defend its borders from attack. After the 1973 Yom Kippur War, its main opponent became the PLO and those Arab states which supported it, such as Syria. To protect its security, in 1978 Israel went as far as bombing a nuclear power station under construction in Iraq for fear that it might be used to manufacture nuclear weapons for the Iraqi leader, Saddam Hussein.

In 1982, under the prime ministership of Menachem Begin, Israel launched the Lebanon War. The aim was to destroy PLO bases within Lebanon. Israel forces reached the outskirts of the Lebanese capital, Beirut. Lebanese Christian forces – with Israeli knowledge – massacred Palestinian refugees in camps at Sabra and Chatila, near Beirut. The war ended with the expulsion of the PLO from Lebanon. Israel also occupied a border zone of southern Lebanon, south of the Litani river as a security zone. Although the war had succeeded in expelling the PLO, it had also plunged Lebanon into a bitter civil war, which involved major intervention by Syria into eastern Lebanon.

Threats to security also came from within Israeli-occupied territory in Palestine. On 8 December 1987 the 'Intifada' (shaking off) began – the Palestinian uprising against Israeli occupation. It was triggered by an incident in the Gaza Strip – a truck crashed into a car at an Israeli military checkpoint, killing four Palestinians. Although an accident, this sparked off demonstrations and street clashes between Palestinians and Israeli troops. The Intifada spread right across Israeli-occupied Palestine, and caught Israel by surprise. Within three weeks, 22 Palestinians had been killed and 320 injured by Israeli troops. On the Israeli side, 56 soldiers and 30 civilians had been injured by stones and bottles.

The Intifada split Israeli society. Many began to demonstrate openly against Israeli occupation of the Palestinian areas. On 23 January 1988, approximately 90,000 people demonstrated against their government in Tel Aviv. Among the Palestinians, the Intifada also saw the appearance of a new radical group, Hamas.

The Israeli government response was twofold. First, it increased its military presence in Palestinian areas, and curfews were introduced. Palestinians were also punished economically, being forbidden to sell their agricultural produce in markets. Secondly, reprisal raids on Palestinian areas became commonplace. Between December 1987 and December 1988, 526 Palestinian homes were demolished as reprisals for attacks on Israeli troops. Israel also launched an air attack on the new PLO headquarters in Tunis, Tunisia.

In 1993, in the Oslo Accords, Israel recognised the PLO and the Palestinian claim to self-government. In return, the PLO recognised Israel's right to exist. This was a landmark move towards solving the Palestinian problem. But for the Israeli prime minister, Yitzhak Rabin, the agreement came at a cost – he was assassinated in 1995, by an Israeli opposed to the agreement. The PLO leader, Yasser Arafat was also criticised by some radical Palestinians for recognising Israel, and the situation contributed to the growth in support for Hamas.

Although the Oslo Accords acted as a milestone towards a lasting settlement, the year 2000 saw a major step in the opposite direction. Israel and the PLO failed to come to an agreement in the Camp David talks of that year. Of a more serious nature, on 28 September, a second Intifada erupted

**Yasser Arafat
(1929–2004)**
Born in Cairo, Egypt to Palestinian parents. In 1958 he founded Fatah, a militant Palestinian organisation, which aimed to liberate Palestine in an armed struggle with Israel. Fatah became the PLO in 1964. After the Six Day War, the PLO was responsible for terrorist attacks on Israel and Israelis around the world. In 1973 the PLO was declared the sole representative of the Palestinian people. Even though he did not represent an independent state, Arafat was allowed to address the UN General Assembly in 1973. In 1988 the PLO declared an independent state of Palestine, even though the area was under Israeli occupation. In the Gulf War of 1990–91 Arafat supported Saddam Hussein.

Major change after the Gulf War came in 1993 in Oslo Accords, when Arafat recognised the state of Israel and renounced violence. He signed a peace agreement with the Israeli government for which he was awarded the Nobel Peace Prize in 1994. In 1996 he was elected head of the Palestinian National Authority by a large majority. In 2000 he failed to reach agreement with Ehud Barak, Israeli Prime Minister, in the Camp David II Summit. From the late 1990s his authority was undermined by the rise of more militant Palestinian groups, such as Hamas.

**Ariel Sharon (1928– )**
Born in Palestine. Served in the Israeli army in the 1956 and 1967 wars. He was held responsible for the massacre in the Sabra and Chatila refugee camps in 1982. (Although the massacre was carried out by Chruistain Arabs, Sharon was believed to have given the orders.) In 2000 his visit to the al-Aqsa Mosque in Jerusalem sparked off the al-Aqsa Intifada. Israeli prime minister 2001–06, and the main person responsible for building the defence wall between Israel and Palestinian areas.

after Israeli politician, Ariel Sharon, accompanied by a thousand Israeli police, visited the al-Aqsa Mosque in Jerusalem. This was the world's third most holy Muslim shrine, after Mecca and Medina. Sharon was the Israeli leader closely linked to the 1982 massacre of Palestinians in the Sabra and Chatila refugee camps, in Lebanon. This new, 'al-Aqsa Initifada' involved radical groups, such as Hamas and Hezbollah. It also involved suicide bombing of targets within Israel (see table).

### Terrorism in Israel

Number of Israelis killed in the al-Aqsa Intifada
(29 September 2000 – 12 January 2004)

| Type of attack | Civilians | Security forces | Total |
|---|---|---|---|
| Rocks | 2 | 0 | 2 |
| Stabbing | 6 | 0 | 6 |
| Run over by vehicle | 1 | 7 | 8 |
| Lynching | 17 | 2 | 19 |
| Shooting | 92 | 103 | 195 |
| Drive-by shooting | 28 | 9 | 37 |
| Shooting at vehicle from an ambush | 59 | 11 | 70 |
| Shooting at towns and villages | 15 | 6 | 21 |
| Shooting at military installations | 0 | 26 | 26 |
| Bombing | 24 | 36 | 60 |
| Suicide bombing | 373 | 43 | 416 |
| Car bombing | 15 | 23 | 38 |
| Mortar bombing | 0 | 1 | 1 |
| Other | 1 | 4 | 5 |
| **Total killed** | **633** | **271** | **904** |
| *Total injured* | *4,290* | *1,773* | *6,063* |

Source: Bernard Reich, *A Brief History of Israel*, Checkmark Books, 2005

The Israeli response to the al-Aqsa Intifada was to build a large wall separating Israel from the West Bank Palestinian area. Condemned internationally, the wall was Sharon's lasting legacy to Israeli–Palestinian relations.

By 2004 Israel had made agreements with Egypt, Jordan, Lebanon and the PLO which resulted in Arab recognition of Israel's right to exist. However, Israel had not made agreements with any other states or with Iran, which after 1979 became increasingly anti-Israeli. Also the two Intifadas led to the rise of radical Palestinian and Islamic groups who undermined the authority of the PLO within Palestinian areas.

---

### 1978 to 2000: The roadmap to peace?

**1978–79**

**Camp David Agreement** between Egypt and Israel (USA acted as mediator) *becomes*

26 March **1979**

**Treaty of Washington**
- Brought an end to the state of war between Egypt and Israel
- Egypt recognised Israel's right to exist
- Diplomatic relations established between Egypt and Israel
- Israel agreed to withdraw from the Sinai Peninsula and to remove Jewish settlements from Sinai.

13 Sept. **1993**

**Oslo Accords** agreement between Israel (Rabin) and PLO leader, Arafat (USA acted as mediator)
- PLO recognised Israel's right to exist in peace and security
- Israel recognised PLO as representative of the Palestinians
- PLO renounced use of terrorism against Israel
- Interim self-government agreement allowed limited Palestinian self-government in Gaza and Jericho as first stage in creation of Palestinian Authority.

26 October **1994**

**Israel–Jordan Peace Treaty** (USA acted as mediator)
- Peace agreement
- Israel recognised Jordan's special role in the Muslim holy shrines in Jerusalem
- Encouraged economic co-operation.

December **1995**

**Oslo Accords (II)** (USA acted as mediator)
- Withdrawal of Israeli forces from Palestinian towns of Jenin, Tulkarm, Nablus, Qalqilya and Bethlehem
- In 1996 Hebron Agreement, Hebron handed over to Palestinian control
- As a result, all large Palestinian towns in West Bank area under Palestinian control.

23 October **1998**

**Wye River Memorandum** between Israel (Netanyahu ) and PLO leader, Arafat (USA acted as mediator)
- Agreed phased removal of Israeli forces from 13% of Palestinian Authority
- Increased area under Palestinian Authority control.

**2000**

**Camp David (II)** summit between Israel (Barak) and PLO leader, Arafat (USA acted as mediator)
*The summit failed.*
Barak offered Arafat
- Recognition of a Palestinian state
- Self-government to Arabs in East Jerusalem.
But Barak wouldn't accept Arafat's request for
- Removal of all Jewish settlements in West Bank since 1967
- Remilitarisation of West Bank and Gaza.
- Return of East Jerusalem to Palestinian control.

A key issue in the Israeli–Palestinian question was the building of Jewish settlements in Palestinian areas following the 1967 Six Day War. From then on, Israeli settlers had established homes in occupied territory, including the Sinai Peninsula (taken from Egypt in 1967), the Gaza Strip, the West Bank and East Jerusalem. These new settlements caused great resentment among Palestinians, whose land had been taken to build them. The settlements were protected by the Israeli army, and the settlers were allowed to carry weapons – a right denied to ordinary Palestinians. Most important of all, the settlements gave the impression that Israel would attempt in the future to incorporate these areas within the Israeli state. This fear was an important issue behind the Intifada.

However, Israel was willing to trade removal of these settlements for peace and security. In the Treaty of Washington, in 1979, Jewish settlements were removed from Sinai, and by 2004 initial agreement had been made to withdraw Jewish settlements from the Gaza Strip. Nevertheless, Israel showed no intention of removing settlements from East Jerusalem or the West Bank. These were major stumbling blocks in the failure to reach agreement at the Camp David II talks of 2000, between Israel and the PLO.

Another major obstacle to a lasting solution to the Palestinian problem was the rise of radical Arab and Islamic groups in the late 1980s. When the PLO began to make concessions to Israel, most notably in the 1993 Oslo Accords, radical Palestinians joined Hamas. It was Hamas that led the terror attacks against Israel in the al-Aqsa Intifada from 2000 to 2004. Also, following the Iranian Revolution of 1979, Iran supported the development of Hezbollah, another radical group based in Lebanon. Hezbollah was against any compromise with Israel. From the Oslo Accords to 2004 the PLO gained international recognition. Also, from the mid-1990s, the Palestinian National Authority – a PLO agency – gained increasing control over large areas of the Gaza Strip and the West Bank. Its position, however, has been undermined by Hamas, which continued the armed struggle against Israel.

**1. Why has the Palestinian problem been so difficult to solve in the period 1948 to 2004?**

## Source-based questions: The UN and the Palestinian refugee problem, 1948–49

### SOURCE A

11 December will mark the 55th anniversary of UN Resolution 194. By this historic act, the world community, speaking through the United Nations, formally acknowledges the right of return to their homes and property of Palestinians who were driven out as a result of Zionist military operations in 1948 that culminated in the declaration of the State of Israel.

Adopted 11 December 1948, Resolution 194 reads:

'Refugees wishing to return to their homes and live in peace with their neighbours should be permitted to do so at the earliest practicable date. Compensation should be paid for loss or damage to property.'

In the context of upholding the UN Charter and international law, Resolution 194 continues to hold great symbolic as well as practical significance. For the first time with regard to a specific conflict, an international body of sovereign states resolved that acts of violation of human rights, such as the right of return, could not be permitted to stand. The world community asserted that individual and collective human rights now stand above the claims of individual states.

Uniquely in the history of the UN, Resolution 194 has been reaffirmed more than 25 times and confirmed more than 130 times. The number of refugees at the time numbered more than 750,000 or 60 per cent of the population of Palestine.

From a television broadcast by Al Jazeera, an Arabic Broadcasting Company, 6 December 2003

## SOURCE B

The key document cited by supporters of a Palestinian right to return is Resolution 194, passed after the first Arab-initiated war against Israel.

Through many years and multiple wars, the Arab states refused ever to recognise Israel, much less to reach a peaceful settlement.

The only clause of the Resolution ever acknowledged by Arabs was Paragraph 11, which suggested that:

'Refugees wishing to return to their homes and live in peace with their neighbours **should be permitted to do so**.'

The requirement that they accept living 'at peace with their neighbours' meant that the Palestinians had to accept Israel's right to exist, something that very few were willing to do. Further, it did not even hint at any return of descendants of refugees.

An article published by the Committee for Accuracy in Middle East Reporting in America, a Jewish American organisation, 1 September 2000

## SOURCE C

The UN first took up the refugee issue and adopted Resolution 194 on 11 December 1948. This called upon Arab states and Israel to resolve all outstanding issues through negotiations either directly, or through the Palestine Conciliation Committee established by this resolution.

Resolution 194 met most of Israel's concerns regarding the refugees, who feared they would be regarded as potential enemies if they were allowed to return unconditionally. The Israelis considered the settlement of the refugee issue as a negotiable part of an overall peace settlement. At the time the Israelis did not expect the refugees to be a major issue. They thought the Arab states would resettle the majority of refugees. The Arabs were not willing to compromise. In fact they unanimously rejected the UN Resolution.

An article on a website called the Jewish Virtual Library, 2005

## SOURCE D

The Arab states demanded a settlement of the refugee question as a precondition of even discussing other matters. Israel, on the other hand, demanded that the matter be discussed as part of general negotiations for a final settlement. The only point on which there was any agreement was a scheme for the return of refugees separated from their families by the Arab–Israeli War. Israel eventually agreed in principle to accept 100,000 refugees. The United States urged Israel, it was reported, to accept about 300,000 refugees but this was rejected by Israel.

A British historian, writing in 1982

## SOURCE E

The central practical issue regarding refugees is the right claimed by the Palestinians. They cite UN Resolution 194, passed in December 1948. Most of the Resolution's provisions regarding refugees, access to holy places, internationalisation of Jerusalem and permanent peace through a UN mediator were never implemented. Palestinians claimed that their rights are based on international law. However, resolutions of the UN General Assembly are not binding in international law. Israelis point out that a consequence of the Arab–Israeli War and the creation of Israel was that about 630,000 Jews fled Arab countries and lost their property. Moreover, there is probably no precedent in international law for forcing a hostile population on a country. After World War II Germans living in the Czech Sudetenland, who had been active in supporting the Nazis, were expelled and lost their property. In 1947, India and Pakistan formed two states, and exchanged populations on a mass scale. No right of return was ever claimed.

From a Mid Eastern Website for Co-existence between Arabs and Jews, 2003

**How far do Sources A–E support the view that the UN's attempt to solve the refugee problem was doomed to failure?**

# 7.5 How did the Iranian Revolution of 1979 affect the Middle East?

**Ayatollah Khomeini
(1902–1989)**
Born in Khomein, Iran.
Ruhollah Khomeini was Grand
Ayatollah of Iran. Ayatollah is
the most senior cleric of Shi'ite
Islam within Iran. A major critic
of the Shah's rule, he was
placed under house arrest in
Iran in 1964, then forced into
exile. In the Iranian Revolution,
he helped to lead opposition to
the Shah from his home near
Paris. He returned to Iran in
1979, after the Shah had fled.
He helped to create the Islamic
Republic of Iran from 1979.

Until 1979 the main area of instability in the Middle East was centred on the Arab–Israeli conflict. But this changed dramatically in 1979 when the Shah of Iran left his country, to be replaced as ruler by Ayatollah Khomeini. Overnight, Iran changed from being the USA's closest ally in the region (along with Israel) to being its most feared enemy.

## The causes of the Iranian Revolution

Shah Mohammad Reza Pahlavi was ruler of Iran from 1941 to 1979. His rule had been interrupted, in 1953, by a power struggle with a national leader, the prime minister, Mohammed Mosaddeq. Mosaddeq disliked Iran's oil industry being under the control of western countries, such as the USA and Britain. However, the Central Intelligence Agency of the USA helped overthrow Mosaddeq and returned the Shah to power. From 1953 to 1979 the Shah maintained complete political control of Iran, using SAVAK, the secret police, to suppress any opposition. He was advised by many western advisers, including the US and British intelligence services.

Unpopularity with the Shah's rule became a major issue in the late 1970s. Resentment was based on a number of factors. The Shah had attempted to modernise the Iranian economy but, by 1977, inflation and unemployment were becoming a problem. He had also tried to modernise – and westernise – Iranian society, causing resentment among the population, the overwhelming majority of whom were Shi'ite Muslims. Finally, the Shah's regime was accused of corruption and oppression. An example of the Shah's lavish use of government money came in 1971 with the celebration of the 2500th anniversary of the founding of the Persian Empire (Persia was the former name of Iran). A huge celebration was held at Persepolis (the ancient capital), costing approximately $100 million – at a time when eastern Iran was suffering a major drought.

Demonstrations against the Shah became serious in January 1978, steadily becoming larger and spreading across the country. By the summer, the Shah had to approach the USA for help, but the Carter administration would not offer him any military support. By September, the SAVAK and Iranian military were finding it increasingly difficult to maintain law and order. In October, a general strike paralysed the country.

On 16 January 1979, the Shah decided to take his family out of the country. For a few weeks, the country was under the control of a moderate prime minister, Shapour Bakhtiar. But the turning-point in this Revolution came on 1 February 1979 when the religious leader of most Iranians, the Ayatollah Khomeini, returned to Iran from exile in Paris. Within ten days of his arrival, Khomeini supporters had ousted Bakhtiar and proclaimed an Islamic Republic.

## The immediate impact of the Iranian Revolution

The instability in the Middle East created by the Iranian Revolution had an immediate impact on the price of oil. By the end of 1979, the world price of oil had doubled (and this followed a fourfold increase in the price in 1973–74). The effect on the world economy was profound – it provoked a worldwide recession. In the USA and Europe, economic growth dropped dramatically and unemployment rose.

The Iranian Revolution also caused an international crisis of a different sort. In October 1979 the exiled Shah entered the USA to receive medical treatment for cancer. This led to widespread anti-American demonstrations in Iran. The most serious aspect of anti-American feeling was the storming of the US embassy in Tehran and the capture of 52 US staff as hostages. The Iran hostage crisis lasted from October 1979 to January 1981, causing a major crisis in Iran–US relations.

From February 1979 the Khomeini regime transformed Iranian society. Strict Islamic law was introduced. For instance, all women had to wear headscarves, and stoning to death was introduced as a punishment for adultery. As a result, much of Iranian society went through a period of profound change and uncertainty in 1979–80. It was feared that Iran might fragment into different political units. Kurds in northern Iran expressed the desire for more self-government, and in south-western Iran, the oil rich province of Khuzestan was being eyed by neighbouring Iraq.

### The Iran–Iraq War, 1980–88

The bloodiest war in the post-war Middle East took place between September 1980 and August 1988. The true death toll is unknown, but is in the region of one and a half million. Fighting was likened to the First World War – static front lines, trench warfare, mass infantry attacks and the use of poison gas. After eight long years, the war ended in stalemate – with a relatively small amount of territory gained by Iran.

The war had many causes. When the Ottoman Empire collapsed in 1920 the new borders of the British mandate of Iraq left unresolved the land claims by the Arab Iraqis over Iranian territory in Khuzestan. Also, when the Iranian Revolution occurred the ruler of Iraq, Saddam Hussein, tried to use the political instability to his own advantage by acquiring Khuzestan, thereby increasing his oil wealth. Also, Sadam wanted to control the whole of the Shatt al-Arab waterway, which was shared by Iraq and Iran. The waterway linked Iraq's main rivers – the Tigris and Euphrates – with the Persian Gulf.

Iraq had religious reasons as well as economic ones. Khuzestan contained a significant number of Sunni Muslims, similar to the majority in Iraq, and Saddam hoped to exploit their fears of Shi'ite domination under Ayatollah Khomeini and win their support.

On the Iranian side there was dislike of the secular state created by Sadam in Iraq. They wanted to see Iraq turned into an Islamic Republic. Also Khomeini hoped to unite all Shi'ite Muslims into one state. Southern Iraq contained a Shi'ite Muslim minority. When Iraq invaded Iran, Khomeini declared a holy war in defence of the Iranian Islamic Revolution.

By 1982 Saddam Hussein had realised that his gamble to acquire Khuzestan had failed. He attempted to make peace but Iran refused, so from 1982 to 1988 the conflict became a war of attrition.

By 1988 the Iranian Revolution was secure. The war had united the country behind Ayatollah Khomeini. Western fear of the Iranian Revolution led Britain and the USA to provide military equipment for Saddam Hussein. He was seen by the USA as their main ally in the defence of the Middle East against the spread of the Islamic revolution.

**1. What do you regard as the main reason why the Iranian Revolution occurred in 1979?**

**2. What has been the most important impact of the Iranian Revolution in the period 1979 to 2004?**

# 7.6  To what extent was Iraq responsible for the crises in the Middle East from 1990 to 2004?

Between 1988 and 1990, Saddam Hussein went from being the west's most important Middle Eastern ally against Iran to being their arch enemy. The turning-point in this relationship occurred in 1990, when Iraq invaded and occupied Kuwait. The invasion provoked an immediate response from the USA and the United Nations, leading to the Gulf War. 'Operation Desert Shield' was immediately put into action to prevent Iraq invading Saudi Arabia, and once this was accomplished 'Operation Desert Storm' was launched. This was a US-led coalition attack on Iraqi-occupied Kuwait and Iraq itself, on behalf of the United Nations. The coalition included Britain, France, Syria and Saudi Arabia. Israel was persuaded by the USA to remain out of the conflict, even though it was attacked by Iraqi missiles. The Gulf War lasted from 2 August 1990 to 28 February 1991, and resulted in a massive victory for the US-led coalition, which recaptured Kuwait. During the war, Iraq lost approximately 100,000 dead, compared to 358 coalition troops.

### What caused the Gulf War of 1990–91?

The causes of the Gulf War were varied. Part of the problem went back as far as 1920, when Kuwait was given territory that was claimed by Iraq. However, the main reasons for the invasion were political and economic. Saddam Hussein had failed in his bid to acquire the oil-rich Iranian province of Khuzestan in the Iran–Iraq War of 1980–88, and the war had caused severe strains on the Iraqi economy. In addition, following that war Kuwait increased its oil production by 40% which had an adverse effect on world oil prices – and on the Iraqi economy in particular.

The main reasons for Saddam's decision to invade Kuwait was to regain prestige and to acquire Kuwait's rich oil reserves. However, one must not underestimate Saddam's belief that other states – the USA in particular – would not intervene. The USA had been a supporter of Iraq in the Iran–Iraq War, providing over $200 million of military aid to Saddam.

### What was the Impact of the war?

The US-led victory was a personal triumph for **President George H. Bush**. However, Bush stopped short of trying to topple Saddam from power, fearing that this would have led to a split in the US-led coalition. Instead Bush encouraged Shi'ite Muslims in southern Iraq to rebel against Saddam. But the Shi'ite uprising was put down ruthlessly by Saddam's army.

From 1991 to 2003 the western powers took alternative steps to contain Saddam. UN-sponsored economic sanctions were introduced. No-fly zones were created over northern and southern Iraq, to protect the Kurds in the north and the Shi'ites in the south from attack by Saddam. US, French and UK air forces prevented the Iraqis from operating military aircraft over approximately 60% of Iraq. From December 1998, under *Operation Desert Fox* US and UK air forces extended their operations and attacked Iraqi anti-aircraft installations across Iraq.

Because it was believed that Saddam was manufacturing chemical, biological and possibly nuclear weapons, UN weapons inspectors were sent to Iraq to locate the manufacturing plants. These inspections began in 1991, at the end of the Gulf War. They involved constant friction between the UN inspectors and Iraq. Sometimes inspectors were forced to leave Iraq but were subsequently reinstated following UN sanctions and US threats of military action. From 1991 to 2003 Iraq was, in many ways, in a 'cold war' with the UN and the western powers.

**George H. Bush (1924– )**
US President from 1989 to 1993. Member of the Republican Party. Father of George W. Bush.

**George W. Bush (1946– )**
US President from 2001 to 2009. Member of the Republican Party. Son of George H. Bush.

### Why did the Iraq War of 2003 take place?

In many ways the Iraq War of 2003 was unfinished business from the Gulf War of 1990–91. George H. Bush had hoped that military defeat in Kuwait would lead to internal revolution against Saddam in Iraq. But in 1991 all attempts to rise up against Saddam by the Kurds in the north and the Shi'ites in the south failed. Therefore, in 2003, George W. Bush was determined to organise 'regime change' in Iraq.

The urgency for removal of Saddam in 2003 was linked to the fear that

**Tony Blair (1953– )**
British Prime Minister from 1997 to 2007. Won three successive general elections, in 1997, 2001 and 2005, before retiring.

**Al-Qaeda**: An extreme Islamic group founded in 1988 by Osama Bin Laden. Aims to create Islamic states across the Muslim world, and is opposed to western influence in the Middle East. Linked to the Taliban in Afghanistan and responsible for the 9/11 terrorist attacks on the USA.

**Taliban**: The Islamic movement in Afghanistan. Before 2002 it formed the government of Afghanistan. Since 2002 it has been involved in a guerrilla war against UN coalition forces there.

**Osama Bin Laden (1957– )**
Founder of al-Qaeda.

**Donald Rumsfeld (1932– )**
US Secretary for Defense. Main policymaker on Iraq in George W. Bush's government from 2001 to 2006. Mainly responsible for planning victory in the Iraq War of 2003 and for the chaos following that war. Dismissed by George W. Bush in 2006.

he was developing weapons of mass destruction (WMD), including chemical, biological and possibly nuclear weapons. Saddam had shown in the Gulf War of 1990–91 that he had the capacity to fire rockets against targets in Israel and Saudi Arabia. Western intelligence sources suggested that WMD were being developed, and that a pre-emptive strike against Saddam was required. This was supported by the daily Iraqi obstruction to the UN weapons inspectors within Iraq. This formed the basis of the Blair Government request that the House of Commons support a war against Iraq. Since 2003, however, it has become clear that Iraq's WMD did not exist. However, there is evidence to suggest that Saddam deliberately leaked information suggesting their existence as a deterrence against attack. This strategy clearly backfired.

However, another important factor was the impact of 9/11 in 2001. The **al-Qaeda** attack on the USA sparked off widespread condemnation, both within and outside the USA. From 2001, President George W. Bush launched 'GWAT', the global war against terror. Part of this strategy was the overthrow of the **Taliban** regime in Afghanistan, which was achieved in 2002.

Bush also claimed that Saddam Hussein had links with al-Qaeda. This also proved to be untrue. Al-Qaeda's leader, Osama Bin Laden, was in favour of creating Islamic states across the Middle East, and disliked secular regimes like Iraq.

Finally, when looking at the causes of the war, one cannot discount economic factors. Iraq possessed huge oil reserves, and the USA was keen to gain at least influence, if not control, over this vital energy source.

### The decision to go to war

Like his father, George H. Bush, George W. Bush attempted to get UN approval for his campaign against Saddam. However, by the end of January 2003 it was clear that France, a permanent member of the UN Security Council would veto any attempt to topple Saddam by force. As a result, George W. Bush went ahead and planned an invasion without UN approval. In the invasion, the USA was joined by the UK, Australia, Spain, Italy and Poland. However, 98% of the coalition forces consisted of US and UK troops. The coalition called it 'Operation Enduring Freedom'. They had vastly superior weaponry and the war lasted only from 20 March to 15 April.

### The aftermath of the Iraq War of 2003

On 1 May 2003 President George W. Bush made a visit to the US aircraft carrier *Abraham Lincoln*, stationed in the Persian Gulf, off Iraq. He proudly announced 'Mission accomplished'.

But the war had not ended – instead it had entered a new phase, a guerrilla war. Once the Saddam regime was overthrown it became clear that the US coalition had not developed a comprehensive plan to restore law and order. (As US Secretary of Defense, Donald Rumsfeld put it, US forces 'don't do nation building'.) The Iraqi army was disbanded and the Saddam administration was removed. In its place, chaos reigned, and the country began to split apart. The Kurds, in the north, set up their own government, then the Shi'ites in the south attempted to follow suit. The Sunni area in mid-Iraq became the centre of guerrilla warfare against coalition forces. The capital, Baghdad became the centre of a civil war between Sunni and Shi'ite with both sides attacking coalition forces. The US and its allies had entered a quagmire from which they could not withdraw. It seemed like the Vietnam War all over again.

George W. Bush on the *Abraham Lincoln* in May 2003.

1. In what ways were the causes of the Gulf War of 1990–91 and the Iraq War of 2003 similar, and in what ways were they different? Explain your answer.

2. Was Saddam Hussein solely to blame for the wars of 1990–91 and 2003? Give reasons for your answer.

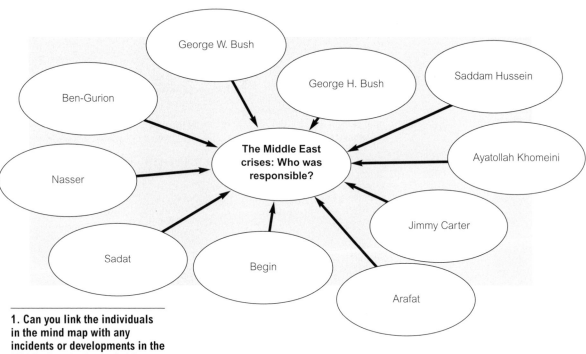

1. Can you link the individuals in the mind map with any incidents or developments in the Middle East in the period from 1945 to 2003?

2. Which of the individuals in the mind map were responsible for creating instability in the Middle East? Give reasons for your choice.

3. Which of the individuals in the mind map was most responsible for trying to achieve peace and stability in the Middle East? Give reasons for your answer.

## Further Reading

*The Arab–Israeli Conflict* by Kirsten E. Schulze (Longman Seminar Studies series, 1999)

*The Palestine–Israel Conflict: A Beginner's Guide* by Dan Cohn-Sherbok and Dawoud El-Alami (One World Books, 2001)

*A Brief History of Israel* by Bernard Reich (Checkmark Books, 2005)

*A History of Israel* by Ahron Bregman (Palgrave Macmillan, 2002)

*A History of Modern Palestine* by Ilan Pappe (Cambridge University Press, Second edition, 2006)

*The Israel–Palestine Question* edited by Ilan Pappe (Routledge, 1999)

*The Iranian Revolution and the Islamic Republic* (Contemporary Issues in the Middle East) by N. Keddie and B. Hoogland (Syracuse University Press, 1986)

*War in the Gulf 1990–1991: The Iraq–Kuwait Conflict and its Implications* by M. Khadarri and E. Ghareeb, Oxford University Press, 1997)

*The George H. W. Bush Years* by J. R. Greene (Facts on File, 2005)

*Power, Faith and Fantasy: America in the Middle East, 1776 to the Present* by M. Oren (W.W. Norton, 2007)

# Index

## Glossary terms

Al-Qaeda   205
Annexation   33
Appeasement   15, 115
Arbitration   54
Atheism   128
Atomic diplomacy   117
Austria   27
Autocratic   28
Autocratic monarch   12
Axis   88

Balkan nationalism   26
Balkans   15
Bipartisan   147
Bi-polar   111
Bizonia   120
*Blitzkrieg*   82
Bohemia and Moravia   16
Brezhnev Doctrine   130
Brinkmanship   152

China lobby   143
Collaboration   96
Collective security   61
Collectivisation   141
Comecon   117
Cominform   120
Conscript   168
Containment   115
Conventional forces   122
Cost-of-living index   104
Coup   174

Dardanelles   34
Defoliants   169
Demagogues   53
*Demiurge*   73
Détente   123
Diplomatic system   22
Disarmament   47

Eastern Rumelia   29
Economic warfare   111
Embargoes   54, 77
Empire and Dominions   93
Eretz-Israel   187
Euphemism   157

Feudalism   139
'Final Solution' (*Endlösung*)   98
Fourteen Points   51
French Indo-China   77

*Gauleiters*   95
General Staffs   33
Gold Standard   59
Great Powers   22

Hamas   197
Hezbollah   197
Hossbach Memorandum   73

Indo-China   15
INF   126
Inflammatory rhetoric   150
Iranian Revolution in 1979   130
Iron Curtain speech   115
Isolationism   46

Joint Chiefs of Staff   160

Khmer Rouge   172
Kremlin   92

Low Countries   85

Maginot Line   48
Mandate   183
Mandated territories   54
Marshall Aid   117
Martial law   130
*Mein Kampf*   76
Memoirs   22
*Milice*   97
Mobilisation   22
Mohacs in 1526   87
Monolithic   175

Napalm   169
Nationalised   181
Nationalism   127
NATO   120
Non-proliferation treaty   125

'Oder-Neisse Line'   125
*Ostpolitik*   125

Partisan movement   100
Passive resistance   56
Pentagon Papers (1971)   165
Pincer movement   84
Protectorate   35
'Puppet' governments   95

Recession   176
'Redskins'   95
Reparations   22

SALT   123
*Sammlungspolitik*   31
Sanctions   54
Satellite states   15, 114
Scuttling   49
Serfs   25
Shi'ite and Sunni Muslims   182
Siege   91
Solidarity   126
Stalinist   144
'Strategic Defence Initiative'   126
Strategic Hamlets Programme   161
'Successor states'   52
Sudetenland   67
Suez Crisis   129
Sultanate   31
Summary execution   96

Taliban   205
Third World   161
TNT   172
Treaty of Versailles   22
Tripartite   107
Tyranny   115

Unilateral   48
United Nations organisation   107

Vichy government   48

Walloons   97
Warsaw Pact   123
*Wehrmacht*   83

## Profiles

Aehrenthal, Aloys von   33
Arafat, Yasser   198

Begin, Menachem   197
Beneš, Edvard   51
Ben-Gurion, David   183
Berchtold, Leopold von   37
Bin Laden, Osama   205
Bismarck, Otto von   25
Blair, Tony   205
Brandt, Willi   125
Brezhnev, Leonid   126
Bush, George H.   204
Bush, George W.   204

Chamberlain, Neville   69
Chiang Kai-Shek   141
Churchill, Winston   87

Daladier, Edouard   69
Dayan, Moshe   190
Delcassé, Théophile   32
Dubček, Alexander   129

Eden, Anthony   195
Eisenhower, Dwight   122, 195

Farouk I, King   194
Franco, Francisco   88
Franz Ferdinand, Archduke   30

Gomulka, Wladyslaw   129
Gorbachev, Mikhail   126
Guderian, Heinz   83

Haile Selassie   62
Henlein, Konrad   68
Herzl, Theodore   183
Ho Chi Minh   153
Hötzendorf, Conrad von   33
Hussein, Saddam   182

Izvolski, Alexander   34

Johnson, Lyndon Baines   159

Kennedy, John Fitzgerald   159
Keynes, John Maynard   52
Khomeini, Ayatollah   202
Kim Il Sung   144
Kleist, Ewald von   85

Lloyd George, David   49

MacArthur, Douglas   139
MacDonald, Ramsay   55
Mao Ze-dong   141
Masaryk, Tomas   51

Naguib, General Muhammad   194
Nagy, Imre   119
Nasser, Gamal Abdel   182
Ngo Dinh Diem   154
Nguyen Van Thieu   171

Poincaré, Raymond   56

Quisling, Vidkun   97

Rabin, Yitzhak   197
Reagan, Ronald   126
Rhee, Syngman   144
Rommel, Erwin   83
Roosevelt, Franklin D.   89
Rumsfeld, Donald   205

Sadat, Anwar   193
Sauckel, Fritz   96
Seyss-Inquart, Arthur   67
Sharon, Ariel   198
Speer, Albert   93

Taylor, General Maxwell   160
Tito (Josef Broz)   118
Todt, Fritz   93
Truman, Harry S.   115

Wałęsa, Lech   130
Wedemeyer, Albert Coady   142
Weizmann, Chaim   185
Wilson, Woodrow   49

Yeltsin, Boris   133

Zhukov, Georgi   91

# MAIN INDEX

Abdul Hamid, Sultan   33
Abyssinia   15, 45, 55, 62–3, 64, 66
Acheson, Dean   115, 142, 143, 149, 153
Adamthwaite, Anthony   53, 78, 84
Addis Adaba   62
Aden   181
Adenauer, Konrad   111
Adowa, Battle of (1896)   62
Adrianople   37
Advisory Committee on Traffic in Women
    and Children (UNICEF)   55
Aehrenthal, Aloys von   33–4
Afghanistan   16, 33, 126, 130, 131, 133,
    205
Africa   13, 15, 24, 30, 114
    Scramble for   13, 62
Agadir Crisis (1911)   20, 21, 35, 36

Åland Islands   55
Albania   37, 116, 118
Alexander III, Tsar   29
Algéçiras Conference (1906)   33
Algeria   15
Alliance system   16, 21, 22, 27–30, 35,
    41, 47–8, 61
Alperovitz, Gar   117
Al-Qaeda   180, 205
Alsace-Lorraine   20, 25, 40, 49, 58
Ambrose, Stephen   115, 149–50, 152,
    162, 171
Amouroux, Henri   100
Andropov, Yuri   111, 126
Anglo-French Alliance (1854)   28
Anglo-Russian Entente (1907)   23
Anglo-Russian Treaty (1942)   107
Angola   133
*Anschluss* (1938)   65, 66–8
Anti-Comintern Pact (1936)   45, 65
Anti-semitism   97, 98–9, 102–3, 106
Antwerp   104
ANZUS Pact (1951)
Ap Bac, Battle of (1963)   163
Appeasement   15, 16, 48, 59, 61, 68–70,
    73–4, 78–9, 85, 115
Appleman, William   115
Arab Higher Committee   187
Arab-Israeli Wars   16, 17, 180, 181,
    187–93
Arab League   182, 192
Arab Revolt (1936)   185
Arabs   181, 182, 183–5, 187–201
Arafat, Yasser   197–9
Ardennes   85, 105
Argentina   59
Armenia   133
Arms control   110, 111, 123, 126, 134–5
Arms race   21, 22, 30, 131, 132, 135
    naval   31, 35
    nuclear   18, 109
Army of the Republic of Vietnam (ARVN)
    155, 161, 163, 166, 168, 170, 171,
    173, 174
Arnhem   105
Asia   114, 136–78
Aswan High Dam   194–5, 196
Atlantic Charter (1941)   46, 81
Atlantic Ocean   76, 88, 89
Atom bomb   18, 81, 109, 110, 116, 117,
    143, 146, 152, 172
Auschwitz   98
Australia   12, 24, 82, 147, 152, 205
Austria   51, 52, 58, 66, 78
*Anschluss*   45, 65, 66–8
    failed Nazi coup   62, 67
    military occupation zones   14, 116,
        121
    unified state   129
Austria-Hungary   12, 13, 20, 26, 33
    alliances   16, 20, 27–8, 37–8
    and Balkans   33–4, 37–9, 43–4
    collapse of   17, 21, 46, 51, 52
    First World War   20–22, 24, 39–40
    Great Power status   12, 25–6
    regional disputes   15, 26
    war guilt   41–2
Austrian State Treaty (1955)   110, 121,
    129
Austro-Prussian War (1866)   17, 24–7

Axis powers   64–5, 88, 103–6
Azerbaijan   133

Babi Yar   96
Bad Godesberg   69
Badoglio, Marshal Pietro   104
Baghdad   205
Baghdad Pact (1954)   113, 149
Bahrain   181
Bakhtiar, Shapour   202
Balance of power   16, 47, 49, 52, 57, 61,
    64, 84
Balfour Declaration (1917)   183
Balkan League (1912)   36
Balkan Wars (1912–13)   20, 21, 36–7
Balkans   28, 36–8, 71
    crises   22, 27, 30, 33–4, 38–40,
        41–2
    nationalism   15, 26
    egional disputes   15, 16, 25
    Second World War   88, 95, 100
Ball, George   166
Ball, Simon J.   125, 130, 132
Baltic States   79, 81, 106, 118, 128, 133
Barak, Ehud   187, 199
Basic Treaty (1972)   125
Battle of the Atlantic (1940)   75, 89
Battle of Britain (1940)   46, 76, 81, 87–8
Battle of the Bulge (1944–45)   105
Battleships   18, 31
Baumont, Maurice   53, 64, 66
Bavaria   52
Beck, General Ludwig   72
Beck-Rzikowsky, General   33
Begin, Menachem   185, 187, 197
Beirut   197
Belgium   13, 24, 29, 49, 122
    colonies   108
    First World War   20, 39
    German occupation   95, 97, 101
    Locarno Pact   58
    occupies Ruhr   56, 58
    Second World War   46, 75, 81, 85
Belgrade   101
Belzec   98
Ben-Gurion, David   183, 185, 187
Beneš, Edvard   51, 68, 69, 120
Berchtesgaden   67, 69, 78
Berchtold, Count Leopold von   37, 38
Berghahn, Volker   23
Berlin   64, 81, 83, 106, 114, 121, 142,
    152, 161
Berlin Airlift (1948)   110, 116, 120–22
Berlin, Congress of (1878)   27
Berlin Crisis (1958–61)   110
Berlin, Treaty of (1878)   16, 27
Berlin Wall   110, 111, 114, 121, 123,
    125, 128, 131
Bessarabia   71
Bethmann-Hollweg, Theobold von   39,
    41
Betts, Richard H.   166
Biltmore Conference (1942)   185
Bin Laden, Osama   205
Bismarck, Otto von   24, 25, 26–30, 66
Bizonia   116, 120
'Black Hand'   38
Black September   192–3
Blair, Tony   205
*Blitzkrieg*   17, 75, 82, 84, 91

Blum, Leon 68
Bohemia and Moravia 16, 46, 70, 95, 100
Bolshevik Revolution (1917) 17, 21, 52, 111, 114
Bolshevism 59, 64–5, 78, 89, 91, 95, 102
Bornet, Vaughn Davis 168
Bosnia-Herzegovina 20, 33–4, 43
Boves 96
Brandt, Willi 111, 125–6
Brazil 59
Brest-Litovsk, Treaty of (1918) 21
Brezhnev, Leonid 111, 123, 126, 130, 133
Brezhnev Doctrine 130, 131
Briand, Aristide 55, 59
Briand-Kellogg Pact (1928) 45, 58–9
Britain
    alliances and treaties 20, 23, 27, 28, 31, 32, 45, 61–3, 70–71, 152
    Anglo–American relations 15, 129
    Anglo–French relations 35, 55
    Anglo–German relations 31, 35, 67, 68
    appeasement 15–16, 68–9, 74, 78
    economy 13, 14, 24, 59
    First World War 13, 20–21, 24, 29, 39
    Great Power status 24–5
    industry 13, 93
    and League of Nations 16, 53
    Lend-Lease agreement 46, 76, 81
    Locarno Pact 58
    mandated territories 181, 184, 186–7, 203
    and Middle East 181, 182–8, 203–5
    military strength 13, 18, 24, 84
    occupying power in Germany 121
    postwar 117
    regional disputes 15, 16
    Second World War 14, 16, 18, 46, 48, 72, 75, 76, 79, 81–2, 87, 106, 108
    and Spanish Civil War 64
    Suez Crisis 181, 189–90, 195
    and Versailles Treaty 48–9
British Army 24–5, 76, 93
British Empire 12, 13, 24–5, 26, 42, 74, 93, 194
    decline of 14, 15, 47, 108, 117, 187
British Expeditionary Force 75
Brogan, Hugh 161
Broszat, Martin 102
Brusilov Offensive (1916) 21
Brussels 104
Bucharest 119
Bucharest, Treaty of (1913) 37
Budapest 129
Bulganin, Nikolai 111, 123
Bulgaria 36–7, 51, 55, 106, 107, 108, 116, 131
Bulgarian Crisis (1885–87) 20, 27, 28, 29
Bullock, Alan 74, 89, 106
Bülow, Bernhard von 30, 33, 34
Bulow, Karl von 44
Bundy, McGeorge 155, 162
Bundy, William P. 162, 166

Burleigh, Michael 89
Bush, George H. 111, 204
Bush, George W. 204–6
Butler, Rohan 73

Caen 104
Caillaux, Joseph 35
Calley, Lt William 169
Calvocoressi, Peter 87, 92
Cambodia 15, 137, 152–4, 159, 170, 172–5
Camp David summits 180, 196, 199–200
Canada 12, 13, 14, 24, 82
Capitalism 14, 42, 47, 58, 59, 111, 114, 141
Caprivi, Leo von 29
Carolinas Islands 139
Carter, Jimmy 111, 126, 202
Catholic Church 128, 130
Caucasus 91
Cecil, Lord David 55
CENTO 113
Chafe, William H. 163, 164, 177
Chamberlain, Neville 69, 72, 78
Chatila refugee camp 197, 198
Chautemps, Camille 68
Chelmno 98
Chernenko, Konstantin 111, 126
Chiang Kai-Shek 137, 141–3, 146, 151, 152
China 12, 13, 18, 123, 137
    alliances and treaties 136, 143
    Communism 14, 137, 138, 139, 141–4
    Japanese occupation 14, 15, 76–7
    Korean War 17, 138, 145–7, 149
    loss of 143–4, 153
    People's Republic 116, 142, 143, 146
    Sino–Soviet relations 138, 143, 175
    Sino–US relations 137, 139–42, 151–2, 171, 175–6
    and Taiwan 137, 151–2
    and Vietnam 154, 175
China Aid Act (1948) 136, 142
'China White Paper' (1949) 143
Chinese Civil War (1949) 114, 116, 136, 139, 141–3, 147
Chinese–Japanese War (1894–95) 45
Churchill, Winston 48, 53, 87, 89, 107, 110, 116, 121
CIA 155, 161, 162, 173, 202
Ciano, Count Galaezzo 64, 65, 67
Clemenceau, Georges 49
Clercq, Staf de 97
Coal production 56, 92–3, 96
Cold War 14, 15, 16
    in Asia 136–78
    end of 132–5
    in Europe 111–35
    Germany and 121–7
    in Middle East 181, 192
    responsibility for 114–18
Collaboration 96–7, 101–2
Cologne 58
Colonialism 12–13, 23, 28, 30–31, 33, 42, 52

Comecon 117, 121, 130
Cominform 120, 127
Comintern 120
Committee of National Reconciliation (Vietnam) 173
Commonwealth of Independent States 133
Communism 14–15, 16, 97, 99, 167
Cold War 114–18
    Eastern Europe 15, 118–21, 127–31
    Far East 137–8, 139–44, 153–5, 160–64, 168–74
    Hitler and 72, 76
    Soviet 14, 17, 52, 70, 111, 114, 133
Concentration camps 83, 98
Concert of Europe 16, 24
Condor Legion 64
Conkin, Paul K. 165
Conscription 13, 17, 24, 30, 45, 61, 105
Constantinople 37, 40, 183
Containment policy 115, 122, 137–8, 141, 142, 144, 145–9, 152, 153, 155, 174
Cooper–Church Amendment 172
CPSU (Communist Party of the Soviet Union) 110
Crete 88
Crimea 105
Crimean War 24, 28
Croatia 51
Crockatt, Richard 140
Cuba 14, 123, 133, 161
Cuno, Wilhelm 56, 57
Czechoslovakia 51, 66, 74, 101, 188, 195
    alliances 58
    coup 110
    destruction of 71, 72
    Prague Spring (1968) 110, 129–30, 131
    socialist republic 108, 116, 119, 120, 128
    Sudetenland 68–70, 78
    Velvet Revolution (1989) 111, 131

D-Day 81, 93, 101, 104
Da Nang 136, 138, 157, 165
Daladier, Edouard 69, 72
Danzig 50, 71, 72, 78, 79
Dardanelles 34
Dawes, Charles 57
Dawes Plan (1924) 45, 57–8, 59
Dawidowicz, Lucy 99, 103
Dayan, Moshe 190
Decolonisation 14, 15
Degrelle, Leon 97
Deir Yassin 187
Delbrück, H. von 40
Delcassé, Théophile 32–3
Denmark 46, 50, 75, 81, 85, 95, 97, 101
'Destroyer Deal' (1940) 89
Détente 110, 123–4, 126, 175
Dien Bien Phu 136, 138, 153
Dimitrievich, Colonel 38
Disarmament 47, 49, 52, 54, 60–61, 84, 134
Disarmament Conference (1932) 60, 61
Dollfuss, Engelbert 67

Domino Theory 138, 154, 157, 160, 161, 164, 168, 174
*Dreadnought*, HMS 18, 31
*Dreikaiserbund* (1873) 20, 26–7, 28, 29
Dresden 105
Dual Alliance (1879) 20, 27–8
Dual Monarchy 33, 34, 37, 38
Dubček, Alexander 129–30, 131
Dulles, John F. 122, 143, 146–7, 151, 152, 153
Dumbarton Oaks conference (1944) 107
Dumbrell, John 177
Dunkirk 75, 76, 81, 85–6, 87
Dutch East Indies 77

East Berlin 114
East Germany 110, 114, 116, 118, 120, 121–5
Eastern Europe 15, 61, 98, 99
    occupied territories 95–6, 97, 100
    political revolution 130–33
    postwar 106, 114, 115, 116, 118
    under Soviets 118–21 , 127–31
Eastern Question 34
Eastern Rumelia 29
Economic sanctions 54, 63
Economic depression 13, 14, 59–60, 117
Economic warfare 111
*Economist* 132
Eden, Anthony 195
Egypt 31, 180, 181–3, 188–90, 192–7, 199
Eilat 190
*Einsatzgruppen*, *see* SS
Eisenhower, Dwight D. 106, 111, 122, 141
    Domino Theory 160, 174
    'New Look' foreign policy 129
    and South East Asia 146, 149, 153–4
    and Suez 195
    and Taiwan 144, 151–2
    and Vietnam 159
El Alamein 81
Ellsberg, Daniel 165
Emirates 181
Encirclement policy (*Einkreisungspolitik*) 33, 40, 41
Entente Cordiale (1904) 20, 23, 31–3
Erhard, Ludwig 111
Eritrea 62
Estonia 71, 75, 118, 128, 133
Ethiopia 13, 62
Eupen 49, 58
Europe 12–14, 83, 111
    balance of power 16, 49, 52, 64, 84
    Cold War in 111–35
    Concert of 16, 24
    decline of 15, 108, 117
    divided 114
    economy 13, 52, 83
    '*Mitteleuropa*' 125
    regional disputes 15
European Defence Community 122–3
European Recovery Programme, *see* Marshall Aid
Evans, Rowland 165
*Exodus 1947* 186
Extermination camps 98–9

Falaise 104
Far East 137–78
Farouk I, King 194
Fascism 59, 62, 64, 97, 103–4, 108
Fascist Grand Council 104
Fay, Sidney Bradshaw 22, 40, 41
Fechter, Peter 125
Fellner, Fritz 41
Ferguson, Niall 38
Fez, occupation (1911) 34–5
FFI (Forces Françaises de l'Intérieur) 101
Fieldhouse, David 42
'Final Solution' 82–3, 98–9, 101, 102
Finland 55, 71, 75, 76, 81, 85, 90
First World War (1914–18) 13, 17–18, 74, 183
    aftermath 46–7
    armistice 48
    causes 15, 20–24, 29, 35, 37–42
    impact of 21–2
    outbreak of 39
    peace treaties 48–53
    reparations 22, 45, 50–53, 55–6
    war guilt 22–4, 39, 40–42, 47, 49–50
Fischer, Fritz 22–3, 35, 38, 40–41
Flemish Legion 95
Foch, Ferdinand 48
Foot, M.R.D. 101
Forced labour 96, 99
Ford, Gerald R. 111
Formosa 136, 137, 142
Formosa Resolution (1955) 152
Four Power Pact (1933) 45, 61–2
France 48
    alliances and treaties 16, 20, 23, 26, 29, 31, 32, 45, 61–3, 66, 69–72, 152
    appeasement 15–16, 68–9, 74, 78
    disarmament proposals 60–61
    empire 12, 13, 14, 15, 25, 28, 30, 31, 33, 47, 74, 108, 153–4, 159
    and European cooperation 122–3
    fall of 75–6, 81, 82, 85–7, 89, 94
    First World War 13, 20–22, 24, 30, 39–40, 74
Franco–American relations 15, 129
Franco–British relations 35, 66
Franco–German relations 20, 26, 56–7, 67
Franco–Russian relations 20, 29, 37, 122
    Great Power status 12, 25, 39
    isolation 27, 28–9
    and League of Nations 16, 53
    Locarno Pact 58
    mandated territories 180, 181, 184
    and Middle East 181, 189–90, 195, 204, 205
    military strength 13, 18, 84
    occupied 95, 96–7, 99–102
    occupies Fez 34–5
    occupies Ruhr 45, 55–7, 58
    occupying power in Germany 121
    postwar 117
    regional conflicts 32–5
    Second World War 16, 17, 46, 48, 72, 74–6, 79, 81, 84–7, 95, 104, 108

and Spanish Civil War 64
and Versailles Treaty 48–50, 53
Vichy government 48
war debts 60
Franco, General Francisco 64, 88
Franco-Austrian War (1859) 24
Franco-Italian Entente (1902) 20
Franco-Prussian War (1870–71) 12, 13, 17, 24, 25, 26
Franco-Russian Alliance (1894) 16, 20, 29
Frank, Hans 95
Frankfurt Treaty (1871) 25
Franz Ferdinand, Archduke 20, 22, 24, 30, 38, 43
Franz Josef, Emperor 25
Free French forces 104
Free trade 28
Free World 111, 114, 134
Freedman, Lawrence 161, 163
French Army 25, 30, 75, 84–5
French Congo 35
French Resistance 99, 100
Frick, Wilhelm 95

Gaddis, John Lewis 117
Galbraith, John Kenneth 160
Gallagher, John 13
Gallipoli 21, 37
Gamelin, Marshal Maurice 78
Gaulle, Charles de 84
Gaza Strip 190, 197, 199, 200
Gdansk 71, 130
Geiss, Immanuel 23, 33, 34, 38, 41
Gelb, Leslie K. 166
Geneva 53, 60
Geneva Accords (1954) 136, 154, 158, 159
Geneva Summit (1985) 134
Genocide 83
Georgia 128, 133
German Air Force, *see* Luftwaffe
German Army (*Wehrmacht*) 13, 25, 37, 40, 49, 83–4
German Democratic Republic, *see* East Germany
German Empire 12, 13, 21, 24, 25, 26
German Federal Republic, *see* West Germany
German Navy 20, 23, 30–31, 48, 49
German Navy Laws 31
German-Soviet Pact (1939) 70–71
Germany:
    alliances 16, 20, 26–8, 37–8, 45, 46, 61–2, 64–5, 70–71
    Axis powers 64–5
    and Balkans 37–8
    and Cold War 114, 121–7
    colonies 13, 23, 30–31, 52, 54
    demilitarisation 49, 52, 60, 84
    division 108, 110, 123
    economy 13, 23, 25, 28, 52–3, 56, 91, 93
    expansionism 45–6, 55, 66–8, 74
    First World War 18, 20–22, 30, 39–40, 47
    Great Power status 12, 25, 61
    Holocaust 82–3, 98–9
    industry 13, 53, 93–5, 96

and League of Nations   16, 54, 59, 61, 62
Locarno Pact   58
military occupation zones   14, 107, 114, 116, 120, 121
military strength   31, 37, 84, 88
Nazi   14, 47, 48, 93–9
partition   14, 15
re-armament   45, 66, 122–3
regional disputes   15, 32–5
relations with Britain   35
relations with France   20, 56–7
reparations   22, 45, 50–51, 60
reunification   111
revolution   17
*Sammlungspolitik*   31
Second World War   14, 15, 17, 18, 46, 74–7, 81–109, 110
territorial changes   49–50, 51–2
unification   24, 25, 26, 66
and Versailles Treaty   48–9
war guilt   22–4, 40–42, 47, 49–50
*Weltpolitik*   21, 23, 30–32, 39
*see also* East Germany; West Germany
Gettysburg, Battle of   22
Gherghiu-Dej, Gheorghe   119
Gibraltar   35
Gierek, Edouard   130
Giglio, James N.   163
Gilbert, Parker   57
*Glasnost*   114, 130, 133
Goering, Hermann   68, 78, 87, 95–6, 102
Golan Heights   191, 192, 193
Gold Standard   59
Goldberger, Leo   101
Goldhagen, David   103
Goldwater, Barry   165
Goluchowski, Count   33
Gomulka, Wladyslaw   129
Gorbachev, Mikhail   15, 111, 114, 126, 130, 133–5
Gottwald, Klement   120
Grand Alliance   114, 115, 117
Great Depression   13, 59–60
Great Patriotic War   76
Great Powers   12–13, 15, 16, 17, 18, 22–7, 121
Greece   36–7, 46, 55, 70, 76, 88, 95, 100, 107, 110, 116, 117, 187
Greek Civil War (1945–49)   115, 116
Green Berets   155, 161, 162, 174
Greenham Common   126
Groza, Petru   119
Guderian, General Heinz   75
Gulf War (1990–91)   16, 18, 180, 181, 203–5

Habsburg Empire   25, 33, 34, 37, 43, 51, 68
Hagganah   185, 188
Haifa   187
Haile Selassie, Emperor   62–3
Halberstam, David   163
Halifax, Lord   78
Hamas   197, 198, 200
Hamburg   107
Harriman, William A.   160
Health Organisation (WHO)   55
Hebron   199

Helsinki Accords (1975)   110, 126
Helwan   194
Henlein, Konrad   68, 69
Herring, George C.   166, 168
Herriot, Édouard   67
Herzl, Theodore   183
Heydrich, Reinhard   95, 100
Hezbollah   197, 198, 200
Higgins, Hugh   135
Hildebrand, Klaus   73
Hillgruber, Andreas   73
Himmler, Heinrich   99
Hindenburg Line   21, 105
Hiroshima (1945)   14, 18, 81, 109, 110, 116
Hitler, Adolf   23, 45
    anti-semitism   98, 103, 106, 184
    appeasement of   48, 69, 78, 115
    and European alliance   61–5
    expansionism   66–9, 72
    and League of Nations   61, 62
    *Lebensraum* policy   79, 89, 106
    *Mein Kampf*   67, 73, 76
    and Mussolini   64, 67
    nervous disease   106
    Pacts   61, 70–71
    regional disputes   15–16
    and Second World War   73–4, 77, 82, 84–9, 91, 95–7, 102, 105, 106
    and Spanish Civil War   64
    suicide   106
    and Versailles settlement   14, 15, 66–8
Ho Chi Minh   138, 153, 154, 159, 167
Hoare, Samuel   63
Holland, *see* Netherlands
Holocaust   82–3, 98–9, 102–3, 185
Holstein, Friedrich von   33
Honecker, Eruch   131
Hoover, Herbert   60
Hoover Moratorium (1931–32)   45, 60
Horowitz, David   115
Horthy, Admiral Miklós   97
Hossbach Memorandum   73
Hötzendorf, Conrad von   33, 34
Human rights   126
Hungarian Workers' Party   120
Hungary   51, 52, 55, 70, 131
    Second World War   76, 88, 97
    socialist republic   107, 108, 116, 119–20, 128
    uprising (1956)   110, 114, 129
Hussein, Saddam   16, 180, 181, 182, 197, 203–5

ICBMs   131, 134
Imperialism   12–13, 14, 15, 23, 30, 42
India   12, 15, 18, 24, 25, 33, 82, 187, 201
Indo-China   15, 48, 77, 136, 138, 149, 152–4, 158–60
Indo-Chinese Communist Party   153
Indonesia   140, 160
Industry   13, 82, 92–3, 96, 118, 128, 140
INF   111, 130
Inter-Allied Reparations Commission   51
International Brigades   64
International Labour Organisation   54
Intifada   197–9, 200

Iran   31, 130, 180–2, 197, 199, 200, 202–3
Iran, Shah of   180, 202
Iran–Iraq War (1980–88)   16, 180, 203, 204
Iranian hostage crisis (1979–81)   202–3
Iraq   16, 17, 180–82, 184, 188, 196, 197, 203–5
Iraq War (2003)   18, 181, 204–5
Irgun   185, 188
Iron Curtain   110, 114, 115, 116, 121, 123, 127
Isaac, J.   40
Islamic fundamentalism   16, 182, 197, 200
Isolationism (USA)   14, 46, 52, 55, 89, 142
Israel   16, 18, 180–82, 196–200, 204
    Arab-Israeli Wars   16, 17, 180, 181, 187–93, 195
    creation of   183–7
    peace treaties   199
    Prime Ministers   187
Israel War of Independence (1948–49)   188–9, 196
Israeli Defence Force   185   188
Italian Social Republic   104
Italy   13, 14, 56, 58, 205
    alliances   16, 20, 27, 28, 45, 46, 48, 61–4
    and *Anschluss*   67
    attacks Tripoli   36
    Axis power   64–5
    colonies   28, 62, 108
    economy   104
    and European cooperation   122
    Fascism   62
    First World War   21, 41
    invades Abyssinia   15, 45, 55, 62–3, 66
    and League of Nations   16, 64
    Locarno Pact   58
    military strength   84
    Second World War   46, 76, 81, 86, 88, 103–4, 108
    and Spanish Civil War   64
    unification   24, 25
    and Versailles Treaty   48
    war with Turkey   20
Iwo Jima   139
Izvolski, Alexander   34, 35

Janina   37
Japan   13, 47, 74, 89
    alliances and treaties   45, 65, 136, 140, 147
    army   141
    economy   139–40, 141
    and League of Nations   16, 54
    occupies China   14, 15, 45, 55, 63, 76–7, 142
    occupies Indo-China   48, 77
    Pearl Harbor   46, 48, 76–7, 81, 89, 137
    relations with China   176
    relations with Russia   20, 33, 141
    Second World War   14, 18, 46, 82, 108, 144
    US and   136, 137, 139–41, 144, 149

Japan-China War (1937)   45
Jaruzelski, General Wojciech   130, 131
Jerusalem   185, 187, 188, 191–2, 199, 200
Jewish United Resistance Movement   185
Jews   14, 96, 97, 101, 102–3
   'Final Solution'   82–3, 98–9, 102
   and Israel   183–7
John Paul II, Pope   110, 111, 128
Johnson, Lyndon B.   111, 130, 138, 147, 157–9, 163–8, 170–71, 174
Jordan   181, 188, 190, 191, 196, 199
Judaism   95
July Crisis (1914)   16, 21, 22, 24, 38–40, 41
Jutland, Battle of (1916)   21

Kampuchea   174
Kania, Stanislaw   130
'Karlsbad Programme' (1938)   68
Katyn massacre   127
Keegan, John   100
Keitel, General Wilhelm   96, 99
Kellogg, William   59
Kennan, George   110, 115, 149, 170
Kennedy, John F.   111, 136, 147, 154–64, 168, 173–4
Kennedy, Paul   133
Kennedy, Robert F.   160, 162, 170
Kent State University   137, 170, 171
Keynes, John Maynard   52–3, 58
Khahn, General   163
Kharkov, Battle of (1943)   105
Khmer Rouge   172, 174–5
Khomeini, Ayatollah   180, 202–3
Khruschev, Nikita   111, 120, 123, 128–9, 152
Khuzestan   203, 204
Kiderlen-Wächter, Alfred von   35
Kiel Canal   107
Kiesinger, Kurt   111
Kiev   90
Kim Il Sung   137, 144, 149, 150–51
Kissinger, Henry   175–6, 193
Kleist, General Ewald von   85
Kluge, Gunther von   106
Koch, H.W.   41
Kohl, Helmut   111
Korea   137, 139, 144
Korean War (1950–53)   16, 17, 18, 110, 114, 122, 136–8, 140, 144–51
Kosygin, Alexander   111
Krenz, Egon   131
Kurds   203, 204, 205
Kursk, Battle of (1943)   81, 105
Kuwait   16, 180, 181, 203–4

Labour force   96, 99, 100
Laos   14, 136, 152–5, 158–60, 162, 165, 172–4
Latvia   71, 75, 118, 128, 133
Lausanne Conference (1932)   45, 60
Laval, Pierre   62, 63, 96, 97, 102
League of Nations   15, 16–17, 59, 60, 107
   Covenant   53–4, 55
   creation of   16, 45
   effectiveness of   53–5
   Italy and   55, 62–4, 66

   major institutions   54
   mandates   184, 185
Lebanon   180, 181, 182, 184, 188, 196, 199
Lebanon War (1982)   197
*Lebensraum*   76, 79, 89, 106
Legion of Volunteers Against Bolshevism   95
Lemnitzer, General Lyman   160
Lend-Lease Agreement (1941/42)   46, 76, 81, 89, 93
Lenin, Vladimir   42
Leningrad   83, 89, 90, 91, 106
Lezaky massacre (1942)   100
Liberal Party (Britain)   38
Liberia   13
Liddell Hart, Sir Basil   38, 84, 105
Lidice massacre (1942)   96, 100
Ligachev, Yegor   133
Linz   67
Lithuania   71, 75, 118, 128, 133
Litvinov, Maxim   70
Lloyd George, David   22, 35, 49
Locarno Pact (1925)   45, 58–9, 61, 66, 72
Lodge, Henry Cabot   163
*Lombardverbot*   29
Lon Nol   174
London   87
London Conference (1945)   116
'Long Telegram'   110, 115
Low Countries   85
Lowe, Peter   150–51
Lublin   119
*Luftwaffe*   75, 76, 84, 87–8, 105
Luxembourg   75, 122

MacArthur, General Douglas   139, 145, 146, 150
MacDonald, Ramsay   55
Macedonia   37
Madagascar   98
Madrid   346
Maginot Line   48, 75, 85
Mahan, Alfred T.   30
Malaya   77, 160, 161
Malenkov, Georgi   111
Malmedy   49, 58
Manchuria   14, 15, 45, 55, 76, 142, 143
Mandated territories   54, 183–7, 203
Mansfield, Mike   161
Manstein, General Erich von   85, 106
Manstein Plan   75
Mantoux, E.   53
Mao Ze-dong   137, 141–2, 143, 151, 152, 167, 176
March Against Death (1969)   137, 170
Marianas Islands   139
Marne, Battle of   21
Marshall, George   117, 142
Marshall Islands   139
Marshall Plan   110, 116, 118, 120, 128
Martin, Joseph   146
Mason, John   13
Martel, Gordon   41
Marxist historians   42
Masaryk, Jan   128
Masaryk, Tomas   51
Mason, John W.   123
Mastny, Vojtech   115

Matsu   151
Mazowiecki, Tadeusz   131
McCarthy, Eugene   170
McCarthy, Joseph   144
McCarthyism   138, 143, 147, 175
McCauley, Martin   132, 134
McNamara, Robert   155, 157, 162, 165, 166
Media   177
Mediterranean   27, 28, 35, 78, 88, 103, 107
*Mein Kampf* (Hitler)   67, 73, 76
Meir, Golda   187
Meretalov, A.   70
Michael, King of Romania   119
Middle East   16, 24, 85, 114, 180–207
Midway, Battle of   77
Mihailovic, Dmitri   97
Mikolajczyk, Stanislaw   119
Milan   104
*Milice*   97
Military Assistance Advisory Group   154
Milward, Alan   73, 91, 100
Mindsentzy, Cardinal   128
Minh, General   163
Minsk   106
'*Mitteleuropa*'   125
Mohacs, Battle of (1526)   87
Moldavia   75, 118
Molotov, Vyacheslav   70–71, 116, 117
Mongolia   14
Monte Cassino   104
Montenegro   27, 36
Morocco   20, 31–3, 34–5, 36, 37
Mosaddeq, Mohammed   181, 202
Moscow   71, 83, 89, 107, 150, 151, 175
Moscow Olympics (1980)   126
Moscow Treaty (1970)   125
Muller, Admiral Georg von   23
Munich Conference (1938)   15, 45, 68–70, 72, 79
Munich Olympics (1972)   193
Murphy, Derrick   117
Muslims   100, 182, 183, 198, 202–5
Mussert, A.A.   97
Mussolini, Benito   55, 61, 62–5, 67, 69, 72, 81, 86, 88, 102
   fall of   103–4, 106
Mutual Security Treaty (1951)   140–41, 143
My Lai Massacre (1968)   136, 169
Myanmar   12, 160

Nagasaki (1945)   14, 18, 81, 110, 116
Naguib, General Muhammad   194
Nagy, Imre   119, 129
Namier, Sir Lewis   73
Narodna Odbrana   43
Nasser, Gamal Abdel   180, 182, 190–91, 194–6
National Front (Czechoslovakia)   129
National Union (Egypt)   194
Nationalism   33, 41, 59, 83, 97, 103
   Arab   194, 195, 196
   Balkan   15, 26, 34, 37
   Eastern European   127–8, 129, 133
   Far East   138, 153, 154, 159, 174
Nationalist Chinese   137, 141–4, 146, 151–2

NATO 110, 113, 116, 120, 123, 125, 129, 149, 150
Naval Defence Act (Britain, 1889) 13
Naval League 38
Nazi Germany 14, 47, 48, 93–9
Nazism 59, 62, 67, 97–9, 106, 108
Netanyahu, Benjamin 187, 199
Netherlands 29, 46, 75, 81, 85, 97, 108, 122
Neuilly 51
Neurath, Constantine von 95
Neutrality Acts (USA, 1935–37) 89
New Imperialism 12
New York 107
New Zealand 12, 147, 152
Ngo Dinh Diem 136, 154–5, 158, 159, 161, 163
Ngo Dinh Nhu 161
Nguyen Van Thieu 171, 172, 173
Nice 86
Nicholas II, Tsar 17, 21
Nicolson, Harold 48, 53
9/11 16, 180, 205
Nixon, Richard M. 111, 123, 165
  in China 137, 151
Nixon Doctrine 171
  and South East Asia 138, 153, 170–71, 173–7
NKVD 91
NLF (National Liberation Front) 154, 155, 158, 159
Normandy landings 81, 93, 101, 104
North Africa 81, 83, 88, 103, 149
North Korea 14, 16, 17, 136, 137–8, 140, 144–50
North Vietnam 138, 154, 157–9, 165–70, 172–3, 175–6
North Vietnamese Army (NVA) 169–70, 171, 174
Norway 46, 75, 81, 85, 95, 97, 101
Novak, Robert 165
Novotny, Antonin 129
Nuclear weapons 17, 18, 143, 146–7, 151, 152, 172, 205
  anti-nuclear protesters 126
  arms control 110, 111, 123, 126, 134–5, 175
  arms race 14, 18, 109
  atomic diplomacy 117, 122
  Hiroshima and Nagasaki 14, 18, 110, 116
  INF 126
Nuremberg Trials 68, 73, 93

October Protocols (1936) 64
Oder-Neisse Line 125
O'Donnell, Ken 161
Oil 63, 77, 85, 91, 130, 137, 181, 202–5
Okinawa 139
Olympic Games 126, 193
Oncken, H. 40
Operation Barbarossa 76, 81
Operation Desert Fox 204
Operation Desert Shield 203
Operation Desert Storm 203–4
Operation Enduring Freedom 205
Operation Linebacker 172, 175
Operation Moked 190
Operation Overlord 104

Operation Rolling Thunder 158, 165, 168
Operation Sealion 76
Operation Shark 185
Oradour sur Glane (massacre, 1944) 96
Orel 106
Orthodox Church 92
Oslo Accords (1993) 180, 197, 199, 200
Osobka, Edward 119
Ostland 95
*Ostpolitik* 125–6
Ottoman Empire 13, 15, 21, 25–6, 27, 28, 31, 183–4, 203
  *see also* Turkey
Overy, Richard J. 74, 78

'Pact of Steel' (1939) 46, 65, 72
Pahlavi, Mohammad Reza, Shah 202
Pakistan 12, 15, 152, 187, 201
Palestine 180, 181, 183–7, 192, 196, 197
Palestinian Arabs 180, 181, 184–5, 187–90, 192, 196–201
Palestinian Liberation Organisation (PLO) 192, 197, 199, 200
Palestinian National Authority 199, 200
Palmiry 96
Pan-German League 35
Papacy 110, 111, 128
Paris 75, 86, 104
Paris Peace Agreement (1920), *see* Versailles Treaty
Paris Peace Agreement (1973) 137, 173, 176, 193
Partisan movements 100–101, 104, 120
Paterson, Thomas G. 150, 151
Patterson, James 150
Pavelic, Ante 97
Pearl Harbor 46, 48, 76–7, 81, 89, 137
Peasant Party (Poland) 119
Peel Commission (1937) 185
Pentagon Papers 165, 167
Peres, Shimon 187
*Perestroika* 114, 130, 133
Perle, Richard 132
Permanent Court of International Justice 54
Persia 33, 202
Pétain, Marshal Philippe 86, 101
Philippines 77, 136, 140, 147, 149, 152
'Phoney War' (1939–40) 48, 74–5, 85
Pilsen 68
Pleiku 136, 157, 165
Pleven, Rene 122
Pleven Plan (1951) 122
Poidevin, Raymond 42
Poincaré, Raymond 35, 37, 57–8, 59
Pol Pot 172, 174–5
Poland 66, 71–2, 111, 128, 205
  alliances and treaties 58, 70, 71–2, 84, 125
  invasion of 16, 17, 46, 48, 65, 74–5, 79, 81, 82, 84
  military strength 84
  non-aggression pact with Germany 45, 61–2
  occupied 95, 98, 101
  post-war 107, 116
  socialist republic 108, 116, 119, 120, 126, 127, 129–31

Solidarity movement 111, 126, 128, 130–31
  territorial changes 50, 51, 55, 71, 118, 125
  uprisings 110
Polaris missiles 112
Polish Home Army 119, 128
Polish corridor 50, 71
Polish United Workers' Party 119
Posen 50
Potsdam Agreement (1945) 81, 107, 110, 116, 121, 122, 144
Poznan Rising (1956) 110, 129
Prague 68, 70, 131
Prague Spring (1968) 110, 129–30, 131
Princip, Gavrilo 38, 43
Propaganda 14, 79, 85, 86, 90, 95, 96, 101, 111, 131, 140
Protectionism 28
Prussia 24, 25, 26, 50, 66, 107
*Punch* 26
Putten 96
Pyongyang 145, 151

Quagmire theory 163
Quemoy 151, 152
Quisling, Vidkun 97

Rabin, Yitzhak 187, 197, 199
Rapallo, Treaty of (1922) 45, 71
Reagan, Ronald W. 111, 126, 132, 134
*Realpolitik* 27, 55
Recession 176, 202
Red Army 14, 15, 90, 92, 99, 105–6
Referendums 67, 68, 119, 194
Refugees 108, 123, 180, 181, 186, 188–9, 196–8, 200–201
Regional disputes 15–16
Reichard, Gary 150
Reichstag 23, 31, 37
Reinsurance Treaty (1887) 20, 27, 29
Remilitarisation 45, 66
Reparations 22, 45, 50–51, 52–3, 55–8, 59, 60
Resistance movements 96, 99–101, 185
Rethondes, Treaty of (1940) 86
Revisionist historians 115, 117
Revolutions 17, 130–31, 133
Rexist movement 97
Reykjavik 134, 135
Rhee, Syngman 137, 144, 146, 150
Rhineland 45, 49–50, 57, 58, 59, 66
Ribbentrop, Joachim von 71
Ribbentrop–Molotov Pact (1939) 46, 70–71, 74–5, 76, 84, 99
Rich, Norman 96
Ritter, Gerhard 41
'Road Map to Peace' (2000) 180, 199
Robertson, E.M. 73
Robinson, Ronald 13
Romania 37, 127
  alliances 27, 28, 70
  political revolution 111, 131
  Second World War 76, 88, 95, 106
  socialist republic 107, 108, 116, 119
Rome 81, 104
Rome Agreements (1935) 62, 63
Rommel, Erwin 83, 106

Roosevelt, Franklin D. 76, 89, 107, 115–17, 142, 147
Rosenberg, Alfred 95
Rotterdam 85
Royal Air Force 76, 79, 88, 93
Royal Navy 13, 14, 23, 24, 31, 79
Ruhr 45, 55–7, 58, 95, 107
Rumsfeld, Donald 205
Rundstedt, Gerd von 106
Rusk, Dean 155, 162, 168
Russia 12
    alliances 16, 20, 23, 27–9, 31
    army 13, 25, 30
    and Bosnia-Herzegovina 34
    Bolshevik Revolution 17, 21, 52, 114
    First World War 20, 22, 24, 30, 39–40, 47
    Great Power status 12, 25
    military power 13, 34
    regional disputes 15, 26
    relations with Austria 28
    relations with Britain 33
    relations with France 20, 28, 29, 37
    relations with Germany 20, 26, 27, 28, 29
    *see also* USSR
Russian Empire 13, 21, 46
Russian Federation 133
Russian Liberation Army 97
Russo-German Pact, *see* Ribbentrop–Molotov Pact
Russo-Japanese War (1905–06) 20, 33, 141
Russo-Turkish War (1877–78) 27
Ruthenia 51, 118

Saarland 45, 54, 107
Sabra refugee camp 197, 198
Sadat, Anwar 180, 193, 196
Saigon 137, 163, 170, 173
St Germain, Treaty of (1919) 45, 51
SALT treaties 110, 111, 123–5, 126, 175
*Sammlungspolitik* 31
San Stefano, Treaty of 27
Sanders, Vivienne 153
Sarajevo 20, 34, 38–9, 43
Sauckel, Fritz 96
Saudi Arabia 181, 182, 188, 203, 204
Savoy 86
Scandinavia 85
Scapa Flow 49
Schlesinger, Arthur M. 160, 161, 165
Schlieffen Plan 21, 29, 30
Schmidt, Helmut 111
Schuschnigg, Kurt von 68
Scutari 37
SDI (Strategic Defence Initiative) 126, 134
Second World War (1939–45) 14, 16–18, 48, 68–77, 81–109
    Axis collapses 103–6
    causes 68–74, 115
    consequences of 107–9, 115
    extension of conflict 87–9
    fall of France 75–6, 85–7, 89
    Far East 144
    Great Patriotic War 76
    and Middle East 185, 194

Normandy landings 104
occupied territories 95–7, 99–102
offensive against USSR 89–91
origins 73–4
outbreak 46, 68–74
peace settlement 106–7
Phoney War 48, 74–5, 85
war production 92–5
Sedan 85
Seoul 144, 145
September Programme 23
Serbia 20, 22, 24, 27, 33–4, 36, 37, 38, 39, 41–4
Serfdom 25
Sevres 51
Seyss-Inquart, Arthur 67
Sforza, Count 57
Shamir, Yitzhak 187
Sharett, Moshe 187
Sharon, Ariel 187, 198
Sheehan, Neil 163, 165
Shirer, William 74
Sicily 103
Siegfried Line 21, 105
Sihanouk, Prince Norodom 174
Silesia 93, 96
Simon, Sir John 61
Sinai Peninsula 188–92, 196, 199, 200
Singapore 77
*Sitzkrieg* 85
Six Day War (1967) 180, 190–92, 194, 195, 200
Skoda arms factories 68, 70
Slavs 95, 97, 99
Slovak National Uprising
Slovakia 51, 70, 72, 76, 97
Slovenia 51
Smallholders' Party (Hungary) 119
Sobibor 98
Social Darwinism 30
Social Democratic Party (Germany) 23–4
Social Democrats (Czechoslovakia) 130
Socialism 38, 64, 111
Solidarity (Poland) 111, 126, 128, 130–31
Somalia 62
Somme, Battle of 21
South Africa 12, 13, 82
South East Asia 153–74
South East Asian Treaty Organisation (SEATO) 113, 136, 149, 152, 154
South Korea 16, 17, 136–8, 140, 144–50, 152
South Vietnam 138, 152, 154–64, 166, 172–3
Soviet Union, *see* USSR
Spain 13, 64, 76, 205
Spanish Civil War (1936) 45, 64, 67, 88
Speer, Albert 93–5
SS 96, 99
Stalin, Josef 70–71, 83, 107, 111, 116, 120, 121
    death 110, 128, 146
    denunciation of 128–9
    and Eastern Europe 115, 118–19, 127
    and Far East 142, 145, 149, 150, 151, 153

Second World War 75, 76, 89, 91, 103
Stalingrad, Battle of 81, 83, 91
Stalinism 129
Stern Gang 185
Stirkwerda, Carl 42
Stone, Norman 38
Stone, Oliver 158
Strandmann, Hartmut Pogge von 41
Strategic Hamlets Programme 155, 158, 161
Stresa Conference (1935) 45, 62
Stresa Front 62, 63, 66
Stresemann, Gustav 55, 57, 58, 59
Students for a Democratic Society 136, 170
Submarines 18, 89, 112
Sudeten Party 68
Sudetenland 45, 67, 68–70, 78, 201
Suez Canal 13, 190, 191, 193–4, 196
Suez Crisis (1956) 129, 180, 181, 194, 195
Suez War (1956) 189–90
Superpowers 14–15, 17, 18, 83, 108–9, 111, 132
Swain, G. and N. 129
Sweden 55, 85, 97, 101
Syria 180–82, 184, 188, 190–93, 195–7, 204

Tachen islands 151
Taiwan 136, 137, 142, 144, 146, 149, 151–2, 176
Taliban 16, 205
Tanks 17, 75, 82, 84, 91, 93
Tariffs 59
Taylor, A.J.P. 22, 37, 40, 41, 51, 67, 71, 72, 73–4, 78, 84
Taylor, General Maxwell 160, 163
Tehran 202
Tehran Conference (1943) 107
Televaag 96
Terrorism 16, 43, 56, 192, 198–9, 200, 205
Teschen 72
Tet Offensive (1968) 136, 158, 169–70
Thailand 140, 149, 152, 155, 160, 162
Third World 154, 161
Three Emperors' League (1873) 20, 26–7, 28, 29
Tiran Straits 190
Tiso, Joseph 97
Tito (Josef Broz) 100, 118, 120, 127
Todt, Fritz 93
Tonkin, Gulf of 136, 157, 158, 165
Tonkin Resolution (1964) 157, 158, 165, 172, 174
Torgau 105
Total war 18, 82, 100, 170
Toul 39
Trade 13, 42
Transjordan 184, 188
Treblinka 98, 102
Trevor-Roper, Hugh 73
Trianon 51
Triple Alliance (1882) 16, 20, 27, 28, 29
Tripoli 36
Truman, Harry S. 111, 115–18, 122, 153
    and China 142–3
    and Korea 137–8, 144, 146–51

Truman Doctrine (1947)   110, 115, 116,
    118, 120, 137, 147–9, 153, 155, 174
Tunis   28, 197
Turkey   20, 21, 27, 33, 36, 51, 87, 110,
    116, 117, 187
    *see also* Ottoman Empire
Twenty Years' Truce   72, 79

Uganda   183
Ukraine   89, 90, 95, 96, 128, 130
United Arab Republic   182, 190, 195,
    196
United Nations (UN)   16, 125, 175, 195
    China and   143, 151, 176
    created   17, 107
    Emergency Force (UNEF)   190
    and Gulf Wars   203–5
    and Korean War   138, 144–7, 149
    and Palestinian refugees   200–201
    Relief and Works Agency (UNRWA)
        188
    Security Council   145, 188, 192,
        205
    Special Committee on Palestine
        (UNSCOP)   186–7
    structure   145
United States   12, 13
    alliances and treaties   113, 137,
        140, 147–9, 151, 152
    and Cold War in Asia   136–78
    and Cold War in Europe   14,
        111–18, 121–7, 131–5
    economy   13, 18, 59, 83, 108, 116,
        176
    First World War   21
    industry   93
    isolationism   14, 46, 52, 55, 89,
        142
    and Korean War   144–9
    and League of Nations   16, 54
    Lend-Lease agreement   46, 76, 81,
        89, 93
    and Middle East   181, 185, 186,
        188, 190, 192–3, 195, 202–4
    nuclear arms race   14, 18
    occupying power in Germany   121
    Presidents   111
    regional disputes   16
    Second World War   14, 18, 46, 48,
        74, 77, 81–2, 89, 93, 104
    superpower status   14–15, 108, 111
    and Taiwan   136, 137, 144, 146,
        151–2
US–Chinese relations   137, 139–42,
    151–2, 171, 175–6
US–Japanese relations   137, 139–41, 144
US–Soviet relations   175
    and Versailles Treaty   48–9
    Vietnam War   138, 157–74
    war against terror   16
    war loans   58, 60
USSR   47, 49, 124
    Afghanistan invasion   126, 130,
        131, 133

alliances and treaties   46, 61, 66,
    70–71, 76, 125, 136
army, *see* Red Army
and Baltic States   81
Communist Party, *see* CPSU
Cold War   14, 111–18, 132
    collapse of   15, 111, 132
    and Eastern Europe   118–21,
        127–33
    economy   13, 18, 114, 132–3
    and Far East   139, 141, 144, 150,
        154, 167
    Great Patriotic War   76
    industry   92–3
    leaders   111
    and League of Nations   16, 54
    Lend-lease   93
    and Middle East   181, 188, 190,
        192–3, 195
    military strength   84
    nuclear weapons   14, 18, 110
    occupied   97, 100
    occupying power in Germany   121
    regional disputes   16
    relations with west   70, 129
    Second World War   14, 17, 46, 48,
        74–6, 81–3, 89–93, 106–8, 115,
        144
    Soviet–Chinese relations   138, 143,
        152, 175
    Soviet–US relations   175
    and Spanish Civil War   64
    superpower status   14–15, 108,
        111, 132
    and Versailles   52
    Winter War   81, 85
    *see also* Russia

Velvet Revolution (1989)   111, 131
Vercors (1944)   100
Verdun, Battle of (1916)   21, 22
Versailles Treaty (1919–20)   22, 40, 45,
    47–53, 56, 60, 61, 89, 184
    Hitler and   66–8, 71
Vichy France   48, 101
Victor Emmanuel III   104
Victoria, Queen   24, 31
Vienna   66, 67, 121
Vienna Congress (1815)   51
Vietcong   138, 154–7, 159, 163, 165,
    169–70
Vietminh   153
Vietnam   14, 15, 133, 136, 153–68
Vietnam War (1964–73)   16, 17, 18, 114,
    115, 136–8, 147, 151, 157–78
    anti-war movement   138, 170–71,
        177–8
    effects of   173–4
    responsibility for   158–68
Vilna   55
Vlasov, General A.A.   97
*Volkssturm*   105

Wal-Wal (1934)   62
Walęsa, Lech   130

Wall Street Crash (1929)   45, 47, 59–61
War Powers Act (USA, 1973)   174
Warfare   17–18
Warsaw   21, 81, 98, 131
    Uprising (1944)   100, 119, 128
Warsaw Pact   110, 113, 123, 125, 129,
    130
Warsaw Treaty (1970)   125
Washington, Treaty of (1979)   199, 200
Watergate   173
Watt, Donald   74
Weapons of mass destructions (WMD)
    205
Weber, Eugen   35
Wedemeyer, General Albert   142
*Wehrmacht*   83–4, 85, 89–90, 91, 95,
    104–6
Weimar Republic   40
Weizmann, Chaim   185
*Weltpolitik*   21, 23, 30–32, 39
Werth, Alexander   99
West Bank   191, 192, 196, 198, 199, 200
West Berlin   121–2, 123
West Germany   110, 116, 120, 121,
    122–5
    Chancellors   111
    *Ostpolitik*   125–6
Westmoreland, General William   155,
    164
Wiesbaden Accords (1921)   55
Wilhelm II, Kaiser   17, 23–4, 30–31, 32,
    35, 37, 41
Williams, T.D.   73
Wilson, Woodrow   21, 49, 52, 53
Wint, Guy   87
Winter War (1939–40)   81, 85
Wiskemann, Elizabeth   65
Woodhead Commission (1938)   185
Woodward, E.L.   73
Wye River Memorandum (1998)   199

Yalta Conference (1945)   81, 107, 110,
    115, 116, 118, 142
Yeltsin, Boris   111, 133
Yemen   195, 196
Yom Kippur War (1973)   180, 192–3,
    196, 197
Young Plan (1929)   45, 58, 60
'Young Turk' movement   33
Ypres, Battle of   21
Yugoslavia   51, 55, 145
    communist state   107, 108, 118,
        120–21, 127
    German occupation   95, 97, 100
    Second World War   46, 76, 88

Zabern incident (1913)   20
Zechlin, Egmont   41
Zeppelins   18
Zhivkov, Topol   131
Zhou En-lai   176
Zhukov, Marshal Georgi   91
Zinn, Howard   178
Zionist Movement   183, 184, 186–7
Zog, King   118